LOGICAL PUZZLES

CHARTWELL
BOOKS, INC.

This edition printed in 2006 by

CHARTWELL BOOKS, INC.
A Division of **BOOK SALES, INC.**
114 Northfield Avenue
Edison, New Jersey 08837

The Collection © 2005 Arcturus Publishing Limited
26/27 Bickels Yard, 151–153 Bermondsey Street,
London SE1 3HA

Individual puzzles © 2005 Puzzler Media Ltd
Puzzler Media Ltd, Stonecroft
69 Station Road, Redhill, Surrey, RH1 1EY

ISBN-13: 978-0-7858-2121-2
ISBN-10: 0-7858-2121-X

Printed in China

INTRODUCTION

Logical Puzzles contains over 300 cracking conundrums. Each has been designed to develop your powers of logical thinking; this compilation includes charts for the standard problems to enable you to assess the possibilities and note down the information you gather from the clues. For some of the more difficult puzzles we have also provided useful tips to get you started.

A full solution for each puzzle is provided at the end of the book.

HAIR LINE

Three friends have jobs in different hairdressing salons in town. From the clues given below, can you identify them, say where each works, and work out their respective ages?

Clues

1 Joy Bunn is older than her friend who works at Marcel's.

2 Frances, whose surname is not Fringe, is employed at The Hairport.

3 The assistant at Making Waves is 19.

	Bunn	Curleigh	Fringe	Making Waves	Marcel's	The Hairport	18	19	20
Bianca			•						
Frances		✓							
Joy	•								•
18									
19									
20									
Making Waves									
Marcel's									
The Hairport									

Forename	Surname	Salon	Age
Joy	Bunn	Making Waves	19
Frances	Curleigh	Hairport	20
Bianca	Fringe	Marcel's	18

THE GENTLE SEX

More and more crime novels are being published which are written by women and feature women sleuths. From the clues given below, can you work out the titles of three such recent ones, naming their women investigators and saying in what city they are set?

Clues

I The Dublin sleuth does not figure in the novel by Jane Shorrocks.

2 Melanie Pierce is not the author of *Deadly Desire* and her investigator is not Dilly Frith. Dilly Frith doesn't operate in Sheffield.

3 Karel Blayne is not the intrepid crime-solver in *Nowhere To Hide*, a thriller by Penelope Gunn.

4 Lila Kreiks, who is a Chicago medical examiner, doesn't display her sleuthing skills in *She Had To Pay*.

	Deadly Desire	Nowhere To Hide	She Had To Pay	Dilly Frith	Karel Blayne	Lila Kreiks	Chicago	Dublin	Sheffield
Jane Shorrocks									
Melanie Pierce									
Penelope Gunn									
Chicago									
Dublin									
Sheffield									
Dilly Frith									
Karel Blayne									
Lila Kreiks									

Author	Title	Investigator	City

A HAIR OF DIFFERENCE

After the robbery at the Storbury Minimart, police took descriptions of the villain from four witnesses. (Luckily, the shop's security video showed clearly that the thief had a shaven head and a fringe beard with no moustache, giving·a clear enough picture for police to recognise the man!) How did each witness describe the colour and length of the thief's coiffure and his facial hair?

Clues

1 Of three of the witnesses, one described the thief as 'a clean-shaven man, bald on top', another was the shopkeeper and a third thought the villain had fair hair.

2 One person told police that the thief had dark-brown hair and a goatee beard. This wasn't the painter (who was redecorating the Minimart at the time of the robbery) or the witness who said the villain's hair was shoulder-length – and neither of these two was the person who thought the villain had a heavy moustache but no beard.

3 The passer-by who saw the thief run out of the Minimart and described him as having greying hair was neither the oldest witness (who said his hair was cut short) nor the youngest witness (who was certain he had a full beard).

	Dark brown	Fair	Greying	Red brown	Bald on top	Cut short	Receding	Shoulder-length	Clean shaven	Full beard	Goatee beard	Moustache
Customer												
Painter												
Passer-by												
Shopkeeper												
Clean shaven												
Full beard												
Goatee beard												
Moustache												
Bald on top												
Cut short												
Receding												
Shoulder-length												

Witness	Hair colour	Hair description	Facial hair

POPPINS-POURRI

Of course every family in London at the end of the 19th Century wanted a nanny like Mary Poppins (even though she was completely fictitious and the books weren't written until years later) but those that could afford a nanny at all still had to settle for second best, or worse. From the clues below, can you identify the two children in each family, and the nanny hired to look after the little darlings?

Clues

1 Coincidentally, each of the four families had given their two children forenames of the same length.

2 Alicia's nanny wasn't Martha Poggins.

3 Sarah's surname wasn't Bagstock.

4 Ralph's nanny was Maud Potiphar.

5 Mr and Mrs Carson named their son Oliver.

6 Mavis Pomfret was nanny to the Dugdale children.

7 The surname of Mabel Ponsonby's employers was one letter longer than that of George and Phoebe's parents.

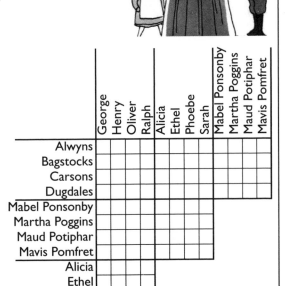

	George	Henry	Oliver	Ralph	Alicia	Ethel	Phoebe	Sarah	Mabel Ponsonby	Martha Poggins	Maud Potiphar	Mavis Pomfret
Alwyns												
Bagstocks												
Carsons												
Dugdales												
Mabel Ponsonby												
Martha Poggins												
Maud Potiphar												
Mavis Pomfret												
Alicia													
Ethel													
Phoebe													
Sarah													

Family	Son	Daughter	Nanny

GONE FISHIN'

The Noah's Ark in Storbury is the unofficial club house of the River Stor Angling Association, and last week four old friends there commiserated about the miserable time each had had on his last fishing trip. Can you work out where on the River Stor each man had fished, how many fish he'd caught, and what incident had really ruined his day?

Clues

1 Sam, whose angling expedition came to an abrupt end when he was bitten by a passer-by's pet dog, caught one fewer fish than the angler who went fishing at Mill Reach.

2 One of the four friends spent all day on the river bank, caught just one fish and then, when he came to return home, discovered his car had been stolen!

3 Chick always goes to Jack's Island when he fishes the Stor.

4 The man who fished at The Pits, where there are several deep craters in the bed of the river, caught two fewer fish than the one whose day's angling was ruined by the loss of his favourite rod, accidentally dropped into the water.

5 Keith's friend caught three fish at Bull's Bridge.

	Bull's Bridge	Jack's Island	Mill Reach	The Pits	None	One	Two	Three	Bitten by dog	Car stolen	Fell in river	Lost rod
Chick												
Keith												
Percy												
Sam												
Bitten by dog												
Car stolen												
Fell in river												
Lost rod												
None												
One												
Two												
Three												

Angler	Fishing spot	Number caught	Incident

RECORD HOLDERS

At a collectors' fair in Northchester, one stall was displaying four classic LP records dating back to the sixties. From the clues below, can you fill in the name of each record, the group who recorded it and the year in which it first came out?

Clues

1 The number one hit album *Bridge Over The Mersey* first came out in 1965.

2 *Hearsay* was originally released in the year before the Scarabs released their album which is shown here.

3 Record A was recorded by the Faunas; record B is called *Born In The UK*.

4 *Far Side Of The Planet*, the Peter's Pilgrims LP, is displayed next to the most recent of the four records.

Titles:
Born In The UK;
Bridge Over The Mersey;
Far Side Of The Planet;
Hearsay

Groups:
Faunas; Peter's Pilgrims;
Rolling Bones; Scarabs

Years:
1963; 1964; 1965; 1966

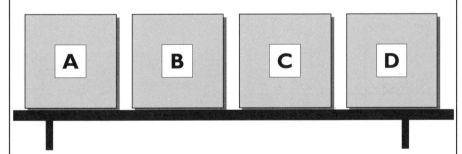

LP	Title	Group	Year
A			
B			
C			
D			

Starting tip:

Work out the title of the 1966 LP.

JUST PHENOMENAL

The five members of the rock band Phenomenon had each received a sack of fan mail, which they had just sat down to answer. Can you match the members with their rôles in the band and say to which fan from which city each was replying at the moment in question?

Clues

1 Martin, who was writing to Sarah, doesn't play the guitar.

2 Jenny had written from her home in Liverpool, but not to Tristan, who is the vocalist with Phenomenon.

3 The letter to which Peter was replying had been posted in Glasgow.

4 The drummer wasn't writing to the girl from Birmingham, who isn't Tina.

5 Bethany had written a fan letter to the Phenomenon's keyboard player.

6 The band's lead guitarist, who isn't Jamie, was answering the fan letter from Manchester.

	Bass guitarist	Drummer	Keyboard player	Lead guitarist	Singer	Bethany	Jenny	Naomi	Sarah	Tina	Birmingham	Glasgow	Liverpool	London	Manchester
Jamie															
Martin															
Peter															
Richard															
Tristan															
Birmingham															
Glasgow															
Liverpool															
London															
Manchester															
Bethany															
Jenny															
Naomi															
Sarah															
Tina															

Band member	Rôle	Fan	City

IN DIVERS PLACES

The Britannic Salvage Company is a world leader in deep-sea recovery and its five ships, with their teams of divers, are constantly busy. Can you identify the captain of each of the vessels and say which sea it's currently in and what kind of wreck it's working on?

Clues

1 Captain Jervis of the Wyvern is the only captain whose surname is the same length as his ship's name. He isn't the man whose divers are bringing up treasure from a schooner wrecked 150 years ago in the Tasman Sea.

2 Orion is engaged in recovering the flight recorder and other material from a crashed airliner.

3 Gipsy is currently in the North Sea. Her divers aren't working on a sunken freighter.

4 Captain Stark's ship isn't the Hunter.

5 Captain Blake, who's in charge of raising a submarine lost in World War Two, doesn't command the vessel which is in the Indian Ocean.

6 Captain Popham's ship is in the Arctic Ocean.

	Captain Blake	Captain Fisher	Captain Jervis	Captain Popham	Captain Stark	Aegean Sea	Arctic Ocean	Indian Ocean	North Sea	Tasman Sea	Airliner	Freighter	Galleon	Schooner	Submarine
Diadem															
Gipsy															
Hunter															
Orion															
Wyvern															
Airliner															
Freighter															
Galleon															
Schooner															
Submarine															
Aegean Sea															
Arctic Ocean															
Indian Ocean															
North Sea															
Tasman Sea															

Ship	Captain	Sea	Wreck

IT'S A DOG'S LIFE

The Police Department of Santa Diega City, California, has five dog teams, referred to collectively as the K9s. Each team comprises a driver, a dog handler and of course, a dog - all the dogs are German Shepherds. Can you identify which team every driver, handler and dog belongs to?

Clues

1 In Team K9-5 the dog is called Columbo, but the driver isn't surnamed Airedale.

2 Officer Dobermann is the driver for Team K9-4.

3 Officer Pointer's team-mates include neither Officer Jack Russell nor Starsky.

4 Officer Russell isn't a member of Team K9-3.

5 Officer Basset's team has a final number one lower than that of Officer Cairn's; the latter team includes Marlowe.

6 Officer Husky is the handler for her team's German Shepherd, Archer.

7 Officer Schnauzer belongs to Team K9-1, but Kojak doesn't.

	Driver					Handler					Dog				
	Airedale	Cairn	Dobermann	Pointer	Vizsla	Basset	Griffon	Husky	Russell	Schnauzer	Archer	Columbo	Kojak	Marlowe	Starsky
K9-1															
K9-2															
K9-3															
K9-4															
K9-5															
Archer															
Columbo															
Kojak															
Marlowe															
Starsky															
Basset															
Griffon															
Husky															
Russell															
Schnauzer															

Team	Driver	Handler	Dog

FOREIGN EXCHANGE

The local school is currently running a Student Exchange programme and five friends have German girls to stay for a week. Can you discover which girl is staying with whom, her home town in Germany and the tourist site or town that each will be visiting this weekend?

Clues

1 Louise's German guest (not Maria) is from Dortmund; they're off to a central London venue.

2 Kathy's guest, whose name begins with 'E', isn't from Frankfurt and she's not taking her to see Windsor Castle or the British Museum.

3 Heidi is from Hamburg. The girl from Stuttgart is off to see the British Museum.

4 Liz's guest (whose name begins with 'H') will be visiting a castle.

5 The girl visiting Stratford-upon-Avon isn't from a town beginning with 'H', nor is she Hannah.

6 Eva is staying with Sarah, but they're not off to visit the British Museum.

	Elsa	Eva	Hannah	Heidi	Maria	Dortmund	Frankfurt	Hamburg	Hannover	Stuttgart	British Museum	National Gallery	Stratford-upon-Avon	Warwick Castle	Windsor Castle
Kathy															
Liz															
Louise															
Natalie															
Sarah															
British Museum															
National Gallery															
Stratford-upon-Avon															
Warwick Castle															
Windsor Castle															
Dortmund															
Frankfurt															
Hamburg															
Hannover															
Stuttgart															

Host	Visitor	Home town	Visiting

GET YOUR BEARINGS

Each of the boxes numbered 1 to 7 in the diagram is of a different colour and contains a different number of ball-bearings. Can you work out the colour of each box and say how many ball-bearings it contains? NB - 'Left' and 'right' are from your point of view as you look at the picture.

Clues

1 Box 2 contains more ball-bearings than box 7, but fewer than the red box.

2 Box 4 is blue and contains half as many ball-bearings as the green box, which is two positions to the left of the white one.

3 The box which holds just one ball-bearing is next to and left of that containing 64.

4 There are eight ball-bearings in box 3 and 32 in the pink box.

5 The brown box hasn't exactly four ball-bearings.

6 There are fewer than ten ball-bearings in box 6.

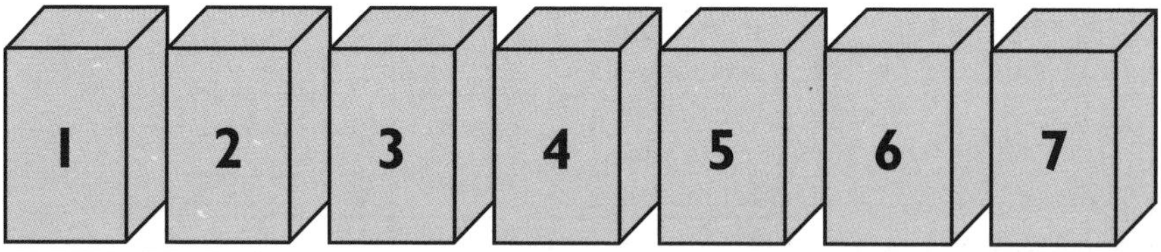

Colours:
Blue; brown; green; pink; red; white; yellow

Quantities:
1; 2; 4; 8;16; 32; 64

Box	Colour	Quantity

Starting tip:

Locate the box which contains the most ball-bearings.

THEIR NUMBER'S UP

Five friends regularly frequent their local bingo club, where last week each won an extra prize on the call of a particular number on a different day of the week. Can you sort out all the details?

Clues

1 Cissie won her prize when the number 24 was called.

2 Neil won his prize two days after the bottle of whisky was won on the call of the number 5.

3 Spencer's lucky day was later in the week than Bunny's and his winning number was lower than the one which won the tin of biscuits.

4 Rose won the portable television set.

5 The microwave oven was Thursday's prize.

6 83 was the lucky number on Tuesday, but 30 wasn't particularly lucky on Saturday.

	Microwave	Portable TV	Tin of biscuits	Umbrella	Whisky	5	24	30	66	83	Monday	Tuesday	Wednesday	Thursday	Saturday
Bunny															
Cissie															
Neil															
Rose															
Spencer															
Monday															
Tuesday															
Wednesday															
Thursday															
Saturday															
5															
24															
30															
66															
83															

Winner	Prize	Number	Day

MACK & MS KNYFE

Last year, hack writer Bob Wheel – writing as Mack Matcho – produced five thrillers featuring a female American private eye called Jakki Knyfe, tailored for the 'sex and violence' end of the market. From the clues below, can you work out in which month he wrote each book, in which US city it was set and what kind of crime Ms Knyfe set out to investigate?

Clues

1 In *Femme Fatale*, Jakki Knyfe is called in to investigate the murder of a tycoon's daughter, while in the book set in Denver (written in the first half of the year) she's hired to find out who's forging paintings in the style of one of America's greatest artists.

2 Bob wrote *Burning Heat* in November.

3 The story set in Pittsburgh, Pennsylvania, isn't *Siren Song* (which wasn't written in January).

4 The case of the burglary at the apartment of a crime boss's mistress didn't take Jakki Knyfe to Pittsburgh.

5 *Temptress* (set in Cleveland) isn't the book about the blackmailing of a corrupt politician, which was written in June.

6 The novel set in Seattle was produced in April.

	January	April	June	August	November	Cleveland	Denver	Miami	Pittsburgh	Seattle	Blackmail	Burglary	Forgery	Kidnapping	Murder
Burning Heat															
Femme Fatale																
Forbidden Fruit																
Siren Song																
Temptress																
Blackmail																
Burglary																
Forgery																
Kidnapping																
Murder																
Cleveland																
Denver																
Miami																
Pittsburgh																
Seattle																

Title	Month	City	Crime

IRRATIONAL EXPLANATIONS

Many people claim to have contact with aliens and other worlds, even very sensible, level-headed people. Here are examples of five – but can you link the year of each claim to the person who made it, his or her occupation and the nature of his or her claim?

Clues

1 Mrs Sobers claims that her body was taken over by aliens, while the bus driver claims that his children are in fact aliens.

2 Mr Featon-Ground (who made the most recent claim) isn't an estate agent.

3 Back in 1981 it was the doctor who reckoned to have had an alien encounter; the librarian made his or her claim four years after someone else spoke of being abducted by aliens and four years before Miss Clerehead told her story.

4 The sighting of alien spacecraft didn't take place in 1989.

5 In 1993, one of the five claimed to have originally come from another planet.

6 Mr Sayne is a teacher.

	Miss Clerehead	Mr Featon-Ground	Mr Normhall	Mr Sayne	Mrs Sobers	Bus driver	Doctor	Estate agent	Librarian	Teacher	Abducted by aliens	Another planet	Body taken over	Children are aliens	Saw alien spacecraft
1981															
1985															
1989															
1993															
1997															
Abducted by aliens															
Another planet															
Body taken over															
Children are aliens															
Saw alien spacecraft															
Bus driver															
Doctor															
Estate agent															
Librarian															
Teacher															

Year	Name	Occupation	Claim

HANGING MATTERS

Painter and decorator Roland Trestle had five paper-hanging jobs last week. From the following information, can you discover which room he tackled on each day, the number of rolls required and the style of paper each house-owner had chosen?

Clues

1 Tuesday's job involved more than four rolls of flowered wallpaper. Neither the striped paper nor that used in the sitting room was hung on Friday.

2 Roland did the hall and stairs on Thursday, using a roll more than he used of the abstract pattern.

3 He hung the five rolls on either Monday or Friday.

4 The kitchen job took the fewest number of rolls.

5 The woodchip paper was for the dining room, which he didn't do on either Monday or Friday.

6 The six rolls were of an embossed wallpaper.

Day	Room	No of rolls	Style

THE GRIMBOLD STORY

Recently, a number of books have been published about the life and work of 1990s financial whizkid Gavin Grimbold, each giving a different opinion as to the reason for his success. From the clues below, can you work out the name and qualification of each of the writers, the title of his or her book and why they say Grimbold made such a huge fortune?

Clues

1 The book (not *Grimbold*) which describes Gavin Grimbold as 'a misunderstood genius' wasn't written by the man's ex-business partner.

2 Mark Lamb wrote *Gold Bug*. David Cory's book isn't *Money Machine*.

3 The economist is a man.

4 Banker George Hall isn't the author of *Profit Without Honour*, which accuses Gavin Grimbold of dishonesty.

5 Ann Bull (who puts Grimbold's acquisition of riches down to sheer luck) used his name in the title of her book: Grimbold's ex-partner did not.

6 The occultist whose book (not *Money Machine*) accuses Grimbold of using black magic to influence the stock market didn't use the man's name in its title.

7 *Grimbold's Millions* is the work of an investigative journalist from a national daily paper.

	Banker	Economist	Ex-partner	Journalist	Occultist	Gold Bug	Grimbold	Grimbold's Millions	Money Machine	Profit W'out Hon	Black magic	Dishonesty	Genius	Hard work	Luck
Ann Bull															
David Cory															
George Hall															
Mark Lamb															
Rita Sharp															
Black magic															
Dishonesty															
Genius															
Hard work															
Luck															
Gold Bug															
Grimbold															
Grimbold's Millions															
Money Machine															
Profit W'out Hon															

Author	Qualification	Book title	Conclusion

PARBRIDGE PARISHES

The ancient town of Parbridge was once a great monastic centre and still boasts five parishes, each with its own historic church building. Can you discover the name of each parish, the name of the thoroughfare in which the parish church stands and the name of its current incumbent?

Clues

1 The Reverend Alan Johnson is rector of the parish marked E on the map, which isn't St Monica's; it doesn't have a common border with the parish named for the church in Guild Lane, which isn't St Hubert's.

2 Parish B is St Anselm's. The vicar of parish C isn't the Reverend Edwin Lucas.

3 The Reverend Oliver Matthews is the parish minister of St Ebba's.

4 The church of parish D is in West Square.

Parish Names:
St Anselm's; St Ebba's; St Hubert's; St Jude's; St Monica's

Street Names:
Barr Hill; Church Street; Guild Lane; Market Street; West Square

Clergy Names:
Revd A Johnson; Revd E Lucas; Revd I Marks; Revd O Matthews; Revd U Paul

5 The Reverend Ursula Paul's church is in Church Street.

6 St Jude's Church, once part of the monastery, is in Barr Hill. The parish of St Jude's, which has the River Par as one of its borders, doesn't have the Reverend Ian Marks as its current incumbent.

Parish	Name	Street	Clergy
A			
B			
C			
D			
E			

Starting tip:

Work out the name of the church in Parish E.

ROGUES' GALLERY

On the wall of the sheriff's office in Lawless Creek, Arizona, were six wanted posters side by side, as illustrated in the diagram and lettered A to F. Can you identify the subject of each poster and match him with his crime and the reward offered for his capture?

A	B	C	D	E	F
WANTED	WANTED	WANTED	WANTED	WANTED	WANTED

Clues

1 The reward offered for the capture of Rusty Nayle was $2,000 less than was offered for the notorious bank robber on poster F.

2 Brad Hall was wanted for murder; the price put on him was $1,000 less than was offered for Billy Cann, who was featured in the poster two places to the right.

3 $3,000 was the price offered for the sheep stealer.

4 The rustler wasn't Hank Artz.

5 The smallest sum was featured on the poster immediately to the left of the one depicting the stagecoach robber.

6 Artie Fishell's capture was worth $4,000 to whoever could bring it about; the kidnapper featured on an adjacent poster.

7 The $5,000 reward was advertised on poster C.

	Artie Fishell	Billy Cann	Brad Hall	Dan Druff	Hank Artz	Rusty Nayle	Bank robbery	Kidnap	Murder	Rustling	Sheep stealing	Stagecoach robbery	$1,000	$2,000	$3,000	$4,000	$5,000	$6,000
Poster A																		
Poster B																			
Poster C																			
Poster D																			
Poster E																			
Poster F																			

Poster	A	B	C	D	E	F
Crook						
Reward						
Crime						

IN THE SOAP

Several of the actors in TV's Eastbrook Street soap opera have been in it for some years. Below are five examples: from the information given, can you work out the name of the character played by each actor, the type of rôle and the number of years each has been in the soap?

Clues

1 James Tyler has been in the soap for four years, but not playing Mr Holland.

2 Jack Stretton plays a shopkeeper but hasn't been in the series for five years.

3 Jean Neville plays Eileen Pascoe; she's been in Eastbrook Street three years longer than the actor who plays the publican.

4 Adam Quinn has been in the programme for an even number of years, while the person who plays the market stallholder has been in it a year longer than Adam.

5 The actor playing Clark Foster has been with Eastbrook Street for six years.

6 The character of Fred Pascoe is a long-distance lorry driver.

	Clark Foster	Eileen Pascoe	Fred Pascoe	Len Hooton	Mr Holland	Café owner	Lorry driver	Market stallholder	Publican	Shopkeeper	Four years	Five years	Six years	Seven years	Ten years
Adam Quinn															
Alan Poole															
Jack Stretton															
James Tyler															
Jean Neville															
Four years															
Five years															
Six years															
Seven years															
Ten years															
Café owner															
Lorry driver															
Market s'holder															
Publican															
Shopkeeper															

Actor	Character	Type of rôle	Years in series

BRANCHES EVERYWHERE

In the back gardens of four neighbouring houses, four fathers have built tree houses (each in a different species of tree) for their sons. Can you name the boy who lives at each house and work out the kind of tree in which his den is built?

Clues

1 Darren's house is built in a beech tree.

2 The sycamore is in the garden of number 7, which isn't where Bradley Woods lives.

3 The horse chestnut, which doesn't house the den of young Forrest, isn't in the garden of number 3.

4 Mr Holt built a tree house in the garden of number 5.

5 Clive lives at number 1.

Forenames:
Andrew; Bradley; Clive; Darren

Surnames:
Forrest; Holt; Spinney; Woods

Trees:
Beech; horse chestnut; sycamore; walnut

No 7   **No 5**   **No 3**   **No 1**

House No	Forename	Surname	Tree
1			
3			
5			
7			

Starting tip: First work out the number of Bradley's house.

NOT TOO CLOSE

Laburnum Close is an exclusive development of four houses, each owned by men formerly eminent in different fields, but now retired. Can you name the man who lives at each of the houses and work out his former profession and the unoriginal name he has given his house?

Clues

1 The Larches, owned by the retired publisher, has a more northerly location than Mr Nutbrown's residence.

2 Mr Ashburton, the retired banker, bought the next house along Laburnum Close after The Oaks as you enter the development from the main road.

3 Mr Firman's house is numbered two lower than the former solicitor's. Mr Birchfield's home isn't number 1.

4 Number 3 is named The Laurels.

Owners:
Ashburton; Birchfield; Firman; Nutbrown

Professions:
Banker; judge; publisher; solicitor

House names:
The Elms; The Larches; The Laurels; The Oaks

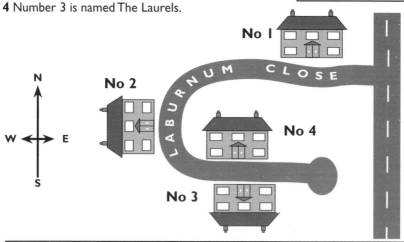

House No	Owner	Profession	House name
1			
2			
3			
4			

Starting tip:

First name the man who lives at number 1.

MEMORY LANE

A group of five friends were reminiscing about the cartoons they used to watch on television when they were children in the sixties. Each had a different favourite series. Can you fully identify the five, work out their present ages and say which cartoon each preferred?

Clues

1 Annie Mason is a year older than the man whose favourite cartoon used to be Bugs Bunny.

2 Roy, who is now 36, isn't two years older than Petula, whose favourite series wasn't Yogi Bear.

3 The Flintstones was the favourite of the person now aged 34.

4 Short is just a year younger than Allen.

5 Bernard, who was a great Tom And Jerry fan, is older than the person named Ryan, but not by a gap of two years.

	Allen	Burton	Mason	Ryan	Short	32	33	34	35	36	Bugs Bunny	Huckleberry Hound	The Flintstones	Tom And Jerry	Yogi Bear
Annie															
Bernard															
Petula															
Philip															
Roy															
Bugs Bunny															
Huckleberry H															
The Flintstones															
Tom And Jerry															
Yogi Bear															
32															
33															
34															
35															
36															

Forename	Surname	Current age	Cartoon

LOOKING AHEAD

Weatherman Wyndham Raine is giving the long-range weather forecast for the week ahead. From the following details, can you discover what the weather will be on each of the five days, the wind direction and the temperature?

Clues

1 'We will see the lowest temperatures of the week on Tuesday...'; this isn't the day to expect the sunshine and showers.

2 'Sunny, with a brisk north-easterly wind...'; on that day it will be warmer than the one with the sunshine and showers.

3 'There will be no sunshine on Wednesday'; nor will the wind be in the west on Wednesday.

4 No rain has been mentioned for Friday or the day when the wind will be in the west. On the unsettled day with 20 degrees, the wind won't be in the south-east.

5 '...winds in the east and a temperature of 21...'; cloud hasn't been mentioned for the day when the temperature will be 19.

6 'On Thursday we'll see cloud and rain...'

	Cloud and rain	Cloudy	Sunny	Sunshine/showers	Unsettled	East	North East	South	South East	West	18C	19C	20C	21C	22C
Monday															
Tuesday															
Wednesday															
Thursday															
Friday															
18C															
19C															
20C															
21C															
22C															
East															
North East															
South															
South East															
West															

Day	Weather	Wind direction	Temperature

NEIGHBOURS

Four couples who live in neighbouring semi-detached houses each have a different make of car. Can you name the pair who live in the houses numbered 1 to 7 and say which make of car they own?

Clues

1 Toby and Janet live in the house attached to the one whose owners drive the Volvo.

2 Shirley is the female half of the couple at number 1.

3 Nick and his wife drive the Peugeot. Their house bears a higher number than the one where Norma lives.

4 The Toyota (which can be seen outside number 5) doesn't belong to Laurie and his wife.

Husbands:
Laurie; Nick; Patrick; Toby

Wives:
Janet; Norma; Shirley; Stella

Cars:
Fiat; Peugeot; Toyota; Volvo

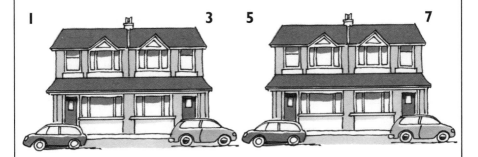

House No	Husband	Wife	Car
1			
3			
5			
7			

Starting tip:

Begin by naming Nick's wife.

WHOOPS!

Last week five waitresses were fired from the exclusive Café Bonaparte in London's West End for committing the worst sin in the Bonaparte's book, that of dropping food (or drink) on a customer. Can you work out who sinned on each of the listed days, what she dropped and on whom?

Clues

1 Donna (who was neither the first nor the second waitress to be fired) got her cards for dropping something all down the front of TV presenter Carol Singer.

2 Dawn Brakes, MP and Junior Transport Minister (who wasn't splattered on Friday), wasn't Rebecca's victim.

3 Gillian departed the Café Bonaparte's employ at 9.15pm on Thursday, shortly after splattering one of the restaurant's most famous customers.

4 Movie hunk Matt Finnish was soaked in red wine the night after Samantha managed to dump an entire sherry trifle in a diner's lap.

5 Olive Tree, the world's favourite romantic novelist, was the victim of Wednesday's accident.

6 The gravy was spilled on Tuesday, but not by Louise.

7 Monday's incident didn't involve chocolate sauce.

	Donna	Gillian	Louise	Rebecca	Samantha	Chocolate sauce	Gravy	Red wine	Tomato soup	Trifle	Carol Singer	Dawn Brakes	Lord Sandladies	Matt Finnish	Olive Tree
Monday															
Tuesday															
Wednesday															
Thursday															
Friday															
Carol Singer																
Dawn Brakes																
Lord Sandladies																
Matt Finnish																
Olive Tree																
Choc sauce						
Gravy						
Red wine						
Tomato soup						
Trifle						

Day	Waitress	Item spilled	Diner

VALERIE'S VALENTINES

Just before Valerie Vargrage left home on 14 February to go to work at the offices of Universal Merchants, the postman popped five Valentine's cards through her door. She only had time for a quick look at them, but was able to tell who had sent each one. Can you work out what was on the front and the inside of each card, how it was signed and who sent it?

Clues

1 The card signed 'John Doe', easily recognised as being from the office boy by the spelling of Valerie as 'Valery', didn't have a picture of a bunch of roses.

2 The card with lovebirds (which contained a cheeky limerick) wasn't signed by 'you-know-who'.

3 The card from the UM sales manager (written in the same green ink he uses for internal memos) contained a two-line verse, but wasn't signed either 'your secret admirer' or 'you-know-who'.

4 There was a four-line verse in the card signed by 'your mystery man'.

5 'Mr X's' card had a heart on the front.

6 The teddy bear card (which, being unstamped, had to be from the postman!), didn't contain four lines of prose. Neither the card with a picture of Cupid nor that with the four lines of prose was from Valerie's boss, whose handwriting she found every bit as easy to recognise as that of her husband.

	Four lines prose	Four lines verse	Greeting only	Limerick	Two lines verse	John Doe	Mr X	Mystery man	Secret admirer	You-know-who	Boss	Husband	Office boy	Postman	Sales manager
Cupid															
Heart															
Lovebirds															
Roses															
Teddy bear															
Boss															
Husband															
Office boy															
Postman															
Sales manager															
John Doe															
Mr X															
Mystery man															
Secret admirer															
You-know-who															

Picture	Contents	Signature	Sender

DOGGY DECISIONS

The four dogs lettered A to D in the diagram were the finalists at the Dog Show. Each of the four judges placed the dogs in a different order on their mark sheets. Can you work out the name and breed of each of the four dogs and the positions in which they were placed?

Clues

1 No judge's name initial matched the letter of the dog in the diagram that he or she placed first and no two dogs were given the same placing by more than one judge.

2 Barry gave first place to the Labrador, while Ann's first choice was Crusty.

3 Chloë placed dog B third in her list, but she didn't give fourth position to the dog immediately to the right of Rusty, as you look at the picture.

4 Trusty, the Samoyed, is directly next to the dog which David placed first.

5 Ann placed dog B higher than Dusty in her marking order.

6 Barry didn't give third place to the Alsatian.

7 The judge who placed dog D first put dog B last.

> **Dogs:**
> Crusty; Dusty; Rusty; Trusty

> **Breeds:**
> Alsatian; Dalmatian; Labrador; Samoyed

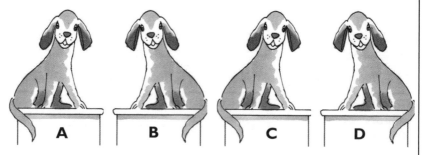

A   **B**   **C**   **D**

Name: _____ _____ _____ _____

Breed: _____ _____ _____ _____

	Ann	Barry	Chloë	David
1st				
2nd				
3rd				
4th				

Starting tip:
First discover which judge is referred to in clue 7.

GASWORKS COTTAGE

Gasworks Cottage isn't a real house, it's the rarest in a set of a hundred miniature buildings marketed by a well-known china company. At a recent convention, five collectors who have been lucky enough to acquire one for less than the normal price of £85.00 compared notes. Can you work out how much each paid and where and in which town it was purchased?

Clues

1 The Gasworks Cottage bought at an auction was more than £3 (but less than £24) cheaper than the one from the antique shop, which wasn't visited by Miss Peabody.

2 The junk shop proprietor and the street market stallholder both charged more for Gasworks Cottage than was demanded in Norwich.

3 Mrs Welburn paid less for her Gasworks Cottage than did Mr Grayson, but more than whoever found one in Hastings, who didn't pay £3.

4 The man who found his Gasworks Cottage in Swindon, but not in a junk shop, didn't pay £27.00. The woman who bought a Gasworks Cottage in St Alban's had to spend more than £27.00.

5 The owner of the second-hand china shop sold a Gasworks Cottage for £3 less than one man paid in Birmingham.

	£3.00	£6.00	£27.00	£30.00	£54.00	Antique shop	Auction	China shop	Junk shop	Street market	Birmingham	Hastings	Norwich	St Alban's	Swindon
Mrs Browning															
Mr Grayson															
Mr Jesmond															
Miss Peabody															
Mrs Welburn															
Birmingham															
Hastings															
Norwich															
St Alban's															
Swindon															
Antique shop															
Auction															
China shop															
Junk shop															
Street market															

Collector	Paid	Bought from	Town

CLASS DISTINCTION

The diagram shows four classrooms leading off a corridor at Netherlipp High School. In each of rooms 1 to 4 a different lesson is being taken by a different year group. Can you insert in the spaces provided the name of the teacher in each room, the year group he or she's teaching and the subject of the lesson? NB – Year numbers increase with the age of the children: year 8 pupils are a year older than year 7 pupils.

Clues

1 The Maths class is in the room between the one where Mr Liddell is teaching on one side and the one where the year 7 pupils are being taught on the other.

2 The pupils learning German are a year older than those in the History class, which isn't Miss Biddle's.

3 The oldest pupils aren't in room 4.

4 Mrs Fiddle is in charge of the English class, who are older than the pupils Mr Diddle is teaching in room 3.

Teachers:
Miss Biddle; Mr Diddle; Mrs Fiddle; Mr Liddell

Years:
Year 7; year 8; year 9; year 10

Subjects:
English; German; History; Maths

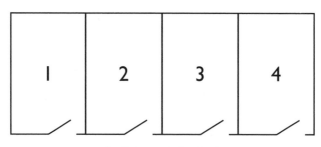

CORRIDOR

Class	Teacher	Year	Subject
1			
2			
3			
4			

Starting tip:

First work out which lesson the year 7 pupils are taking.

JUBILEE TERRACE

Five couples who figure prominently in the TV soap Jubilee Terrace have recently found their marriages under stress for various reasons. Can you fully identify each pair and say why their marriage is in trouble?

Clues

1 Gordon's compulsive gambling is putting a great strain on his marriage. He's not Mr Renshaw.

2 The Listers, whose marriage is crumbling because of uncontrolled violence, have forenames of equal length.

3 Shirley (whose surname immediately follows Darren's in the alphabetical list) isn't the woman who has just discovered an unpleasant secret from her husband's past.

4 Denise is Mrs Fenner.

5 Shane isn't married to Penny. Penny isn't Mrs Markham.

6 Arnold's surname is Gibson.

7 Mandy is having an affair with her husband's best friend.

	Denise	Diane	Mandy	Penny	Shirley	Fenner	Gibson	Lister	Markham	Renshaw	Affair	Arguments	Gambling	Past secret	Violence
Arnold															
Darren															
Gordon															
Pete															
Shane															
Affair																
Arguments																
Gambling																
Past secret																
Violence																
Fenner																
Gibson																
Lister																
Markham																
Renshaw																

Husband	Wife	Surname	Problem

A REWARDING TIME

In due course five of the villains featured in Logic Puzzle 18, Rogues' Gallery, were brought to book. From the clues given below and the information obtained by solving the earlier problem, can you name the man who collected each reward, work out his description and say in which order each of the crooks was captured?

Clues

1 Lou Tennant collected the reward offered on poster B; he wasn't the mortician, who made a later claim.

2 The apothecary claimed the reward offered for the sheep stealer.

3 Bob Binns made his claim next after the farmhand.

4 Jack Knife, the bounty hunter, wasn't the second man to benefit, who denounced the man featured on poster F.

5 Jim Crack made the third claim for reward money; he didn't turn in the crook featured on poster D.

6 The oil prospector's reward was an odd number of thousands of dollars.

7 Chad Valley didn't make the fourth claim, which didn't involve the rustler.

	Bob Binns	Chad Valley	Jack Knife	Jim Crack	Lou Tennant	Apothecary	Bounty hunter	Farmhand	Mortician	Oil prospector	First	Second	Third	Fourth	Fifth
Artie Fishell															
Brad Hall															
Dan Druff															
Hank Artz															
Rusty Nayle															
First															
Second															
Third															
Fourth															
Fifth															
Apothecary															
Bounty hunter															
Farmhand															
Mortician															
Oil prospector															

Crook	Claimant	Description	Order

JUST FETED

Last summer five fêtes were held at various locations in our neighbourhood in successive months, each of which suffered an unfortunate mishap. Can you work out the venue for each month's fête, say by which group it was organised and identify the mishap?

Clues

1 The church fête was held in the grounds of the vicarage as usual, but the Junior Soccer League's fête in July wasn't staged at the football stadium.

2 The Women's Institute guest of honour failed to turn up to open their fête, which took place the month before the one held in the Town Hall.

3 The village green was the location chosen for the August fête, which wasn't run by the tennis club.

4 The fête affected by the power cut took place later than that spoiled by heavy rain.

5 The preparations for the June fête were badly disrupted when the hired marquee wasn't delivered as arranged.

6 The loudspeaker system failed at Valley Farm the month after the fête run by the scouts was held.

	Football stadium	Town Hall	Valley Farm	Vicarage	Village green	Church	Jnr Soccer League	Scouts	Tennis club	Women's Institute	No guest	No marquee	Power cut	Rain	Speakers failed
May															
June															
July															
August															
September															
No guest															
No marquee															
Power cut															
Rain															
Speakers failed															
Church															
Jnr Soccer															
Scouts															
Tennis club															
Women's Inst															

Month	Venue	Organisers	Mishap

TAKING STOCK

Money-market guru Gordon Gerbil was in a buying mood this morning. Scanning the movements of the money market, he bought five blocks of shares in up and coming companies. Can you work out at what time during the first hour's work each purchase was made, the name of the company, the price paid per share and the number bought?

Clues

1 At 9.30 Gordon picked up the phone to buy shares in Euro-Amalgamated, paying less per share than for those he acquired in Imperial Holdings; and he bought one hundred more of the former than the latter.

2 The AD&G shares (of which he didn't buy exactly 300 or 500) were at 126p and weren't bought first.

3 The largest number of shares (purchased last) weren't the cheapest per share.

4 Gordon acquired shares in the Albion Group ten minutes before he bought those in BBF.

5 The shares bought at 9.50 were priced at 110p each.

6 He bought 400 shares in one company at 73p per share.

	AD&G	Albion Group	BBF	Euro-Amalgamated	Imperial Holdings	40p	73p	110p	126p	142p	200	300	400	500	600
9.00am															
9.20am															
9.30am															
9.50am															
10.00am															
200											
300											
400											
500											
600											
40p						
73p						
110p						
126p						
142p						

Time	Company	Price per share	Quantity

BATTLESHIPS

This puzzle is based on the old game of battleships. Your task is to find the vessels in the diagram. Some parts of boats or sea squares have already been filled in, and a number next to a row or column refers to the number of occupied squares in that row or column. The boats may be positioned horizontally or vertically, but no two boats or parts of boats are in adjacent squares – horizontally, vertically or diagonally.

Aircraft Carrier:

Battleships:

Cruisers:

Destroyers:

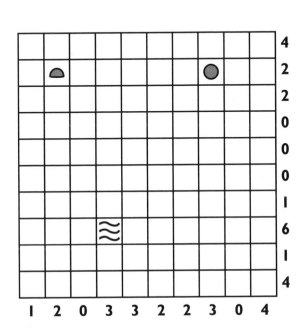

LOGI-5

Every row across and column down should contain five letters:
A, B, C, D and E, appearing once each. Also every shape (shown by the
thick lines) must contain each of the letters A, B, C, D and E, appearing
once each. Can you fill the grid?

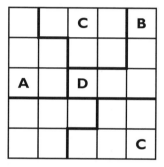

ABC

Every row across and column down is to have each of the letters A, B and
C and two empty squares. The letter outside the grid shows the first or
second letter in the direction of the arrow. Can you fill the grid?

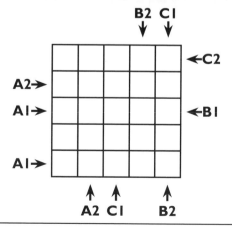

NOT-SO-GRAND PRIX

Only seven competitors entered the Balonia Grand Prix this year. Can you work out each one's pit number (one to seven), together with his starting position and finishing place and enter them in the table below?
NB – The three numbers for each of the drivers were all different.

Clues

1 Girling's pit number was one lower than that of the man who started in sixth position and one higher than that of the man who finished in third place.

2 Croft is the only competitor who had even numbers for his pit number, starting number and finishing position; he finished in a better position than the one in which he started.

3 Fetterman started in the same position as Downes finished and finished in the same position as Girling started; his pit number was one lower than that of the man who finished in second position.

4 Armendez started one ahead of Stottski, who wasn't in pit seven and finished two places ahead of him.

5 Both Ortiz and Girling started two places behind their finishing positions.

6 Downes' pit number was two less than his starting position; his finishing position had a smaller number than both.

7 The competitor who had pit number one finished sixth, while the one who started sixth finished first.

Driver	Pit number	Starting position	Finishing place
Armendez			
Croft			
Downes			
Fetterman			
Girling			
Ortiz			
Stottski			

Starting tip:

Work out Croft's starting position.

CURSING THE CURSE

The tomb of Queen Nem-Isis is said to have a curse on it and five recent visitors have reason to think this may be true. Can you work out their full names, the day of each one's visit and the misfortune which befell them soon after?

Clues

1 The visitor who developed a stomach upset saw the tomb the day after the one who had his wallet stolen; the visit of Mrs King, who isn't Julia, was earlier than both.

2 Peter's visit was more than a day earlier than that of the person surnamed Holliday but next after that of the visitor whose spectacles were lost.

3 Rowena's visit was the day after Julia's but the person who had the misfortune to fall in the Nile saw the tomb later, but not next after Rowena.

4 The visitor with the surname Sands suffered no medical consequences but the next day's visitor had the stomach upset.

5 Barry saw the tomb the day after Cave. Marjorie saw it later than the two people who lost possessions.

	Cave	Holliday	King	Palmer	Sands	Monday	Tuesday	Wednesday	Thursday	Friday	Broke ankle	Fell in river	Lost spectacles	Lost wallet	Stomach upset
Barry															
Julia															
Marjorie															
Peter															
Rowena															
Broke ankle															
Fell in river															
Lost spectacles															
Lost wallet															
Stomach upset															
Monday															
Tuesday															
Wednesday															
Thursday															
Friday															

Forename	Surname	Day	Misfortune

THE ICING ON THE CAKE

Betty was an expert in cake icing and decorating and was often asked by her friends to produce cakes for special occasions. Can you work out the full details of her five most recent assignments, saying for what occasion she made a cake in each month, its shape and which colour of icing she used for the inscription on each cake?

Clues

1 The heart-shaped cake was chosen for the engagement party, which was a later one than the one for which Betty used the yellow icing for the lettering.

2 The blue inscription on the horse-shoe shaped cake didn't refer to anyone's birthday; this cake was made earlier than the rectangular one.

3 The wedding cake was produced in November.

4 The square cake was made the month before that with an inscription in pink.

5 The cake Betty made in August wasn't round in shape and it wasn't for the 18th birthday celebrations.

6 Green was the colour selected for the inscription wishing the recipient a long and happy retirement; this wasn't the December cake.

	18th birthday	40th birthday	Engagement	Retirement	Wedding	Heart-shaped	Horse-shoe	Rectangular	Round	Square	Blue	Green	Orange	Pink	Yellow
August															
September															
October															
November															
December															
Blue															
Green															
Orange															
Pink															
Yellow															
Heart-shaped															
Horse-shoe															
Rectangular															
Round															
Square															

Month	Occasion	Shape	Colour

JUST THE TICKET

Five worthy causes were running tombola stalls at the local village fête and a visiting VIP had at least one go on each. Luckily she also won a prize on each, drawing a ticket that ended in either a 0 or a 5. From the following information, can you discover how many tickets were bought at each stall, the number of the winning ticket in each case and the prize?

Clues

1 The number of the winning ticket from the Drama Group stall was higher than that which won the table mats, but lower than that on the winning ticket from amongst the twelve bought (not in aid of a church fund) at one stall.

2 The number on the winning ticket from the batch of six was higher than that from the batch of ten, but five lower than the ticket which won the bottle of lemonade.

3 The number on the winning ticket from the two bought at one stall was ten higher than that which won the vase, but ten lower than the winning ticket from the batch of five.

4 The number on the winning ticket from the Scouts stall was lower than that from the School Association stall.

5 The prize from the Scouts tombola was neither the bottle of lemonade nor the bottle of wine.

6 The batch of five tickets won a bottle, but not in the tombola in aid of church restoration.

	Two	Five	Six	Ten	Twelve	25	30	35	40	50	Lemonade	Table mats	Tin of beans	Vase	Wine
Church Hall															
Church Rest'n															
Drama Group															
School Assoc															
Scouts															
Lemonade															
Table mats															
Tin of beans															
Vase															
Wine															
25															
30															
35															
40															
50															

Organiser	No of tickets	Winning No	Prize

ON MANOEUVRES

Five members of a military vehicle club set off for a rally. Each was driving a different type of vehicle, manufactured in a different year and each was unfortunately late in arriving at the rally by a different number of minutes. Can you sort out all the details?

Clues

1 The Land-Rover, which was made in 1951, wasn't as late to the rally as Barry's vehicle.

2 Geoff's lorry was manufactured the year before the vehicle which arrived just five minutes late.

3 Mike's vehicle wasn't built in 1943.

4 Dave was all of twenty-five minutes behind time when he finally turned up.

5 Stephen was later arriving than the owner of the Jeep.

6 The vehicle produced in 1945 was fifteen minutes late arriving at the rally.

7 The oldest of the five vehicles wasn't the motor-cycle.

	Jeep	Land-Rover	Lorry	Motor-cycle	Staff car	1942	1943	1944	1945	1951	5 minutes	10 minutes	15 minutes	20 minutes	25 minutes
Barry															
Dave															
Geoff															
Mike															
Stephen															
5 minutes															
10 minutes															
15 minutes															
20 minutes															
25 minutes															
1942															
1943															
1944															
1945															
1951															

Name	Vehicle	Year	Minutes late

LONELY VIGILS

In the later years of the Roman occupation of Britain, the garrisons in the legionary fortresses were much depleted. In Deva, for example, they could spare only one man at a time to guard each of the four walls. Can you indicate in the diagram the name of the soldier on each wall, his home country and the number of years he had served in his legion?

Clues

1 The wall patrolled by Blunderbuss was opposite the one whose guard had twelve years' service; he wasn't Rictus.

2 The man on the south wall was neither Voluminus nor the one from Syria.

3 The man from Gallia had been assigned to the west wall; the one from Africa had eleven years' service behind him and the man on the north wall had served for nine years.

4 The duty centurion making a clockwise tour of the walls would have come across Hiatus next after the man from Germania, neither of whom was the longest serving legionary.

Names:
Blunderbuss; Hiatus; Rictus; Voluminus

Countries:
Africa; Gallia; Germania; Syria

Years' service: 9; 10; 11; 12

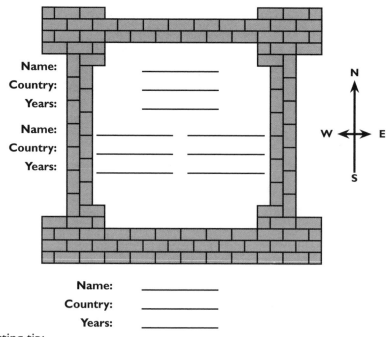

Name:
Country:
Years:

Name:
Country:
Years:

Name:
Country:
Years:

Name:
Country:
Years:

N
W ← → E
S

Starting tip:

Work out who has served for twelve years.

SECOND THOUGHTS

Desmond the Ditherer recently spent a day at the races. You can well imagine the agonies he went through deciding which horses to back. And at every race, when he had reached his decision, at the very last second he switched to another horse, to his disadvantage. Can you fill in the table below, naming the horse he had first picked and the one to which he switched for each race and adding the positions each achieved?

Clues

1 Desmond's first choice for the 3.30 came in one place lower than that of his first choice for the 2.00, but three places higher than his second choice for the 2.30.

2 Rallentando was the horse to which he switched from the one which won its race, which was next before the race in which he rejected the horse which finished second in favour of Claredown.

3 If he had not switched to Dinkum Lad, Desmond would have had a third-placed horse in the race preceding the one where his original choice was Trottophan.

4 Great Scott's finishing position was higher than that of his first choice two races earlier.

5 The finishing position attained by Big Cheese was double that gained by the horse from which he switched to Big Cheese.

6 He backed Brunski in the next race after the one where he discarded Arivale, whose position was one higher than that of the horse rejected in favour of Brunski.

7 The horse he backed in the 3.00 reached one place better than the one he backed in the 4.00 after rejecting Cynosure.

First choices:
Arivale; Cynosure; Great Scott; Grey Mist; Trottophan

Second choices:
Big Cheese; Brunski; Claredown; Dinkum Lad; Rallentando

Positions of 1st choices:
First; second; third; fourth; fifth

Positions of 2nd choices:
Sixth; seventh; eighth; ninth; tenth

RACE CARD				
	First choice	**Place**	**Backed**	**Place**
2.00				
2.30				
3.00				
3.30				
4.00				

Starting tip:
Work out in which race Desmond's original choice was the winner.

SPORTING SCHOLARS

Five young men are currently attending different American universities on sports scholarships. Each is involved in a different game or sport. Can you identify the five young sportsmen, say which university each attends and name his sport?

Clues

1 Neither Boyd Greaves nor his friend at Harwell are majoring in athletics or ice hockey.

2 Lincoln's scholarship is at Parkleigh. His surname isn't Lambert.

3 The tennis player isn't at Cornford.

4 Nicholas is a promising young baseball player.

5 O'Driscoll (not Franklin) is studying at Gayle University. His subject there isn't athletics.

6 Jones is the football player (American football not soccer, of course). The name of his university has one more letter than that of the one where Howard is a student.

| | Surname | | | | | University | | | | | Sport | | | | |
---	Greaves	Howard	Jones	Lambert	O'Driscoll	Cornford	Gayle	Harwell	Parkleigh	Stanburg	Athletics	Baseball	Football	Ice hockey	Tennis
Boyd															
Franklin															
Lincoln															
Nicholas															
Warren															
Athletics															
Baseball															
Football															
Ice hockey															
Tennis															
Cornford															
Gayle															
Harwell															
Parkleigh															
Stanburg															

Forename	Surname	University	Sport

RAPID REPERTORY

The X-Pres Players recently performed five different plays, one in each of the weeks of their five-week tour. Can you work out who wrote each play and where and in what order it was performed?

Clues

1 The name of the author of the comedy is next alphabetically after that of the author of the play which was put on fourth and next before that of the author of the farce; none of these three plays was performed at the Playhouse.

2 The play performed at the Alhambra came after the one written by Flatt and before the farce.

3 The comedy (not performed second) was played more than a week before the company appeared at the Coliseum.

4 There were bigger audiences for the whodunnit (not by Archer) than for either Penman's play or the one performed at the Forum (which was next but one after Penman's).

5 The kitchen-sink play was earlier in the repertoire than the one by Lines but later than that at the Playhouse.

6 The costume drama immediately preceded the play at the Royal.

	Archer	Boarder	Flatt	Lines	Penman	Alhambra	Coliseum	Forum	Playhouse	Royal	First	Second	Third	Fourth	Fifth
Comedy															
Costume drama															
Farce															
Kitchen-sink															
Whodunnit															
First															
Second															
Third															
Fourth															
Fifth															
Alhambra															
Coliseum															
Forum															
Playhouse															
Royal															

Genre	Playwright	Theatre	Order

LOTS AND LOTS

In the office of the auctioneers Hammer and Tongs there is a chart showing the categories and numbers of articles to be auctioned next week. Can you discover what type(s) of articles will be auctioned and in what quantity on each of the listed days?

Clues

1 The quantity of books and folios to be auctioned is higher than the items of jewellery, but lower than the number of articles earmarked for Tuesday's auction.

2 The auction of furniture is to be held the day after that of the 294 items which outnumber the items of furniture by more than 50.

3 The number of stamps for auction is next after the number of pictures, but both are smaller than the number due for Thursday's auction.

4 The Saturday number is next after the number of stamps, but next before the number of books and folios.

5 Monday's quota is next below Friday's.

6 Every digit in Wednesday's number of lots appears at least once in the numbers for all the other days; this isn't the case for Friday's lot number.

	Books & folios	China & glass	Furniture	Jewellery	Pictures	Stamps	132	167	185	223	271	294
Monday												
Tuesday												
Wednesday												
Thursday												
Friday												
Saturday												
132												
167												
185												
223												
271												
294												

Day	Category	Number

LOGI-PATH

Use your deductive reasoning to form a pathway from the box marked 'START' to the box marked 'FINISH', moving either horizontally or vertically (but not diagonally) from square to adjacent square. The number at the beginning of every row or column indicates exactly how many boxes in that row or column your pathway must pass through. The small diagram at the bottom of the page is given as an example of how it works.

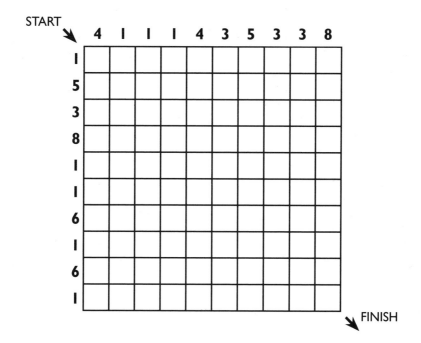

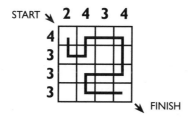

ON THE BALL

It was a day of great excitement at the Eventide Home, when England ran out for their first match in 2002's World Cup. Six residents grabbed the front row of seats in the TV lounge, some wearing scarves, some sporting replica shirts and some nursing old-style rattles dug out for the occasion. Can you name the occupant of each seat and work out his or her age?

Clues

1 Harold still has clear memories of his team, Brentford, playing Grimsby Town in the old First Division. He has Mrs Finney immediately to his left and the 91-year-old immediately to his right.

2 Alice watched Arsenal when they won five League Championships and two FA Cups in the 1930s and is occupying seat E, wearing her red and white scarf, to show her continuing support.

3 The dearest wish of Mr Carter (who is 83) is to see Preston North End back where they belong, at the top of the Premier League.

4 The 80-year-old resident (not Mavis) whose surname isn't Franklin, was the first to reach the lounge and book seat C for an ideal view of the game.

5 Stanley (a former Wolves supporter and now in his eighties) sat waving an old gold and black rattle, two places to Edith Swift's right.

6 The 95-year-old wasn't in seat B.

7 The resident surnamed Matthews sat between a man and a woman.

	Alice	Edith	Harold	Mavis	Stanley	Ted	Carter	Finney	Franklin	Matthews	Swift	Wright	78	80	83	86	91	95
Seat A																		
Seat B																			
Seat C																			
Seat D																			
Seat E																			
Seat F																			

Seat	A	B	C	D	E	F
Forename						
Surname						
Age						

DOMINO SEARCH

A standard set of dominoes has been laid out, using numbers instead of dots for clarity. With the aid of a sharp pencil and a keen brain, can you draw in the lines to show where each domino has been placed? You may find the check grid useful – crossing off each domino as you find it.

6	6	4	4	4	3	6	6
5	0	1	2	5	4	0	2
0	0	3	4	5	2	5	0
1	5	1	1	1	2	5	2
1	4	3	0	6	1	4	3
2	5	5	2	2	3	3	1
6	6	0	3	4	0	6	3

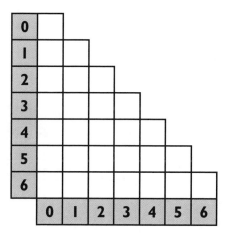

SCOTCH MIST

Three couples who went on holiday last year encountered very different weather conditions. Can you match the pairs, say where each couple went and work out the weather each encountered?

Clues

1 One couple encountered the infamous Scotch mist.

2 Patrick's holiday destination wasn't in Spain.

3 Jenny, whose husband isn't Peter, found the heat wave a bit too much for comfort.

4 Paul and Joyce are one of the three couples.

5 Joan's holiday wasn't interrupted by the floods.

Husband	Wife	Location	Weather

SAY IT WITH FLOWERS

Daisy received birthday cards from her three granddaughters, each having pictures of different numbers of flowers. Can you work out where each granddaughter lives and the quantity and type of flowers on every card?

Clues

1 The card from the Preston granddaughter, who isn't Karen, hasn't five flowers.

2 There were more than three freesias on Janet's card. Janet doesn't live in Lincoln.

3 The card with four roses wasn't from Daphne.

	Bristol	Lincoln	Preston	Freesias	Roses	Sunflowers	Three	Four	Five
Daphne									
Janet									
Karen									
Three									
Four									
Five									
Freesias									
Roses									
Sunflowers									

Granddaughter	Home town	Flower	Number

A WALK IN THE SUN

Last Saturday, Adam Walker spent the day strolling on the moors near his home town, stopping off at four villages for a drink and a snack at the local pub. From the clues below, can you work out the order in which he visited the villages, the name of each one's pub and what Adam ate there? (His drinks order was always the same – one pint of bitter.)

Clues

1 At the King's Head Adam drank a pint of bitter and ate one of the landlady's delicious home-made sausage rolls.

2 Adam stopped at one other village after Moortop (where the pub isn't called the Fox and Pheasant) before he reached Beckford, where he enjoyed a pork pie at the local.

3 Adam's third stop was at Cragfoot, where the pub's name includes a colour.

4 The second pub Adam visited, which was where he ate a cheese roll, wasn't the Red Cow.

	Beckford	Cragfoot	Moortop	Tarnside	Black Bear	Fox and Pheasant	King's Head	Red Cow	Cheese roll	Ham sandwich	Pork pie	Sausage roll
First												
Second												
Third												
Fourth												
Cheese roll												
Ham sandwich												
Pork pie												
Sausage roll												
Black Bear												
Fox and Pheasant												
King's Head												
Red Cow												

BLACK BEAR

Order	Village	Pub name	Snack

SUNKEN SUBS

The UXS class of submarines, or U-boats as they were known, were an unsuccessful German Navy experiment dating from 1912. Only four were built and all sank within a year of being launched. Can you work out the name of each U-boat's captain and where and why it sank?

Clues

1 The UXS-3 went down in the mouth of the harbour at Cuxhaven.

2 UXS-4, which went down for the last time after being caught in a fierce storm, wasn't Kapitan Von Nadose's vessel.

3 The U-boat which sank in the Irish Sea after being attacked – if that's the word – by an amorous whale wasn't the UXS-2.

4 Kapitan Von Kee's U-boat was numbered between the one which sank after springing a leak and the one that went down in the Wash while on a visit to England.

5 Kapitan Von Derful's boat sank in the Skagerrak on its way up into the Baltic.

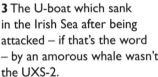

	Von Atatime	Von Derful	Von Kee	Von Nadose	Cuxhaven	Irish Sea	Skagerrak	Wash	Attacked by whale	Collision	Sank in storm	Sprang leak
UXS-1												
UXS-2												
UXS-3												
UXS-4												
Attacked by whale												
Collision												
Sank in storm												
Sprang leak												
Cuxhaven												
Irish Sea												
Skagerrak												
Wash												

U-boat	Captain	Where sunk	How sunk

TRANSPORTS OF DELIGHT

Photographer Len Scapp provides the cover pictures for the quarterly magazine *Vintage Transport* and already has all the shots for next year. From the clues below, can you work out which model posed for each issue's cover, over what kind of vehicle she's draping her not-always-fully-dressed self and what's in the background?

Clues

1 The issue of Vintage Transport with a dilapidated barn on the cover, which won't be the one for the first quarter, won't appear immediately after the one with the old country pub on the front.

2 The 1929 Midget sports car with Roberta at the wheel will feature on the *Vintage Transport* cover in an even-numbered quarter of the year.

3 The traditional gypsy caravan passing a working windmill (Len and his model had to go a long way to find one of those) will appear on the front of *Vintage Transport* the quarter before Michelle is featured.

4 Jackie, who wasn't photographed outside the pub or the windmill, isn't pictured with the pony and authentic Victorian trap.

5 Denise's picture will be seen the quarter after the model sitting in a World War II Jeep.

	Denise	Jackie	Michelle	Roberta	Gypsy caravan	Jeep	Pony and trap	Sports car	Barn	Pub	Railway station	Windmill
Jan–March												
April–June												
July–Sept												
Oct–Dec												
Barn								
Pub								
Railway station								
Windmill								
Gypsy caravan				
Jeep				
Pony and trap				
Sports car				

Issue	Model	Transport	Background

FOUR MEN IN A BOAT

The diagram shows an aerial view of three boats lined up for the start of a coxless fours race. Can you identify the men who occupy positions 1 to 4 in each of the boats lettered A to C?

NB – Remember that the front man in each boat is number 1, as they row facing the opposite way to the direction in which the boat travels.

Clues

1 By coincidence Lewis is immediately behind Carroll in one of the boats.

2 Anson's position in boat B is numbered one higher than that of Edwards' position in boat C.

3 Davies is number 2 in boat A.

4 Kelly is a member of the same crew as Farrow.

5 Harding is two positions in front of Jakeman in boat B.

6 Morgan's boat is indicated by a later letter of the alphabet than Giles'.

7 Baker is rower 1 in boat C, whose number 3 has a six-letter surname.

Names:
Anson; Baker; Carroll; Davies; Edwards; Farrow; Giles; Harding; Jakeman; Kelly; Lewis; Morgan

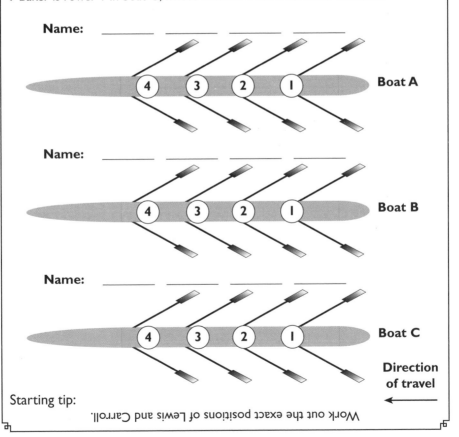

Name: ＿＿＿ ＿＿＿ ＿＿＿ ＿＿＿

Boat A

Name: ＿＿＿ ＿＿＿ ＿＿＿ ＿＿＿

Boat B

Name: ＿＿＿ ＿＿＿ ＿＿＿ ＿＿＿

Boat C

Direction of travel
←

Starting tip:

Work out the exact positions of Lewis and Carroll.

CRIMINAL MASTERMINDS

Well, they're not criminals themselves, but five scriptwriters have been commissioned by Albion TV to turn out two-part whodunnits set in different parts of England. Can you work out the title of each writer's work, their detective's name and the location in which the story is set?

Clues

1 The script set in rural Norfolk doesn't feature Superintendent Nick Verges.

2 Sergeant Luke Tyrrel's male creator has chosen his own home town of Newcastle-upon-Tyne as a setting.

3 *Walk In Fear* is set in and around Brighton. It isn't Ted Wallace's script featuring Inspector Chris Gower.

4 Chief Inspector Samantha Denny tracks down the killer in *Sons Of Eve*.

5 Anna Creasey, whose detective isn't police surgeon Dr Jennifer Evans, is the writer of *Out Of Sight*.

6 Damon Gardner's script has a Liverpool location; Paul Sayers' script isn't entitled *Born To Die*.

	Born To Die	Life For Life	Out Of Sight	Sons Of Eve	Walk In Fear	Chief Insp Denny	Dr Evans	Insp Gower	Sgt Tyrrel	Supt Verges	Brighton	Liverpool	Newcastle	Rural Devon	Rural Norfolk
Anna Creasey															
Damon Gardner															
Kate Marsh															
Paul Sayers															
Ted Wallace															
Brighton															
Liverpool															
Newcastle															
Rural Devon															
Rural Norfolk															
Chief Insp Denny															
Dr Evans															
Insp Gower															
Sgt Tyrrel															
Supt Verges															

Writer	Title	Detective	Location

PUB ENTERTAINMENT

Lots of pubs offer entertainment as well as drink and food, but tonight the London hostelries listed here are providing some very special – not to mention obscure – performances. From the clues below, can you work out the location (street and postal district) of each pub, together with the entertainment it is offering?

Clues

1 The W1 pub, which isn't in Knight Street, isn't the one which is putting on a display of Micronesian fruit-juggling by the Farounkhi Brothers.

2 The Hansom Cab (which isn't in Paxton Court), is in a lower-numbered postal district than both of the pubs with one-word names and is offering patrons the chance to see one of the world's very few indoor boomerang throwers.

3 Mildmay Place is in London EC4. It's in NW3 that the authentic Victorian flea circus will be performing.

4 Angela Ostroj and her Performing Fish have been booked for tonight by the pub in Oslo Square.

5 The Wellington's postal district is numbered two higher than that of the Antelope.

6 The Duke of Dorset is at the top end of Bute Terrace.

	Bute Terrace	Knight Street	Mildmay Place	Oslo Square	Paxton Court	EC4	NW3	SW5	W1	WC2	Albanian folk music	Flea circus	Fruit-juggling	Indoor boomerangs	Performing fish
Antelope															
Duke of Dorset															
Hansom Cab															
Old Hat															
Wellington															
Alb'n folk music															
Flea circus															
Fruit-juggling															
Indoor b'rangs															
Performing fish															
EC4															
NW3															
SW5															
W1															
WC2															

Pub	Street	Postal district	Entertainment

BANNS SUBSTANCE

There are five marriages pending in our parish and the vicar announced the banns on Sunday. From the following information, can you discover the full names of the bride and groom in each case?

NB – Surnames are those of their respective parents.

Clues

1 Paul Wright is marrying neither Rachel nor her best friend, who is the daughter of Mr and Mrs Ramsey.

2 Jonathan's bride (not Miss Ramsey) has a name which begins with a C.

3 Laura will shortly become Mrs Searle, while Miss Tucker will become Mrs McLaren, but not by marrying Jonathan.

4 Philip and Tara are tying the knot; he's not Mr Hobbs and Mr Hobbs isn't marrying Miss Newman.

5 Mark is engaged to Miss Piper; she will become neither Mrs Walton nor Mrs Hobbs.

6 Catherine is the daughter of Mr and Mrs Brennan.

	Hobbs	McLaren	Searle	Walton	Wright	Catherine	Charlotte	Laura	Rachel	Tara	Brennan	Newman	Piper	Ramsey	Tucker
Jonathan															
Mark															
Michael															
Paul															
Philip															
Brennan															
Newman															
Piper															
Ramsey															
Tucker															
Catherine															
Charlotte															
Laura															
Rachel															
Tara															

Groom	His surname	Bride	Her surname

JUMP-OFF

Five riders went through with clear rounds in the show-jumping competition, but in the jump-off against the clock only one managed a clear round to take the prize. From the information given below, can you work out who was riding which horse, the time each took for the round and how many faults the runners-up scored?

Clues

1 George Farrow went round faster than Jane Warwick.

2 Anne Melton scored 3 faults and was 4 seconds slower than Silver King.

3 Coral River scored the most faults.

4 The horse that got round in 2 minutes 20 seconds had 8 faults.

5 Miss Maggie had the fastest round, but didn't go clear; her rider wasn't George Farrow.

6 Malcolm Quinn rode Shadow Lad.

	Coral River	Diamante	Miss Maggie	Shadow Lad	Silver King	Clear	3 faults	4 faults	8 faults	12 faults	2 min 14 sec	2 min 16 sec	2 min 18 sec	2 min 20 sec	2 min 22 sec
Anne Melton															
George Farrow															
Graham Stewart															
Jane Warwick															
Malcolm Quinn															
2 min 14 sec															
2 min 16 sec															
2 min 18 sec															
2 min 20 sec															
2 min 22 sec															
Clear															
3 faults															
4 faults															
8 faults															
12 faults															

Rider	Horse	Faults	Time

DOMINO THEORY

The diagram shows six standard dominoes laid face up on the table, lettered A to F. Can you work out and insert the correct number of spots on each of the twelve visible faces?

Clues

1 The only 2 on view is on the lower half of domino C.

2 The total number of spots on domino A is four; one of its two ends can also be seen on domino B, but not in the same position.

3 One 4 is on the upper section of domino E, while the other is somewhere further left, accompanying one of the two 1s.

4 No number of spots occurs more than three times in the whole layout.

5 The number of spots on the upper half of domino C is twice that on the upper half of domino A and the same as that on one half of domino E.

6 Only one blank end appears in the layout and only one domino is a double; the former is further left than the latter.

7 All seven possible ends from blank to 6 spots are represented somewhere in the layout.

8 There is no 5 on domino F, nor is 5 the number of spots that can be seen on the upper half of domino D.

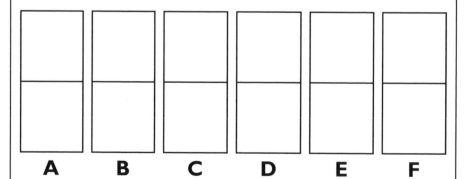

Starting tip:

Work out the number of spots on domino A.

LE AUTRES MOUSQUETAIRES

Contrary to what some believe, there were more than three – or even four – Musketeers serving King Louis XIII; in fact, there were hundreds of them and details of five are given below. Can you work out which province of France each Musketeer came from, the most distinctive aspect of his appearance and the vice which occupied most of his spare time?

Clues

1 The name of the Musketeer with big ears began with a consonant.

2 It was, of course, the overweight Musketeer whose vice was eating too much; the one who drank heavily wasn't from Picardy.

3 Silvis found himself totally unable to resist beautiful women; it wasn't Damos who was a persistent gambler.

4 Archamos, the Norman, was a compulsive consumer. The red-haired Musketeer drank only a little wine and never touched spirits.

5 Maximos was the largest of the Musketeers, towering six inches above the man from Provence, who had built up a fearsome reputation as a duellist who would fight for any reason – or none at all.

6 The bow-legged Burgundian Musketeer wasn't a great drinker and neither he nor Uramis gambled.

	Burgundy	Normandy	Picardy	Provence	Touraine	Big ears	Bow-legged	Overweight	Red hair	Very large	Drinking	Duelling	Eating	Gambling	Women
Archamos															
Damos															
Maximos															
Silvis															
Uramis															
Drinking															
Duelling															
Eating															
Gambling															
Women															
Big ears															
Bow-legged															
Overweight															
Red hair															
Very large															

Name	Province	Feature	Vice

BATTLESHIPS

This puzzle is based on the old game of battleships. Your task is to find the vessels in the diagram. Some parts of boats or sea squares have already been filled in, and a number next to a row or column refers to the number of occupied squares in that row or column. The boats may be positioned horizontally or vertically, but no two boats or parts of boats are in adjacent squares – horizontally, vertically or diagonally.

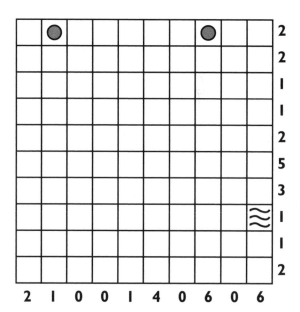

Aircraft Carrier:

Battleships:

Cruisers:

Destroyers:

PILE UP

These piles of bricks aren't the random results of a child's play but clues to a final, at present blank, pile on the right. Like the rest, that one has six bricks each with a different one of the six letters.

The numbers below the piles tell you two things:

(a) The number of adjacent pairs of bricks in that column which also appear adjacent in the final pile.

(b) The number of adjacent pairs of bricks that make a correct pair but the wrong way up.

So: would score one in the 'Correct' row if the final pile had an A directly above a C and a one in the 'Reversed' row if the final pile had a C on top of an A. From all this, can you create the final pile before it topples?

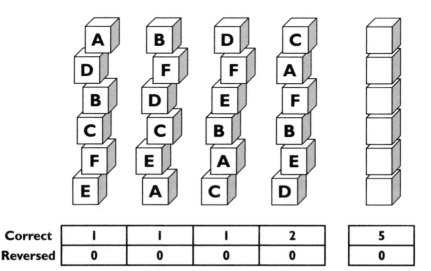

Correct	1	1	1	2		5
Reversed	0	0	0	0		0

DOGGY DO

This year's Spring fête at All Saints Parish Church, Storbury, included a dog show. Can you work out the name and breed of the dog which took each of the first five places and the name of the owner who showed it?

Clues

1 Spots, a Dalmatian – what else? – didn't win second prize.

2 First place went to the Irish setter which isn't Robin Scott's Mickey.

3 Frank Grey's dog came one place behind Bosun, who doesn't belong to Liz Pope, but one place ahead of the poodle.

4 The English springer spaniel was shown by Ann Darling.

5 Liz Pope's dog, which took second place, isn't called Topsy.

	Bosun	Fitz	Mickey	Spots	Topsy	Boxer	Dalmatian	Irish setter	Poodle	Springer spaniel	Ann Darling	Frank Grey	John Lamb	Liz Pope	Robin Scott
First															
Second															
Third															
Fourth															
Fifth															
Ann Darling															
Frank Grey															
John Lamb															
Liz Pope															
Robin Scott															
Boxer															
Dalmatian															
Irish setter															
Poodle															
Springer spaniel															

Prize	Name	Breed	Owner

A QUESTION OF QUIZZES

Five men have been hired to front new quizzes for Albion TV. Can you work out what each man has been doing up till now, the title of the quiz he'll be mastering and the subject of the questions he'll be asking?

Clues

1 The name of the Comeback quizmaster is listed alphabetically more than one place after that of the man (not Alan Ashley) who was formerly a TV presenter.

2 The man who will present Quizzicle, who has a longer first name than the one who will be asking show business questions, isn't an actor.

3 Don Darrell isn't the actor who's had a regular rôle in a TV soap opera; neither he nor Roy Rumford has ever worked as a presenter on TV or radio.

4 Tony Turpin will ask questions about famous people. The man asking about events in recent history has never worked as a presenter.

5 The quizmaster who'll be asking general knowledge questions is neither the one who'll be running Third Degree nor the former film actor.

6 The questions on Double, Double will concern either showbiz or famous people. Neither Martin Moor's nor those on Quizzicle will test general knowledge.

	Film actor	Newsreader	Radio presenter	TV actor	TV presenter	Comeback	Double, Double	Quizzicle	Third Degree	Under Pressure	Famous people	Gen knowledge	Recent history	Showbiz	Sport
Alan Ashley															
Don Darrell															
Martin Moor															
Roy Rumford															
Tony Turpin															
Famous people															
Gen knowledge															
Recent history															
Showbiz															
Sport															
Comeback															
Double, Double															
Quizzicle															
Third Degree															
Under Pressure															

Quizmaster	Former occ	Quiz title	Subject

SIGNS OF THE TIMES

Five couples who were all friends and neighbours each had different star signs. Can you work out who is married to whom and name their respective signs of the Zodiac?
NB – Animal signs are Aries, Capricorn, Leo and Taurus.

Clues

1 Hazel is a Libra subject, while her husband was born under an animal sign.

2 Holly isn't the wife of Alan, whose birth sign is Pisces, while Arthur wasn't born under Capricorn.

3 The Taurus subject isn't married to the Scorpio.

4 Hetty and her husband Alfred aren't the pair whose respective signs are Sagittarius and Cancer.

5 Albert is married to a Gemini subject.

6 Hilda's husband was born under the sign of Aries.

		Her sign									His sign				
		Gemini	Leo	Libra	Sagittarius	Taurus	Alan	Albert	Alfred	Anthony	Arthur	Aries	Cancer	Capricorn	Pisces	Scorpio
	Hazel															
	Helen															
	Hetty															
	Hilda															
	Holly															
	Aries															
H	Cancer															
I	Capricorn															
S	Pisces															
	Scorpio															
	Alan															
	Albert															
	Alfred															
	Anthony															
	Arthur															

Wife	Her sign	Husband	His sign

CENSUS SENSIBILITY

At a family history centre, all six of the computers provided for the public are being used by people searching for their ancestors amid the 1881 census records from different areas. Can you discover the name of the patron using each machine and the area they're researching? NB – 'Left' and 'right' are from the point of view of the people using the computers.

Clues

1 No two women are seated at adjacent computers.

2 William Dane isn't using computer 2.

3 Tom Wheeler is using machine 4.

4 John Alden isn't looking for ancestors from London.

5 The patron at computer 5 is male.

6 The person using machine 6 isn't searching the census records for North London.

7 Harriet Smith is seated immediately to the right of the person examining the records from Newcastle.

8 The Leeds census records are displayed on the computer immediately to the left of the one John Alden's using.

9 The man who is examining the Bristol records is seated immediately right of a patron who's trying to trace an ancestor from London.

10 Lucy Graham is seated two places to the left of Esther Lyon.

Names:
Esther Lyon; Harriet Smith; John Alden; Lucy Graham; Tom Wheeler; William Dane

Census Areas:
Bristol; Leeds; Newcastle; North London; Salisbury; West London

1	2	3	4	5	6

Computer	Researcher	Area
1		
2		
3		
4		
5		
6		

Starting tip:

Work out where Lucy Graham and Esther Lyon are seated.

SUFFERING CATS

Five cat owners were waiting with their pets to see the vet for various reasons. Can you match the owners with their pets, say why each pet had been brought to see the vet and work out in which order they were invited into the surgery?

Clues

1 The cat which was due for some routine injections was seen by the vet later than Sam, but some time before Michael's pet.

2 Catullus was the first animal in the waiting room queue; he isn't Sarah's cat.

3 Mitzi was the cat with a broken tooth.

4 Hannah and her pet were the third pair to be invited into the surgery.

5 David's pet is called Tiny Tim.

6 The second pet to be seen by the vet was diagnosed as suffering from cat flu.

7 Katy was the owner of the animal with the cut paw, who was seen immediately before Oedipus.

	Catullus	Mitzi	Oedipus	Sam	Tiny Tim	Abscess	Broken tooth	Cat flu	Cut paw	Injections	First	Second	Third	Fourth	Fifth
David															
Hannah															
Katy															
Michael															
Sarah															
First															
Second															
Third															
Fourth															
Fifth															
Abscess															
Broken tooth															
Cat flu															
Cut paw															
Injections															

Owner	Pet	Problem	Order seen

IN THE FRAME

There were only four runners in the 3.30 at Shingledown the other day. The diagram shows a head-on view of them lined up for the start. Can you name the horse in each of the starting-stalls lettered A to D and fully identify its jockey?

Clues

1 As they wait for the off in the starting-stalls Jackie has Mr Jingle immediately on one side of him and the rider named Silk immediately on the other.

2 Derek Raynes is riding a horse somewhere to the left of Placebo as you look at the diagram.

3 Nigel, who is ready for the off in stall C, isn't riding Sea Fret.

4 Paddy, whose surname isn't Mount, is riding Saturday Night.

Horses:
Mr Jingle; Placebo; Saturday Night; Sea Fret

First names:
Derek; Jackie; Nigel; Paddy

Surnames:
Mount; Raynes; Ryder; Silk

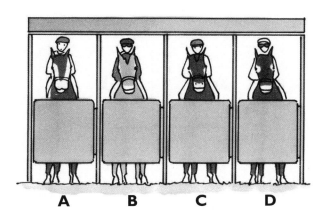

Stall	Horse	Forename	Surname
A			
B			
C			
D			

Starting tip:

First work out which stall Jackie is in.

IN BUSINESS

The diagram shows the centremost pages of the village church magazine, which contain four large advertisements paid for by local tradespeople. From the given clues, can you name the person who inserted each advert, work out his trade and locate his business?

Clues

1 Mr Bailey, the decorator, placed the advertisement diagonally opposite the one in which Main Street is referred to.

2 Kilroy's trading address is South Lane.

3 The business advertised in box A is located in Station Road.

4 Andrews, who isn't the florist, paid for the advert in box C.

5 The plumber (whose advert appears in box D) isn't Mr Rogers.

Names:
Andrews; Bailey; Kilroy; Rogers

Businesses:
Decorator; florist; landscape gardener; plumber.

Addresses:
Church Street; Main Street; South Lane; Station Road

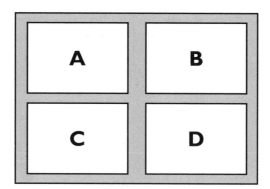

Advert	Name	Business	Address
A			
B			
C			
D			

Starting tip:

Begin by working out the name of the plumber.

I DO... AGAIN

Socialite Ga-Ga Zabor has been married five times, each time to a wealthy husband. From the information given below, can you discover the order in which she married the five men, his business and his personal wealth?

Clues

1 Husband number one wasn't the computer baron worth $18 million, while Ga-Ga's second husband had a personal wealth of $14 million.

2 Dean Richland took Ga-Ga up the aisle for the third time.

3 Her fifth husband was big in oil; he wasn't Buck Pyle.

4 Ga-Ga divorced Barney Silverspoon in favour of the property magnate, who was worth more than Buck Pyle.

5 Financier Oscar Lavisch was worth less than $20 million.

6 Harvey Cashmore had a personal wealth of $20 million.

	Barney Silverspoon	Buck Pyle	Dean Richland	Harvey Cashmore	Oscar Lavisch	Computers	Financier	Oil	Property	Shipping	$14 million	$16 million	$18 million	$20 million	$22 million
First															
Second															
Third															
Fourth															
Fifth															
$14 million															
$16 million															
$18 million															
$20 million															
$22 million															
Computers															
Financier															
Oil															
Property															
Shipping															

Order	Husband	Business	Wealth

THEY ALSO SERVE

Tennis fans will be aware that when the Trimbledon championships are on television, the producer is fond of highlighting the speed at which players' serves travel. Five of the fastest servers in last year's championships were each eliminated in a different round of the competition. Can you fully identify the five players, work out the speed of each man's fastest recorded serve and say how far he advanced in the tournament?

Clues

1 The measured speed of the fastest serve by the defeated finalist, Martin, wasn't less than 130mph.

2 Mark Svensson, the Swede, was eliminated in the round immediately before the man whose speed of serve was 131mph.

3 Charles wasn't knocked out in the second round; his surname appears earlier in the alphabetical list than that of Harry, whose best serve was 1 mph slower.

4 The man whose Trimbledon exit came in the third round served at a maximum speed of 130mph.

5 Paul reached the semi-final before bowing out of last year's competition.

6 A service speed of 129mph was recorded by the man whose elimination came next after that of Simon, who isn't Jourdain.

	Bradley	Jourdain	Martin	Svensson	Willis	128 mph	129 mph	130 mph	131 mph	132 mph	First round	Second round	Third round	Semi-final	Final
Charles															
Harry															
Mark															
Paul															
Simon															
First round											
Second round											
Third round											
Semi-final											
Final											
128 mph						
129 mph						
130 mph						
131 mph						
132 mph						

Forename	Surname	Speed	Round

OVER THE GARDEN WALL

Four women who live in neighbouring houses are each chatting over the garden wall to the rear of their homes to one of their neighbours, in the positions shown in the diagram. Can you fully identify the four and say which member of her family each woman is discussing with her friend?

Clues

1 Madge is telling her neighbour Mrs Gossip, who doesn't have a daughter, about all the latest misdeeds of her sister.

2 Mrs Gabbey lives at number 10.

3 Pat Chatham isn't chatting to Annie over the garden wall.

4 Her husband is the person about whom the resident of number 6 is expatiating at great length.

5 The woman at number 12 has no sons.

Forenames:
Annie; Madge; Pat; Zoë

Surnames:
Chatham; Gabbey; Gossip; Tattle

Subjects:
Daughter; husband; sister; son

Number	Forename	Surname	Subject
6			
8			
10			
12			

Starting tip:

Identify the relative about whom the woman at number 12 is speaking.

STRANGERS IN TOWN

The Marshal of Crossroads, Texas, was mighty worried to see, one night in the summer of 1876, that there were five tough-lookin' strangers in town, but a few polite – mighty polite! – questions made sure they were all honest men jest passin' through. From the clues below, can you figure out each man's job, where he'd ridden from and where he was goin'? (NB – Of course, nobody was headin' back where he'd jest come from.)

Clue

1 The buffalo hunter and the gambler both went by nicknames (shown in quotation marks); the buffalo hunter had come from Eagle Ridge but wasn't on his way to the town the Texas Ranger had just left.

2 The Ranger was headin' for Spanish Springs, on the trail of an outlaw called Frank Jessey.

3 The man travellin' from Fort Hood to Eagle Ridge wasn't Joe Jarvis.

4 'Alabama' Abney was on his way to see a guy in Comanche Butte.

5 Frank Forman, who'd come into Crossroads from Comanche Butte, wasn't the rancher, who had never visited Mustang City and reckoned that, from what he'd heard of it, he never would.

6 Cal Coulan was a bronco buster, hired by the boss of the Bar K ranch to break a bunch of wild horses.

	Bronco buster	Buffalo hunter	Gambler	Rancher	Texas Ranger	From Comanche Butte	Eagle Ridge	Fort Hood	Mustang City	Spanish Springs	To Comanche Butte	Eagle Ridge	Fort Hood	Mustang City	Spanish Springs
'Alabama' Abney															
Cal Coulan															
Frank Forman															
'Grizzly' Gates															
Joe Jarvis															
TO Comanche B															
Eagle Ridge															
Fort Hood															
Mustang C															
Spanish Sp															
FROM Comanche B															
Eagle Ridge															
Fort Hood															
Mustang C															
Spanish Sp															

Name	Job	Comin' from	Goin' to

EDUCATIONAL EXCURSION

Prof Liggett was a Professor of Mathematics who was convinced that he had invented an infallible system for winning at games of chance. To test out his theories he spent a week in Las Vegas, where he visited a different casino and played a different game on each night of the week, with varying results. Can you name the casino he went to each night, say which game he played there and work out how much he won or lost on each occasion?

Clues

1 Prof Liggett was a little nettled that his largest profit, of $35, came from the Wheel of Fortune, which offered the least scope for individual skill.

2 When he played at the Golden Nugget on Tuesday, the professor (or rather, the University) ended up out of pocket.

3 The biggest loss was incurred two nights after the professor played roulette at the Sahara.

4 Thursday was a more successful night than Friday, when the professor didn't play video poker.

5 The night out at the Treasure Island ended in a loss of $15.

6 Baccarat was the game Prof Liggett played on Wednesday; this wasn't at the Circus Casino.

	Circus	Golden Nugget	Mirage	Sahara	Treasure Island	Baccarat	Black jack	Roulette	Video poker	Wheel of Fortune	Lost $22	Lost $15	Lost $12	Won $25	Won $35
Monday															
Tuesday															
Wednesday															
Thursday															
Friday															
Lost $22															
Lost $15															
Lost $12															
Won $25															
Won $35															
Baccarat															
Black jack															
Roulette															
Video poker															
Wheel of F															

Night	Casino	Game	Result

DOMINO SEARCH

A standard set of dominoes has been laid out, using numbers instead of dots for clarity. With the aid of a sharp pencil and a keen brain, can you draw in the lines to show where each domino has been placed? You may find the check grid useful – crossing off each domino as you find it.

1	0	3	4	5	1	2	4
6	5	0	0	0	2	3	4
3	1	6	1	2	4	4	6
6	1	5	5	0	3	3	2
6	4	0	4	5	6	3	5
5	3	2	1	3	1	0	5
6	0	1	6	2	2	2	4

	0	1	2	3	4	5	6
0							
1							
2							
3							
4							
5							
6							

RETIRING TYPES

Five friends recently retired from the same company. Can you discover which department each worked for, the number of years each had been with the company and his or her retirement gift?

Clues

1 Derek Gordon (who received a CD player) had been with the company for over 30 years, but not in the Export department.

2 Jean Kelly wasn't in Personnel and neither she nor her friend (retiring from Export) had been with the company for the least number of years.

3 The man (not Len Rogers) retiring after 18 years received a camera; the former Personnel employee did not.

4 George Doughty worked in Sales; Beryl Peacock had been with the company for 24 years and didn't get the video player.

5 The longest-serving employee was in Accounts.

6 The colleague retiring from Purchasing was given a clock.

	Accounts	Export	Personnel	Purchasing	Sales	16	18	24	31	33	Camera	CD player	Clock	Garden furniture	Video player
Beryl Peacock															
Derek Gordon															
George Doughty															
Jean Kelly															
Len Rogers															
Camera															
CD player															
Clock															
Garden furniture															
Video player															
16															
18															
24															
31															
33															

Name	Department	Years of service	Gift

PUNNET OF STRAWBERRIES

Gregory Punnet, who died in 1949, was the last squire to occupy the Manor House of the village of Strawberries, but all five of his children still live in the village. Can you work out the address (house name and street name) and telephone number of each?

Clues

1 Julian Punnet isn't the occupant of Oakhurst; the telephone number for Oakhurst isn't 100670.

2 Prudence Borthwick, née Punnet, lives at Valley View. Her phone number isn't 100845.

3 The phone number for the house in Snow Hill ends in a zero.

4 To speak to the people at Rose Cottage, which isn't in Church Green, you call 100775; the occupants of Rose Cottage are the family of one of Gregory's twin children Bernard and Felicity.

5 Felicity's phone number is a lower one than Bernard's.

6 Vernon Punnet, whose home is in Mill Lane, has a phone number thirty-five higher than that of his sibling whose home is in Badger's Holt, The Street, Strawberries.

	Badger's Holt	Moonrakers	Oakhurst	Rose Cottage	Valley View	Church Green	London Road	Mill Lane	Snow Hill	The Street	100635	100670	100740	100775	100845
Bernard															
Felicity															
Julian															
Prudence															
Vernon															
100635										
100670										
100740										
100775										
100845										
Church Green					
London Road					
Mill Lane					
Snow Hill					
The Street					

Punnet	House name	Street	Phone number

SQUARE DANCES

London's popular Nunnery Square Market attracts many different street entertainers to amuse the holiday crowds. From the following information, can you discover whereabouts in the Square each is, the nature of the five performances in progress and the sizes of their respective audiences?

Clues

1 Carly is on the south side of the Square; she doesn't have an audience of 80 people.

2 The smallest audience is watching the performance in the centre of the Square; it isn't the unicyclist and the unicyclist isn't Darren.

3 The crowd of 120 people is either on the east or west of the Square; they're not watching Wizzo the Magician.

4 The juggler is entertaining people on the east side.

5 Danny has the biggest audience; he's not on the north side.

6 Neither Lisa nor the tumbler has more than 100 people watching them; Lisa isn't on the north side of the Square.

	Centre	East side	North side	South side	West side	Juggler	Magician	Mime artist	Tumbler	Unicyclist	30	60	80	120	140
Carly															
Danny															
Darren															
Lisa															
Wizzo															
30															
60															
80															
120															
140															
Juggler															
Magician															
Mime artist															
Tumbler															
Unicyclist															

Performer	Position	Entertainment	Audience

HOOKE, LYNE, SINKER (AND ALL)

Six men were fishing round the perimeter of a large pond, in the positions lettered A to F in the diagram. Can you fully identify each of the six and say how many fish each caught that afternoon?

Clues

1 Sinker, who had a totally unsuccessful afternoon's fishing, can be seen two positions clockwise of Fergus round the pond.

2 Hooke was in position A. The man who caught just one fish was in either position B or position F.

3 Tony (not Mr Lyne) is angler B.

4 Man C caught fewer fish than Bates, who isn't his immediate neighbour.

5 Grant Reel caught two more fish than angler D.

6 The man in position E, who isn't Dave, caught two fish during the afternoon.

7 Paul caught three fish.

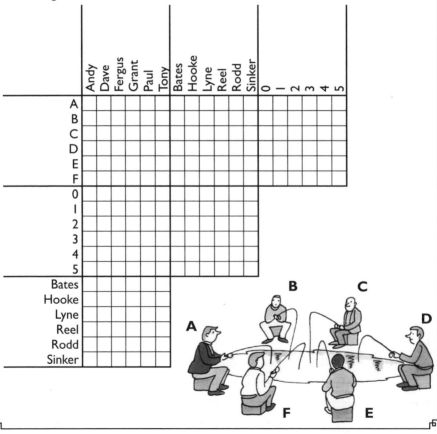

BY A BABBLING BROOK

Last summer four couples on camping holidays found a good spot to pitch their tents, two on each side of a small stream in the positions numbered 1 to 4 in the diagram. Can you name the pair using each tent and work out the latter's colour? NB – Tent No 1 is directly north of tent No 3; and tent No 2 is directly north of tent No 4.

Clues

1 The green tent is either directly north or directly south of the tent which is occupied by John and Sally.

2 The female sharing tent 2 is Lesley.

3 The grey tent is on the same side of the stream as the one occupied by Tara, whose camping companion isn't Patrick.

4 Jason and his partner are using tent 4.

5 Tent 1 is blue.

Males:
Alan; Jason; John; Patrick

Females:
Kelly; Lesley; Sally; Tara

Colours:
Blue; brown; green; grey

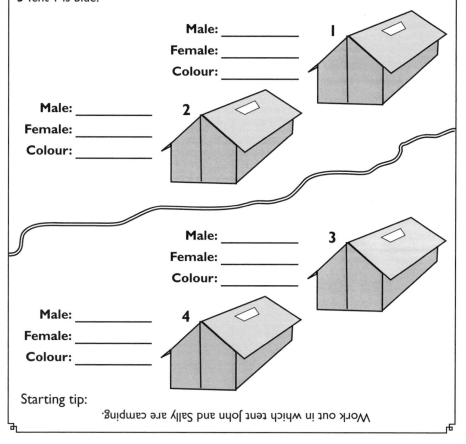

Male: _____
Female: _____
Colour: _____

1

Male: _____
Female: _____
Colour: _____

2

Male: _____
Female: _____
Colour: _____

3

Male: _____
Female: _____
Colour: _____

4

Starting tip:

Work out in which tent John and Sally are camping.

FIRST IMPRESSIONS

Five contenders appeared on the *Stars In Their Minds* television programme featuring amateur impressionists. From the clues, can you work out the order in which the five appeared, say which star each impersonated and name the job each normally does?

Clues

1 Each contestant impersonated a star of his or her own sex.

2 Rod, the mechanic, appeared next after the Madonna impersonator.

3 Colin was on some time after the performer who mimicked Cilla Black and some time before the Stevie Wonder impersonator.

4 The fourth impressionist to be seen by the viewers wasn't a chiropodist.

5 The person who delivers the milk did an impression of Jon Bon Jovi.

6 The cook was the third impressionist to perform.

7 Sally was the second contestant to appear.

Name	Order	Star	Job

MINE'S A MINI

Five friends, all enthusiastic members of the Mini Owners Club, meet each year at the annual convention on Brighton seafront. Can you match each member with the colour in which their Mini is now painted, together with its year letter and the special feature each has added?

Clues

1 The pink Mini with nudge bars was registered more recently than Dave's car.

2 Sally's Mini has been re-sprayed in shiny silver paint.

3 The yellow Mini is newer than both Anne's car and the one with the extra range of headlights.

4 Jeremy has bought a Mini whose year letter is J to match his initial.

5 Patriotic Pat has painted the roof of his Mini as a huge Union Jack.

6 The year letter of the red Mini is K.

7 The most recent of the five Minis is resplendent with a set of new chrome wheel-trims.

	Green	Pink	Red	Silver	Yellow	B	F	J	K	M	Chrome w-trims	Extra lights	Musical horn	Nudge bars	Union Jack
Anne															
Dave															
Jeremy															
Pat															
Sally															
Chrome w-trims															
Extra lights															
Musical horn															
Nudge bars															
Union Jack															
B															
F															
J															
K															
M															

Owner	Colour	Year letter	Feature

PARTY LINES

June sells jewellery by party plan and below are details of five parties she had last week. From the information given, can you discover the name of each evening's hostess, the value of sales at each party and the gift claimed by each woman?

Clues

1 Sales at Jade's party amounted to £165, while the hostess on the previous evening had chosen the wine glasses as her gift.

2 It wasn't Beryl who hosted the Monday party and chose the ring.

3 Ruby chose the candelabra, which was a gift available for a party with sales of less than £200.

	Beryl	Gemma	Jade	Pearl	Ruby	£140	£165	£180	£230	£260	Candelabra	Clock	Cuddly toy	Ring	Wine glasses
Monday															
Tuesday															
Wednesday															
Thursday															
Friday															
Candelabra															
Clock															
Cuddly toy															
Ring															
Wine glasses															
£140															
£165															
£180															
£230															
£260															

4 The cuddly toy was chosen by the hostess the evening after Pearl's party and the evening before the £180 party.

5 The £140 sales total entitled the hostess to a clock as a gift.

6 The Wednesday evening party achieved the highest sales.

Evening	Hostess	Total sales	Gift chosen

HITTING THE HEADLINES

Five people were featured for different reasons on successive days in the local paper. Can you identify the five, say on which day their story appeared in the paper and work out in which event each was involved?

Clues

1 Daniel Perry's name appeared in the paper the day after that of the person who had been injured in a paragliding accident.

2 Holtby was the subject of the Friday feature.

3 Janice formed an action group to combat problems on an estate.

4 Edgar's story was published later in the week than Chambers', but earlier than the feature on the newly-appointed bishop.

5 Vernon's story wasn't told on Wednesday.

6 Ronald was featured in the Thursday edition.

7 Tuesday's issue featured the retirement of someone who had been with the same firm for forty-five years.

	Chambers	Holtby	Leeson	Perry	Vernon	Monday	Tuesday	Wednesday	Thursday	Friday	Action group	Named bishop	Paragliding accident	Retirement	Stopped horse
Daniel															
Edgar															
Emma															
Janice															
Ronald															
Action group															
Named bishop															
Para accident															
Retirement															
Stopped horse															
Monday															
Tuesday															
Wednesday															
Thursday															
Friday															

Forename	Surname	Day	Story

A-HAUNTING WE WILL GO

We are indebted to Mr S Pook for supplying the information for this problem. From the clues given, can you work out what ghostly apparition haunts which building, in what village and the year it was first seen?

Clues

1 Neither the building in Aarghyll (not an abbey) nor the hall is haunted by the large baying mastiff. The Aarghyll apparition wasn't the first to be seen, but was recorded in the century before the mastiff's sighting.

2 The Dredleigh ghost was first seen in the century preceding that in which the white boar was first seen. The spook in the manor was seen later than both.

3 The monk (who doesn't haunt a rectory or monastery) was first seen later than the abbey apparition but earlier than that in Fantoume (seen later than the ghost which haunts the monastery).

4 An animal apparition was first recorded in 1670. The rectory ghost was first seen later than that in Raith but earlier than the grey lady (of Grimlyn), who was seen later than the apparition which haunts the hall.

5 The headless man was first seen a century before the monk.

	Abbey	Hall	Manor	Monastery	Rectory	Aarghyll	Dredleigh	Fantoume	Grimlyn	Raith	1493	1549	1670	1721	1807
Grey lady															
Headless man															
Large mastiff															
Monk															
White boar															
1493															
1549															
1670															
1721															
1807															
Aarghyll															
Dredleigh															
Fantoume															
Grimlyn															
Raith															

Apparition	Building	Village	Year

ON THE BEACH

The seaside resort of Brightbourne hasn't really opened for the season yet, but four couples have decided to take an early trip down to the beach and are now huddled in their coats with the wind whistling past as they eat their sandwiches and wish they hadn't bothered. From the clues below, can you fill in the first name and surname of the male and female partners in each couple and say how they got to Brightbourne?

Clues

1 Alan isn't the man in couple D and Gary isn't the one who arrived in Brightbourne by train.

2 Mr Kidd brought his girlfriend to the seaside in a van he 'borrowed' from his employers.

3 Kate's surname is Swan.

4 Couple B are neither Tony and his girlfriend (Ms Clay) nor Dawn and her boyfriend (Mr Burr).

5 Jack is the male half of couple A.

6 Jane, who drove to Brightbourne in her own car and now wishes she and her boyfriend had gone somewhere else, is sitting somewhere to Mr and Mrs Ross's right (from their point of view).

Men's forenames:
Alan; Gary; Jack; Tony

Men's surnames:
Burr; Kidd; Ross; Watt

Women's forenames:
Dawn; Jane; Kate; Zena

Women's surnames:
Clay; Hunt; Ross; Swan

Transport:
Car; coach; train; van

A   **B**   **C**   **D**

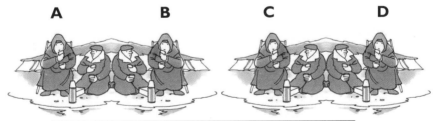

Couple	Man		Woman		Transport
	Forename	Surname	Forename	Surname	
A					
B					
C					
D					

Starting tip:

Work out the surname of Jane's partner.

GIVE ME A RING

Five couples who recently became engaged each visited a jeweller's shop on the same day to buy an engagement ring. Can you match the couples, say which stone each woman chose for her ring and work out in which order they visited the shop?

Clues

1 Graeme and Natalie were earlier visitors to the jeweller's than the couple who bought the emerald ring.

2 Sharon's ring had a large ruby as its stone; she and her fiancé visited the shop immediately after Darren and his intended partner.

3 Miranda and her fiancé were the first pair to buy a ring.

4 The second couple chose the sapphire ring.

5 Jonathan's fiancée chose the opal ring on the visit before Penny's.

6 Adam was the third man to buy his fiancée a ring.

	Miranda	Natalie	Penny	Sharon	Zoë	Diamond	Emerald	Opal	Ruby	Sapphire	First	Second	Third	Fourth	Fifth
Adam															
Darren															
Gareth															
Graeme															
Jonathan															
First															
Second															
Third															
Fourth															
Fifth															
Diamond															
Emerald															
Opal															
Ruby															
Sapphire															

Man	Woman	Stone	Order

LOGI-5

Every row across and column down should contain five letters: A, B, C, D and E, appearing once each. Also every shape (shown by the thick lines) must contain each of the letters A, B, C, D and E, appearing once each. Can you fill the grid?

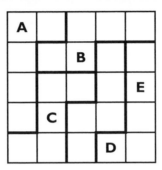

ABC

Every row across and column down is to have each of the letters A, B and C and two empty squares. The letter outside the grid shows the first or second letter in the direction of the arrow. Can you fill the grid?

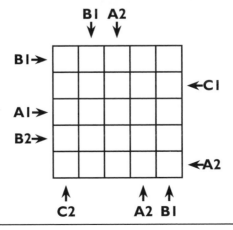

HOUSE POINTS

Our local junior school is divided into five houses and they've just had their sports day. In each event there were five competitors, one from each house and each house won a race, came second in another and third in another. From the following information, can you discover which house won which event and which houses came second and third?

Clues

1 In the skipping race Herons came second; Kingfishers weren't third.

2 Peacocks won the egg and spoon race; Mallards weren't second.

3 Eagles came third in the sprint, which wasn't won by Kingfishers; Peacocks weren't second in the race won by Kingfishers.

4 Herons didn't win the relay race and Kingfishers weren't third.

5 Kingfishers came second in the race won by Mallards.

6 Peacocks came third in the race won by Herons.

	First					Second					Third				
	Eagles	Herons	Kingfishers	Mallards	Peacocks	Eagles	Herons	Kingfishers	Mallards	Peacocks	Eagles	Herons	Kingfishers	Mallards	Peacocks
Egg and spoon															
Relay															
Sack															
Skipping															
Sprint															
THIRD Eagles															
THIRD Herons															
THIRD Kingfishers															
THIRD Mallards															
THIRD Peacocks															
Eagles															
Herons															
Kingfishers															
Mallards															
Peacocks															

Event	First	Second	Third

INTERNATIONAL CALLS

Hack writer Bob Wheel sells a lot of his work abroad, so he's used to getting international phone calls. Last week he received five. Can you work out who called each day, where from and their relationship to Bob?

Clues

1 Bob's old friend – who rang to report the progress of a round-the-world trip – didn't call on Wednesday; the agent of the celebrity for whom Bob had agreed to ghostwrite an autobiography rang later in the week than the publisher.

2 Kate Nilson (not in New York) made Saturday's business call. Cliff Brown's call was immediately before the one from New York and immediately after that from Bob's stepchild.

3 Sally Thynn's call, which came from the USA, was earlier in the week than the one from the publisher, who was also in America.

4 Bob's lawyer rang more than two days before the person in Chicago; neither of these was the business call from Rick Plotkin, who rang from the USA.

5 Jim Hart phoned Bob from Bombay two days before he received the call from Los Angeles.

	Cliff Brown	Jim Hart	Kate Nilson	Rick Plotkin	Sally Thynn	Bombay	Chicago	Los Angeles	New York	Sydney	Client's agent	Lawyer	Old friend	Publisher	Stepchild
Sunday															
Tuesday															
Wednesday															
Thursday															
Saturday															
Client's agent															
Lawyer															
Old friend															
Publisher															
Stepchild															
Bombay															
Chicago															
Los Angeles															
New York															
Sydney															

Day	Caller	City	Relationship

PANDEMONIUM ENTERPRISES

A new block of four units was added to the existing ones at Pandemonium Industrial Park. Can you determine which firm occupied each unit, the name of the firm's proprietor and how many workers it employed?

Clues

1 The firm owned by Extranius was next left to the one with 24 workers.

2 The Herbal Remedies firm was further left than both the one owned by Uncius and the one which employed 18 hands.

3 Unit 3 had fewer staff than Fitted Furniture but more than the firm owned by Nonplus.

4 Venison Burgers was further right than Surplus's company and had six more workers.

5 Mosaic Tiles had a staff six greater than unit No 4.

Firms:
Fitted Furniture; Herbal Remedies; Mosaic Tiles; Venison Burgers

Proprietors:
Extranius; Nonplus; Surplus; Uncius

Workers:
12; 18; 24; 28

Unit	Firm	Proprietor	Workers

Starting tip:

Start by deciding who owns the firm with 24 workers.

CRAFTY LADIES

Five women exhibited their craft work in a local gallery, each operating in a separate room. From the clues given, can you indicate in the diagram which room each occupied, what craft each specialised in and how many items of her work she displayed? NB – 'Left' and 'right' are from your point of view as you look at the picture.

Clues

1 The hand-knitting display was in the room next to and right of that where 30 items were exhibited; Gillian's room was further left than either.

2 The room labelled D had five fewer items than the one which was displaying the work of the hand-weaver.

3 Susan had the room next to and left of that used by the quilting expert.

4 Angela (who doesn't knit) had the room next to and left of that used for the exhibition of oil paintings but further right than that housing the exhibition of tapestry work.

5 Christine, who displayed at least three fewer examples of her work than Marie, had the room next to and right of that where 23 items were on show.

6 Room C accommodated 25 pieces of work.

Women:
Angela; Christine; Gillian; Marie; Susan

Crafts:
Hand-knitting; hand-weaving; oil paintings; quilting; tapestry

Numbers of items:
20; 23; 25; 28; 30

Gallery	Woman	Craft	No of items

Starting tip:

Work out the room in which the 30 items were displayed.

WHEELIE DIFFICULT

The annual bicycle trials over a stiff course in the Netherlipp area had their customary crop of disappointed participants, among them the five in this problem. Can you work out the number each wore, the cause of each one's withdrawal and the number of miles each completed before having to drop out?

Clues

1 Treddwell dropped out next before No 32 but later than whoever fell in a ditch.

2 The man who skidded on an icy patch had a higher number than the one who dropped out after 16 miles; neither was Saddler, whose number was between those of the two.

3 The competitor who got a puncture dropped out next before Chayne, who had the next lower number.

4 The man who collided with a thorny hedge had a number which was more than twice the number of miles he completed.

5 The man whose chain snapped withdrew next after Peddler, whose number was lower but not next lower.

6 Spokesworth travelled in excess of six miles further than Chayne.

7 The incident which caused a man's withdrawal at 19 miles wasn't due to a problem with a specific part of his bike, unlike that which caused the withdrawal at 31 miles.

	6	21	32	40	53	Chain snapped	Collided/hedge	Fell in ditch	Puncture	Skidded on ice	14 miles	16 miles	19 miles	25 miles	31 miles
Chayne															
Peddler															
Saddler															
Spokesworth															
Treddwell															
14 miles															
16 miles															
19 miles															
25 miles															
31 miles															
Chain snapped															
Collided/hedge															
Fell in ditch															
Puncture															
Skidded on ice															

Cyclist	Number	Cause	Miles covered

HOME AND AWAY

Five reporters from the *Daily Planet* were sent by the sports editor to cover different rugby matches last weekend. Can you identify the five and name the home and away teams involved in the games each man reported?

Clues

1 Gordon's assignment took him to Rawfleet.

2 Pass was sent to cover the match where the visitors were Sandfield.

3 Fenborough's away game wasn't reported by Mr Ruck or Mr Tackle.

4 The match covered by Danny Ruck wasn't the needle game between Winstone and Markwell.

5 Dagford didn't take part in the rather uneventful match at Boringham, which was watched for The Planet by the reporter whose surname appears next but one either before or after that of Chris.

6 Tackle reported on the match at Tibleigh.

7 The away team in the match watched by Bill was Lingmoor.

	Boot	Maul	Pass	Ruck	Tackle	Boringham	Rawfleet	Thrumley	Tibleigh	Winstone	Dagford	Fenborough	Lingmoor	Markwell	Sandfield
						Home					**Away**				
Bill															
Chris															
Danny															
Gordon															
Sandy															
Dagford															
Fenborough															
Lingmoor															
Markwell															
Sandfield															
Boringham															
Rawfleet															
Thrumley															
Tibleigh															
Winstone															

Reporter	Surname	Home	Away

AN ALL-ROUND TEST

The favourite form of cricket in Balonia is a seven-a-side game in which one player is the wicket-keeper and the other six face a maximum of 18 balls and bowl three overs. Can you work out the batting order of the Pravitch team in their most recent match, the runs scored by each of the team's six members and the runs scored by the opposing team off each one's bowling? Please ignore the wicket-keeper, who batted seventh.

Clues

1 Whereas Cloutov, who didn't bat first, scored one more run than he conceded, batsman No 4 conceded one more run than he scored.

2 Pullov was the only man with two odd-numbered figures. No 1 (the men batted in the order of their numbers) was the only man with two even figures.

3 The man who scored most runs did not concede either most or fewest and the man who conceded most did not score most or fewest runs.

4 Smitov gave away two more runs than were scored by Nokov, who batted more than one place after him, while Pinchitov, who batted earlier then Smitov, gave away two more than Smitov scored.

5 Swipov batted next after the man who scored 12 and next before the one who conceded 14; Swipov scored and conceded fewer than No 5.

6 Nokov's combined figures were one less than Pullov's and one more than Pinchitov's.

Names:
Cloutov; Nokov; Pinchitov; Pullov; Smitov; Swipov

Runs scored:
10; 12; 15; 17; 18; 21

Runs conceded:
11; 13; 14; 16; 19; 20

Order	Name	Runs scored	Runs conceded
No 1			
No 2			
No 3			
No 4			
No 5			
No 6			

Starting tip:

Work out who batted first, then the possibilities for his order of batting.

AFTER HOURS

Our local History Society recently arranged a series of talks, held in the Village Hall. From the clues given, can you work out the full names of the speakers, the subject each covered and the number in the audience on each occasion?

Clues

1 Mr Copeland's talk drew a bigger audience than the one on the Geology of Yorkshire but a smaller one by more than two than the talk by Kenneth.

2 Mr Wanstead's forename is alphabetically next before that of the speaker on Steam Railways. The surname of the man whose topic was Local Castles is next before that of Philip.

3 John's audience was next largest after that of Mr Britton and both were larger than the Steam Railways audience.

4 The audience for Philip's talk (not on the River Tees), wasn't the largest or smallest, but it was smaller by more than three than that of Mr Granger, whose first name is the next shortest after that of the man whose talk was attended by 41.

5 More people listened to the talk by Mr Richards than the one by Bertrand but still more listened to the one on Local Castles.

	Britton	Copeland	Granger	Richards	Wanstead	Coastal Erosion	Local Castles	River Tees	Steam Railways	Yorkshire	36	38	41	43	46
Bertrand															
David															
John															
Kenneth															
Philip															
36															
38															
41															
43															
46															
Coastal Erosion															
Local Castles															
River Tees															
Steam Railways															
Yorkshire															

Speaker	Surname	Subject	Audience size

FAST FORWARD

I recently spent a week as a guest of the NHS. For the first few hours I was in a mixed bay of the Admissions and Assessment Ward, where the rapidity of change of bed occupancy was almost electrifying. I noticed the situation at three stages: on my arrival, about halfway through my stay and just before I was moved to more permanent quarters. Can you indicate on the diagram the sex of the patient who occupied every bed at each stage?

Clues

1 No bed apart from mine (number 5), had a patient of the same sex throughout the three stages.

2 At no stage were beds 1, 2 and 3 all occupied by patients of the same sex. At only one stage was there a woman in the bed opposite mine.

3 There were two stages when a man's bed was between two women's beds.

4 Only at the second stage were there two women patients in beds opposite each other, but there were men opposite each other at all three stages, though never more than one pair at any stage.

5 Bed 3 acquired its first woman patient later than bed 6, whose first stage patient was of a different sex to the one in bed 3. The sequence of sex occupancy of bed 6 was the reverse of that of bed 1. Bed 4 hadn't two male patients in successive stages.

Stage 1: _____   _____   _____

Stage 2: _____   _____   _____

Stage 3: _____   _____   _____

Stage 1: _____   _____

Stage 2: _____   (My bed)   _____

Stage 3: _____

FIGURE IT OUT

Each of the squares in the grid below should be filled with a single digit number from 1 to 9 – each of those numbers being used four times. Use the clues (and the number already placed) to complete the square, bearing in mind that the same number must not appear in two adjacent (touching) squares either across or down. If the same number is used more than once in any row across or column down it is stated in the relevant clue.

Clues

Across:

1 Two threes are the only odd numbers.
2 Total twenty-one.
3 Two eights. No two.
4 Two fives.
5 Consecutive numbers placed in order.
6 Two sevens.

Down:

1 Two nines.
2 No nine. Three is the lowest number.
3 No three. Two eights.
4 Consecutive numbers placed in order.
5 Two fives. No even numbers.
6 Two fours. One is the only odd number.

	1	2	3	4	5	6
1						
2						2
3						
4						
5						
6						

1
2
3
4
5
6
7
8
9

LOGI-PATH

Use your deductive reasoning to form a pathway from the box marked 'START' to the box marked 'FINISH', moving either horizontally or vertically (but not diagonally) from square to adjacent square. The number at the beginning of every row or column indicates exactly how many boxes in that row or column your pathway must pass through. The small diagram at the bottom of the page is given as an example of how it works.

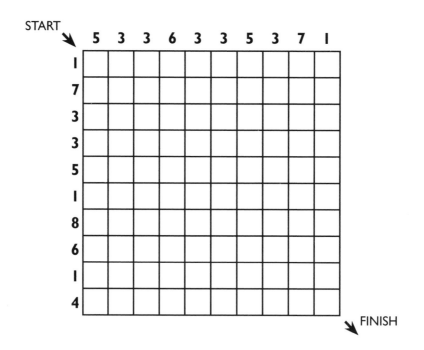

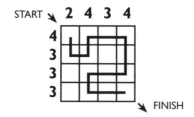

DRONES AT ASCOT

One fine day in the 1920s, five friends (collectively known as the Drones) each escorted a different girl to Royal Ascot. Can you fully identify the girl who went with each Drone and state the colour of the hat she sported?

Clues

1 The girl in the pink hat (not the Hon Sybilla Ponsonby) went to Ascot with Archie Fotheringhay.

2 Miss Beauchamp's blue hat caused much comment amongst racegoers.

3 None of the five girls has a surname which occupies the same position in its alphabetical list as her first name does in its own.

4 Caroline isn't Miss Rockingham, whose forename occurs later in the list than that of the girl in the cream hat.

5 Montague Ffolliott and Caroline made up a foursome for their day at the races with Caroline's friend in the beige hat and her escort (not Rupert de Grey).

6 Edward Tanqueray went to Ascot with Miss Wotherspoon.

7 Diana's hat was a delightful shade of primrose yellow.

	Ariadne	Caroline	Diana	Heather	Sybilla	Beauchamp	Cullompton	Ponsonby	Rockingham	Wotherspoon	Beige	Blue	Cream	Pink	Primrose
Archie Fotheringhay															
Edward Tanqueray															
Gerald Huntington															
Montague Ffolliott															
Rupert de Grey															
Beige															
Blue															
Cream															
Pink															
Primrose															
Beauchamp															
Cullompton															
Ponsonby															
Rockingham															
Wotherspoon															

Drone	Forename	Surname	Hat colour

FLORAL TRIBUTES

Three women were recently bought a bunch of their favourite flowers by their respective husbands. Can you fully identify the three, match them with their husbands and say which favourite flowers each was bought?

Clues

1 None of the three women had a favourite flower which matched her first name.

2 John Flowers didn't buy his wife the violets.

3 Jeremy didn't buy roses for his wife Violet.

4 Mr Bloom didn't buy the lilies.

	Bloom	Flowers	Plant	James	Jeremy	John	Lilies	Roses	Violets
Lily									
Rose									
Violet									
Lilies									
Roses									
Violets									
James									
Jeremy									
John									

Forename	Surname	Husband	Flowers

SACKCLOTH AND ASHES

It was a black day in the history of Netherlipp Nomads Football Club. Not only were they beaten in the first round of the Frewty Mewsly Cup but they also had three men sent off. Can you work out the time of each one's dismissal, the position each occupies and the offence for which each was sent off?

Clues

1 The striker was sent off after 65 minutes, but not for jabbing his elbow into an opponent.

2 Midfielder Foote wasn't sent off for tripping.

3 The man responsible for a blatant trip got his marching orders before Legge.

4 McNee's participation in the match ended after 40 minutes.

	25 minutes	40 minutes	65 minutes	Jostling referee	Tripping	Use of elbow	Defender	Midfield	Striker
Foote									
Legge									
McNee									
Defender									
Midfield									
Striker									
Jostling referee									
Tripping									
Use of elbow									

Player	Time	Offence	Position

LOGI-5

Every row across and column down should contain five letters: A, B, C, D and E, appearing once each. Also every shape (shown by the thick lines) must contain each of the letters A, B, C, D and E, appearing once each. Can you fill the grid?

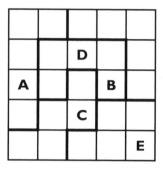

ABC

Every row across and column down is to have each of the letters A, B and C and two empty squares. The letter outside the grid shows the first or second letter in the direction of the arrow. Can you fill the grid?

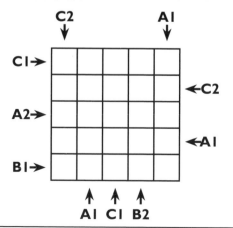

MAYDAY!

Four hired motor-cruisers are in trouble in different places on the Norfolk Broads and the hirers have sent out distress signals – well, actually, they've telephoned the boatyard. Can you work out the name and size of each boat, where it is and the nature of its problem?

Clues

1 The 5-berth Orchid isn't the boat that's tied up at Wroxham with a damaged hull after colliding with another boat.

2 The hirer of the 2-berth boat phoned the boatyard from Oulton Broad.

3 The Cygnet, whose propeller has become fouled with waterweed, has one less berth than the boat whose engine has failed due to water in the diesel fuel – the hirer got the respective filler caps confused.

4 The Neptune, which is moored at Ludham Bridge, hasn't a jammed rudder.

	2-berth	3-berth	4-berth	5-berth	Burgh Castle	Ludham Bridge	Oulton Broad	Wroxham	Collision	Propeller fouled	Rudder jammed	Water in fuel
Cygnet												
Emerald												
Neptune												
Orchid												
Collision									
Propeller fouled								
Rudder jammed								
Water in fuel								
Burgh Castle					
Ludham Bridge					
Oulton Broad					
Wroxham					

Boat	Size	Location	Problem

TUNG STREET

Four women from Tung Street met at the corner shop and each had a juicy item of gossip to pass on about one of the other residents in the street. Can you work out where in Tung Street each woman lives, about whom she told her friends and what she said about them?

Clues

1 'That Mrs Robinson is carrying on again,' said one of the four gossips.

2 Mrs Jones lives at 1 Tung Street; Mrs Smith's home isn't number 5.

3 Mrs Brown, who told the others about a person who was months behind with the rent, lives at a house numbered two lower than that occupied by the woman who passed on a secret about Miss Taylor.

4 Mrs Williams told the others about Mrs Davies, but didn't allege that she was in trouble with the law.

	No 1	No 3	No 5	No 7	Mrs Davies	Mr Miller	Mrs Robinson	Miss Taylor	Behind with rent	Carrying on	Drinking again	Trouble with law
Mrs Brown												
Mrs Jones												
Mrs Smith												
Mrs Williams												
Behind with rent												
Carrying on												
Drinking again												
Trouble with law												
Mrs Davies												
Mr Miller												
Mrs Robinson												
Miss Taylor												

Gossiper	House No	Gossiped about	Story

CAR-RY ON RALLYING

As final preparations for a classic car rally went ahead, four of the vehicles arrived at the site almost simultaneously. Can you work out the make and colour of each, to whom it belonged and how it arrived at the event?

Clues

1 Iris James' blue car isn't the 1949 Connaught L2.

2 Harry Innes' car is the 1932 Alvis Speed 20.

3 Ron Stirling's vehicle, which isn't white, appears in the alphabetical list immediately before the classic car which arrived at the rally on a trailer towed behind its owner's latest car, a Jaguar Sovereign.

4 The 1946 Delahaye Type 135 was towed to the event on a trailer behind a Ford Transit van.

5 The yellow car, which was the only one to be driven to the event on its own wheels, is two places away from Frank Graham's vehicle in the alphabetical list.

	Blue	Green	White	Yellow	Frank Graham	Harry Innes	Iris James	Ron Stirling	Driven	On car trailer	On lorry	On van trailer
Alvis												
Bristol												
Connaught												
Delahaye												
Driven												
On car trailer												
On lorry												
On van trailer												
Frank Graham												
Harry Innes												
Iris James												
Ron Stirling												

Car make	Car colour	Car owner	Arrival mode

INDIAN FILE

Many Native Americans had intriguing names when translated from their language into English. Below are four (invented) examples, but can you discover the three-word meaning of each when translated?

Clues

1 Kiawewe means Black something, but not Singing or Feather; nor is it the name that includes Desert and Flower.

2 The name Tecume has nothing to do with Big or Singing.

3 The translation of Gantuma involves the word Yellow but not Happy.

4 One of the names in English is Happy something Wind.

5 Another begins Long Mountain.

6 The name Haranto is to do with Thunder.

	Big	Black	Happy	Little	Long	Desert	Mountain	Running	Singing	Yellow	Elk	Feather	Flower	Thunder	Wind
Chalako															
Gantuma															
Haranto															
Kiawewe															
Tecume															
Elk															
Feather															
Flower															
Thunder															
Wind															
Desert															
Mountain															
Running															
Singing															
Yellow															

Name	First word	Second word	Third word

PILE UP

These piles of bricks aren't the random results of a child's play but clues to a final, at present blank, pile on the right. Like the rest, that one has six bricks each with a different one of the six letters.

The numbers below the piles tell you two things:

(a) The number of adjacent pairs of bricks in that column which also appear adjacent in the final pile.

(b) The number of adjacent pairs of bricks that make a correct pair but the wrong way up.

So:

would score one in the 'Correct' row if the final pile had an A directly above a C and a one in the 'Reversed' row if the final pile had a C on top of an A. From all this, can you create the final pile before it topples?

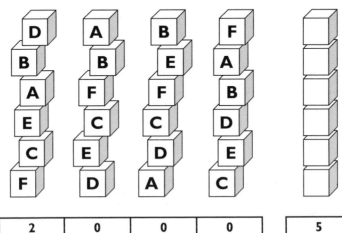

Correct	2	0	0	0	5
Reversed	0	0	0	1	0

THE CHIPS ARE DOWN

It is a tense moment in the casino as five eminent high-rolling gamblers await the spinning of the roulette wheel. From the following information, can you discover the glamorous companion standing at the arm of each gambler, the number he has bet on and the size of the wager?

Clues

1 Francesca looks on as her companion Count Zaleski places his bet on a number that is four less than that chosen by the gambler placing the £10,000 bet.

2 Sir Brian Ranby has placed the highest bet, while Prince Werther has placed his chips on number 32.

3 Isabella's companion has bet less than £15,000 on number 24.

4 Lisette's companion has bet £15,000.

5 The smallest bet is on number 12.

6 Cecilia has not come to the casino with a Sir.

	Cecilia	Francesca	Isabella	Lisette	Sacha	12	16	20	24	32	£5,000	£10,000	£15,000	£20,000	£25,000
Count Zaleski															
Lord Langridge															
Prince Werther															
Sir Brian Ranby															
Sir Vincent Tate															
£5,000											
£10,000											
£15,000											
£20,000											
£25,000											
12						
16						
20						
24						
32						

Player	Companion	Number	Size of wager

MISS RAFFLES AT THE ROYAL

The new musical Miss Raffles, based loosely on the life of the Amateur Cracksman's criminal sister, is playing at London's Royal Theatre and the five star dressing-rooms there are occupied by the performers taking the leading parts, all of whom are better known for their TV work. Can you work out who's in each dressing room, in which TV series they appear and whom they play in Miss Raffles?

Clues

1 Dressing room 1 is occupied by the performer known to the public as tough DS Sandy Morrow in the long-running cop show The Law; this isn't Vince Young.

2 Peter Stone's dressing room is numbered one higher than that of the soap opera star from Londoners, but one lower than that occupied by the person playing master criminal Vorzinski.

3 Glenda James plays Miss Amy Raffles.

4 Kirk Mooney is changing in dressing room 5.

5 The actor playing Tom Wright has been assigned dressing room 2. The man in room 3 hasn't been cast as Scotland Yard man Inspector McKee.

6 Brian Davis is the only British actor with a rôle in the top US series Z Files, while the man playing Amy's famous brother A J Raffles is one of the stars of the 'laddish' sitcom Chaps Misbehaving.

	Brian Davis	Glenda James	Kirk Mooney	Peter Stone	Vince Young	Chaps Misbehaving	Hammerdale	Londoners	The Law	Z Files	A J Raffles	Inspector McKee	Miss Raffles	Tom Wright	Vorzinski
Room 1															
Room 2															
Room 3															
Room 4															
Room 5															
A J Raffles															
Inspector McKee															
Miss Raffles															
Tom Wright															
Vorzinski															
Chaps Misbehaving															
Hammerdale															
Londoners															
The Law															
Z Files															

Dressing room	Star	TV series	Rôle

MISSION ACCOMPLISHED

Five First World War pilots, each returning from separate missions of varying types, were forced to crash land on the airfield for different reasons at a different time on the same day. Can you match each pilot with his mission and say why each had to make an emergency landing and at what time he did so? (You will be pleased to know that all five landed successfully and none was seriously injured.)

Clues

1 The man who blacked out following his balloon-busting mission managed to recover sufficiently to bring his aircraft down, landing next after Billy.

2 It was during the afternoon that Rick limped home on a wing and a prayer after his rudder was shot off.

3 The plane which ran short of fuel made its emergency landing at 1340 hours.

4 Dennis (not the last to land) had been on a mission to spot the enemy's latest artillery positions.

5 One plane made an emergency landing at 1520 hours, after strafing enemy lines. Its pilot's name occupies an odd-numbered position in the alphabetical list.

6 The shot-away undercarriage wasn't the cause of the first or last emergency.

7 The pilot whose engine seized up had not been on escort patrol.

	Artillery spotting	Balloon busting	Escort patrol	Reconnaissance	Strafing enemy lines	Blacked out	Engine seized	Ran out of fuel	Rudder shot off	U'carriage shot off	1030 hours	1115 hours	1340 hours	1520 hours	1705 hours
Ben															
Billy															
Dennis															
Jim															
Rick															
1030 hours															
1115 hours															
1340 hours															
1520 hours															
1705 hours															
Blacked out															
Engine seized															
Ran out of fuel															
Rudder shot off															
U/c shot off															

Pilot	Mission	Reason	Time

INTER RELATIONS

In a village churchyard, three sisters are buried in adjacent graves. Each sister was married and the stones also commemorate their respective husbands. Can you work out the first names and surnames inscribed on each headstone and the year in which each of the six died?

Clues

1 Ellen isn't commemorated by the inscription on headstone 1.

2 Samuel's wife departed this life in 1894; their surname wasn't Stones.

3 Adam died in 1891, whilst the date 1896 doesn't appear on headstone 3.

4 Constance is buried between her sister who died in 1887 and the one who married Mr Graves.

5 The wife of Mr Tombs died in 1899.

6 Maud's husband wasn't called James, nor is her headstone immediately to the left of his.

Surnames:
Graves; Stones; Tombs

Husbands:
Adam; James; Samuel

Wives:
Constance; Ellen; Maud

Dates of death:
1884; 1887; 1891; 1894; 1896; 1899

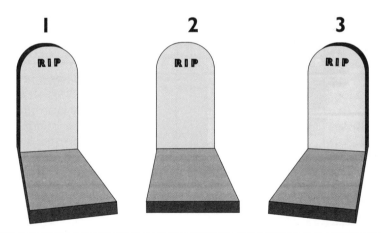

Stone	Surname	Husband	He died	Wife	She died
1					
2					
3					

Starting tip:

First decide where Constance is buried and then Ellen.

BACKING OUT

Five teenagers, who had each recently passed their driving test, badgered their reluctant fathers into lending them the family car. Unfortunately, each ran into something in their own driveway before ever reaching the road. Can you match the drivers with their fathers, say what each hit and work out exactly how long it was since each had passed the test?

Clues

1 Michael's son said that he wasn't to know that next door's dog had decided to cross the drive just as he was backing out.

2 It was a full ten days since Diane had been awarded a full driving licence.

3 Robin was convinced that the garage door had blown into his path just as he emerged, although the evidence was somewhat against him, as there wasn't a breath of wind that day.

4 Twelve days had elapsed since the teenager who hit the lawn mower had celebrated passing the test; the car in question didn't belong to Roger.

5 Henry's offspring had been granted a driving licence just five days previously.

6 Greg's son Mark had been officially driving longer than James, but not as long as the teenager whose brother's new bike was reduced to a mangled heap.

Father	Teenager	Object hit	Days since test

THE HIGH LIFE

Five amateur climbers of different nationalities attempted to climb Mont Blanc (4,807 metres), but all gave up their attempt for various different reasons when they had reached a height not too far from the summit. Can you work out the full details?

Clues

1 Dieter, the German climber, abandoned his attempt 200 metres short of the height attained by the man who suffered the severe nose bleed.

2 Frank isn't the Frenchman, who achieved a greater height than the Dutch climber.

3 The intense cold wasn't responsible for the abandonment at 4,000 metres.

4 The asthma attack was a crushing blow for the climber who had already reached 4,600 metres, with a mere 200 to go.

5 Peter's attempt took him further up Mont Blanc than most, ending only when he was about 400 metres short of the summit.

6 The Belgian climber suddenly felt desperately homesick and turned back forthwith.

7 Paul's attempt was defeated by severe gales.

8 The British mountaineer aborted his climb at 4,200 metres.

	Belgian	British	Dutch	French	German	3,800 metres	4,000 metres	4,200 metres	4,400 metres	4,600 metres	Asthma	Cold	Gales	Homesick	Nose bleed
Dieter															
Frank															
Paul															
Peter															
Richard															
Asthma															
Cold															
Gales															
Homesick															
Nose bleed															
3,800 metres															
4,000 metres															
4,200 metres															
4,400 metres															
4,600 metres															

Climber	Nationality	Height reached	Reason

LOGI-PATH

Use your deductive reasoning to form a pathway from the box marked 'START' to the box marked 'FINISH', moving either horizontally or vertically (but not diagonally) from square to adjacent square. The number at the beginning of every row or column indicates exactly how many boxes in that row or column your pathway must pass through. The small diagram at the bottom of the page is given as an example of how it works.

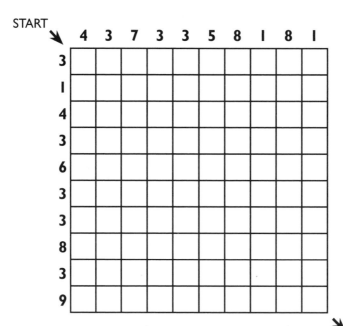

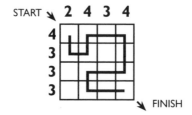

EN GARDE, MOUSQUETAIRE!

One fine morning in the summer of 1640, five musketeers had to make an early visit to a secluded spot by the Seine to fight a duel with a member of Cardinal Richelieu's Guard. Can you work out which Musketeer fought at which time, name his opponent and find the reason that he had challenged the man?

Clues

1 The first Musketeer to fight wasn't the one who had challenged the Guardsman who made an insulting remark about his personal appearance.

2 Silvis and his adversary fought at 8 o'clock.

3 Maximos wasn't the Musketeer who had challenged the man who carelessly splashed red wine on his new tunic.

4 The duel at 6.30 was with the man who'd called the King an 'incapable lout'. This wasn't Sergent Dingue, who fought immediately before Damos.

5 Lieutenant Gorille and his opponent began their fight at half past seven.

6 Caporal Balourd had upset one of the Musketeers by kicking his horse.

7 Brigadier Bourricot fought Archamos.

8 Uramis, who had challenged his opponent on the excuse that he had an ugly beard, wasn't the first to fight; Capitan Laideron wasn't the Guardsman who lost the 8 o'clock duel.

	Musketeer					Guardsman					Insulted King	Kicked horse	Personal insult	Splashed tunic	Ugly beard
	Archamos	Damos	Maximos	Silvis	Uramis	Balourd	Bourricot	Dingue	Gorille	Laideron					
6.00															
6.30															
7.00															
7.30															
8.00															
Insulted King															
Kicked horse															
Personal insult															
Splashed tunic															
Ugly beard															
Balourd															
Bourricot															
Dingue															
Gorille															
Laideron															

Time	Musketeer	Guardsman	Reason

PLAYING AWAY

This season I travelled to five away matches, each with a different friend. From the following verses, can you discover who my companion was on each occasion, the team we were playing against, the name of the ground and the final score?

Clues

I went with Pete to Denton;
Their ground isn't Old Mill.
It also isn't Horton Road,
Where the game was lost three nil.

The winners there weren't Armley;
We beat St Johns two one.
With Keith I saw us draw two all;
To The Elms I went with Don.

The game against Westhampton
I didn't see with Paul;
He also missed the one nil game,
Which wasn't at Craven Hall.

The game we saw at Benfield
Was played at Stamford Green –
Now try and sort the details
Of all the matches seen!

	Armley	Benfield	Denton	St Johns	Westhampton	Craven Hall	Horton Road	Old Mill	Stamford Green	The Elms	0-2	1-0	1-2	2-2	3-0
Don															
Keith															
Paul															
Pete															
Steve															

Companion	Team	Ground	Score

FEBRUARY FUN

Each of the numbers 1 to 28, representing the days of February, appears once in the 28 squares in the diagram. Can you place them all in their correct positions?

Clues

1 26 is in square C2, 3 is in F4 and 18 is in E1.

2 The horizontal sequence 5, 20, 14 appears in the layout, but not in row 3.

3 None of the two-digit numbers in row 4 is divisible by 3.

4 The number in A1 is twice that in G1, while G4 contains an odd number.

5 The odd number in F2 is two higher than the one in C4, while E2 contains a single digit.

6 There are no odd numbers in column E and the numbers in column D total 56.

7 The 7 is two places to the left of the 11 and immediately above the 12, while the 17 is two to the left of the 9 and immediately below the 6.

8 Four of the seven numbers in row 1 have two digits, one of these being 13; the total of all the numbers in this row doesn't end in 3 or 6.

9 The number in B4 is five higher than the one in B1 and five lower than the one in B2.

10 The 21 is somewhere in column B and the 27 somewhere in column F, but the 19 isn't in column G.

11 The 1 is somewhere above the 9 in the same column.

12 The 24 and 28 are both in the same column as the 2.

13 The number in G2 is higher than the number in G3.

	A	B	C	D	E	F	G
1							
2							
3							
4							

Starting tip:

Place the sequence related in clue 2.

LOGI-5

Every row across and column down should contain five letters: A, B, C, D and E, appearing once each. Also every shape (shown by the thick lines) must contain each of the letters A, B, C, D and E, appearing once each. Can you fill the grid?

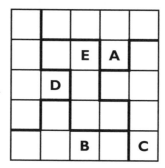

ABC

Every row across and column down is to have each of the letters A, B and C and two empty squares. The letter outside the grid shows the first or second letter in the direction of the arrow. Can you fill the grid?

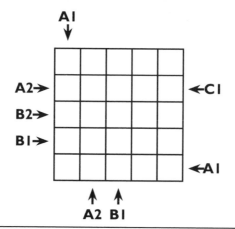

DETECTIVE WORKS

Here are details of five popular and successful fictional sleuths. From the information given, can you work out who is the creator of each and the number of books they have written featuring their detective, together with the part of the country where the investigations are set?

Clues

1 Charlotte Neill has written two more Rosie Rycroft novels than have been written about the Norfolk-based detective.

2 Philippa Dean's books are set in London and she has written at least eight featuring her popular sleuth.

3 Ernest Bradley (not the creator of Lady Lavinia Poole) doesn't write stories which take place around Manchester.

4 The Sgt Currie stories, set in Scotland, are written by a woman. The eight books are the work of a man.

5 The detective about whom ten books have been published operates in Cornwall.

6 Inspector Crisp has featured in the fewest books.

	Henry Madison	Inspector Crisp	Lady Lavinia Poole	Rosie Rycroft	Sgt Currie	4	6	8	10	12	Cornwall	London	Manchester	Norfolk	Scotland
Charlotte Neill															
Ernest Bradley															
Ian Lenton															
Philippa Dean															
Susan Dewar															
Cornwall															
London															
Manchester															
Norfolk															
Scotland															
4															
6															
8															
10															
12															

Author	Sleuth	No of books	Setting

DOMINO SEARCH

A standard set of dominoes has been laid out, using numbers instead of dots for clarity. With the aid of a sharp pencil and a keen brain, can you draw in the lines to show where each domino has been placed? You may find the check grid useful – crossing off each domino as you find it.

1	3	6	2	4	0	5	6
5	2	0	2	1	1	0	2
4	4	0	2	4	6	0	3
5	0	6	5	6	3	5	5
2	3	0	4	1	4	5	0
1	6	6	6	2	1	3	1
1	2	3	4	4	5	3	3

0							
1							
2							
3							
4							
5							
6							
	0	**1**	**2**	**3**	**4**	**5**	**6**

WATER BABIES

At the school swimming gala the girls' medley relay race was reaching an exciting climax as the four swimmers on the final leg neared the finish in the positions shown in the diagram. Can you fully identify the swimmer in each lane and work out the colour of the house she was representing?

Clues

1 Sonia Herring's position at the point in the race pictured in the diagram is immediately ahead of the green house's representative.

2 Samantha is the swimmer shown in lane 3.

3 Wendy, whose surname isn't Fish, isn't swimming for the yellow house, which isn't using lane 4.

4 The blue team has been allocated lane 1 for this year's medley race.

5 Jenny and the girl named Codd are in adjacent lanes.

Forenames:
Jenny; Samantha; Sonia; Wendy

Surnames:
Codd; Fish; Herring; Seal

Colours:
Blue; green; red; yellow

Direction of swimming ⟶

Lane	Forename	Surname	Colour
1			
2			
3			
4			

Starting tip:

Work out in which lane the green house is racing.

BUSKING IN THE SUN

Four students spent their last vacation busking in the main thoroughfare of town. Each was reading a different subject and each played a different musical instrument. Can you name each busker lettered A to D in the diagram and match them with their subjects and instruments? NB – It's a long street and they are far enough apart to be heard separately, but we have brought them closer together for the benefit of the diagram.

Clues

1 From left to right, Rosalie occupies the next pitch after the pan-pipe playing Science student.

2 Classicist Jonathan doesn't play the harmonica.

3 Eleanor operates from pitch B.

4 The ukulele player doesn't have pitch D.

5 The violin is the instrument used by busker C, whose university course isn't Theology.

Students:
Donald; Eleanor; Jonathan; Rosalie

Subjects:
Classics; Law; Science; Theology

Instruments:
Harmonica; Pan pipes; ukulele; violin

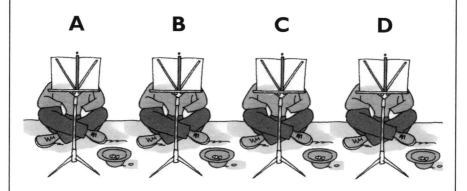

A   **B**   **C**   **D**

Busker	Name	Subject	Instrument
A			
B			
C			
D			

Starting tip:

First identify the pitch occupied by the pan pipes player.

LECTURE TOUR

The college lecture rooms are all busy this morning, with five lecturers giving talks on their particular subjects. Can you discover the starting time and room number of each lecture and the subject?

Clues

1 Dr Garvey's lecture on Medieval History, which isn't in room 5, starts before and is in a room numbered higher than Dr Keenan's talk.

2 The starting time of Mr Blake's lecture is immediately after that of the Romantic Poets lecture in room 1, but his isn't the 9.15 lecture in room 2.

3 Mrs Newell is lecturing in room 3, but not on Calculus.

4 Dr Searle's lecture begins at 10 o'clock.

5 The 9 o'clock lecture is being given by a Doctor.

6 The French Literature lecture starts at 10.45.

	Room 1	Room 2	Room 3	Room 4	Room 5	Dr Garvey	Dr Keenan	Dr Searle	Mr Blake	Mrs Newell	Biophysics	Calculus	French Literature	Medieval History	Romantic Poets
9.00															
9.15															
10.00															
10.45															
11.00															
Biophysics											
Calculus											
French Literature											
Medieval History											
Romantic Poets											
Dr Garvey						
Dr Keenan						
Dr Searle						
Mr Blake						
Mrs Newell						

Time	Room	Lecturer	Subject

JUST MANAGING

Six buildings are situated in the very heart of town, in the positions numbered 1 to 6 in the diagram. Can you identify each building and work out the full name of its manager?

Clues

1 The jewellers and the building under the management of Nathan Lucas share a common wall.

2 Terry's computer store bears a number twice that indicating the furniture store, which is on the opposite side of the main street.

3 Mervyn is the manager of the business in building 3.

4 The travel agency bears a higher number than the bank; one of these is managed by Brett and the other by Barrymore.

5 Building 6 is the Majestic Hotel.

6 The building where Coombes is in charge bears a number one higher than the one managed by Gilroy.

7 Arnold is the cousin of the man named Nesbitt, who runs the business in building 2.

	1		2	3
	4		5	6

	Bank	Computer store	Furniture store	Hotel	Jewellers	Travel agency	Arnold	Brett	Mervyn	Nathan	Robert	Terry	Barrymore	Coombes	Gilroy	Lucas	Nesbitt	Walker
Building 1																		
Building 2																		
Building 3																		
Building 4																		
Building 5																		
Building 6																		

Building	Business	Manager	Surname

LOGI-5

Every row across and column down should contain five letters: A, B, C, D and E, appearing once each. Also every shape (shown by the thick lines) must contain each of the letters A, B, C, D and E, appearing once each. Can you fill the grid?

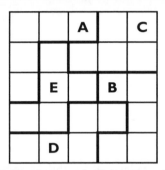

ABC

Every row across and column down is to have each of the letters A, B and C and two empty squares. The letter outside the grid shows the first or second letter in the direction of the arrow. Can you fill the grid?

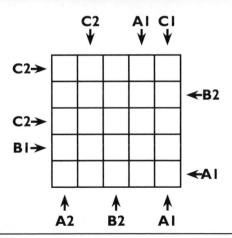

THRILLING WORDS

The books numbered 1 to 4 in the diagram are all thrillers by best-selling author Agatha Marsh standing on a shelf at the local branch library. Each book was taken out by a different fan of Agatha's works on the same day last week. Can you work out the title of each book and the name and occupation of the woman who borrowed it?

Clues

1 Wendy is the optician.

2 The position on the shelf of Death In The Rough, a mystery set on a golf course, was immediately between the book Joyce borrowed and the one chosen by the barmaid.

3 The nurse took out Killer At Large.

4 Olive borrowed the book numbered 3 in the diagram, which has a title consisting of an even number of words.

5 Book number 2 on the shelf was selected by the vet.

Books:
Death In The Rough; Killer At Large; Mayday Murder; Nemesis

Borrowers:
Joyce; Mary; Olive; Wendy

Occupations:
Barmaid; nurse; optician; vet

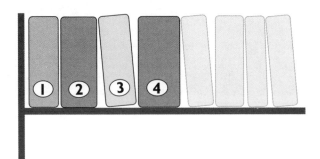

Book	Title	Borrower	Occupation
1			
2			
3			
4			

Starting tip:

Work out Olive's occupation.

BUENOS DIAS

Val Encier is a London-based Spanish interpreter and each day last week she assisted a different Spanish-speaking visitor engaged in professional discussions with their British contacts. Can you work out the name of her client on each day, where they were from and their occupation?

Clues

1 On Wednesday Val was interpreting for the Uruguayan visitor and on Thursday for Maria Benavento.

2 Val translated for Rosita Jimenez the day after she had worked with the visitor from Costa Rica; Carlos Perez wasn't from the Philippines.

3 On Monday, Val acted as interpreter for a civil engineer who had come to London for discussions about a road-building project.

4 Val worked with Pablo Machado from Mexico City more than one day after she translated for the surgeon attending a one-day conference.

5 The policeman's name was Felipe San Martin; the novelist, who was in London to sort out a publishing deal, was Spanish.

	Carlos Perez	Felipe San Martin	Maria Benavento	Pablo Machado	Rosita Jimenez	Costa Rica	Mexico	Philippines	Spain	Uruguay	Banker	Engineer	Policeman	Novelist	Surgeon
Monday															
Tuesday															
Wednesday															
Thursday															
Friday															
Banker															
Engineer															
Policeman															
Novelist															
Surgeon															
Costa Rica															
Mexico															
Philippines															
Spain															
Uruguay															

Day	Visitor	Homeland	Occupation

LOCAL MISGOVERNMENT

Sleazington's citizens are as honest and moral as anyone, so it's pure coincidence that the mayors of the town over a five-year period all become involved in scandals. From the clues below, can you work out the name and normal occupation of each year's Mayor and the nature of the scandal in which they were implicated?

Clues

1 George Flint, a director of a local manufacturing company, wasn't the Mayor who had an affair with the Town Clerk.

2 Susan Ryde was Mayor of Sleazington in 1994.

3 The 1995 Mayor wasn't the publican who ran the Sleazington Arms.

4 Trevor Wells wasn't the garage owner who was Mayor in 1998.

5 The estate agent was found to be running a property racket selling dilapidated buildings to the council for inflated prices.

6 The person found to be a member of a smuggling ring bringing in cheap booze and tobacco from the Continent was Mayor in an even-numbered year.

7 Ann Chester, who was deemed to be misusing the mayoral limousine by loading it with second-hand goods and taking it off to boot-sales on Sundays, was Mayor the year before the solicitor.

	Ann Chester	George Flint	John Lincoln	Susan Ryde	Trevor Wells	Company director	Estate agent	Garage owner	Publican	Solicitor	Affair/Town Clerk	Embezzlement	Misused car	Property racket	Smuggling ring
1994															
1995															
1996															
1997															
1998															
Affair/T Clerk															
Embezzlement															
Misused car															
Property racket															
Smuggling ring															
Co director															
Estate agent															
Garage owner															
Publican															
Solicitor															

Year	Name	Occupation	Scandal

VEE SHORT INTERVIEWS

Last week Radio Eastland presenter Vee Aitcheff had the chance to travel up to London to tape interviews with five celebrities, each of whom has some sort of connection with the Eastland area – but, as you can see from her appointment times, she had to keep her interviews short. Can you work out whom she interviewed in each time slot, their claim to fame and their connection with the Eastland area?

Clues

1 Alison Byrd's first job after leaving school was as a trainee with Radio Eastland.

2 Vee's appointment with Louise Mann, whose latest novel Little Gentlemen is top of the best-seller lists, was ninety minutes after the one with the celebrity who had been educated at a boarding school in Edwinsbury near the Eastland studios.

3 The round-the-world balloonist was born in the Radio Eastland reception area but moved away when she was six.

4 At 12.30pm, Vee had an interview with Paul Quiller.

5 Vee talked to the American-born celebrity whose grandfather had emigrated from a village near Storbury in 1920 immediately after interviewing the inventor and immediately before meeting Jill Keevil.

6 Vee's 9.30am interview was with the person whose mother lives in a retirement home in Edwinsbury; that person wasn't the pop singer.

	Alison Byrd	Jill Keevil	Louise Mann	Paul Quiller	Simon Tees	Balloonist	Inventor	Novelist	Pop singer	Tennis player	Birthplace	First job	Grandfather	Mother	School
9.30am															
11.00am															
12.30pm															
2.00pm															
3.30pm															
Birthplace															
First job															
Grandfather															
Mother															
School															
Balloonist															
Inventor															
Novelist															
Pop singer															
Tennis player															

Appointment	Celebrity	Occupation	Connection

UNCLE DEREK'S CLUB

The children's column in the local newspaper, edited by Uncle Derek, contains a birthday section listing the members of Uncle Derek's Club who celebrate their birthdays that day. We have selected one name at random from each of last week's five lists. Can you work out the full name of the child who celebrated on each day and say how old he or she became?

Clues

1 Hannah's eleventh birthday was celebrated later in the week than the day Waites' name appeared in the paper.

2 Uncle Derek's list included Adam's name on Wednesday.

3 Cheryl Vickers is a year older than the child featured on Monday.

4 The party at the Temples' house took place on Tuesday, the day of the Temple child's birthday.

5 The ninth birthday was recorded in Thursday's edition.

6 The surname of the child who is now twelve is MacMahon, whose first name isn't Dean.

7 The child who had a birthday on Friday is two years older than Fellowes.

	Adam	Belinda	Cheryl	Dean	Hannah	Fellowes	MacMahon	Temple	Vickers	Waites	8	9	10	11	12
Monday															
Tuesday															
Wednesday															
Thursday															
Friday															
8															
9															
10															
11															
12															
Fellowes															
MacMahon															
Temple															
Vickers															
Waites															

Day	Child	Surname	Age

CLUBLAND

Five gentlemen are sitting in the hush of the Library at the Albion Club in London's Pall Mall. Can you discover which newspaper each is reading, the drink each has ordered and his line of business?

Clues

1 Sir Anthony Grant is reading The Times and Sir Peter Rowse is enjoying a whisky.

2 Lord Redman's chosen newspaper isn't the Independent and neither he nor the reader of the Herald Tribune is drinking sherry.

3 Neither Mr Golding nor the man reading the Independent is the banker (not a lord) who has a gin and tonic.

4 Lord Newbury, who isn't in shipping, has a brandy and soda. Sir Peter Rowse, who isn't in horse-racing, isn't reading the Herald Tribune.

5 The whisky and soda drinker is reading the Daily Telegraph.

6 The industrialist is reading the Guardian. The shipping magnate isn't reading the Independent.

	Daily Telegraph	Guardian	Herald Tribune	Independent	The Times	Brandy and soda	Gin and tonic	Malt whisky	Sherry	Whisky and soda	Banker	Economist	Horse-racing	Industrialist	Shipping
Bernard Golding															
Lord Newbury															
Lord Redman															
Sir A Grant															
Sir P Rowse															
Banker															
Economist															
Horse-racing															
Industrialist															
Shipping															
Brandy/soda															
Gin/tonic															
Malt whisky															
Sherry															
Whisky/soda															

Gentleman	Newspaper	Drink	Business

BATTLESHIPS

This puzzle is based on the old game of battleships. Your task is to find the vessels in the diagram. Some parts of boats or sea squares have already been filled in, and a number next to a row or column refers to the number of occupied squares in that row or column. The boats may be positioned horizontally or vertically, but no two boats or parts of boats are in adjacent squares — horizontally, vertically or diagonally.

Aircraft Carrier:

Battleships:

Cruisers:

Destroyers:

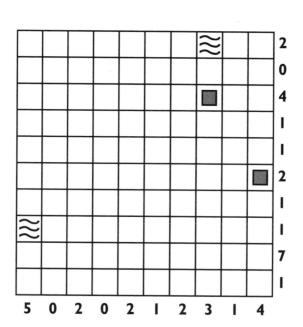

DOMINO SEARCH

A standard set of dominoes has been laid out, using numbers instead of dots for clarity. With the aid of a sharp pencil and a keen brain, can you draw in the lines to show where each domino has been placed? You may find the check grid useful – crossing off each domino as you find it.

1	5	0	5	6	5	6	2
3	2	4	3	0	5	3	0
1	5	1	3	2	3	1	6
4	6	0	0	0	4	1	4
4	2	2	2	5	3	4	5
1	6	4	6	6	1	2	0
5	2	3	1	4	3	6	0

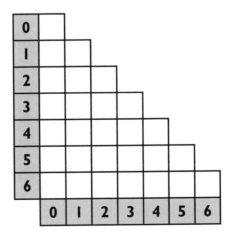

FLOOR SHOW

Four exercises were taking place simultaneously at a gymnastics competition. Can you name the gymnast in each of the positions lettered A to D, say which activity was taking place there and work out the highest mark each was awarded by the judges for her performance in it?

Clues

1 The girl performing the floor exercises in area B obtained a top score 0.2 higher than Gerda.

2 Natalie is performing her exercise in the area marked D on the plan.

3 Lara is performing on her favourite piece of apparatus, the parallel bars.

4 The girl in area C received a top mark of 9.9.

5 The beam exercise isn't taking place in area A.

Gymnasts:
Barbara; Gerda; Lara; Natalie

Exercises:
Bars; beam; floor; vault

Top marks:
9.6; 9.7; 9.8; 9.9

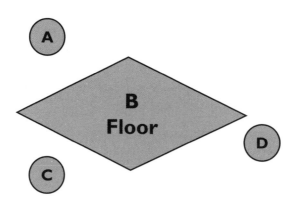

Area	Gymnast	Exercise	Top mark

Starting tip:

Work out the top mark given to the girl doing the floor exercises.

FOREIGN FOOD

In the 24th century Luna City – capital of what was Earth's moon before it became independent – is a large underground community which boasts, among other things, a number of restaurants serving alien cuisine. Can you work out the name of each, its address in the city, the type of food it serves and the reason the restaurant doesn't get any Terran (Earth-human) customers?

Clues

1 Only one of the two restaurants with atmospheres unbreathable by Terrans (who require oxygen) is in a Dome; it is neither the establishment in the Port Dome by the rocket terminal nor the one serving Adomphan food.

2 The restaurant in Tunnel J3A, which Terrans avoid because they find it distressing to be served with food that's still alive, isn't the Violet Planet.

3 Neither the restaurant with a chlorine atmosphere nor the one in the Old Dome offers Adomphan cuisine.

4 The Green Fort (which is Slanian) and Agich and Ruom's are both in Domes.

5 Neither the restaurant in the Port Dome nor that serving Purian food is Proj-Ka's, kept in total darkness because the aliens to whom it caters 'see' using vibrations.

6 The restaurant serving Graypecian food has a methane atmosphere, unlike Agich and Ruom's.

	Market Dome	Old Dome	Port Dome	Tunnel C7	Tunnel J3A	Adomphan	Graypecian	Karakatian	Purian	Slanian	Chlorine atmosphere	Live food	Methane atmosphere	Poisonous food	Totally dark
Agich and Ruom's															
Green Fort															
19 Brothers															
Proj-Ka's															
Violet Planet															
Chlorine atmos															
Live food															
Methane atmos															
Poisonous food															
Totally dark															
Adomphan															
Graypecian															
Karakatian															
Purian															
Slanian															

Restaurant	Address	Cuisine	Disadvantage

OVER THE DITCH

In 1944 in preparation for the D-Day invasion, five British agents, trained as radio operators, were parachuted into occupied France to work with different Resistance groups. Can you work out each agent's name, where they were dropped and the codename and occupation of the Resistance leader with whom they were sent to work?

Clues

1 The group led by the dentist codenamed Faucon didn't operate in the Dijon area.

2 The nom de guerre of the man for whom Alec Cooper acted as radio operator was the same length as that of the leader who ran the Café Moulin Noir.

3 Levrier wasn't a policeman. The police sergeant's group wasn't that in Rouen, which was assigned a radio operator with a longer surname than that of the one who went to Toulouse.

4 Trudy Vane, who went to Dijon, didn't work with the police sergeant. Jack Moody was attached to the group whose leader was a mechanic.

5 Guy Fenton was radio operator for Argent, who wasn't the police sergeant. Dinah Ewart didn't work with Pelerin or Serin (whose base was in Lille).

	Avignon	Dijon	Lille	Rouen	Toulouse	Argent	Faucon	Levrier	Pelerin	Serin	Café owner	Dentist	Mechanic	Police inspector	Police sergeant
Alec Cooper															
Dinah Ewart															
Guy Fenton															
Jack Moody															
Trudy Vane															
Café owner															
Dentist															
Mechanic															
Police inspector															
Police sergeant															
Argent															
Faucon															
Levrier															
Pelerin															
Serin															

Agent	City	Leader	Occupation

ON AND OFF

A bus route runs through a busy town centre. Five successive stops account for the largest number of passengers getting on or off the bus. Given the details of just one journey, can you work out at what time the bus reached every stop and how many passengers got on and off there?

Clues

1 The same number of people didn't get on and off the bus at any of the stops.

2 Odeon Corner was reached three minutes after the stop where three passengers boarded the bus and three minutes before the one where nine alighted.

3 Two passengers got on the bus at the stop where eight got off.

4 Six people alighted at the shopping mall.

5 Exactly four people didn't get on at the central library, which was where the bus stopped at 10.14.

6 Five passengers got on the bus at the first stop.

7 One more person left the bus at the Post Office than at the 10.11 stop.

		10.05	10.08	10.11	10.14	10.17	**ON** 2	3	4	5	6	**OFF** 5	6	7	8	9
Library																
Odeon Corner																
Post office																
Shopping mall																
Station																
O	5															
F	6															
F	7															
	8																
	9																
O	2															
N	3															
	4																
	5																
	6																

Stop	Time	No on	No off

GONE VIKING

In the year 913 AD, in the Norse village of Litendalvik, there lived five sisters whose husbands had gone raiding in their longships and not returned. Can you work out the name of each woman's husband and longship and say how long – in 913 AD – he had been missing?

Clues

1 Bjarni the Red was captain of the longship Ice Dragon.

2 Eyjolf the Swift's ship had been missing for a shorter period than the one commanded by Snorri the Stout, husband of Gudrid the Gentle, but for more than the one year Thorhild the Slender had been waiting for her husband to return.

3 Sigrid Fairhair's husband had been missing two years longer than the Stormrider, the longship of Vigdis the Singer's spouse.

4 The Black Shark had sailed out of Litendalvik in 906 AD and had never returned.

5 Thorwald had been missing for three years.

6 The husband of Freydis Squinteye had named his ship after a kind of dragon.

7 Eric Longshanks had been missing longer than the captain of the Seasnake, who wasn't Sigrid Fairhair's husband.

	Bjarni	Eric	Eyjolf	Snorri	Thorwald	Black Shark	Great Dragon	Ice Dragon	Seasnake	Stormrider	1 year	3 years	5 years	6 years	7 years
Freydis															
Gudrid															
Sigrid															
Thorhild															
Vigdis															
1 year															
3 years															
5 years															
6 years															
7 years															
Black Shark															
Great Dragon															
Ice Dragon															
Seasnake															
Stormrider															

Sister	Husband	Longship	Years missing

DOWN UNDER

Five French underwater explorers made expeditions to different ocean areas last year in different months. Can you fully identify the five and work out the details of each man's voyage?

Clues

1 The Antarctic expedition was scheduled for December to take advantage of the summer weather.

2 Didier Pieuvre mounted the next expedition following that to the South Pacific.

3 Auguste led the April expedition, which wasn't to an Atlantic area.

4 Hippocampe's expedition took place in October.

5 Requin, who isn't Bruno, headed for the South Atlantic to carry out his explorations; this wasn't the expedition which immediately preceded Calmar's.

6 Victor's chosen location was the Indian Ocean.

	Calmar	Hippocampe	Pieuvre	Requin	Soumarin	Antarctic	Indian	North Atlantic	South Atlantic	South Pacific	March	April	July	October	December
Auguste															
Bruno															
Didier															
Emmanuel															
Victor															
March															
April															
July															
October															
December															
Antarctic															
Indian															
North Atlantic															
South Atlantic															
South Pacific															

Explorer	Surname	Ocean	Month

BAR OF JUDGMENT

Four friends have gone to the Royal Theatre in London's West End to see the new musical Miss Raffles as described in puzzle 110 and during the interval have retired to the bar for a drink and to discuss the show. Can you fill in on the drawing the name of the person occupying each seat at the table, what they're drinking and their opinion of Miss Raffles?

Clues

1 It isn't Jack who thinks the show is 'disappointing – the idea's good but it could have been better handled'.

2 Matt is in seat 3.

3 The glass in front of the person in seat 2 – who's driving the others home later – contains only mineral water.

4 Alison, who thinks that the show is 'excellent, it couldn't possibly be better', is sitting in a lower-numbered seat than the gin-and-tonic drinker.

5 The theatregoer who considers that Miss Raffles is 'not bad - they've taken a lot of trouble with the costumes and sets' has a seat number between those of Tracey, who's not in seat 4 and the person with the glass of red wine.

Names:
Alison; Jack; Matt; Tracey

Drinks:
Gin and tonic; mineral water; red wine; white wine

Opinions:
'Disappointing'; 'excellent'; 'not bad'; 'rubbish'

Seat	Name	Drink	Opinion
1			
2			
3			
4			

Starting tip:

Work out who is sitting in seat 4.

LOGI-PATH

Use your deductive reasoning to form a pathway from the box marked 'START' to the box marked 'FINISH', moving either horizontally or vertically (but not diagonally) from square to adjacent square. The number at the beginning of every row or column indicates exactly how many boxes in that row or column your pathway must pass through. The small diagram at the bottom of the page is given as an example of how it works.

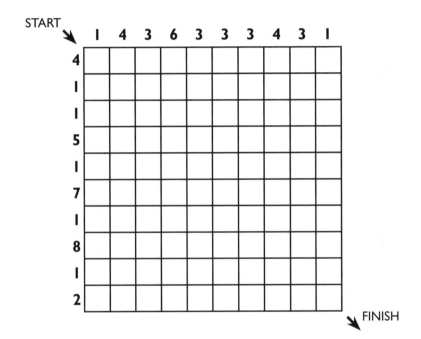

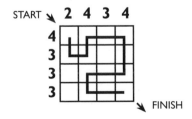

BECAUSE IT WAS THERE

Five 19th Century explorers each made an expedition to a different part of the world. Can you identify the five and say where each man went to and in which year his expedition was mounted?

Clues

1 Wickstead's trip to the Amazonian rain-forests took place in the same decade as Solomon's expedition, which wasn't the last of the five.

2 Leopold Handyside mounted his expedition four years after the man who chose the northern regions of Canada as his scene of operations.

3 Horatio set off on his travels in 1861.

4 The expedition to Darkest Africa and Prothero's venture were separated by a period of eight years.

5 Rathbone's expedition set out in 1857.

6 Gideon, who wasn't Boswell, ventured into hitherto unexplored territory in Western Australia.

	Boswell	Handyside	Prothero	Rathbone	Wickstead	Amazon forest	Canadian north	Darkest Africa	Tibet	Western Australia	1849	1853	1857	1861	1865
Gideon															
Horatio															
Leopold															
Marmaduke															
Solomon															
1849															
1853															
1857															
1861															
1865															
Amazon forest															
Canadian north															
Darkest Africa															
Tibet															
W Australia															

Explorer	Surname	Place	Year

TEA TIME

While on holiday, the Eatwell family treat themselves to a cream tea or similar in a village tea-room. They did particularly well last week…! Can you discover which tea-room they patronised each day, the village in which it is situated and what particular item on the menu they would heartily recommend (should you ever go there)?

Clues

1 Clotted cream was the speciality of the Wishing Well, which the Eatwells visited earlier than the tea-room in Stoneybrook.

2 They called in at Millwood two days after sampling the home-made jam at the Inglenook Tea-Rooms.

3 The Eatwells enjoyed superb home-made fruit cake on Sunday afternoon and wonderful meringues in Oakmeadow, which wasn't their Saturday venue.

4 The chocolate cake wasn't eaten at Copper Kettle (which is exactly five miles from the tea-room visited on Tuesday).

5 They didn't have tea at the Tudor Cottage on Wednesday.

6 On Monday afternoon the Eatwells had tea in Ashdene.

	Copper Kettle	Inglenook	Mulberry Tree	Tudor Cottage	Wishing Well	Ashdene	Millwood	Oakmeadow	Stoneybrook	Thatchleigh	Chocolate cake	Clotted cream	Home-made fruit cake	Home-made jam	Meringues
Saturday															
Sunday															
Monday															
Tuesday															
Wednesday															
Chocolate cake															
Clotted cream															
Fruit cake															
Jam															
Meringues															
Ashdene															
Millwood															
Oakmeadow															
Stoneybrook															
Thatchleigh															

Day	Tea-room	Village	Item

PUZZLE IT OUT

Five crossword addicts each had a particular favourite type of puzzle, which is published once a week, on a different day, in their regular daily paper. Can you match each solver with his or her crossword preference and say on which day and in which paper it appears?

Clues

1 The general knowledge crossword is published every Thursday; it isn't tackled by the woman who takes the Bugle.

2 Caroline's favourite crossword only appears in the Sunday edition of her paper.

3 Rodney's cryptic crossword appears later in the week than the one in the Watchman.

4 The skeleton crossword doesn't appear on a Monday.

5 The giant crossword is in the Planet and appears later in the week than Kevin's favourite puzzle.

6 Wednesday is the day the Clarion reader's favourite puzzle is printed.

7 Emma never buys any other paper but the Globe.

	Cryptic	General knowledge	Giant	Skeleton	Thematic	Sunday	Monday	Wednesday	Thursday	Saturday	Bugle	Clarion	Globe	Planet	Watchman
Caroline															
Emma															
Janice															
Kevin															
Rodney															
Bugle															
Clarion															
Globe															
Planet															
Watchman															
Sunday															
Monday															
Wednesday															
Thursday															
Saturday															

Solver	Crossword	Day	Paper

AIMING HIGH

Last year there were several undistinguished attempts by countries to launch rockets. Can you name the countries and the rockets they launched on the five specified dates and say what height each rocket attained?

Clues

1 DZQ attained a greater height than the rocket launched on March 29th but a lower height than Ruritania's rocket.

2 Neither Gondwanaland's rocket nor Hybus, which was sent up next after it, gained as much height as the one launched on July 10th.

3 Rekniz made its attempt earlier than Banania's rocket but later than the one which malfunctioned at 5.5 miles.

4 The first of the five to be launched was less successful than the last; the least successful attempt took place next before the one which went up 8.5 miles.

5 Balonia launched its rocket next after Superlox V and both were earlier than that which rose 10 miles.

6 Lopez II was launched next before Columnia's rocket; the height it reached was over two miles more than that of the latter.

	Balonia	Banania	Columnia	Gondwanaland	Ruritania	DZQ	Hybus	Lopez II	Rekniz	Superlox V	3 miles	5.5 miles	6 miles	8.5 miles	10 miles
January 7															
March 29															
May 16															
July 10															
September 21															
3 miles															
5.5 miles															
6 miles															
8.5 miles															
10 miles															
DZQ															
Hybus															
Lopez II															
Rekniz															
Superlox V															

Date	Country	Rocket	Height

PRODIGY CLOSE

The six families who live in Prodigy Close each have a child who has a remarkable talent in a different field. From the clues given below, can you name the family which lives in each of the houses numbered 1 to 6, identify their child, and say at what each excels?

Clues

1 Young Bright, the chess player, lives directly across the Close from Jamie.

2 Linda is an outstanding sprinter.

3 The Marvell family live at number 3, Prodigy Close.

4 Matthew Best lives next door to the violinist, but the swimmer lives on the opposite side of the Close.

5 The girl at number 2, whose surname is not Tallant, is an excellent pianist, but the child at number 6 is not a musician.

6 Kieron's house is number 5.

7 The tennis player's house has a lower number than that of the Nonesuch family, while Mary lives next door to the Dazzlers.

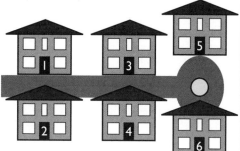

	Best	Bright	Dazzler	Marvell	Nonesuch	Tallant	Jamie	Kieron	Linda	Mary	Matthew	Naomi	Chess	Piano	Running	Swimming	Tennis	Violin
No 1																		
No 2																			
No 3																			
No 4																			
No 5																			
No 6																			

House No	Family	Child	Activity

WHO GOES THERE?

Four drivers were held up at the traffic lights in Dimbourne Road. By chance, only one of them was going straight along the road to Dimbourne, village D, while each of the others were about to turn off on a different one of the three side roads leading to villages A, B and C. Can you name the driver of each of the cars numbered 1 to 4, work out its make, identify all four villages and say who was going to which?

Clues

1 Neither of the first two drivers in the line was going to take a left turn. One of these two drivers was John and the other owns the Fiat.

2 Dick's Vauxhall was immediately behind the car which was heading for Dimbourne.

3 Betty was going to take the turn for Kidwell, which is the next after the one the driver of car 4 would take.

4 Maggie's car was somewhere ahead in the line at the lights of the one heading for Walbury.

5 The Citroën was immediately behind the car whose driver had an appointment in Brigthorpe.

Drivers:
Betty; Dick; John; Maggie

Cars:
Citroën; Fiat; Rover; Vauxhall

Villages:
Brigthorpe; Dimbourne; Kidwell; Walbury

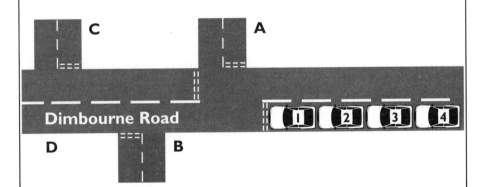

Car	Driver	Make	Village	Village name
1				
2				
3				
4				

Starting tip:

Identify the driver of car 4.

THE EMPIRE LOOKS BACK

The drawing below shows an advertisement for the Classic Film Festival at the Empire Theatre, Storbury; the central panel gives details of dates, times and prices, while the panels round the edge show pictures of the stars of the featured films. Can you determine the name of each star pictured, the rôle in which they're pictured and the film from which the picture comes?

Clues

1 The star in B (who wasn't in Henry VI) has a forename and surname with the same initial. C shows a woman.

2 The star in D is shown playing psychiatrist and amateur detective Dr Boswell, a rôle for which he or she received an Oscar.

3 The picture of the star playing the alien Xantipon is immediately clockwise of that depicting Michelle Hammond.

4 The star of The Bird From Gozo (in E) didn't play Sergeant Fox.

5 The man in A is Kevin Kaye.

6 The still of Tom Briscoe in Whitehouse is one place clockwise from that showing a star playing Kit Shannon and one place anticlockwise from the shot of Sandra Singer. One of these was in Comrade Abel.

7 The picture of Charlie Cotman as French airman Jean Gaudier is directly opposite the shot from The Third Woman.

Star names:
Charlie Cotman; Emma Eastley; Kevin Kaye; Michelle Hammond; Sandra Singer; Tom Briscoe

Rôle names:
Dr Boswell; Ginger; Jean Gaudier; Kit Shannon; Sergeant Fox; Xantipon

Film titles:
Comrade Abel; Henry VI; The Bird From Gozo; The 40th Step; The Third Woman; Whitehouse

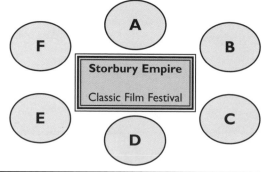

Picture	Star	Rôle	Film
A			
B			
C			
D			
E			
F			

Starting tip:
Work out the position of the picture of Tom Briscoe.

BATTLESHIPS

This puzzle is based on the old game of battleships. Your task is to find the vessels in the diagram. Some parts of boats or sea squares have already been filled in, and a number next to a row or column refers to the number of occupied squares in that row or column. The boats may be positioned horizontally or vertically, but no two boats or parts of boats are in adjacent squares — horizontally, vertically or diagonally.

Aircraft Carrier:

Battleships:

Cruisers:

Destroyers:

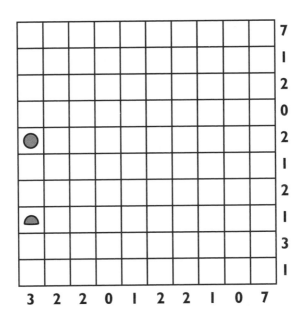

LOGI-5

Every row across and column down should contain five letters: A, B, C, D and E, appearing once each. Also every shape (shown by the thick lines) must contain each of the letters A, B, C, D and E, appearing once each. Can you fill the grid?

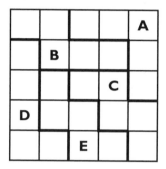

ABC

Every row across and column down is to have each of the letters A, B and C and two empty squares. The letter outside the grid shows the first or second letter in the direction of the arrow. Can you fill the grid?

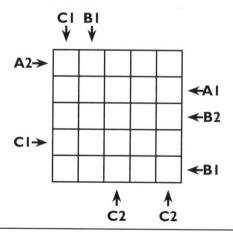

CUTTING REMARKS

Our talkative and long-established village barber, Dan Druff, has recently retired from full-time work and now opens only on Monday mornings. Last Monday he had five customers. Can you work out their full names, their nicknames and the times Dan dealt with each.
NB – The nicknames are all accurate descriptions of their owners' hair.

Clues

1 In no instance does the alphabetical order of first names coincide with that of surnames or nicknames (eg Fred isn't Dowson or Baldie).

2 Pybus, who has long, straight hair, arrived immediately after Peter.

3 Farmer received attention more than half an hour after Harry; and neither has ginger hair. Ginger's turn was immediately between Blondie's and Jack's.

4 Spoors (who wasn't first) had his turn earlier than Curly.

5 The turn of Shorty (not Mr Dowson) was more than an hour after Walker's, but Roy's was later still. Fred's turn came immediately after Blondie's and immediately before Baldie's.

	Dowson	Farmer	Pybus	Spoors	Walker	Baldie	Blondie	Curly	Ginger	Shorty	9.20	9.50	10.30	11.00	11.40
Fred															
Harry															
Jack															
Peter															
Roy															
9.20															
9.50															
10.30															
11.00															
11.40															
Baldie															
Blondie															
Curly															
Ginger															
Shorty															

Customer	Surname	Nickname	Time

PHOTO DEVELOPMENT

Granny Bromley has photographs of her grandchildren all over the house; the ones on the bookcase are of her youngest grandchild, Emma, taken on five different holidays. For each picture, can you determine the location and Emma's age at the time? NB – 'Left' and 'right' are from your point of view as you look at the pictures.

Clues

1 The photograph of Emma when she was six is next to and left of the one taken at Salcombe.

2 Emma was a year older when she went to Tenby than in photograph D.

3 The Little Haven picture is next to and right of the one taken when she was three years old.

4 She was older when she holidayed in Milford-on-Sea than in photograph at A but younger than when she was at Swanage.

Locations:
Little Haven; Milford-on-Sea; Salcombe; Swanage; Tenby

Ages:
1; 3; 4; 5; 6

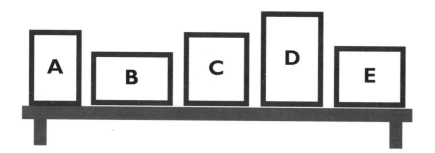

Picture	Location	Age

Starting tip:

Work out the holiday location shown in photo A.

THE ENGINE ROOM

A recent conference on engineering education was attended by some of the foremost engineering experts in Western Europe. Can you work out the age and specialisation of each and say where each is currently working?

Clues

1 The engineer working in France is three years older than the expert in marine salvage but younger than the expert in reinforced concrete.

2 Kurt Manners is younger than the man working in Sweden but older than Mark Thyme; but the specialist in road construction is younger than any of these.

3 Adolph Finn is three years younger than the man working in Scotland but more than three years older than the one currently employed in Germany.

4 Kon Fetti isn't as old as the man working in England (who is younger than the aircraft designer).

5 The specialist in railway engines is three years older than the man in Sweden.

	38	41	44	47	50	Aircraft design	Marine salvage	Railway engines	Reinforced concrete	Road construction	England	France	Germany	Scotland	Sweden
Adolph Finn															
Fitz Anstarts															
Kon Fetti															
Kurt Manners															
Mark Thyme															
England															
France															
Germany															
Scotland															
Sweden															
Aircraft design															
Marine salvage															
Railway engines															
Reinforced concrete															
Road construction															

Engineer	Age	Specialisation	Country

FARMERS' ARMS

A representative group of farmers met to formulate strategy for their campaign against the latest regulations from Brussels. Can you deduce the name and speciality of the farmer at each place around the table?

Clues

1 The numerical order of the seats doesn't at any point tally with the alphabetical order of the names of the farmers who sat in them.

2 Chook sat directly opposite the poultry farmer and next to and right of Barlie, who was directly opposite the potato grower; the latter was next clockwise after Stockman, while the pig farmer sat directly opposite Syloh.

3 The cattle farmer was next to and right of Giles and next to and left of Barlie.

4 The man with the corn crop sat with the farmer who has extensive orchards on his left and Syloh on his right. Oates was on the same side of the table as the corn grower and directly opposite the wheat specialist, who was next to and right of Grayne, who sat directly opposite the fruit grower.

5 The name of the farmer in seat 3 is alphabetically next after that of the man in seat 1, but alphabetically next before that of the man in seat 4.

Farmers:
Barlie; Chook; Giles; Grayne; Haynes; Oates; Stockman; Syloh

Specialities:
Cattle; corn; fruit; pigs; potatoes; poultry; rapeseed; wheat

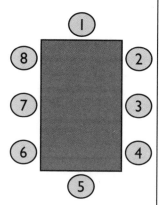

Seat No	1	2	3	4
Farmer				
Speciality				

Seat No	5	6	7	8
Farmer				
Speciality				

Starting tip:

Work out who occupied seat 3.

DOMINO SEARCH

A standard set of dominoes has been laid out, using numbers instead of dots for clarity. With the aid of a sharp pencil and a keen brain, can you draw in the lines to show where each domino has been placed? You may find the check grid useful – crossing off each domino as you find it.

1	6	3	6	0	6	0	2
6	2	2	6	6	5	3	1
2	4	1	2	4	4	0	0
0	5	5	3	0	4	5	3
4	1	3	1	4	5	3	3
1	5	0	0	1	6	4	2
6	2	3	2	1	4	5	5

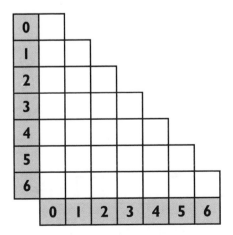

LOGI-5

Every row across and column down should contain five letters:
A, B, C, D and E, appearing once each. Also every shape (shown by the
thick lines) must contain each of the letters A, B, C, D and E, appearing
once each. Can you fill the grid?

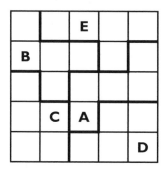

ABC

Every row across and column down is to have each of the letters A, B and
C and two empty squares. The letter outside the grid shows the first or
second letter in the direction of the arrow. Can you fill the grid?

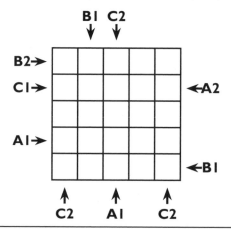

DOWN ON THE FARM

Three men are each employed on neighbouring farms. Can you identify each man, name the farmer he works for and the farm he works on?

Clues

1 Farmer Stiles owns Toft Farm.

2 Harrow doesn't work on Nutwood Farm.

3 Eddie Drill isn't employed by Farmer Giles.

4 Farmer Wiles regards Plowman as one of his best workers.

5 Ben isn't an employee of Hilltop Farm.

	Drill	Harrow	Plowman	Giles	Stiles	Wiles	Hilltop Farm	Nutwood Farm	Toft Farm
Ben									
Eddie									
Jack									
Hilltop Farm									
Nutwood Farm									
Toft Farm									
Giles									
Stiles									
Wiles									

Forename	Surname	Farmer	Farm

ANNUAL EVENT

Three neighbours from Primrose Avenue happened to meet at the check-out of the local garden centre where each had bought two different kinds of bedding plants. Can you work out the number of each man's house and the two types of plant each bought?

Clues

1 The nemesia were bought by the resident of No 17.

2 Mr Green lives next door to the man who bought the pansies.

3 Mr Raikes has a lower-numbered house than the man who bought the geraniums.

4 The occupant of No 15 didn't buy the begonias; the one who did also purchased the lobelia.

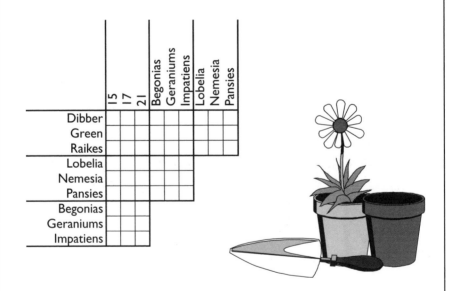

Name	Number	First choice	Second choice

PILE UP

These piles of bricks aren't the random results of a child's play but clues to a final, at present blank, pile on the right. Like the rest, that one has six bricks each with a different one of the six letters.

The numbers below the piles tell you two things:

(a) The number of adjacent pairs of bricks in that column which also appear adjacent in the final pile.

(b) The number of adjacent pairs of bricks that make a correct pair but the wrong way up.

So:

 would score one in the 'Correct' row if the final pile had an A directly above a C and a one in the 'Reversed' row if the final pile had a C on top of an A. From all this, can you create the final pile before it topples?

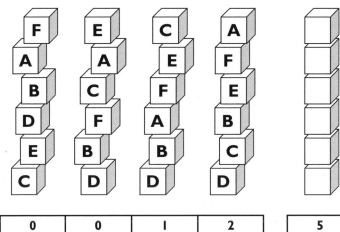

Correct	0	0	1	2		5
Reversed	0	1	0	1		0

TAME SHRINK

Dr Rhonda Twist is a psychiatrist who seldom sees a patient – she makes her living as a psychiatric advisor (or tame shrink as she's irreverently called) for a number of radio and TV stations. On Thursday, for instance, she was on four different day-time shows, talking on various topics. Can you work out to whom she talked in each time-slot, on which station and what about?

Clues

1 Dr Twist's discussion with Clair Payne was broadcast on City Radio.

2 At 4.00pm, Dr Twist was talking about triskaidekaphobia – which is, of course, the fear of the number 13.

3 It was at 12 noon that the good Doctor made her appearance on Albion TV.

4 Dr Twist's report on 'Chocolate - sweet treat or mindbender?', which wasn't made on the Kay Sampson Show, went out two hours after her chat about stress and its effects.

5 Dr Twist's discussion on UFOs – 'alien visitors or hallucinations?' – with Alison Reid and her broadcast on Radio 29 were just two hours apart.

Time	Presenter	Station	Topic

MISSES GRUNDY

As you might expect Mr and Mrs Grundy were extremely strait-laced people and intended each of their four daughters to follow a respectable career. However, the girls had other ideas. From the clues below, can you work out each girl's name, the career which her parents expected her to take up, the one she chose instead and what each has done this month to attract public attention and parental disapproval?

Clues

1 Cherry isn't the leading actress who posed (discreetly) nude for a painting to be shown at the National Academy's summer exhibition.

2 Daphne is a journalist for a trendy lifestyle magazine; her sister who was expected to become a banker is a photographer whose portraits of celebrities often appear in the same publication.

3 Angela, who has just embarked on her fourth attempt to attain lasting marital bliss, was never intended to be a lawyer and knows nothing about photography.

4 The sister who is involved in a torrid and very public affair with a pop star is a qualified accountant but has never practised as such.

	Accountancy	Banking	Law	Medicine	Advertising	Journalism	Photography	Theatre	Affair with pop star	Fourth marriage	Kiss and tell memoirs	Nude portrait
Angela												
Brenda												
Cherry												
Daphne												
Affair/pop star												
Fourth marriage												
Kiss/tell memoirs												
Nude portrait												
Advertising												
Journalism												
Photography												
Theatre												

Name	Intended	Chosen	Scandal

IF MUSIC BE THE FOOD...

Jack took his girlfriend Gill out to dinner four times last week. Can you work out where they went on each occasion, how much Jack paid for the meal and what sort of musical accompaniment they enjoyed whilst eating?

Clues

1 Jack and Gill went to the Blue Moon Restaurant two days before they ate at the Old Bull, which wasn't where Jack spent £50 on dinner.

2 Sunday's dinner bill was £48; the music that night wasn't provided by the Shamrock Folk Trio.

3 Pianist Bebe Grand didn't tinkle the ivories at the restaurant where Jack and Gill dined on Tuesday.

4 The Magnolia, where Jack's bill came to £44, didn't provide a folk group to entertain the diners.

5 At Trivett's Jack spent two pounds less than he did at the restaurant where he and Gill had dinner on Thursday, where they listened to authentic Hungarian gipsy violinist Janos Ferenczy – well, he seemed authentic until he spoke with an unmistakable Birmingham accent.

	Blue Moon	Magnolia	Old Bull	Trivett's	£44	£46	£48	£50	Folk trio	Gipsy violinist	Pianist	String quartet
Sunday												
Tuesday												
Thursday												
Saturday												
Folk trio												
Gipsy violinist												
Pianist												
String quartet												
£44												
£46												
£48												
£50												

Day	Restaurant	Bill	Musicians

XX MD

In the bad old days of the Cold War, the British Secret Service's elite XX section had its own Medical Officer, known for security reasons as Dr XX, to deal with wounded or sick agents returning from assignments. The drawing below reproduces Dr XX's appointments book for a typical Wednesday morning in 1962. Can you fill in the agent-patients' names, from what they were suffering and from where they had recently returned?

Clues

1 The agent who had been on assignment in Tangiers saw Dr XX immediately after Sally Leamas and immediately before the person with a minor bullet wound in the shoulder.

2 Basil Oakes was convalescing after a tough job in Rio de Janeiro.

3 The patient who saw Dr XX at 11.30am was recovering from a knife wound in the side.

4 Rex Hannay saw Dr XX in the same hour as the agent who had cracked a rib while escaping from a KGB prison in Moscow.

5 The man who had recently returned from an assignment in Hong Kong had an appointment with Dr XX at 10.00am.

6 Walter Ashenden, who had a broken arm, wasn't the agent who had been working undercover in the Hungarian Secret Police headquarters in Budapest.

7 Julian Bond, whose appointment was at 9.30am, wasn't the agent who had suffered a broken leg.

Agents:
Basil Oakes; Helen Palmer; Julian Bond; Rex Hannay; Sally Leamas; Walter Ashenden

Suffering from:
Broken arm; broken leg; bullet wound; common cold; cracked rib; knife wound

Returned from:
Budapest; East Berlin; Hong Kong; Moscow; Rio de Janeiro; Tangiers

Time	Agent	Suffering from	Returned from
9.00am			
9.30am			
10.00am			
10.30am			
11.00am			
11.30am			

WEDNESDAY APPOINTMENTS

Starting tip:

Work out the time of Sally Leamas' appointment.

NURSERY RHYME

Five customers have just each bought a plant and another item from the garden centre. From the following verses, can you discover who bought what and what the bill came to?

Clues

Mrs McKay got something for her weeds
Somebody bought a rose bush and some seeds
The seeds were not for Mr Moore,
He spent eight pounds eighty-four.
The person with the mint spent three pounds ten.
Who bought the bulbs? It wasn't Mrs Benn.

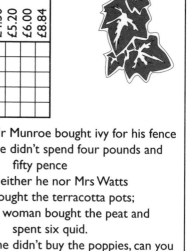

	Bulbs	Ivy	Mint	Poppies	Rose bush	Packet of seeds	Peat	Terracotta pots	Watering-can	Weedkiller	£3.10	£4.50	£5.20	£6.00	£8.84
Mr Moore															
Mr Munroe															
Mrs Benn															
Mrs McKay															
Mrs Watts															
£3.10															
£4.50															
£5.20															
£6.00															
£8.84															
Packet of seeds															
Peat															
Terracotta pots															
Watering-can															
Weedkiller															

Mr Munroe bought ivy for his fence
He didn't spend four pounds and
 fifty pence
Neither he nor Mrs Watts
Bought the terracotta pots;
A woman bought the peat and
 spent six quid.
She didn't buy the poppies, can you
 tell who did?

Customer	Plant	Other item	Price

IT'S TRUE...

...it's in the paper. *The Sunday Cesspit* recently published a story in which Member of Parliament Lothario Paramour was accused of having no fewer than five mistresses over a short period of time. Can you identify each of the women in question, describe her and say in what order each was alleged to have succumbed to Lothario's blandishments?

Clues

1 According to the Cesspit, Lothario's second mistress was an air hostess.

2 Marilyn, the dancer, was alleged to have been Paramour's next mistress after Mrs Oliver.

3 The surname of the Parliamentary researcher was Sefton; her affair with Lothario was said to have taken place next but one after the one with Ann.

4 Helen, who was mentioned as the fifth mistress in the Cesspit's article, wasn't the businesswoman, who wasn't Paramour's alleged first mistress.

5 Beatrice Macfarlane, according to the Cesspit's story, was an earlier mistress than Carol.

6 The fourth of Lothario's reputed affairs was with Miss Philpott.

	Large Macfarlane	Oliver	Philpott	Sefton	Air hostess	Businesswoman	Dancer	Researcher	Secretary	First	Second	Third	Fourth	Fifth
Ann														
Beatrice														
Carol														
Helen														
Marilyn														
First														
Second														
Third														
Fourth														
Fifth														
Air hostess														
Businesswoman														
Dancer														
Researcher														
Secretary														

Forename	Surname	Description	Order

PETTS' TEACHERS

If like me, you were a pupil at Petts' Lane Junior Mixed School in the 1970s you'll remember the teachers listed here, the nicknames we gave them, the after-hours groups they were responsible for running and the exotic backgrounds we attributed to them – on no very good evidence. If you weren't, can you work out those details from the clues given below?

Clues

1 Mr Ennion wasn't Ginger, who was believed to be a bigamist – after all, my mate Danny had been to Ginger's home and seen two wedding pictures.

2 Freckles ran the Cycling Club, bicycles being even more popular with kids then than now. It was a man who ran the football team.

3 We were sure that the teacher who ran the school orchestra was an ex-convict. The one who ran the Drama Club wasn't The Yank, who had once holidayed in the USA but wasn't credited with having performed in a circus.

4 We were all certain that Miss Cudlipp had been a beautiful spy in World War II.

5 Mrs Bowsher ran the Camera Club. Mrs Dancey, who had nothing to do with the Drama Club, was free of suspicion of bigamy, because we knew she was a widow.

6 Mr Acroyd, who was completely bald, was nicknamed Curly. We thought that one of the women was the poet responsible for all the awful verses in greetings cards.

Teacher	Nickname	Activity	Background

VISITORS

The diagram shows four adjacent tables at Parkmoor Prison, where four inmates are currently receiving female visitors. Can you identify the prisoners at each of tables A to D, say for what offence each was convicted, name his visitor and work out her connection with him?

Clues

1 Dick Crippen occupies the table between the fraudster's and that of the man being visited by his mother, Gloria.

2 As you look at the diagram, Cyril is somewhere to the left of Bobby.

3 The criminal at table D is talking to his daughter.

4 Sean is sitting two positions to the right of the car thief.

5 Adams isn't the inmate serving time for assault.

6 The sister visiting Peace is sat at a table adjacent to the one being used by Sandra, who isn't the burglar's visiting girlfriend.

7 Debbie isn't the visitor who has come to visit the man at table B.

Forenames:
Bobby; Cyril; Dick; Sean

Surnames:
Adams; Christie; Crippen; Peace

Crimes:
Assault; burglary; car theft; fraud

Visitors:
Amy; Debbie; Gloria; Sandra

Relationships:
Daughter; girlfriend; mother; sister

Table	A	B	C	D
Forename				
Surname				
Crime				
Visitor				
Connection				

Starting tip:
First work out the relationship between Dick and his visitor.

BATTLESHIPS

This puzzle is based on the old game of battleships. Your task is to find the vessels in the diagram. Some parts of boats or sea squares have already been filled in, and a number next to a row or column refers to the number of occupied squares in that row or column. The boats may be positioned horizontally or vertically, but no two boats or parts of boats are in adjacent squares — horizontally, vertically or diagonally.

Aircraft Carrier:

Battleships:

Cruisers:

Destroyers:

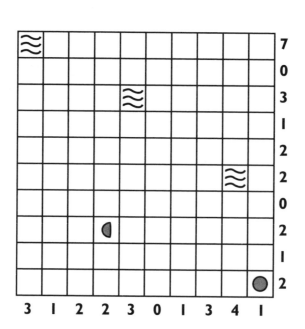

LOGI-5

Every row across and column down should contain five letters:
A, B, C, D and E, appearing once each. Also every shape (shown by the
thick lines) must contain each of the letters A, B, C, D and E, appearing
once each. Can you fill the grid?

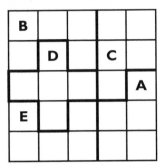

ABC

Every row across and column down is to have each of the letters A, B and
C and two empty squares. The letter outside the grid shows the first or
second letter in the direction of the arrow. Can you fill the grid?

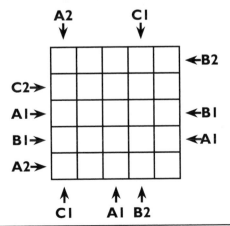

COME RAIN, COME SHINE

Harry Kirrie, an inveterate marathon runner, was in strict training for a forthcoming race and went for an early morning run on each day of the week, regardless of the weather. On each day he chose to run the round trip to a different village within ten miles of home. Can you name the village to which he ran on each day, say how many miles the round trip covered and work out the weather on each occasion?

Clues

1 It rained steadily all day the day before Harry tackled the 17-mile round trip to Springwell.

2 Harry Kirrie's Tuesday run took him to Woodtoft and back, a distance two miles shorter than the round trip to Broadleigh.

3 It wasn't frosty on the morning of Harry's 16-mile run.

4 The 18-mile run was completed beneath an overcast sky.

5 It was fine all day on Wednesday, when Harry covered an even number of miles.

6 Harry Kirrie ran 19 miles on his Thursday training run, when he didn't run through Thorpe Green, which is further from his home than Jerningham.

	Broadleigh	Jerningham	Springwell	Thorpe Green	Woodtoft	16 miles	17 miles	18 miles	19 miles	20 miles	Fine	Frosty	Overcast	Showery	Steady rain
Monday															
Tuesday															
Wednesday															
Thursday															
Friday															
Fine															
Frosty															
Overcast															
Showery															
Steady rain															
16 miles															
17 miles															
18 miles															
19 miles															
20 miles															

Day	Village	Round distance	Weather

HAVE I SHOWN YOU THESE?

Five women at a church social event were showing each other photos of their latest grandchildren. Can you identify the five proud grandmothers, name each woman's grandchild and say how many months old the latter is?

Clues

1 Mrs Gushing is the proud grandma of Rebecca.

2 Mrs Boast has a seven-month-old grandchild.

3 Betty Proudley's grandchild is two months older than Elizabeth.

4 Mrs Bragg's grandchild isn't the one aged five months.

5 Laura's grandchild is now eleven months old.

6 Nellie's daughter named her new arrival Esther.

7 Jack is the newest arrival of the five, having just clocked up three months; his grandma isn't Amy.

	Boast	Bragg	Gushing	Proudley	Strutt	Elizabeth	Esther	Jack	Rebecca	Thomas	3 months	5 months	7 months	9 months	11 months
Amy															
Betty															
Laura															
Nellie															
Stella															
3 months															
5 months															
7 months															
9 months															
11 months															
Elizabeth															
Esther															
Jack															
Rebecca															
Thomas															

Forename	Surname	Grandchild	Age

TAKEN FOR A RIDE

Five girlfriends went to the fair last night and each went on a different ride with one of the others, also paying for the ride. From the following information, can you discover who rode with whom and the order in which the rides were taken?

Clues

1 Cathy paid for Sam on one of the amusements, but neither it nor the Chairplanes was the second ride.

2 One of the other girls paid for Liz on the fourth ride, but it wasn't Laura.

3 Sam paid for her and her friend on the Dodgems.

4 Debbie's ride on the Waltzer was paid for by her companion.

5 Liz paid on the third ride.

6 The fifth ride was the Ghost Train, which Cathy didn't go on.

	Payer					Companion					First	Second	Third	Fourth	Fifth
	Cathy	Debbie	Laura	Liz	Sam	Cathy	Debbie	Laura	Liz	Sam					
Big Wheel															
Chairplanes															
Dodgems															
Ghost Train															
Waltzer															
First															
Second															
Third															
Fourth															
Fifth															
Cathy															
Debbie															
Laura															
Liz															
Sam															

Ride	Payer	Companion	Order of ride

AVANT LES MOUSQUETAIRES

Of course, the names by which the Other Musketeers were known were – like those of their comrades in the regiment – assumed ones and none had originally been intended for a military career. From the clues below, can you work out the real first name and surname of each Musketeer and say what he might have become if things had worked out differently?

Clues

1 Augustin, whose surname didn't include 'Saint', hadn't intended to become a physician or a priest; Fernand's surname was Rollin.

2 Nicolas had wanted to be a poet and even after an unfortunate misunderstanding had seen him thrown out of the Sorbonne and pushed into becoming a Musketeer, would occasionally dash off a (usually rude) rhyme.

3 Neither the man surnamed Saint-Denis nor his friend Damos had ever desired to be an architect.

4 Gaston (alias Maximos) wasn't a scion of the De La Fresnay family. Neither he nor Archamos had been studying medicine before scandals (one financial, one romantic) pushed them into joining up.

5 Silvis' real surname was Saint-Simon, but – despite the coincidence of initials – Archamos' first name wasn't Augustin.

6 Uramis (not Pierre) gave up his theological studies when he found he preferred swordsmanship to the scriptures.

	Augustin	Fernand	Gaston	Nicolas	Pierre	De La Fresnay	Du Bartas	Rollin	Saint-Denis	Saint-Simon	Architect	Courtier	Physician	Poet	Priest
Archamos															
Damos															
Maximos															
Silvis															
Uramis															
Architect															
Courtier															
Physician															
Poet															
Priest															
De La Fresnay															
Du Bartas															
Rollin															
Saint-Denis															
Saint-Simon															

Musketeers	Forename	Surname	Intended career

CARVED IN STONE

Although the village of Stone is only small, its parish church, St Chad's, contains six magnificent medieval tombs, each with swords and a coat of arms relating to the husband and wife interred within. Can you decide the names of the two persons represented on each tomb?

Clues

1 The tombs of Sir Bruce Baynard and Sir Guy Gargrave are adjacent on the same side of the aisle; Sir Guy's isn't next to that of Lord Sanglier.

2 Lord Dealtry's tomb is numbered two higher than Lady Helen's.

3 Lady Margaret and her husband who was a knight, are in the tomb directly across the aisle from that of Lady Muriel.

4 Lord Bovill's tomb is directly opposite that of Lady Anthea.

5 The couple whose coat of arms is on tomb 5 had a shorter surname than those people interred in tomb 4.

6 Lady Elfreda Sanglier is lying in tomb 2.

Husbands:
Lord Bovill; Lord Dealtry; Lord Sanglier; Sir Bruce Baynard; Sir Guy Gargrave; Sir Rhys Redlaw

Wives:
Lady Anthea; Lady Elfreda; Lady Helen; Lady Margaret; Lady Muriel; Lady Vanessa

Tomb No	1	2	3
Husband			
Wife			

Tomb No	4	5	6
Husband			
Wife			

Starting tip:

Work out the name of the man in tomb 4.

WEB SITES

The five spiders named here have been busy building webs in the garden. Can you work out between which two garden features each has built his web and the number of flies each has caught?

Clues

1 Webley started his web from the apple tree, while Webbington's stretched to the trellis.

2 Webster caught eight more flies in his web than the one between the conifer and the rose bush.

3 The web attached to the wall caught fewer flies than the one stretching from the bicycle.

4 The web attached to the fence snared the largest number of flies.

5 The web starting from the shed caught 16 flies.

6 Webfield was quite pleased with his catch of 20 flies.

	Apple tree	Bicycle	Conifer	Shed	Wheelbarrow	Fence	Garage	Rose bush	Trellis	Wall	8 flies	12 flies	16 flies	20 flies	24 flies
Webber															
Webbington															
Webfield															
Webley															
Webster															
8 flies															
12 flies															
16 flies															
20 flies															
24 flies															
Fence															
Garage															
Rose bush															
Trellis															
Wall															

Spider	From	To	No of flies

HELLO, CAMPERS

At the height of the season in the heyday of holiday camps, four neighbouring chalets at Cutlin's were all occupied by families from different parts of London. Can you name the family in each of the chalets numbered 1 to 4, say where they lived and work out how many people in all were in each chalet?

Clues

1 Mrs Castle, who was a single parent with two young children, had a chalet next door to the one where the family from Ealing was staying.

2 There were four people in chalet 2.

3 The Plaistow family, who were not the Buckets, were booked into chalet 3; there were fewer of them than there were of their neighbours in chalet 4.

4 The family from Islington was housed two chalets to the right of the Beaches as you look at the row in the diagram.

5 The smallest family wasn't staying in chalet 1.

Families:
Beach; Bucket; Castle; Spade

Homes:
Dulwich; Ealing; Islington; Plaistow

Numbers in families:
2; 3; 4; 5

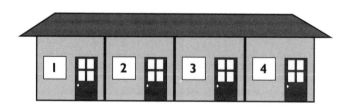

Chalet	Family	Home	No in family
1			
2			
3			
4			

Starting tip:

First work out the number of people in chalet 4.

IT'S QUICKER BY TUBE

Several travellers are queueing at the ticket office of an Underground station on the Piccadilly line. Each is buying a ticket for a different westbound destination. Can you identify just those travellers numbered 1 to 4 in the queue and say for which station each is buying a ticket?

Clues

1 Norbert, who is buying a ticket to Acton Town, is somewhere behind the passenger named Crisp in the queue.

2 The person travelling to Earl's Court, who isn't Easton, is somewhere behind Edmund.

3 Passenger number 4 is heading for South Ealing.

4 Kirk is third in line; he isn't Roberts, who isn't standing immediately in front of Mills.

Forenames:
Denzil; Edmund; Kirk; Norbert

Surnames:
Crisp; Easton; Mills; Roberts

Destinations:
Acton Town; Earl's Court; Hammersmith; South Ealing

Traveller	Forename	Surname	Destination
1			
2			
3			
4			

Starting tip:

Begin by placing Norbert.

FOLLOW THE SIGNS

Five friends, who all have different birth signs, each regularly consult their horoscopes in the local paper. Can you fully identify them, say under which sign each was born and match them with the comment offered to each in last night's issue?

Clues

1 None of the five friends was born under the sign suggested by her surname.

2 Glenda was advised to make no commitments.

3 Rosemary Archer wasn't warned of impending domestic squalls.

4 The Sagittarius subject was urged to follow her instincts.

5 Patricia's star sign isn't Libra and her surname isn't Scales.

6 Sybil, who was born under Pisces, isn't Mrs Crabbe, who was told it would be a good day for her finances.

7 Mrs Fish was born under the sign of Taurus.

	Archer	Bull	Crabbe	Fish	Scales	Cancer	Libra	Pisces	Sagittarius	Taurus	Domestic squalls	Expect phone call	Follow instincts	Good day for finances	Make no commitments
Glenda															
Marjorie															
Patricia															
Rosemary															
Sybil															
Domestic sq															
Expect ph call															
Follow instincts															
Good/finances															
No c'ments															
Cancer															
Libra															
Pisces															
Sagittarius															
Taurus															

Forename	Surname	Sign	Comment

DOMINO SEARCH

A standard set of dominoes has been laid out, using numbers instead of dots for clarity. With the aid of a sharp pencil and a keen brain, can you draw in the lines to show where each domino has been placed? You may find the check grid useful – crossing off each domino as you find it.

1	3	0	3	3	5	4	6
2	0	0	1	1	4	4	2
5	2	2	4	3	6	5	5
2	0	6	6	4	0	5	2
4	0	6	3	1	0	1	4
5	3	6	3	5	6	1	4
1	2	1	5	2	3	6	0

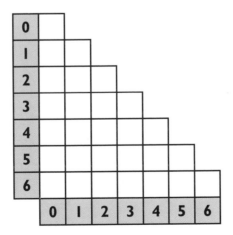

LOGI-PATH

Use your deductive reasoning to form a pathway from the box marked 'START' to the box marked 'FINISH', moving either horizontally or vertically (but not diagonally) from square to adjacent square. The number at the beginning of every row or column indicates exactly how many boxes in that row or column your pathway must pass through. The small diagram at the bottom of the page is given as an example of how it works.

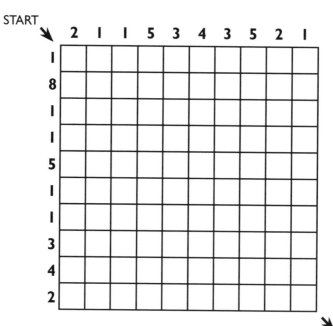

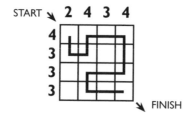

SPACED OUT

En route to the planet Xaramlon via one of the established spacelanes through the Ombran asteroid belt the starship *Endeavour* finds herself in company with five alien vessels. Can you work out the name of each, the English translation of that name, what class of vessel it is and which space-faring race it belongs to?

Clues

1 The Bodian spacecraft isn't the one whose name translates into English as Conquest; the former has twice the engine power of the survey ship – though that's not difficult, as she's the lowest-powered of the alien vessels.

2 Zapikniar is a mining ship. The name of the freighter means Short Shift in English.

3 The Jarromian vessel – her name means Not Scared By Anything – has, thanks to her nanometric drive, the most powerful engines of any of the alien ships, though, of course, she's not as powerful as the Endeavour.

4 Csertik is a Mostian ship. Hosadifi translates as Gigantic.

5 Quaroquep, whose engines deliver less power than those of the Novilmu, isn't the Rigarthic ship nor the one whose name means Evening Star; the latter isn't the survey ship.

6 The Vortican spaceliner has a name one letter shorter than that of the battlecruiser.

	Conquest	Evening Star	Gigantic	Not Scared By Anything	Short Shift	Battlecruiser	Freighter	Mining ship	Spaceliner	Survey ship	Bodian	Jarromian	Mostian	Rigarthic	Vortican
Csertik															
Hosadifi															
Novilmu															
Quaroquep															
Zapikniar															
Bodian															
Jarromian															
Mostian															
Rigarthic															
Vortican															
Battlecruiser															
Freighter															
Mining ship															
Spaceliner															
Survey ship															

Ship name	Translation	Ship type	Ship origin

ON THE MAT

Six friends were drinking in the saloon bar of the Red Dragon, seated round a table in the positions lettered A to F in the diagram. By coincidence, each was using a beer mat printed in a different main colour and bearing a different design. Can you say who sat in each seat and work out the full details of his beer mat?

Clues

1 Bryn's beer mat, which isn't the one lettered F, featured the teddy bear.

2 Rhys sat directly across the table from his friend whose green beer mat featured a bottle, the latter being indicated by an earlier letter of the alphabet.

3 The mat with a girl design has an earlier letter of the alphabet than that on the brown mat.

4 Carl's beer mat is the one lettered B in the diagram.

5 Beer mat A was a bright red colour.

6 Cliff's orange beer mat was next to (and on the same side of the table as) that with the horseshoe motif.

7 The car was the design on beer mat C, which wasn't the blue one and which wasn't being used by Gareth. The cat didn't adorn beer mat E.

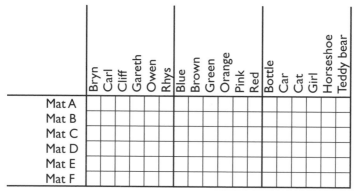

	Bryn	Carl	Cliff	Gareth	Owen	Rhys	Blue	Brown	Green	Orange	Pink	Red	Bottle	Car	Cat	Girl	Horseshoe	Teddy bear
Mat A																		
Mat B																		
Mat C																		
Mat D																		
Mat E																		
Mat F																		

Mat	Drinker	Colour	Design

WALLINGFEN BUSTS

The diagram shows the central staircase in the hall at Wallingfen Castle, with four busts on the plinths lettered A to D. Each bust was collected by a different 19th-century Duke of Wallingfen during his travels in Europe. Can you name the subject of each bust, say which Duke acquired it and work out in which country he bought it?

Clues

1 No bust was acquired in the country most closely associated with its subject.

2 The 3rd Duke bought the bust from France.

3 The 6th Duke purchased the bust of Aristotle. The 4th Duke's acquisition wasn't bust A (which isn't of Galileo).

4 A bust was bought in Italy by the Duke who was succeeded by his eldest son (who bought bust D).

5 The 5th Duke added one of the two busts closest to the foot of the stairs.

6 Bust C isn't of Napoleon.

Subjects:
Aristotle; Beethoven; Galileo; Napoleon

Dukes:
3rd; 4th; 5th; 6th

Countries:
France; Germany; Greece; Italy

Bust	Subject	Duke	Country
A			
B			
C			
D			

Starting tip:

First work out where the 6th Duke acquired his bust.

SILLY SEASON

There's a shortage of hard news in Barsetshlre at the moment, so reporters from all the county's newspapers have been sent out to follow up on silly season stories which will at least keep readers interested. Can you work out which paper each reporter works for, which village they've been sent to and what the story there is?

Clues

1 None of the reporters has a surname which begins with the same letter as that of the village to which he or she was sent.

2 The journalist from the Barsetshire Inquirer isn't in Fenfield.

3 The Barsetshire Times reporter is checking out the alleged sighting of a prehistoric pterodactyl flying over the peaceful countryside – but not in Hillwood.

4 The reporter on the story of the tiger roaming loose at Downbury works for a paper with a name one letter shorter than that (not the Barsetshire Free Press) whose representative is working on the ghost monk story.

5 Ian Jones works for the Herald. Geoff Hall has been assigned the story of the monster living in one of the county's lakes.

6 Annie Brown has gone to Jugford. The Barsetshire Gazette reporter who's been sent to Barstead isn't Edna Finch.

	Free Press	Gazette	Herald	Inquirer	Times	Barstead	Downbury	Fenfield	Hillwood	Jugford	Ghost	Monster	Pterodactyl	Tiger	UFOs
Annie Brown															
Colin Dawes																
Edna Finch																
Geoff Hall																
Ian Jones																
Ghost																
Monster																
Pterodactyl																
Tiger																
UFOs																
Barstead																
Downbury																
Fenfield																
Hillwood																
Jugford																

Reporter	Newspaper	Village	Story

WANTED NO MORE

During one week in the Roaring Twenties, five of the gangsters on the FBI's Most Wanted list were arrested, to their shame, on trivial charges by small-town lawmen who didn't even know whom they had picked up until they checked their fingerprints. Can you work out who was arrested each day, where and why?

Clues

1 Big Al Baddman was arrested on Thursday.

2 The notorious Gorilla Gieriger was charged with illegal parking; this didn't happen in Fairview, Massachusetts, nor on Monday.

3 Tuesday's arrest was for passing a forged dollar bill, in either Fairview Massachusetts or Fairview New York.

4 Lucky LeBase was arrested the day before one of his fellow criminals was detained in Midway, New Jersey.

5 Scarface Sporco was taken into custody in Oak Grove, Illinois, but not for swearing in public; the arrest for swearing didn't take place on Wednesday.

6 The Village Constable of New Hope, Michigan, made his arrest for littering the day after Machinegun McSwine was locked up.

	Big Al Baddman	Gorilla Gieriger	Lucky LeBase	Machinegun McSwine	Scarface Sporco	Fairview (Mass)	Fairview (NY)	Midway	New Hope	Oak Grove	Illegal parking	Littering	Passing forged dollar	Speeding	Swearing
Monday															
Tuesday															
Wednesday															
Thursday															
Friday															
Illegal parking															
Littering															
Passing forged $															
Speeding															
Swearing															
Fairview (Mass)															
Fairview (NY)															
Midway															
New Hope															
Oak Grove															

Day of arrest	Gangster	Place	Charge

POP SHOTS

Five teenage friends are all avid fans of different pop stars and vie with each other to collect photos of their favourites. Can you fully identify the five singers, match each with his or her admirer and say how many photos of him or her this fan possesses?

Clues

1 The girl whose favourite singer is Alma Lincoln has already collected over fifty photos of her.

2 Garry is Julia's heart-throb.

3 Fewer photos of Rick are owned by his fan than the fan of Hyssop possesses of that star.

4 The highest number of photos in any of the collections are of the singer named Rackstraw, whose first name isn't Melanie.

5 Hannah has a larger collection of photos than Angie, whose favourite has a shorter first name than Kerry's.

6 Rachel has 54 photos of the young man she adores, whose surname isn't Malone.

7 Kerry raves about the singer named Hawkes, of whom she doesn't possess 47 photos.

	Hawkes	Hyssop	Lincoln	Malone	Rackstraw	Angie	Hannah	Julia	Kerry	Rachel	42	47	54	58	65
Alma															
Calvin															
Garry															
Melanie															
Rick															
42															
47															
54															
58															
65															
Angie															
Hannah															
Julia															
Kerry															
Rachel															

Forename	Surname	Fan	No of photos

ON THE MARCH

The 24 letters listed make up five words, each associated with the word MARCH. Can you insert each letter into its correct square in the layout shown in the diagram? When you have done this, you might like to try to work out the five words, two of which have four letters, two five letters and one six letters.

Letters: A; A; A; C; C; D; E; E; F; H; I; K; O; O; P; Q; R; R; S; S; S; T; U; U

Clues

1 No horizontal row contains its own identifying letter and no letter occurs more than once in any horizontal row.

2 The letter in A6 immediately precedes alphabetically the one in D1 and is itself immediately preceded by the one in C3.

3 The same letter is to be placed in squares A5, B2 and D3.

4 The K is two squares to the right of an A.

5 There is a U two places to the left of an R.

6 The downward sequence A, U, F appears in one of the odd-numbered columns.

7 One R and one O appear in row D, neither of them being in D6.

8 The column with an S at the top has the Q as its bottom letter.

9 B3 contains a vowel, as does C4.

10 Neither R is directly below an A, nor is either R in column 4 or column 5.

11 The sequence C, O, H can be read horizontally from left to right, but not starting in A1 or B4.

12 The I is somewhere in column 2, the T is somewhere in row C and the P somewhere in row A.

13 To give you a start on the five words, one of them is spelt out by A4, B1, B6, A6.

	1	2	3	4	5	6
A						
B						
C						
D						

March words: _____ _____ _____ _____ _____

Starting tip:

Begin by identifying the letter referred to in clue 3.

BLITZ

During one month of the Blitz on London in 1940, five families occupying neighbouring houses in Targett Street were made homeless by damage of various kinds. (Nobody was hurt, everyone was in the shelters when it happened.) Can you identify each family, the number of their house, the date on which it was hit and what did the damage?

Clues

1 The Wilsons' home was numbered two lower than the house which was totally destroyed by a direct hit from a 250-kilogram high-explosive bomb.

2 The Lee family lived at number 6 Targett Street; the Hills' home was numbered two higher than the house which was hit by a 50-kilogram high-explosive bomb and lost most of its front wall.

3 The Browns were made homeless on the 9th and those at number 4 on the 17th.

4 The Smiths' house was narrowly missed by a big bomb, but was wrecked by the blast; this happened on an even-numbered night of the month.

5 On the 14th, one of the houses in Targett Street was burned down by an incendiary bomb.

6 Ironically, it was shrapnel from shells fired by the anti-aircraft guns defending London that damaged the roof of number 10 so badly that the residents had to move out of their home.

Family	House No	Date	Cause of damage

GOING FOR A SONG

Below are details of five successful bids in a local auction of household effects. From the information given, can you work out who bid for which lot, what it was and how much was paid for it?

Clues

Lot 77 and the bookcase
Were not bid for by Mrs Bryce;
Neither her lot nor 77 fetched 100,
Nor was £60 77's price.

77 wasn't the set of old golf-clubs,
It wasn't the table and chairs –
Those were knocked down to Miss Langham,
While lot number 10 went to Ayres.

The £60 lot was a bookcase,
The £100 lot wasn't 30,
While lot 56 was a
    tea-set, although
Incomplete and a little
    bit dirty.

The clock wasn't bid
    for by Dawson,
He spent the 200 quid;
The clubs didn't go for
    one-fifty,
And that wasn't what
    Miss Newton bid.

	Bookcase	Clock	Golf-clubs	Table and chairs	Tea-set	Miss Langham	Miss Newton	Mr Ayres	Mr Dawson	Mrs Bryce	£60	£100	£150	£180	£200
Lot 10															
Lot 30															
Lot 47															
Lot 56															
Lot 77															
£60															
£100															
£150															
£180															
£200															
Miss Langham															
Miss Newton															
Mr Ayres															
Mr Dawson															
Mrs Bryce															

Lot No	Description	Bidder	Price

PILE UP

These piles of bricks aren't the random results of a child's play but clues to a final, at present blank, pile on the right. Like the rest, that one has six bricks each with a different one of the six letters.

The numbers below the piles tell you two things:

(a) The number of adjacent pairs of bricks in that column which also appear adjacent in the final pile.

(b) The number of adjacent pairs of bricks that make a correct pair but the wrong way up.

So:

would score one in the 'Correct' row if the final pile had an A directly above a C and a one in the 'Reversed' row if the final pile had a C on top of an A. From all this, can you create the final pile before it topples?

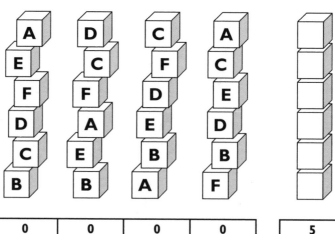

Correct	0	0	0	0	5
Reversed	1	1	0	2	0

OUT OF COURT

Close by the Law Courts is a squash club, to which various luminaries from the courts resort after hours to wind down from their labours in the cause of justice. At the moment depicted in the diagram, all three courts are occupied by such worthies. Can you identify the players numbered 1 to 6 and work out their court-room rôles?

Clues

1 The QC, who isn't Rushby, is playing on a court indicated by a higher number than the one on which the barrister is playing against Henry Barlow.

Court 1 Court 2 Court 3

1 2 3 4 5 6

2 The court usher is playing the solicitor, whose first name is Philip; they aren't on court 3.

3 Marcus is player number 3, while player 1's surname is Douglas.

4 Wilmott, the judge, is one of the odd-numbered players; his forename isn't Bryan.

5 The judge's clerk (who isn't player 5 or player 4) is numbered lower than Rushby; the latter isn't Wilfred, who is numbered two lower than Horne (whose opponent isn't Christopher).

	Bryan	Christopher	Henry	Marcus	Philip	Wilfred	Barlow	Douglas	Horne	Price	Rushby	Wilmott	Barrister	Court usher	Judge	Judge's clerk	QC	Solicitor
Player 1																		
Player 2																		
Player 3																		
Player 4																		
Player 5																		
Player 6																		

Player	Forename	Surname	Court rôle

LOGI-5

Every row across and column down should contain five letters: A, B, C, D and E, appearing once each. Also every shape (shown by the thick lines) must contain each of the letters A, B, C, D and E, appearing once each. Can you fill the grid?

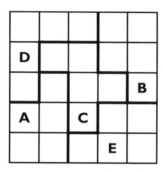

ABC

Every row across and column down is to have each of the letters A, B and C and two empty squares. The letter outside the grid shows the first or second letter in the direction of the arrow. Can you fill the grid?

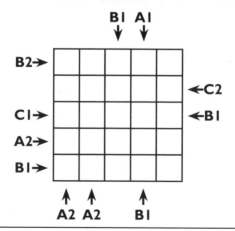

MULTIPLE CHOICE

Last Monday evening, no fewer than five good programmes were on television at the same time. When Desmond Ditherer got his TV guide on Wednesday of the previous week, he made a decision about which of the five to watch and which to video-tape. Of course, (being a Ditherer!) he amended this decision the following day and then again on Friday, Saturday and Sunday. Can you enter each day's decisions in the table below?

Clues

1 No programme featured in his choices on consecutive days.

2 He had decided to tape the consumer advice programme the day after he planned to watch the archaeology documentary.

3 The day when he made the decision to watch the Hitchcock film was earlier than the one when he elected to record it.

4 When it came to Sunday he decided he would watch the programme which on Friday he had planned to record.

5 On no day did he plan to have consumer advice and gardening as his two programmes; the latter didn't first figure in his choices until more than a day later than the former.

6 The day when he decided to watch the holiday programme was next but one after the one when he decided he would prefer to tape it.

Programmes:
Archaeology documentary; consumer advice; garden design; Hitchcock film; holiday choice

	What to watch	**What to tape**
Wednesday		
Thursday		
Friday		
Saturday		
Sunday		

Starting tip:
Work out when he decided to tape/watch the gardening programme.

ON THE ROAD

One week in every summer, Radio Eastland's afternoon show goes on the road, being broadcast by different presenters from the major seaside resorts in the region. From the remarks below, quoted from trailers being broadcast in advance, can you work out which town the show will come from each day, who'll be presenting it and where in the town Radio Eastland's mobile studio will be set up?

Clues

1 '..and the day after Fay D'Oute has presented the show, the Radio Eastland boys and girls will be on the North Quay, outside the new Fishermen's Museum...'

2. 'Hi, I'm Mike Stand and I'll be presenting the show on Wednesday; all you Vee Aitcheff fans, don't forget she'll be running things the day before our mobile studio sets up by the bandstand in King's Park...'

3 'Our broadcast from the Pier at Tickton this year won't be on Friday, but it will be later in the week than our visit to King's Park...'

4 'On Tuesday, we're in Luckstowe: remember how Fay D'Oute got caught in a storm there last year? Maybe that's why she won't be going back...'

5 'I'm Lynne Cupp and I'll be presenting the show from Marine Parade earlier in the week than both our visit to Baddon and Fay's broadcast...'

6 '...and Radio Eastland's own beauty queen, Ann Ouncer, will be taking the mobile studio to Great Aymouth...'

	Baddon	Deepstoft	Great Aymouth	Luckstowe	Tickton	Ann Ouncer	Fay D'Oute	Lynne Cupp	Mike Stand	Vee Aitcheff	King's Park	Marine Parade	North Quay	Pier	The Croft
Monday															
Tuesday															
Wednesday															
Thursday															
Friday															
King's Park															
Marine Parade															
North Quay															
Pier															
The Croft															
Ann Ouncer															
Fay D'Oute															
Lynne Cupp															
Mike Stand															
Vee Aitcheff															

Day	Resort	Presenter	Location

IN THEORY

Everyone has heard of Albert Einstein and his Theory of Relativity, though few could tell you what it is all about. More obscure, however, are five other scientists who came up with equally abstruse theories in the middle years of this century, none of which is ever referred to today. Can you identify the five men, match them with their theories and say in which year they were published?

Clues

1 Bierstein's Theory of Proclivity was published three years earlier than Harry's work.

2 Theodore Rothstein wasn't the scientist who revealed the Theory of Sensitivity to an unheeding world in 1936.

3 Malachi's brainchild was the Theory of Inactivity, which stated that all problems left untackled would eventually solve themselves; unfortunately, he did nothing about it.

4 The Theory of Passivity wasn't published in 1942.

5 Rubinstein's Theory was first aired in a rather obscure scientific journal in 1933.

6 Goldstein's Theory was published three years before Isaac's.

	Bierstein	Epstein	Goldstein	Rothstein	Rubinstein	Inactivity	Passivity	Proclivity	Productivity	Sensitivity	1930	1933	1936	1939	1942
Harry															
Isaac															
Malachi															
Rudolf															
Theodore															
1930															
1933															
1936															
1939															
1942															
Inactivity															
Passivity															
Proclivity															
Productivity															
Sensitivity															

Forename	Surname	Theory	Year

THAT'S MY LINE

We're mad about logic problems in our house! Mum can even turn washday into a teaser for us. Today she chose five items on the washing-line, one belonging to each of us and asked us to work out what item of clothing it was, its colour, to whom it belonged and its position on the line. From the information she gave us, can you work it out too?

Clues

1 Terry, yours was a red item and it was more than seven places nearer the top of the line than the white shirt.

2 My item was seventh from the top of the line, but it wasn't the T-shirt, which was further down the line than the pink item.

3 Adam, yours wasn't the green item.

4 Rachel's item of clothing was her nightie.

5 The shorts were either 16th or 18th on the line and they weren't blue.

6 None of us owns pink trousers.

	Nightie	Shirt	Shorts	T-shirt	Trousers	Blue	Green	Pink	Red	White	Adam	Caroline	Mum	Rachel	Terry
1st															
7th															
9th															
16th															
18th															
Adam															
Caroline															
Mum															
Rachel															
Terry															
Blue															
Green															
Pink															
Red															
White															

Position	Item	Colour	Owner

INTO BATTLE

Some years ago it wasn't unusual to see members of the Salvation Army selling their newspaper *War Cry* in the bars of public houses. Five women Salvationists ventured into different hostelries on the same evening, each managing to sell a different number of papers. Can you identify the five, say in which pub each sold her papers and work out how many?

Clues

1 Ruth, who visited the Coronet and Paperweight, sold two more copies than her friend named Rank.

2 The Toad and Harrow received a visit from Major Van Guard; she sold an even number of papers there.

3 The Salvationist named Fyle sold fewer copies of War Cry than her colleague named Patsy.

4 Miss Phalanx sold the fewest papers.

5 Naomi sold more copies of War Cry than the woman who went into the Lady of Shallott.

6 Lucy, who managed to sell ten papers, wasn't to be found in the Ironmonger's Arms.

	Cannon	Fyle	Phalanx	Rank	Van Guard	Coronet and Paperweight	Grey Donkey	Ironmonger's Arms	Lady of Shallott	Toad and Harrow	5 copies	7 copies	8 copies	10 copies	12 copies
Lucy															
Naomi															
Patsy															
Rose															
Ruth															
5 copies															
7 copies															
8 copies															
10 copies															
12 copies															
Coronet and P															
Grey Donkey															
I'monger's Arms															
Lady of Shallott															
Toad and Harrow															

Forename	Surname	Pub	No sold

BOOK TRADE

Phil Shelves is a book trade rep selling new titles to bookshops. Yesterday he had five appointments; from the following information, can you discover for which time each appointment had been made, the name and location of the shop and the value of the order taken?

Clues

1 His first appointment was in Reading; neither that call nor the one at Speak Volumes resulted in the smallest order.

2 Phil's 11.30 appointment wasn't in Leafield, but he took an order worth over £200; the Booker shop gave him an order worth £100.

3 The Chapterhouse bookshop is in Pagie Hill; Phil called there in the afternoon.

4 He called at The Bookshelf at 3.00pm and took away an order worth an even number of pounds more than the final order of the day.

5 The £300 order wasn't taken in Wordsley nor from the New Leaf bookshop.

6 Brought to Book placed the largest order.

	Brought to Book	Chapterhouse	New Leaf	Speak Volumes	The Bookshelf	Booker	Leafield	Pagie Hill	Reading	Wordsley	£25	£100	£175	£300	£500
9.30															
11.30															
1.30															
3.00															
4.30															
£25															
£100															
£175															
£300															
£500															
Booker															
Leafield															
Pagie Hill															
Reading															
Wordsley															

Time	Shop	Location	Order value

PISA THE ACTION

The Pisa Building on the campus of the University of Goatsferry is divided into six studios which are used by graduate students with artistic leanings – hence its name. Can you work out the full name of the artist currently occupying each studio and say what kind of artworks they produce?

Clues

1 Joan's studio isn't 1B or 3A.

2 Martin's studio is indicated by a letter A after the number, while the person who produces screen-printed textiles uses a studio indicated by a B.

3 Studio 3B is used by the artist who creates ceramics.

4 Patrick, who works in studio 2B, doesn't print textiles; his surname is longer than that of the tenant of studio 2A.

5 The artist surnamed Millais has studio 1B.

6 Dorothy Landseer's studio is on the opposite side of the building to that used by Ellen the sculptress, which isn't 2A; Ellen's surname isn't Beardsley.

7 The artist surnamed Browne, who produces action paintings by the time-honoured method of throwing buckets of paint at a canvas and then rolling in it, doesn't use studio 1A.

8 Sickert's studio and the one used by the etcher are on the same floor.

Forenames:
Dorothy; Ellen; Joan; Martin; Patrick; Winnie

Surnames:
Beardsley; Browne; Landseer; Millais; Sickert; Turner

Art forms:
Action paintings; ceramics; collages; etchings; sculptures; textiles

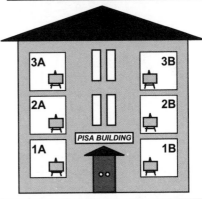

Studio	Forename	Surname	Art form
1A			
1B			
2A			
2B			
3A			
3B			

Starting tip:

Work out in which studio the textiles are being created.

JUST FINE

Five motorists were dealt with in rapid succession in the magistrates' court the other morning. Each man was found guilty of a different offence and each received a different fine. Can you name the defendants in the order in which they appeared, say what offence each had committed and work out the size of the fine each received?

Clues

1 Hogg's failure to observe a stop sign at a road junction cost him a fine £10 higher than the one given to the fifth offender to appear.

2 Knott-Fussey was fined a smaller amount than the driver found to have two defective tyres, who was the first to face the magistrates.

3 Pratt was fined £60 for his transgression; his case was heard immediately before the careless driving charge.

4 Riskett was the fourth man to be fined by the bench; he didn't have to pay as much as the second defendant.

5 The smallest fine wasn't imposed on the man caught speeding in a built-up area.

	Blythe	Hogg	Knott-Fussey	Pratt	Riskett	Careless driving	Defective lights	Defective tyres	Ignoring stop sign	Speeding	£40	£50	£60	£70	£75
First															
Second															
Third															
Fourth															
Fifth															
£40															
£50															
£60															
£70															
£75															
Careless driving															
Defective lights															
Defective tyres															
Ig'ing stop sign															
Speeding															

Order	Driver	Offence	Fine

BATTLESHIPS

This puzzle is based on the old game of battleships. Your task is to find the vessels in the diagram. Some parts of boats or sea squares have already been filled in, and a number next to a row or column refers to the number of occupied squares in that row or column. The boats may be positioned horizontally or vertically, but no two boats or parts of boats are in adjacent squares – horizontally, vertically or diagonally.

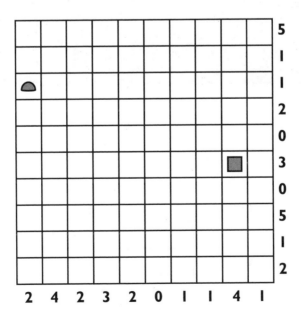

Aircraft Carrier:

Battleships:

Cruisers:

Destroyers:

										5
										1
										1
										2
										0
										3
										0
										5
										1
										2

2 4 2 3 2 0 1 1 4 1

LOGI-5

Every row across and column down should contain five letters:
A, B, C, D and E, appearing once each. Also every shape (shown by the
thick lines) must contain each of the letters A, B, C, D and E, appearing
once each. Can you fill the grid?

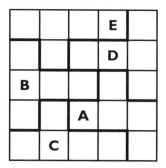

ABC

Every row across and column down is to have each of the letters A, B and
C and two empty squares. The letter outside the grid shows the first or
second letter in the direction of the arrow. Can you fill the grid?

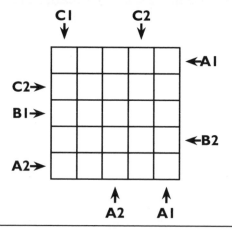

GIG GUIDE

Each day our local radio station has a feature telling listeners which bands can be seen at which venues that evening. Here is today's listing – from the information given below, can you work out which band is at which pub or club, the address and the time their set starts?

Clues

1 The Rosettes are on half an hour before the band appearing at McGinty's, while the band at the Stag's Head in Wharf Lane are on immediately before them.

2 Stir are performing in Newland Square, starting half an hour after the band at the Leather Bottle and an hour before the gig starts in Cambridge Street.

3 Cobra are not the band playing at the Cambridge Street venue.

4 Stir's gig isn't at the Five Bells, which isn't in Market Street.

5 Relish do not have the earliest or latest gig.

6 Unlike the gig in Wood Street, the show at the Britannia is either the first or last of the night.

	Britannia	Five Bells	Leather Bottle	McGinty's	Stag's Head	Cambridge St	Market St	Newland Square	Wharf Lane	Wood St	8.00	8.30	9.00	9.30	10.30
Cobra															
Relish															
Shock Troupe															
Stir															
The Rosettes															
8.00															
8.30															
9.00															
9.30															
10.30															
Cambridge St															
Market St															
Newland Sq															
Wharf Lane															
Wood St															

Band	Venue	Address	Time

PARISH PUMPS

Five villages in a northern county publish local news-sheet magazines. Can you work out the full name of the editor at each village and the title of each one's publication?

Clues

1 None of the villages has a name whose initial letter is the same as that of its publication, or of either the first or surname of the editor.

2 The editor of the Crayston journal isn't Mr Kitson or Mrs Young.

3 Newthorpe's journal's editor has the same number of letters in her first name and surname.

4 The person surnamed Attwater doesn't edit the Clarion.

5 Neither the title of Sarah's magazine nor her village is alphabetically fourth in its respective list.

6 The name of Alan's village is alphabetically next before Johnson's and next after that of the editor of the Courier; the title of Alan's publication is next alphabetically before that of Sarah and next after that of the one circulated in Newthorpe.

7 The Dunsford editor isn't Thomas.

	Alan	Dorothy	Keith	Sarah	Thomas	Attwater	Johnson	Kitson	Pybus	Young	Bugle	Clarion	Contact	Courier	Grapevine
Barnby															
Crayston															
Dunsford															
Kelwick															
Newthorpe															
Bugle															
Clarion															
Contact															
Courier															
Grapevine															
Attwater															
Johnson															
Kitson															
Pybus															
Young															

Village	Forename	Surname	Title

RULING CLASSES

A recent concerted effort by a team of archaeologists has unearthed details of some of the lesser-known ancient rulers of Upper Egypt. Can you work out which dynasty each belonged to, how long each ruled and how many wives each had?

Clues

1 The king who didn't marry was of an earlier dynasty (not the XVth) than that of the one who ruled for 12 years; neither was Tip-Re-Bel, who belonged to the dynasty which came next after the one whose king had three wives.

2 Pelmel-Motif's reign was two years shorter than that of the king who belonged to the XIVth dynasty; and neither had two wives.

3 Rum-Chef's dynasty was later than that of the man with four wives, but earlier than that of the 10-year ruler.

4 Hot-Instep had one fewer wife than the ruler from the XVth dynasty and ruled for more than two fewer years.

5 The king who had one wife belonged to the dynasty which preceded that of the 8-year ruler. Snafu-Pet ruled longer than and had more wives than both but belonged to an earlier dynasty than both, though not the XVth or as early as that of the king who ruled for 14 years.

6 The ruler with three wives reigned two years longer than the one from the XVIth dynasty.

	XIIIth	XIVth	XVth	XVIth	XVIIth	8 years	10 years	12 years	14 years	16 years	No wives	One wife	Two wives	Three wives	Four wives
Hot-Instep															
Pelmel-Motif															
Rum-Chef															
Snafu-Pet															
Tip-Re-Bel															
No wives															
One wife															
Two wives															
Three wives															
Four wives															
8 years															
10 years															
12 years															
14 years															
16 years															

King	Dynasty	Reign	No of wives

LOGI-PATH

Use your deductive reasoning to form a pathway from the box marked 'START' to the box marked 'FINISH', moving either horizontally or vertically (but not diagonally) from square to adjacent square. The number at the beginning of every row or column indicates exactly how many boxes in that row or column your pathway must pass through. The small diagram at the bottom of the page is given as an example of how it works.

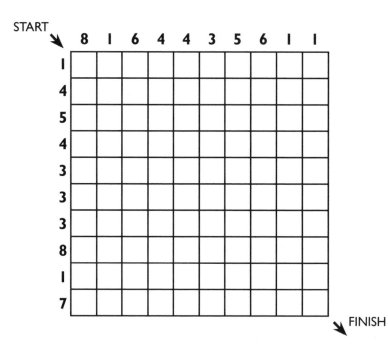

START

8 1 6 4 4 3 5 6 1 1

1
4
5
4
3
3
3
8
1
7

FINISH

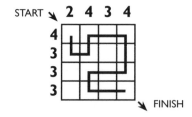

START

2 4 3 4

4
3
3
3

FINISH

DOMINO SEARCH

A standard set of dominoes has been laid out, using numbers instead of dots for clarity. With the aid of a sharp pencil and a keen brain, can you draw in the lines to show where each domino has been placed? You may find the check grid useful – crossing off each domino as you find it.

6	6	1	2	1	3	6	5
3	2	0	1	2	2	3	6
6	0	0	0	5	4	2	6
6	4	0	0	3	1	5	6
2	2	4	4	3	5	1	4
5	5	5	3	3	2	5	4
3	4	4	1	1	1	0	0

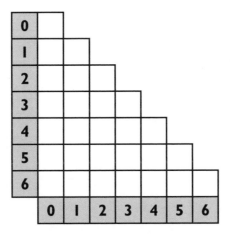

CHAIN OF COMMAND

The Kutprice chain store has an outlet in each of the six main towns in the county, numbered 1 to 6 on the plan. Can you name each town and the street in which the store has a branch there and identify its manager?

Clues

1 The manager of the Newfield store is Landers; this town is somewhere south of the one where the store is in Scott Street.

2 The store in King's Parade, Stackley, bears an odd number on the plan.

3 The manager of the Kutprice store in town number **2** is Middleton.

4 Nelson Avenue isn't in town number 6, nor is it in Rockbury, where the manager's name doesn't begin with an F.

5 The town numbered 5 is Maywell.

6 Stokes' branch in Market Square is in a town south-west of Dilby.

7 The High Street branch is in town number 3.

8 Fowler's branch is further east than Fulton's.

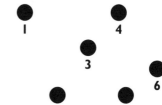

	Dilby	Maywell	Newfield	Rockbury	Stackley	Warnford	High Street	King's Parade	Lincoln Lane	Market Square	Nelson Avenue	Scott Street	Fowler	Fulton	Landers	Middleton	Riches	Stokes
Store 1																		
Store 2																			
Store 3																			
Store 4																			
Store 5																			
Store 6																			

N
W ← → E
S

Store	Town	Street	Manager

GOING UP

The diagram shows four hotel guests going up to their respective rooms in the lift. Can you name each of the guests numbered 1 to 4 in the lift and match them with their rooms on the fifth and sixth floors?

Clues

1 As you look at the diagram, the occupant of room 61 is immediately to the left of Alice Sibley in the lift.

2 Dixon is passenger number 3 in the lift; Rowland doesn't have the room immediately above or below the former's.

3 Roberta's room is number 69.

4 Position 4 in the lift is occupied by Monica, whose room isn't on the same floor as that of the guest named Collins.

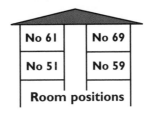

Room positions

Forenames:
Alice; Genevieve; Monica; Roberta

Surnames:
Collins; Dixon; Rowland; Sibley

Woman	Forename	Surname	Room No
1			
2			
3			
4			

Starting tip:
Begin by working out the first name of the guest who has room 61.

UNMATCHED PAIRS

Five engaged couples were going to a fancy dress dance and each man informed his fiancée which costume he would be wearing, assuming that she'd turn up as the obvious partner! But, determined to teach their boyfriends not to take them for granted, the women all chose to dress as characters of their own choice. Can you work out what costume each man wore, who his partner was and as whom she dressed?

Clues

1 Rosemary Weston's fiancé, Adrian Towers, didn't dress as Tarzan.

2 Robin Hood found himself escorting a Queen of whom he'd never heard.

3 Both the forename and surname of Sir Lancelot's partner are longer than those of Superman's partner; the former woman wasn't dressed as Queen Edith (wife of Edward the Confessor) and the latter wasn't Joanne Brock, who wore the uniform of Hannah Snell, the female Marine who joined the Navy undetected in the 18th century.

	Robin Hood	Romeo	Sir Lancelot	Superman	Tarzan	Denise Moody	Joanne Brock	Pauline Wolfe	Rosemary Weston	Virginia Sampson	Aphra Behn	Hannah Snell	Julia Cameron	Queen Edith	Queen Maria
Adrian Towers															
Christian Spicer															
Jason Carey															
Nigel Ward															
Sebastian White															
Aphra Behn															
Hannah Snell															
Julia Cameron															
Queen Edith															
Queen Maria															
Denise Moody															
Joanne Brock															
Pauline Wolfe															
Rosemary W															
Virginia S															

4 The man (not Denise Moody's fiancé) dressed as Tarzan found himself partnering Julia Cameron, a 19th-century pioneer photographer.

5 The woman who went as the writer Aphra Behn and her fiancé both have first names one letter longer than their surnames.

6 Queen Maria of Portugal and her partner were the only couple to share a surname initial.

Man	His costume	Woman	Her costume

ROUGH ROUNDS

George Wood is a very indifferent golfer but he tries hard and is certainly keen. Now that he's retired he gets in 18 holes every day. Can you work out his total score for each day last week, the number of his worst hole and the number of shots he took at that hole?

Clues

1 George's total score when his worst hole was the tenth was higher than on Friday, when he took one more shot at his worst hole than he took on his tenth.

2 His lowest total (which was on the day after his highest) didn't coincide with either his highest or his lowest score at his worst hole or with the highest or lowest worst hole numbers; his highest total didn't happen on the same day as his worst hole number was the highest or lowest.

3 His worst hole score was 11 the day before he had a round of 114 (during which his worst hole was the fifteenth) and his worst hole score was 9 the day before he had a round of 121. His worst hole had a higher number on the day his worst hole score was 9 than on the 121 round day.

4 His worst hole score on Tuesday was two more than on Monday; on neither of these days was his worst hole the twelfth. His Thursday worst hole score was lower than on Wednesday. His Monday total was lower than his Tuesday one.

5 Tuesday was the only day when all his figures were odd numbers; and there was no day when they were all even.

6 The day when his worst hole number was two higher than his worst hole score was next after one when his worst hole number was one lower than his worst hole score.

	109	114	116	121	127	Third	Sixth	Tenth	Twelfth	Fifteenth	7	8	9	10	11
Monday															
Tuesday															
Wednesday															
Thursday															
Friday															

Day	Total score	Worst hole	Worst hole score

ON SHOW

The diagram shows six cars being offered for sale in the showroom of a garage specialising in second-hand cars. Can you say who bought each of the models lettered A to F and how much he or she paid for it? Just in case (perish the thought!) you might be tempted to have recourse to a used car guide, we shall not reveal the ages or makes of the vehicles, but will ask you instead to work out the colour of each car.

Clues

1 The red car bought by Mrs Austin cost more than the one to its left as you look at the showroom, but less than the one to its right.

2 Mr Ford's car cost him £3,750. Mr Rolls didn't buy the car (not car A) priced at exactly £4,000. Car A isn't light blue.

3 The price of the grey car is £4,250.

4 Mr Bentley's car is two places to the left of the most expensive of the six vehicles, as you look at the diagram.

5 £3,500 was the price displayed on the windscreen of car D, which wasn't blue.

6 The man who bought car E paid £500 less than the price of the green vehicle.

7 Mrs Morris didn't buy car C.

	Mrs Austin	Mr Bentley	Mr Ford	Mrs Jowett	Mrs Morris	Mr Rolls	£3,500	£3,750	£4,000	£4,250	£4,500	£4,750	Dark blue	Green	Grey	Light blue	Red	White
Car A																		
Car B																		
Car C																		
Car D																		
Car E																		
Car F																		

Car	Buyer	Price	Colour

NUMBERS UP

The six winning numbers in a recent lottery were: 7, 19, 23, 31, 38 and 47. Five friends had each chosen three of these numbers, though none had three identical choices. Can you enter in the table below each man's three successful numbers?

Clues

1 Each of the numbers 19, 31 and 47 were chosen by only two of the five men; 7, 23 and 38 were each selected by three men; no one had three consecutive numbers.

2 Arthur, who didn't choose 19, had no numbers in common with Charles.

3 Charles didn't select 7.

4 Neither Arthur nor Philip had 23 and neither Eric nor Thomas had 19; Eric's lowest number was higher than Thomas' lowest.

5 Of the three who selected 38, two have alphabetically consecutive names, with the third one's name being alphabetically later.

	Chosen numbers		
Arthur			
Charles			
Eric			
Philip			
Thomas			

Starting tip:

Work out Eric's lowest number.

GUIDED TOUR

Some friends recently had relatives from abroad staying with them for a few days and took them to various places of interest in the area. Can you work out to what village they went on each day, which building they went round and at what inn they had lunch?

Clues

1 They visited the church the day after going to Belham, but the day before lunching at the Black Lion.

2 Wadby has no ecclesiastical buildings of note; the ruins of the priory in another village engaged their interest the day before they had lunch at the Wheatsheaf.

3 They lunched at the Pheasant Inn the day after visiting the castle; neither of these days was Thursday. They went to the Pheasant Inn earlier in the week than their visit to Storton.

4 Egton was the village they went to the day before seeing the abbey; their lunch at the Travellers' Rest was on an earlier day.

5 They had a wander round the Newholm area the day before they looked at the art collection at the hall; neither of these visits was on the Wednesday, when they had lunch at the King's Head.

	Belham	Egton	Newholm	Storton	Wadby	Abbey	Castle	Church	Hall	Priory	Black Lion	King's Head	Pheasant Inn	Travellers' Rest	Wheatsheaf
Monday															
Tuesday															
Wednesday															
Thursday															
Friday															
Black Lion															
King's Head															
Pheasant Inn															
Travellers' Rest															
Wheatsheaf															
Abbey															
Castle															
Church															
Hall															
Priory															

Day	Village	Building	Inn

PILE UP

These piles of bricks aren't the random results of a child's play but clues to a final, at present blank, pile on the right. Like the rest, that one has six bricks each with a different one of the six letters.

The numbers below the piles tell you two things:

(a) The number of adjacent pairs of bricks in that column which also appear adjacent in the final pile.

(b) The number of adjacent pairs of bricks that make a correct pair but the wrong way up.

So: would score one in the 'Correct' row if the final pile had an A directly above a C and a one in the 'Reversed' row if the final pile had a C on top of an A. From all this, can you create the final pile before it topples?

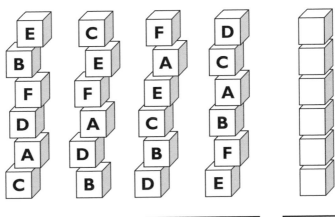

Correct	1	0	0	0	5
Reversed	0	0	2	0	0

PENNY WHISTLE

Penny Whistle, a peripatetic music teacher, visits five centres (the names of which are given in the clues) three times a week each, once in the morning, once in the afternoon and once for an evening class. Can you fill in her timetable for the week?

Clues

1 None of the five centres is visited twice on the same day.

2 The afternoon session at Dunford is the day after the morning one at Cragleigh and the day before the evening class at Branbury.

3 The Wednesday evening class and the Friday afternoon one are at different centres.

4 Encastle is the centre Penny visits on a Wednesday morning.

5 The three visits to Angleton are not on three consecutive days.

6 Branbury isn't visited at all by Penny on Wednesdays.

7 The Encastle evening class isn't on Tuesday.

8 The Cragleigh evening class is on the same day as the afternoon session at Branbury.

9 The morning session at Branbury is later in the week than the one at Angleton, but not on the following day.

Day	Morning	Afternoon	Evening
Monday			
Tuesday			
Wednesday			
Thursday			
Friday			

Starting tip:

First work out the day on which Penny spends the afternoon in Dunford.

GENERATION GAME

Mary's three daughters are each married, with one child. Can you place the daughters in their order of seniority in Mary's family and name each woman's husband and child?

Clues

1 David's wife is younger than William's mother.

2 Janet's child is called Bridget.

3 Alan is married to Mary's youngest daughter.

4 Emma was Mary's next-born daughter after the one who is now Peter's wife.

	Eldest	Middle	Youngest	Alan	David	Peter	CHILD Bridget	Eleanor	William
Emma									
Janet									
Rachel									
Bridget									
Eleanor									
William									
Alan									
David									
Peter									

Daughter	Order in family	Husband	Child

CLINICAL COMMITMENTS

Tim Weekes has three appointments with clinics at the Netherlipp General to keep in the coming months. Can you work out which consultant in which department he has to see in which month and also establish how many previous visits he has made to each clinic?

Clues

1 Mr Weekes has not seen the cardiologist as often as he has seen Dr Patel; his appointment with the latter is earlier than with the former.

2 The appointment with Dr Ryder is a month earlier than the one with the orthopaedic consultant, whom he has seen more times.

3 The July appointment is with the doctor he has already seen four times.

	Patel	Philips	Ryder	Cardiology	General medical	Orthopaedic	Two	Three	Four
July									
August									
September									
Two										
Three									
Four									
Cardiology									
General medical									
Orthopaedic									

Month	Consultant	Department	Previous visits

MESSING ABOUT IN BOATS

It was a bright, sunny Saturday and four lads from Storbury decided to take their girlfriends boating on the River Stor – but it turned out not to be such a brilliant idea. Can you work out the names of each couple, what sort of boat they chose and what happened to ruin the day?

Clues

1 Graham was engaged to Rachel when they started out on Saturday morning – by the end of the day she was saying she never wanted to see him again!

2 The sailing dinghy in which Carol and her boyfriend took to the river wasn't the boat which overturned, dumping both its occupants into the muddy water.

3 It was Helen and her companion who had to dive into the Stor and swim for their lives when she lit a picnic stove to make tea and accidentally set fire to the boat.

4 John ran his boat, which wasn't the sailing dinghy, aground on a mudbank and couldn't refloat it, so he and his soon-to-be-former young lady had to wade ashore and walk home.

5 David took his girlfriend out in a canoe; Amanda didn't go out in the rowing boat.

	Amanda	Carol	Helen	Rachel	Canoe	Motor boat	Rowing boat	Sailing dinghy	Caught fire	Overturned	Ran aground	Sank
Alan												
David												
Graham												
John												
Caught fire												
Overturned												
Ran aground												
Sank												
Canoe												
Motor boat												
Rowing boat												
Sailing dinghy												

Boy	Girl	Boat	Mishap

LOGI-PATH

Use your deductive reasoning to form a pathway from the box marked 'START' to the box marked 'FINISH', moving either horizontally or vertically (but not diagonally) from square to adjacent square. The number at the beginning of every row or column indicates exactly how many boxes in that row or column your pathway must pass through. The small diagram at the bottom of the page is given as an example of how it works.

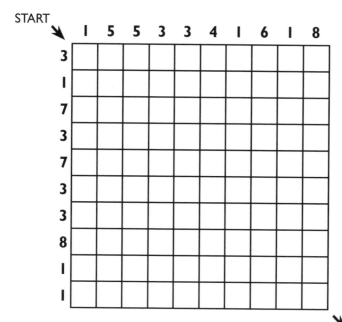

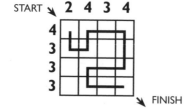

WINNERS

Jockey Ivor Norse had a good day at Epsfield races yesterday, winning four successive races. Can you work out the name of the horse on which he won each race, the name of its owner and the owner's colours Ivor wore?

Clues

1 Ivor won on Mrs Steed's Autumn Venture in the race immediately preceding the one in which he rode in Mr Dobbin's colours.

2 Ivor wasn't wearing the purple and pink stripes when he won the 3 o'clock race on Coral Dancer.

3 For the 3.30 race, Ivor's silks were hooped in mauve and white.

4 Ivor rode Lord Palfrey's horse between the race in which he wore blue with orange spots and the one which he won on Marshal Hart.

	Autumn Venture	Coral Dancer	Golden Gain	Marshal Hart	Lord Palfrey	Miss Colt	Mr Dobbin	Mrs Steed	Blue and orange	Mauve and white	Purple and pink	Red and gold
2.00												
2.30												
3.00												
3.30												
Blue and orange												
Mauve and white												
Purple and pink												
Red and gold												
Lord Palfrey												
Miss Colt												
Mr Dobbin												
Mrs Steed												

Race time	Horse	Owner	Colours

ON ASSIGNMENT

It's early evening in London and four reporters from the *Daily Lantern*, accompanied by photographers, have been sent to various parts of the city to cover different stories. Which photographer is going with each reporter, where have they been sent and what story are they covering?

Clues

1 Amy Burton has been assigned to report on a railway accident, which, although it caused an enormous amount of damage, involved no injuries to passengers or train crews.

2 Photographer Mick Nash is accompanying the reporter going to North London.

3 The photographer assigned to go with Gordon Hope isn't Wally Young.

4 Don Ellis won't be photographing the celebrities at the film premiere in West London.

5 Rob Shelley's covering a story in South London; he's not accompanied by photographer Hannah Jay, who'll be taking pictures at the boxing match.

	Don Ellis	Hannah Jay	Mick Nash	Wally Young	East London	North London	South London	West London	Boxing match	Film premiere	Political speech	Railway accident
Amy Burton												
Gordon Hope												
Kate Lister												
Rob Shelley												
Boxing match									
Film premiere									
Political speech									
Railway accident									
East London					
North London					
South London					
West London					

Reporter	Photographer	Area	Story

BUSH RANGERS

The picture below represents a wanted poster for the Ballarat Boys, a gang of Australian bushrangers contemporary with the more famous Kelly Gang. Can you work out the forename, nickname and surname of each of the infamous four?

Clues

1 Bushranger 3 was named Edward.

2 The man shown in picture 1, the gang's leader, was nicknamed Tiger because of his fierceness in a fight.

3 Alfred Darwin was the only one of the gang to evade eventual capture – he's believed to have gone to the United States in 1880.

4 Sailor Hobart, a deserter from the Royal Navy, is pictured next to the man named Nicholas.

5 The picture of the Glasgow-born bandit known as Jock is immediately right of the one showing the man nicknamed Bluey because of his flaming red hair, who wasn't surnamed Cairns.

Forenames:
Alfred; Edward;
Nicholas; William

Nicknames:
Bluey; Jock; Sailor;
Tiger

Surnames:
Bendigo; Cairns;
Darwin; Hobart

Picture No	Forename	Nickname	Surname

Starting tip:
Work out the nickname of the bushranger in picture 4.

FLAVOUR OF THE LUNCH

Five children are comparing their packed lunches. Each has a sandwich filled with a different flavoured spread, a differently flavoured packet of crisps and a differently flavoured yoghurt. From the following information, can work out which child has which combination of flavours?

Clues

1 Anne isn't the child with the curried chicken spread sandwich and smoky bacon crisps and that child also doesn't have the mango-flavoured yoghurt; neither Anne nor Ben has the roast chicken-flavoured crisps.

2 Jessica has prawn spread in her sandwich but not the prawn cocktail-flavoured crisps; the name of the possessor of the latter is later in alphabetical order than that of the child with the smoked ham spread sandwich.

3 One of the girls has the chicken spread sandwich and the raspberry yoghurt; Claire has cheese and onion crisps.

4 David doesn't like tuna.

5 One of the children has salt and vinegar crisps and a strawberry yoghurt.

6 Ben's yoghurt is black cherry flavour.

	Chicken	Curried chicken	Prawn	Smoked ham	Tuna	Cheese and onion	Prawn cocktail	Roast chicken	Salt and vinegar	Smoky bacon	Banana	Black cherry	Mango	Raspberry	Strawberry
Anne															
Ben															
Claire															
David															
Jessica															
Banana															
Black cherry															
Mango															
Raspberry															
Strawberry															
Cheese/onion															
Prawn cocktail															
Roast chicken															
Salt and vinegar															
Smoky bacon															

Child	Sandwich	Crisps	Yoghurt

FIRST SCENES

Five young people who have just taken the plunge and become actors have all won rôles in the new horror film Night Of The Creeping Death – one of them will actually be on screen for as long as thirty seconds! Can you work out each one's real name, original occupation, professional name and rôle in the movie?

Clues

1 It's Alice Bowells who has changed her name to Liz Monroe and Cedric Doone who used to be a dustman.

2 The ex-bank clerk who has decided to call himself Nick Maxim isn't Victor Wallop or the hopeful who has been cast as a cyclist.

3 Cleo Blaize, formerly known as Muriel Nutter, has never worked in a shop; the man who has been cast as a pub customer has decided to adopt the stage name Sean Turpin.

4 Victor Wallop has been awarded the rôle of second soldier.

5 The former cleaner who will appear as third gipsy isn't (and never has been) Muriel Nutter.

	Bank clerk	Cleaner	Dustman	Shop assistant	Traffic warden	Carl Dumain	Cleo Blaize	Liz Monroe	Nick Maxim	Sean Turpin	Cyclist	First Zombie	Pub Customer	Second Soldier	Third Gipsy
Alice Bowells															
Cedric Doone															
Joseph Kettle															
Muriel Nutter															
Victor Wallop															
Cyclist															
First zombie															
Pub customer															
Second soldier															
Third gipsy															
Carl Dumain															
Cleo Blaize															
Liz Monroe															
Nick Maxim															
Sean Turpin															

Real name	Occupation	Screen name	Rôle

PARADROPS

During the war, certain special squadrons of the Royal Air Force flew numerous missions dropping agents into occupied Europe. Below are some details of one flight in 1942 which dropped five agents in France. Can you work out the order in which the agents jumped, where they were dropped and what they took with them for the French Resistance?

Clues

1 The agent codenamed Javelot (javelin), who dropped with a container of medicines and surgical supplies for the Resistance, didn't leave the plane over St Andre.

2 The third agent to jump carried a very large sum of money, to be used to bribe corrupt officials of the occupying forces.

3 Perroquet (parrot) was the fourth agent to leave the aircraft.

4 The second parachute drop took place over the outskirts of Honbert.

5 The agent codenamed Loir (dormouse), who jumped over Lancy, left the plane immediately before the one who was carrying explosives to be used to blow up a railway line.

6 Vaurien (rascal) left the plane immediately before the agent who dropped into Doubourg with a powerful radio transmitter.

	Choriste	Javelot	Loir	Perroquet	Vaurien	Doubourg	Honbert	Lancy	St Andre	Touriers	Explosives	Guns	Medicines	Money	Radio
First															
Second															
Third															
Fourth															
Fifth															
Explosives											
Guns											
Medicines											
Money											
Radio											
Doubourg						
Honbert						
Lancy						
St Andre						
Touriers						

Order	Agent	Town	Carrying

TRAIL DRIVE

In the late 1860s, five owners of small ranches around the town of Silver Springs, Texas, banded together to take their cows up the trail to sell at the railhead in Kansas, where they would get a much better price. Can you identify the nickname and surname of each rancher, the name of his ranch and the number of animals he contributed to the joint herd?

Clues

1 Paddy O'Reilly, whose family had left Ireland in the potato famine of 1846–7, provided an odd number of cattle for the trail herd.

2 Mr Morgan, whose ranch's name consisted of a single word, didn't contribute the smallest number of cows to the herd.

3 Dusty provided 93 head of cattle in prime condition.

4 Mr Young, whose ranch, which wasn't the Lazy K, bordered that of the man nicknamed Lobo (Spanish for wolf), was the second-largest contributor to the trail herd.

5 Mr Fraser of the Rocking B provided more cattle than Hickory, whose contribution was, however, the next largest.

6 The ex-Confederate cavalry officer who ran the Sabre ranch wasn't nicknamed Buffalo.

7 Hickory's ranch was the Diamond Star.

	Fraser	Morgan	O'Reilly	Smith	Young	Cactus	Diamond Star	Lazy K	Rocking B	Sabre	68	84	93	145	187
Buffalo															
Dusty															
Hickory															
Lobo															
Paddy															
68															
84															
93															
145															
187															
Cactus															
Diamond Star															
Lazy K															
Rocking B															
Sabre															

Nickname	Surname	Ranch	No of cattle

BATTLESHIPS

This puzzle is based on the old game of battleships. Your task is to find the vessels in the diagram. Some parts of boats or sea squares have already been filled in, and a number next to a row or column refers to the number of occupied squares in that row or column. The boats may be positioned horizontally or vertically, but no two boats or parts of boats are in adjacent squares – horizontally, vertically or diagonally.

Aircraft Carrier:

Battleships:

Cruisers:

Destroyers:

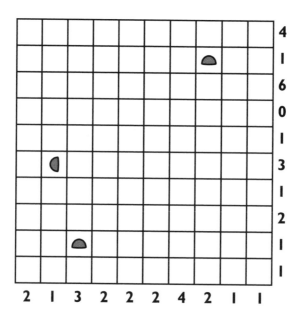

TO BE A PILGRIM

The diagram shows a line of mediæval pilgrims making their way to the shrine of Thomas à Becket in Canterbury. Can you identify each of the men numbered 1 to 7 and work out his occupation?

Clues

1 The shepherd is immediately behind Lionel and immediately ahead of Robin in the line of pilgrims.

2 Geoffrey is a soldier taking advantage of a truce in the wars to make a pilgrimage to the shrine of St Thomas.

3 Simon is two places behind the baker in the procession.

4 Pilgrim 2's name has the same initial letter as that of the potter.

5 Hugh is pilgrim number 4.

6 The man in third position in the line isn't the farmer.

7 Pilgrim number 6 is a humble, but devout, woodcutter.

Names:
Geoffrey; Gilbert; Hugh; Jacob; Lionel; Robin; Simon

Occupations:
Baker; farmer; farrier; potter; shepherd; soldier; woodcutter

To Canterbury

Pilgrim No	Name	Occupation
1		
2		
3		
4		
5		
6		
7		

Starting tip:

First work out the name of the potter.

THE PRODIGIES

Mozart wasn't the only infant classical music prodigy and below are details of five other juvenile composers from roughly the same era. From the information given, can you discover what kind of piece each wrote at which early age and the instrument of which each was a virtuoso?

Clues

1 Joachim Kiddi was a clarinet virtuoso; he wrote his first piece when he was just two years older than the composer of the symphony.

2 The precocious young pianist penned a piano concerto – it wasn't Wolfgang Todlür.

3 Antonio Bambino was only six when he wrote his first masterpiece; he wasn't the virtuoso violinist.

4 Josef Neubörn wasn't the oldest of the five when he wrote his nursery overture.

5 The oboist was two years younger than the writer of the opera.

6 The tone poem was written by a nine-year-old.

Composer	Age	Piece	Instrument

FIRM FOUNDATIONS

The ancient University of Goatsferry has many colleges, some of which date back to the 14th and 15th centuries. Five such colleges are featured in this pair of problems. Can you match each college with the name of its current Master, work out the year of its foundation and name the particular feature for which it is noted?

Clues

1 Alfred Chaplain is the present Master of Plantagenet, which was the next college to be founded after the one with the tower.

2 The Lazarus Library is the envy of all the other Goatsferry colleges; Colin Fellows is Master of an older institution.

3 St Peter's College was founded in 1426.

4 Cordwainers is a more recent foundation than the college with the long-established gardens, whose Master isn't Robert Proctor.

5 Lionel Don presides over the college dating back to 1440.

6 The oldest of the colleges at Goatsferry, founded in 1385, is noted for its magnificent chapel.

	Alfred Chaplain	Angus Dean	Colin Fellows	Lionel Don	Robert Proctor	1385	1401	1426	1440	1463	Chapel	Fountain	Gardens	Library	Tower
Cordwainers															
Lazarus															
Plantagenet															
Princes															
St Peter's															
Chapel															
Fountain															
Gardens															
Library															
Tower															
1385															
1401															
1426															
1440															
1463															

College	Master	Founded	Feature

STEEPED IN HISTORY

Each of the five colleges featured in the previous problem has a famous historian on its academic staff. From the clues here, plus information obtained by solving the previous puzzle, can you identify the five, work out each man's specialist area and match them with their colleges?

Clues

1 Arthur Old isn't the historian whose special subject is the Civil War, whose college Master is Colin Fellows.

2 Theodore's college is the one noted for its tower.

3 The man named Dry lectures at the college founded in 1401.

4 Cedric's special area is Europe in the 19th Century.

5 Neither Sebastian nor Fossil is on the staff of the college with the famous chapel, nor does the latter serve under Lionel Don.

6 Fogey is the specialist on Roman Britain.

7 The man at the college with the attractive gardens shares a surname initial with one of the other four.

8 The social historian isn't based at the college with the fountain.

	Arthur	Basil	Cedric	Sebastian	Theodore	Dry	Fogey	Fossil	Old	Yore	19th C Europe	Civil War	Roman Britain	Social History	The Reformation
Cordwainers															
Lazarus															
Plantagenet															
Princes															
St Peter's															
19th C Europe															
Civil War															
Roman Britain															
Social History															
The Reformation															
Dry															
Fogey															
Fossil															
Old															
Yore															

College	Forename	Surname	Speciality

THE REGULARS

The ABC Cab Company in Storbury has five Friday night regulars (passengers picked up every week from the same spot to go to the same destination). Who is being picked up by each of the designated cabs this week, where will he/she be collected and where is he/she going?

Clues

1 The passenger who will be picked up from the Mill Hotel, who isn't Mrs Usher, won't be going to the address in Chaucer Road.

2 The person going from Saxby House to a house in East Street won't be picked up by a cab with a Bravo call-sign.

3 Alpha 2 will be taking one of the regulars home to Bridge House. Mr Lang isn't being picked up by Alpha 1 or Alpha 2.

4 Mr Todd will be picked up by Bravo 2, but not from outside the Post Office; his destination won't be in York Road.

5 Colonel O'Dowd's cab always takes him straight home to Stag Lodge.

6 The cab which picks Councillor Clark up from Storbury Town Hall after the town council's weekly meeting won't have an Alpha call-sign.

	Colonel O'Dowd	Councillor Clark	Mr Lang	Mr Todd	Mrs Usher	Mill Hotel	Post Office	Railway station	Saxby House	Town Hall	Bridge House	Chaucer Road	East Street	Stag Lodge	York Road
Alpha 1															
Alpha 2															
Bravo 1															
Bravo 2															
Charlie 1															
Bridge House															
Chaucer Road															
East Street															
Stag Lodge															
York Road															
Mill Hotel															
Post Office															
Railway station															
Saxby House															
Town Hall															

Taxi	Passenger	From	To

CAR BOOT TALE

The eight cars lettered A to H in the diagram are in the car park of a large DIY store on the outskirts of town. By coincidence, each of the drivers has just returned to his vehicle, having bought a different item from the store. Can you match the cars with their owners and say what each man is loading in his car boot? NB – 'Left' and 'right' are from your point of view as you look at the picture.

Clues

1 Tim, whose car is denoted by a consonant, is parked two places to the left of the man who bought the doors.

2 Henry, who bought the wallpaper, is parked immediately right of Vince, who didn't buy the paint.

3 The owner of car E had some difficulty in stowing his new ladder aboard to drive home.

4 Neil's car is immediately next to and right of Owen's.

5 Alec's left-hand neighbour in the car park bought a cupboard and his right-hand neighbour bought the tiles.

6 Car D belongs to Rob.

7 The name of the owner of car B is longer than that of the man who bought the electric drill, whose car isn't next to it.

8 Car A isn't owned by a man with a five-letter name.

Owners:
Alec; Henry; Mac; Neil; Owen; Rob; Tim; Vince

Items bought:
Cupboard; doors; electric drill; ladder; paint; shelves; tiles; wallpaper

	A	B	C	D	E	F	G	H

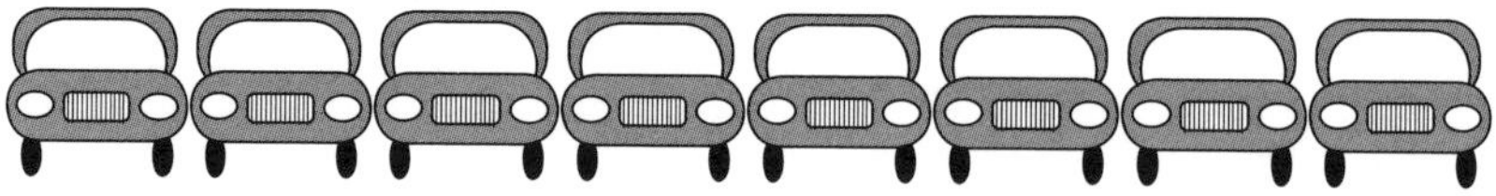

Car	Owner	Item
A		
B		
C		
D		
E		
F		
G		
H		

Starting tip:

Start by working out which car is Tim's.

NOT FROM DOCK GREEN

Most of us remember veteran police officer George Dixon of Dock Green but at a recent Police Federation meeting there were five G Dixons, none from Dock Green or even the Metropolitan Police. Can you work out the rank of each G. Dixon, which force they were from and how many years they had been in the police? (NB – Please note that a Police Constable, like the other ranks, can be a male or a female officer.)

Clues

1 Gordon Dixon had served for two years less than Geoffrey Dixon and a year more than the officer from the Devon and Cornwall Constabulary.

2 The Detective Sergeant had served longer than the member of the South Yorkshire police but a shorter time than Georgina Dixon.

3 Neither Graham Dixon nor the officer who had served the longest was a uniformed Police Constable.

4 Grace Dixon, who didn't belong to the West Midlands force, had served for a year longer than the uniformed Sergeant.

5 The Detective Inspector had served longer than Georgina Dixon but not as long as the officer from Norfolk.

	Detective Inspector	Detective Sergeant	Inspector	Police Constable	Sergeant	Devon and Cornwall	Norfolk	South Yorks	Thames Valley	West Midlands	10 years	11 years	13 years	14 years	16 years
Geoffrey Dixon															
Georgina Dixon															
Gordon Dixon															
Grace Dixon															
Graham Dixon															
10 years															
11 years															
13 years															
14 years															
16 years															
Devon/Cornwall															
Norfolk															
South Yorks															
Thames Valley															
West Midlands															

Name	Rank	Force	Years of service

ON YOUR BIKE

The diagram shows four young lads taking an outing on their bikes. Each bike is a different make and each has a different colour. Can you work out who is on each bike, as well as its make and colour?

Clues

1 Colin's blue bike is immediately ahead of the Rambler as they ride along.

2 Clint's bike isn't yellow.

3 The Mountie is bike number 4 in the diagram; its rider isn't Clyde.

4 The bike leading the line on the outing is resplendent in its new red paint.

5 Craig is riding the bike with the very apt model name Mudlark.

Lads:
Clint; Clyde; Colin; Craig

Makes of bike:
Comet; Mountie; Mudlark; Rambler

Colours:
Blue; green; red; yellow

4   3   2   1

Bicycle	Name	Make	Colour

Starting tip:

Work out which numbered bike is Colin's.

VINTAGE STUFF

The other day I came across an old cigarette card album containing a full set of 50 vintage cars. It fell open at the page illustrated in the diagram, featuring cards 17 to 20 in the series. Can you name the make, colour and year of the car depicted on each card?

Clues

1 The Gentley was depicted in the slot above the one containing the red car.

2 The green car was the right-hand neighbour on the page of the one built in 1912.

3 Card 18 in the series depicted the car built in 1905.

4 The yellow Deauville's number is one higher than that of the 1908 model, (not the Mascara).

5 The Stackard was built in 1903.

Cars:
Deauville; Gentley; Mascara; Stackard

Colours:
Black; green; red; yellow

Years:
1903; 1905; 1908; 1912

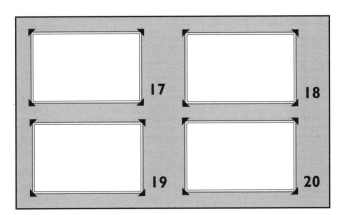

Number	Car	Colour	Year
17			
18			
19			
20			

Starting tip:

Start by identifying the 1908 model.

ANOTHER DOOR OPENS

Five Members of Parliament who lost their seats at the 1997 election have now managed to find alternative employment. Can you identify the five, name the seat each lost and say what he's now doing?

Clues

1 The late Member for Gowing West, whose first name has six letters, is now prospering in his new job as chairman of a merchant bank.

2 Carroll has joined the board of directors of one of the privatised electricity companies.

3 Pearce isn't Morgan, whose former constituency had a single-word name.

4 Walter was the man rejected by the burghers of Onyerbyke in 1997.

5 Terence, who is now in publishing, isn't O'Leary, the former Member for Upson Downs.

6 Lester's surname is Burns.

7 Noel isn't the man who has resumed his pre-Parliamentary career as a barrister; the latter isn't Reeves, who didn't represent Cutloose in the previous Parliament.

	Burns	Carroll	O'Leary	Pearce	Reeves	Casterside	Cutloose	Gowing West	Onyerbyke	Upson Downs	Bank chairman	Barrister	Co director	Publisher	TV pundit
Lester															
Morgan															
Noel															
Terence															
Walter															
Bank chairman															
Barrister															
Co director															
Publisher															
TV pundit															
Casterside															
Cutloose															
Gowing West															
Onyerbyke															
Upson Downs															

Forename	Surname	Constituency	New job

CUT FOR DEAL

Four people about to play cards cut for deal. The cards, which were all of different suits, are shown in the diagram, numbered 1 to 4 in the order in which they were cut. Can you work out the denomination and suit of each card and name the player who drew it?

Clues

1 Clara made her cut immediately before the king was drawn.

2 The diamond was cut next but one after the 3, a male player making the intervening cut.

3 Betty's card, which wasn't a club, was a lower one than card 4.

4 Adam, whose card was a heart, drew it some time before the 10 was cut.

5 The second card to be drawn was a black one, ie either a club or a spade.

Denominations:
3; 7; 10; king

Suits:
Clubs; diamonds; hearts; spades

Players:
Adam; Betty; Clara; Dave

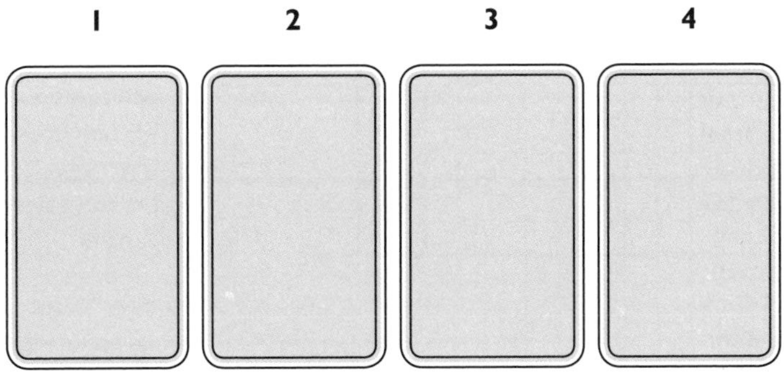

| | 1 | 2 | 3 | 4 |

Card	Denomination	Suit	Player
1			
2			
3			
4			

Starting tip:

Begin by working out who cut card 4.

WINDOWS OF OPPORTUNITY

The Post Office is very busy today – all five service windows are open, with a queue at each. From the following information, can you work out the length of the queue at each window, who is at the head of each queue and what their transactions are?

Clues

1 Mrs O'Brien is paying her phone bill at the head of a queue of fewer than five people; she isn't at window 4.

2 Mr Malone is at the head of a queue of five at a lower-numbered window than the one where the parcel is being weighed; the parcel isn't being sent by Mrs Greenwood.

3 The stamps are being bought at window 3, but not by Miss Evans, who is also not at the head of a queue of six people.

4 The number of people in the line at window 5 is a multiple of the number in the line headed by the person paying their car tax.

5 Mr Shelton is at window 1, but he's not drawing his pension.

	Three people	Four people	Five people	Six people	Ten people	Miss Evans	Mr Malone	Mr Shelton	Mrs Greenwood	Mrs O'Brien	Car tax	Parcel	Pension	Phone bill	Stamps
Window 1															
Window 2															
Window 3															
Window 4															
Window 5															
Car tax															
Parcel															
Pension															
Phone bill															
Stamps															
Miss Evans															
Mr Malone															
Mr Shelton															
Mrs Greenwood															
Mrs O'Brien															

Window No	Queue length	Head of queue	Transaction

HOLY ROTA

Below are details of part of the church rota for St Mary's as printed in the parish magazine. From the information given, can you work out who is responsible for the church flowers each Sunday, who will be the sidesman and who will be reading one of the lessons?

Clues

1 Mrs Newton is due to do the church flowers on the 2nd; Mrs Leonard will not be doing the flowers on either of the Sundays when the Robertson brothers are sidesmen.

2 Mrs Fox will be doing one of the readings on the 9th. On one Sunday Mr R Robertson is both sidesman and reader.

3 Mr Talbot won't be required either on the 16th or the Sunday when his wife is doing the flowers. Miss Woodcock is reading later in the month than Mr Talbot's sidesman duty, but not on the Sunday when she's responsible for the flowers.

4 Mr Howe will be doing his reading the Sunday after Mrs Talbot does the flowers.

5 Miss Stark will be on flower duty and Mr Webb as sidesman the Sunday before Mrs Gray does her reading.

6 Mr S Robertson will be sidesman on the 30th.

	Miss Stark	Miss Woodcock	Mrs Leonard	Mrs Newton	Mrs Talbot	Mr R Robertson	Mr S Robertson	Mr Swain	Mr Talbot	Mr Webb	Miss Woodcock	Mr Howe	Mr R Robertson	Mrs Fox	Mrs Gray
2nd															
9th															
16th															
23rd															
30th															
Miss Woodcock															
Mr Howe															
Mr R Robertson															
Mrs Fox															
Mrs Gray															
Mr R Robertson															
Mr S Robertson															
Mr Swain															
Mr Talbot															
Mr Webb															

Sunday	Church flowers	Sidesman	Reader

DOMINO SEARCH

A standard set of dominoes has been laid out, using numbers instead of dots for clarity. With the aid of a sharp pencil and a keen brain, can you draw in the lines to show where each domino has been placed? You may find the check grid useful – crossing off each domino as you find it.

3	2	3	3	5	3	2	3
6	4	2	1	1	0	1	2
2	2	6	6	6	3	2	5
2	3	0	4	1	1	0	0
1	5	5	0	5	4	0	0
6	1	4	5	5	1	4	4
3	4	6	0	6	6	5	4

0						
1						
2						
3						
4						
5						
6						

| | 0 | 1 | 2 | 3 | 4 | 5 | 6 |

WILLING WORKHORSE

Aristide Percheron, the famous French private detective, solved several baffling cases last year. Can you work out the location and nature of the crime he investigated in each of the listed months and say which seemingly insignificant clue proved crucial to his theory?

Clues

1 The discarded butt of a Gauloise was the key to Percheron's solution of the kidnapping case, which didn't centre on Orleans.

2 The smell of perfume put Aristide on the scent of the criminal in the affair at Clermont-Ferrand.

3 The robbery in Bordeaux took place on the 31st of the month.

4 It was a complicated case of fraud which occupied Percheron's attention for most of August.

5 The broken wine glass led to the arrest of the man involved in the next case after the blackmail inquiry.

6 Aristide spent most of July working on the case in Marseille.

7 The Champagne cork didn't figure in May's inquiry.

8 It was with zest that Percheron tackled a murder case the month after he had made a deduction based on a piece of discarded orange peel.

	Bordeaux	Clermont-Ferrand	Marseille	Nantes	Orleans	Blackmail	Fraud	Kidnap	Murder	Robbery	Broken wine glass	Champagne cork	Gauloise butt	Orange peel	Smell of perfume
May															
June															
July															
August															
September															
Broken wine glass															
Champagne cork															
Gauloise butt															
Orange peel															
Smell of perfume															
Blackmail															
Fraud															
Kidnap															
Murder															
Robbery															

Month	Location	Crime	Clue

GREAT EXPECTATIONS

The diagram shows four expectant mothers awaiting their turn for a check-up at the prenatal clinic. Can you identify the women lettered A to D, name the job each does and say which numbered child she's expecting?

Clues

1 The teacher, who isn't Penny, is in seat A; she isn't expecting her second child.

2 The woman in seat C has the most children already.

3 Suki's two neighbours as she sits waiting are the saleswoman and the woman expecting her first child.

4 Michelle, the social worker, isn't in seat D.

5 The woman in seat B isn't the nursery nurse.

Names:
Eleanor; Michelle; Penny; Suki

Jobs:
Nursery nurse; saleswoman; social worker; teacher

Child expected:
First; second; third; fourth

Mother	Name	Job	Child expected
A			
B			
C			
D			

Starting tip:

First work out Suki's occupation.

PLEASE REPEAT

A group of five friends are all avid viewers of every repeat on television of the classic musical films, though each has her own individual preference. Can you identify the five, work out their respective ages and name each one's favourite film?

Clues

1 Norma, whose favourite film is South Pacific, is two years younger than Mrs Stein, whose favourite isn't The King And I.

2 Sally is 54 and Mrs Lowe is 56.

3 The youngest of the five women prefers The Sound Of Music.

4 Rhoda's surname is Hammer.

5 Mrs Lerner has lost count of the number of times she has watched her favourite film, My Fair Lady.

6 Jill isn't yet 60.

7 The woman who just loves watching Oklahoma isn't 58.

	Hammer	Lerner	Lowe	Rogers	Stein	52	54	56	58	60	My Fair Lady	Oklahoma	South Pacific	The King And I	The Sound Of Music
Greta															
Jill															
Norma															
Rhoda															
Sally															
My Fair Lady																
Oklahoma																
South Pacific																
The King And I																
The Sound Of Music																
52																
54																
56																
58																
60																

Forename	Surname	Age	Favourite film

PILE UP

These piles of bricks aren't the random results of a child's play but clues to a final, at present blank, pile on the right. Like the rest, that one has six bricks each with a different one of the six letters.

The numbers below the piles tell you two things:

(a) The number of adjacent pairs of bricks in that column which also appear adjacent in the final pile.

(b) The number of adjacent pairs of bricks that make a correct pair but the wrong way up.

So:

would score one in the 'Correct' row if the final pile had an A directly above a C and a one in the 'Reversed' row if the final pile had a C on top of an A. From all this, can you create the final pile before it topples?

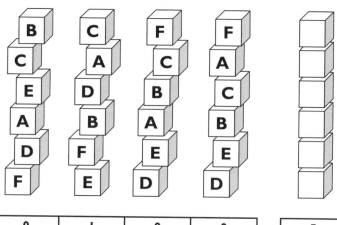

Correct	0	I	0	0		5
Reversed	0	I	2	0		0

PUPPY LOVE?

Buddy, our new puppy, is causing havoc around the house! In the first week that we had him he chewed up various objects, helped himself to items of food and not yet being house-trained, disgraced himself in several unfortunate locations. From the following information, can you work out what he did on each day?

Clues

1 One day – Thursday or Saturday – he did a puddle in the washing-basket, but didn't steal any meat or chew any footwear.

2 He chewed my welly in the incident immediately before he pinched a chocolate biscuit and weed on the armchair.

3 The day he chewed a slipper and helped himself to some bacon wasn't Thursday or the day when he had an accident on the hearth-rug.

4 He left a puddle under the dining-table the day after he chewed up the newspaper.

5 The day (not Monday) when he left teeth-marks in the TV remote control and did a puddle in the kitchen wasn't the day he had the sausage.

6 Saturday wasn't the day that Buddy had an illicit cherry cake.

	Chair leg	Newspaper	Slipper	TV remote control	Welly	Bacon	Cheese sandwich	Cherry cake	Chocolate biscuit	Sausage	Armchair	Hearth-rug	Kitchen	Under dining-table	Washing-basket
Monday															
Wednesday															
Thursday															
Saturday															
Sunday															
Armchair															
Hearth-rug															
Kitchen															
Under dining-table															
Washing-basket															
Bacon															
Cheese sandwich															
Cherry cake															
Chocolate biscuit															
Sausage															

Day	Item chewed	Item stolen	Accident location

BOUNCING ABOUT

Roger is the proud owner of a Bouncy Castle, which he rents out as a sideline to various events in the area where he lives. Last year he had five bookings in successive months at different villages. Can you work out which event he attended in which month at which venue and say what its official starting time was (though, of course, Roger was there well in advance to set things up)?

Clues

1 A group of parents in one village had got together to organise a holiday gala to keep their offspring out of mischief in the first week of August.

2 The wedding party, which a large number of children had been invited to attend, was held in Bloomwell.

3 Oakdown was the venue to which Roger had to travel in July; the event started earlier in the day than the birthday party.

4 The April event had a 4pm start, but the one in May didn't start at 1.30pm.

5 The starting time for the garden party was 2pm.

6 The Brookfield event was held later in the year than the one at Fernleigh.

7 The opening of the village carnival was half an hour later than the start of the event at Glebeton, which wasn't held the following month.

	Birthday party	Garden party	Holiday gala	Village carnival	Wedding party	Bloomwell	Brookfield	Fernleigh	Glebeton	Oakdown	10.30am	11.00am	1.30pm	2.00pm	4.00pm
April															
May															
June															
July															
August															
10.30am															
11.00am															
1.30pm															
2.00pm															
4.00pm															
Bloomwell															
Brookfield															
Fernleigh															
Glebeton															
Oakdown															

Month	Event	Village	Time

ON THE TRAIL

It was 20 miles across rough moorland from the Youth Hostel at Stonebeck, where Dave and his fellow hikers had spent Wednesday night, to the one at Eaglescrag where they planned to be the next evening, so they set out early and made only three short rest-stops en route. Can you work out who ate which snack at each stop?

Clues

1 Nobody ate the same type of snack twice and no two hikers ate the same type of snack at the same stop.

2 The walker who had a ham roll at the 9.00am stop beside the Black Tarn didn't eat a doughnut at the midday stop.

3 Whoever ate the chocolate bar at the first stop had a ham roll at midday.

4 Jack ate his cheese roll last.

5 Mick, who had a doughnut at the 9.00am stop, wasn't the walker who ate a chocolate bar at midday.

6 Gilly ate a sausage roll at the midday stop, but wasn't the one who ate the ham roll last.

7 Patsy didn't have a sausage roll beside the Black Tarn or a ham roll last. The hiker who did have the sausage roll at the first stop had a doughnut at the third.

	9.00am					Midday					3.00pm				
	Cheese roll	Chocolate bar	Doughnut	Ham roll	Sausage roll	Cheese roll	Chocolate bar	Doughnut	Ham roll	Sausage roll	Cheese roll	Chocolate bar	Doughnut	Ham roll	Sausage roll
Dave															
Gilly															
Jack															
Mick															
Patsy															
3.00pm — Cheese roll															
Chocolate bar															
Doughnut															
Ham roll															
Sausage roll															
MIDDAY — Cheese roll															
Chocolate bar															
Doughnut															
Ham roll															
Sausage roll															

Hiker	9.00am	Midday	3.00pm

THE RHYME'S THE THING

Since these matters are top secret, not a lot of people know that five of James Bond's predecessors weren't good enough to cover their tracks and were killed in various locations by the forces of evil. Can you match each man with his code number, and the year and location of his demise? NB – To comply with the Official Secrets Act, locations have been (slightly) disguised – the description of the demise rhymes with the location.

Clues

1 Agent 028, Charles, was the next to meet his doom after his erstwhile colleague who was killed while in his pyjamas.

2 Bruce, whose career came to an untimely end in 1944, had a code number 007 higher than that of the man dispatched by an enemy agent disguised as a Mother Superior.

3 Arthur, who was assassinated by a villainous lascar, was the next agent to fall victim after Dennis.

4 Agent 042's demise took place in 1961.

5 It was in 1938 that one agent was seduced and subsequently murdered by a girl in a sarong.

6 It wasn't in 1955 that an agent was killed after a chase by the secret police.

	014	021	028	035	042	1938	1944	1949	1955	1961	Algeria	Bahamas	Greece	Hong Kong	Madagascar
Arthur															
Bruce															
Charles															
Dennis															
Edgar															
Algeria															
Bahamas															
Greece															
Hong Kong															
Madagascar															
1938															
1944															
1949															
1955															
1961															

Agent	Code No	Year	Location

SCREENED OFF

Back in the 1930s in the golden age of the movies, five cinemas were opened in town, but they've all since closed. From the following information, can you discover the opening and closing dates of each and what the buildings are used for today?

Clues

1 Neither the Palace (which didn't close in 1979) nor the cinema that opened in 1931 (but didn't close in 1979) is now used as a Salvation Army Citadel or a Community Church.

2 The old Essoldo is now a furniture store, but the 1934-built cinema isn't in use for light engineering.

3 The Astoria didn't close its doors in 1979 and the cinema that did isn't now a Salvation Army Citadel; the cinema that closed in 1984 was built the year before the Astoria, but isn't currently the Salvation Army Citadel.

4 The cinema opened in 1933 closed in 1974; the most recently closed is now a Community Church.

5 The Rivoli didn't close in 1967.

6 The Empire opened in 1936.

	1931	1933	1934	1935	1936	1967	1974	1979	1984	1992	Car showroom	Community Church	Furniture store	Light engineering	Salvation Army Citadel
Astoria															
Empire															
Essoldo															
Palace															
Rivoli															
Car showroom															
Comm church															
Furniture store															
Lt engineering															
Salvn Army Citadel															
1967															
1974															
1979															
1984															
1992															

Cinema	Year built	Year closed	Present use

A TASTE FOR LITERATURE

The five Smith boys, born between 1910 and 1920, each had a favourite book in childhood and each grew up to develop a taste for detective fiction in adult life. Can you work out in which year each boy was born and match them with their childhood books and the sleuth whose adventures each devoured in later life?

Clues

1 The Smith who combined a liking for Robin Hood with an affection for Doctor Thorndyke was neither the oldest nor the youngest of the five.

2 The boy whose preference was *Treasure Island* was born in 1913.

3 The lad who favoured *Tarzan*, who wasn't Adrian, wasn't born in 1910.

4 Clarence's adult favourite was Hercule Poirot, while Benjamin, whose childhood choice was *Robinson Crusoe*, wasn't born during the 1914–18 war.

5 Ellery Queen was the adult choice of the Smith boy born in 1915, who wasn't Percival.

6 The Smith who read and re-read *Swiss Family Robinson* was immediately junior in the family to Charles, who didn't grow up to enjoy the Father Brown stories of G K Chesterton.

	1910	1913	1915	1917	1920	Robin Hood	Robinson Crusoe	Swiss Fam Robn	Tarzan	Treasure Island	Dr Thorndyke	Ellery Queen	Father Brown	Hercule Poirot	Lord P Wimsey
Adrian															
Benjamin															
Charles															
Clarence															
Percival															
Dr Thorndyke															
Ellery Queen															
Father Brown															
Hercule Poirot															
Lord P Wimsey															
Robin Hood															
R Crusoe															
Sw Fam Robn															
Tarzan															
Treasure Island															

Name	Year of birth	Childhood book	Detective

FIRE!

Four fire engines from the same station were called out to different incidents on the same afternoon. Can you name each of the places numbered 1 to 4 and say which driver drove his team there and with what type of incident each team dealt?

Clues

1 The factory fire at Blazeborough was in the next location clockwise from the one attended by Frank.

2 Jim drove his fire engine to location 1.

3 Gordon and his team had to rescue a cat stuck up a tree at a location with a lower number on the plan than Scorchford.

4 The chimney fire at location 3 wasn't attended by Reg's crew.

5 Sparkton isn't marked 2 on the map.

Locations:
Blazeborough; Flamewell; Scorchford; Sparkton

Drivers:
Frank; Gordon; Jim; Reg

Incidents:
Cat up tree; chimney fire; chip pan fire; factory fire

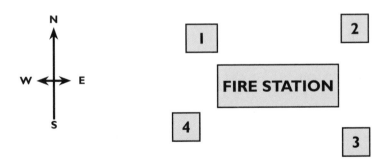

Map reference	Location	Driver	Incident
1			
2			
3			
4			

Starting tip:

First work out the number of the location attended by Gordon's team.

TRIANGULATION

Each of the sixteen small equilateral triangles forming the large equilateral triangle in the diagram contains either one of the letters of the word TRIANGULATION or, in three instances, 60°, representing each of the three angles in each of the triangles. Can you insert all letters and numbers into their correct places?

Clues

1 The letter in triangle 1 is identical with that in triangle 12.
2 One triangle containing an A has a common side with the one to its right containing the G.
3 The triangles containing the 60° legend are all in different horizontal rows, none of them sharing a common side.
4 Triangles 10 and 16 both contain letters not repeated elsewhere, the latter's appearing earlier in the alphabet.
5 Both the Is appear in inverted triangles.
6 Triangle 6 doesn't contain a vowel.
7 There is an N in triangle 8.
8 Triangle 15 contains a letter from the second half of the alphabet.
9 There is a difference of eight between the numbers of the two triangles which contain a T.
10 The triangle in which O appears is numbered four lower than that with the U.

Letters:
A; A; G; I; I; L; N; N; O; R; T; T; U

Symbols:
60°; 60°; 60°

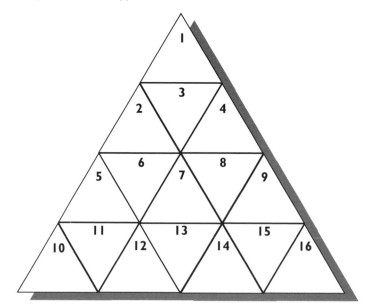

Starting tip:

Begin by placing the letters in triangles 1 and 12.

CRIMINAL PURSUIT

When I called on my friend Alice the other day, she told me about the four new crime novels she had acquired, which occupy the extreme left end of one of her shelves. Can you work out each book's title and the names of its author and the detective it features?

NB – 'Left' and 'right' are from your point of view as you look at the picture.

Clues

1 Jayne D'Eath's novel is next left to the one in which the crime is solved by Superintendent Blair; *Love Lies Bleeding* is further left still.

2 Simon Gore isn't the author of *The Melon Seller*, which stands next right to the book introducing Sergeant Spotforth.

3 The author of the book at 4 isn't Dulcie Coughen.

4 The detective in *The Aspidistra Deaths* has a lower rank than the one who appears in the book in position 3.

5 *Murder At Twilight* is next right to Gore's book but further left than the one in which the detective is Sharp.

Titles:
Love Lies Bleeding; Murder At Twilight; The Aspidistra Deaths; The Melon Seller

Authors:
Al Leith; Dulcie Coughen; Jayne D'Eath; Simon Gore

Detectives:
Superintendent Blair; Chief Inspector Clewes; Inspector Sharp; Sergeant Spotforth

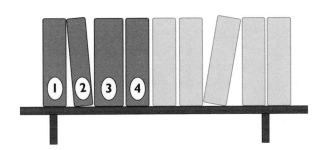

Book	Title	Author	Detective
1			
2			
3			
4			

Starting tip:

Work out the author of book 4.

RAISING CANES

Three friends who have neighbouring allotments each specialise in growing one particular vegetable and one type of soft fruit. Can you identify them and work out the full details of their respective crops?

Clues

1 Derek's artichokes are much admired.

2 Mr Delving is noted for the excellence of his blackcurrants, but he doesn't grow marrows.

3 Michael Trench isn't the gardener who grows the strawberries.

4 One man combines raising raspberry canes with growing parsnips.

	Delving	Mulch	Trench	Artichokes	Marrows	Parsnips	Blackcurrants	Raspberries	Strawberries
Derek									
Michael									
Robin									
Blackcurrants									
Raspberries									
Strawberries									
Artichokes									
Marrows									
Parsnips									

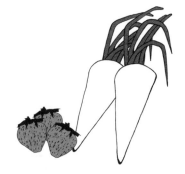

Forename	Surname	Vegetables	Fruit

PILE UP

These piles of bricks aren't the random results of a child's play but clues to a final, at present blank, pile on the right. Like the rest, that one has six bricks each with a different one of the six letters.

The numbers below the piles tell you two things:

(a) The number of adjacent pairs of bricks in that column which also appear adjacent in the final pile.

(b) The number of adjacent pairs of bricks that make a correct pair but the wrong way up.

So: would score one in the 'Correct' row if the final pile had an A directly above a C and a one in the 'Reversed' row if the final pile had a C on top of an A. From all this, can you create the final pile before it topples?

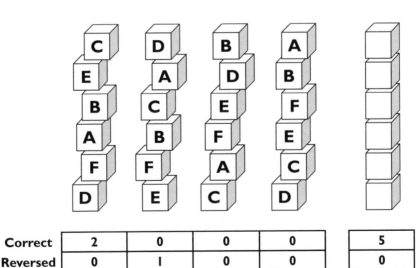

Correct	2	0	0	0	5
Reversed	0	1	0	0	0

STEADY DOES IT

Sid had a gentle flutter at Kempfield Park the other day. He isn't an adventurous punter and backed only three favourites. From the clues given, can you work out in which race Sid's horses ran, in what position each finished and what was each one's starting price?

Clues

1 The horse which Sid backed in the 2.30 wasn't the winner; nor was the winner's price 3-1.

2 Mr Gilly was better placed than the 6-4 horse, which ran in an earlier race.

3 The 7-2 horse, Franchard didn't run in the 3.30 race.

	Franchard	Klondyke	Mr Gilly	First	Second	Third	7-2	3-1	6-4
2.30									
3.00									
3.30									
7-2									
3-1									
6-4									
First									
Second									
Third									

Race time	Horse	Position	Odds

COURSE YOU CAN!

As part of an open day at the Territorial Army base in Edwinsbury, four local celebrities were given the chance to attempt the assault course, but, even though each was assisted by a sergeant from the TA, none of them managed to finish. Can you work out in what field each was a celebrity, who helped and why he or she didn't finish?

Clues

1 Sergeant Wood accompanied the locally-born swimmer who has represented England in international competitions. Fiona Niven isn't the writer of adventure thrillers, who lives in a village just outside the town.

2 Donna Lyons dropped out of the assault course after getting tangled in the scramble net she was supposed to climb.

3 Eddie March, who was helped by Sergeant Grant, wasn't the rather plump Chairperson of the local District Council, who got jammed while crawling through a narrow tunnel.

4 Carl Kirkby wasn't the celebrity who, despite encouragement from Sergeant Hart, refused to even try to climb the ten-foot wall.

	Council Chairperson	Novelist	Radio reporter	Swimmer	Sergeant Grant	Sergeant Hart	Sergeant Moore	Sergeant Wood	Fell into pond	Jammed in tunnel	Refused to climb wall	Tangled in net
Carl Kirkby												
Donna Lyons												
Eddie March												
Fiona Niven												
Fell into pond									
Jammed in tunnel									
Refused to climb									
Tangled in net									
Sergeant Grant					
Sergeant Hart					
Sergeant Moore					
Sergeant Wood					

Name	Status	Helped by	Mishap

SEEING THE SIGHTS

Capital Coaches run four special tours from their central London headquarters every weekday in spring and summer. Can you work out the details of last Friday's trips – the number of each coach, its driver's name, where it went and how many passengers it carried?

Clues

1 Capital's X1 excursion runs to Brighton; Jim Guy didn't drive the X4 last Friday.

2 Billy Dennis' coach carried more passengers than the vehicle Pete Van Hool took to Windsor.

3 Mick Leyland had 51 passengers on his coach, which wasn't doing the circular tour of Historic London.

4 The coach on the Oxford excursion route carried three fewer passengers than the X3; the driver of the former has a shorter surname than the man who went to Brighton.

	Billy Dennis	Jim Guy	Mick Leyland	Pete Van Hool	Brighton	Historic London	Oxford	Windsor	45 passengers	48 passengers	51 passengers	54 passengers
X1												
X2												
X3												
X4												
45 passengers												
48 passengers												
51 passengers												
54 passengers												
Brighton												
Historic London												
Oxford												
Windsor												

Excursion	Driver	Destination	Passengers

TOO MANY CHIEFS

At a convention of law enforcement officers in Washington DC, the Police Chiefs of four small American towns gathered to discuss their respective forces. Can you work out from which town and state each Chief had come and how many officers he had in his force?

Clues

1 The Riverside Police Department had six more officers than the force commanded by the Chief from Kentucky.

2 Chief Durkin was head of a force which contained six more officers than the one from the town in Arkansas.

3 The Pleasant Hill Police Force had four more officers than the one headed by Chief Gore.

4 The Georgetown force had more officers than Chief Panzer's.

5 The town in Minnesota had a police department four officers stronger than the one commanded by Chief Keems.

	Five Points	Georgetown	Pleasant Hill	Riverside	Arkansas	Kentucky	Minnesota	Texas	8 officers	12 officers	14 officers	18 officers
Chief Durkin												
Chief Gore												
Chief Keems												
Chief Panzer												
8 officers												
12 officers												
14 officers												
18 officers												
Arkansas												
Kentucky												
Minnesota												
Texas												

WELCOME TO
PLEASANT HILL

Chief	Town	State	Size of force

THE FORTUNE WHEEL

The diagram shows six segments of the wheel used in the TV game show Lucky Spin. From the clues given below can you work out the number of points shown on each of the segments lettered A to F and the background colour in which each segment is painted?

Clues

1 BANKRUPT is appropriately enough printed on a black background in white letters; this isn't the segment lettered A in the diagram.

2 The yellow segment is immediately clockwise of the one bearing the figure 500.

3 Segment D carries the largest number of points.

4 The first digit of the number on segment E is an even one.

5 The tan background colour is on the segment lettered F.

6 The points offered on segment B are not a multiple of a hundred.

7 The orange segment is immediately anti-clockwise of the pink one.

8 The green segment isn't adjacent to the one bearing the number 450 on the circumference of the wheel.

Legends:
BANKRUPT; 250; 300; 450; 500; 800

Colours:
Black; green; orange; pink; tan; yellow

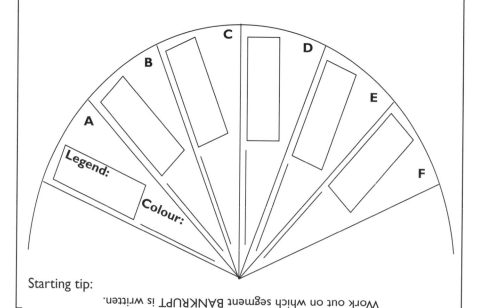

Starting tip:

Work out on which segment BANKRUPT is written.

HOTSHOTS

Below are details of the results of our local Photographic Society landscape photograph competition. From the information given, can you discover, the title of each person's photograph, plus which prize, from 1st down to Commended, was awarded to each photographer and the make of camera used?

Clues

1 Otto Folkus was given the Commended award for his work.

2 Fourth prize wasn't awarded to Sandy Shore, which wasn't Len Scapp's work.

3 Bleak Mid-winter won second prize.

4 The first prize was awarded to the photograph taken with a Gunn camera; it wasn't Poynton Shute's Golden Harvest.

5 Ivor Leitmeter's work was placed one position lower than the one taken with the Zeus.

6 White Water was taken with a Sushi, while F Stopp uses a Nippon.

	Bleak Mid-winter	Golden Harvest	Morning Mist	Sandy Shore	White Water	1st	2nd	3rd	4th	Commended	Gunn	Hitax	Nippon	Sushi	Zeus
F Stopp															
Ivor Leitmeter															
Len Scapp															
Otto Folkus															
Poynton Shute															
Gunn											
Hitax											
Nippon											
Sushi											
Zeus											
1st					
2nd					
3rd					
4th					
Commended					

Photographer	Title	Prize	Camera

PUBLIC DEMONSTRATIONS

Five manufacturers had demonstrators working in Horne & Bollingsworth's department store on Saturday. From the following information, can you work out the product being demonstrated on each floor, the name of each demonstrator and the number of shoppers watching at each location at precisely three o'clock last Saturday afternoon?

Clues

1 The smallest audience was watching the ground floor demonstration.

2 More people were watching the Emotions perfumery demonstrator Sandra than were gathered on the 1st floor.

3 On the 2nd floor Derek was hard at work, but had not attracted the largest audience at three o'clock.

4 Clout power tools were being demonstrated on the 3rd floor, attracting six fewer potential customers than Suzanne's presentation.

5 Paul wasn't addressing nine people nor showing them how effective Shimmer window-cleaner is.

6 A dozen people were watching the demonstration of Markaway easy-clean carpet.

	Clout power tools	Emotions perfume	Markaway carpet	Pinnacle cookware	Shimmer w-cleaner	Clive	Derek	Paul	Sandra	Suzanne	6	9	12	15	18
Basement															
Ground															
1st floor															
2nd floor															
3rd floor															
6										
9										
12										
15										
18										
Clive					
Derek					
Paul					
Sandra					
Suzanne					

Floor	Product	Demonstrator	No of people

LOGI-5

Every row across and column down should contain five letters: A, B, C, D and E, appearing once each. Also every shape (shown by the thick lines) must contain each of the letters A, B, C, D and E, appearing once each. Can you fill the grid?

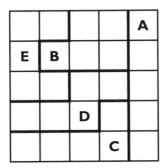

ABC

Every row across and column down is to have each of the letters A, B and C and two empty squares. The letter outside the grid shows the first or second letter in the direction of the arrow. Can you fill the grid?

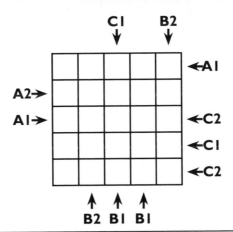

EXTRA TIME

Noel Ines is a part-time film extra and gets occasional work in crowd scenes in a varied selection of films. Below are details of several recent engagements; from the information given, can you work out in which type of film he appeared in which month, the part he played and the number of days' work each provided?

Clues

1 The film adaptation of the classic novel required more days' filming than the romance.

2 Noel played a soldier in the historical epic, spending twice as many days on location as on the August job.

3 He spent more time filming in the rôle of a pub customer than as a footballer.

4 He spent one day fewer filming the thriller in April than he did on the August engagement.

5 His two days of filming as an extra in a restaurant were not for the comedy; in the latter Noel wasn't employed to people a pub.

6 He played the footballer in May; the historical epic wasn't filmed in June.

	Classic novel	Comedy	Historical epic	Romance	Thriller	Footballer	Market trader	Pub customer	Restaurant patron	Soldier	1	2	3	4	5
April															
May															
June															
July															
August															
1															
2															
3															
4															
5															
Footballer															
Market trader															
Pub customer															
Rest'nt patron															
Soldier															

Month	Type of film	Part played	No of days

SNOWSAURUSES

Stone Age winters were quite severe and provided plenty of snow for making into, not just snowmen, but snow creatures of a much larger size. Five old friends Agg, Egg, Igg, Ogg and Ugg entered into the spirit of things with enthusiasm, each building a different snow creature for the benefit of his admiring son. Can you match each hero with the snow sculpture he produced and work out the name and age of each man's son?

Clues

1 None of the sons' names has the same vowel sound in it as his father's.

2 Agg, who made the snow mammoth, has a son two years older than Pigg.

3 The snow pterodactyl was produced by the father of the son aged 5, though he found its massive wing-span a bit of a tricky problem.

4 Cogg, who wasn't the lad for whom the snow brontosaurus was built, isn't 6 years old and his father isn't Egg.

5 Legg was delighted with the snow sabre-toothed tiger his father made for him; he isn't the youngest child, whose father isn't Ogg.

6 Igg is the father of the oldest child.

7 Ugg wasn't the man who made the snow stegosaurus, which wasn't produced for Wagg.

	Brontosaurus	Mammoth	Pterodactyl	Sabre-toothed tiger	Stegosaurus	Cogg	Dugg	Legg	Pigg	Wagg	3	4	5	6	7
Agg															
Egg															
Igg															
Ogg															
Ugg															
3															
4															
5															
6															
7															
Cogg															
Dugg															
Legg															
Pigg															
Wagg															

Hero	Snow creature	Son	Age

SAY CHEESE

GOUDA, the Goatsferry University Dramatic Association, is mounting a production of Romeo and Juliet. Can you fully identify the student selected to play each of the listed rôles and say which subject he or she's reading at Goatsferry? NB – Mercutio, Romeo and Tybalt are male rôles and Juliet and the Nurse are female rôles.

Clues

1 Tooley, who plays Mercutio, isn't Tim. Tim is reading geology.

2 Rosamund's surname isn't Ostler.

3 Adam Benfield's character is listed next but one in the alphabetical list after the one being played by the English student.

4 Hemmings isn't the surname of the student who plays the Nurse.

5 The medical student's rôle in the play is Tybalt.

6 Jenny is reading Spanish at Goatsferry; her surname is shorter than that of the student cast as Romeo.

	Adam	Jenny	Rosamund	Simon	Tim	Benfield	Cooke	Hemmings	Ostler	Tooley	Classics	English	Geology	Medicine	Spanish
Juliet															
Mercutio															
Nurse															
Romeo															
Tybalt															
Classics															
English															
Geology															
Medicine															
Spanish															
Benfield															
Cooke															
Hemmings															
Ostler															
Tooley															

Rôle	Forename	Surname	Subject

YOU'RE NICKNAMED!

All our teachers had nicknames when I was at school and I remember five from one particular year. From the information given below, can you work out the nickname of each member of staff who taught on the listed days, as well as his or her real name and the subject each taught?

Clues

1 Not surprisingly, 'Froggy' taught us French, but not on Monday or Tuesday.

2 We had 'Dalek' on a Wednesday.

3 Mr Benton taught us PE the day before we had 'Gromit'.

4 We had 'Delia' Smith the day before the lesson with 'Bunny'.

5 We had English on Thursday and the teacher's surname was longer than that of the maths teacher.

6 Mrs Waren wasn't the history teacher and the Tuesday tutor wasn't Mr Thorn.

	'Bunny'	'Dalek'	'Delia'	'Froggy'	'Gromit'	Mr Benton	Mrs Johnson	Mr Smith	Mrs Waren	Mr Thorn	English	French	History	Maths	PE
Monday															
Tuesday															
Wednesday															
Thursday															
Friday															
English															
French															
History															
Maths															
PE															
Mr Benton															
Mrs Johnson															
Mr Smith															
Mrs Waren															
Mr Thorn															

Day	Nickname	Teacher	Subject

GRANDSONS' TREAT

Mr and Mrs Fardel had their grandsons Ricky and Billy to stay with them in Storbury last week and each day they took them to another town on the River Stor where they visited two attractions, one in the morning and one in the afternoon. Can you work out where they went each day and the attractions they visited there?

Clues

1 On Friday, the Fardels took their grandsons to Broadwell.

2 Highstone was visited later in the week than the safari park.

3 Everyone enjoyed the afternoon spent on the beach at Longsands.

4 The Norman castle and the country park were visited on the morning and afternoon of the day two days after the Fardels took Ricky and Billy to the cinema.

5 It wasn't on Wednesday morning that they visited the safari park and it wasn't on Thursday morning that they went to the motor museum at Widebridge.

6 Monday afternoon was spent at the aircraft museum and on Tuesday morning they took a boat trip on the Stor, which didn't start from Deepford or Highstone.

	Broadwell	Deepford	Highstone	Longsands	Widebridge	Boat trip	Castle	Motor museum	Safari park	Windmill	Aircraft museum	Beach	Cinema	Country park	Funfair
Monday															
Tuesday															
Wednesday															
Thursday															
Friday															
Aircraft museum															
Beach															
Cinema															
Country park															
Funfair															
Boat trip															
Castle															
Motor museum															
Safari park															
Windmill															

Day	Town	Morning	Afternoon

MISS RAFFLES' SECRET

Miss Raffles purchased a number of homes in different parts of England around the turn of the century where she could hide from the police or just rest from her busy criminal career, where she assumed identities which gave her an excuse for living alone and having frequent long absences. Can you work out what sort of home she lived in under each name, where it was and what the local people thought she was?

Clues

1 In Birmingham, Miss Raffles pretended to be an actress who was frequently away from home working in theatres in distant parts of the country.

2 In Liverpool, where she was known as Mrs Morris, Miss Raffles' home wasn't the quaint 19th-century cottage.

3 When in her semi-detached house in York, Miss Raffles wasn't Miss Forbes.

4 In Oxford, Miss Raffles took the title 'Mrs' and lived in her own modern house but didn't pretend to be a novelist.

5 As Miss Porter, Miss Raffles lived in a flat, but not in Bristol.

6 When living in the terraced house where she said she was the sister of the Bishop of Cardiff, Miss Raffles didn't use the name Mrs Atkins.

7 As the widow of Colonel Wilson, Miss Raffles didn't occupy the detached house.

	Cottage	Detached house	Flat	Semi-det house	Terraced house	Birmingham	Bristol	Liverpool	Oxford	York	Actress	Bishop's sister	Colonel's widow	Novelist	Peer's mistress
Mrs Atkins															
Miss Forbes															
Mrs Morris															
Miss Porter															
Mrs Wilson															
Actress															
Bishop's sister															
Colonel's widow															
Novelist															
Peer's mistress															
Birmingham															
Bristol															
Liverpool															
Oxford															
York															

Name	Type of home	Town	Identity

TO THE OUACHE BASIN

An expedition, sponsored by a major media group, is about to set out for River Ouache in South America (the Ouache Basin is still largely terra incognita) and five of its members are taking part in a press conference. Can you work out where each man is from, his profession and what, in addition to filling his professional rôle, he'll be doing on the expedition?

Clues

1 The man (not a reporter) who will act as the expedition's chief cook, who is neither Heinrich Von Haller nor Mikhail Novikov, comes from a city where French is spoken as a native language.

2 The experienced explorer, the only one of the group who has been to the Ouache Basin before, will naturally be in charge of navigation.

3 Jacques Laplace, who comes from Brussels, isn't the photographer.

4 The man in charge of first aid for the expedition isn't from Montreal.

5 Raoul St Simon is in charge of communications, operating and maintaining the expedition's vital satellite radio link.

6 The party's geologist comes from Cape Town.

7 Biologist Heinrich Von Haller isn't the Parisian who will be the party's language specialist.

	Brussels	Cape Town	Montreal	New York	Paris	Biologist	Explorer	Geologist	Photographer	Reporter	Communications	Cooking	First aid	Languages	Navigation
Andre Benoit															
H Von Haller															
Jacques Laplace															
M Novikov															
Raoul St Simon															
Comms															
Cooking															
First aid															
Languages															
Navigation															
Biologist															
Explorer															
Geologist															
Photographer															
Reporter															

Name	City	Profession	Other rôle

TOWERS OF STRENGTH

The diagram shows a plan of a Norman castle with its four towers. Can you name each tower, say in which year it was built, as well as identify its original use?

Clues

1 The Lion Tower was built at an earlier date than the south tower, neither being used as the armoury.

2 The servants' quarters are in the Jerusalem Tower, renamed by a returning Crusader, which is next clockwise from the one built in 1080.

3 Rollo's Tower stands at the northernmost point of the castle.

4 The east tower was completed just at the turn of a century.

5 The food store wasn't in the Prince's Tower.

Towers:
Jerusalem; Lion; Prince's; Rollo's

Years:
1080; 1100; 1120; 1140

Original uses:
Armoury; food store; guardhouse; servants' quarters

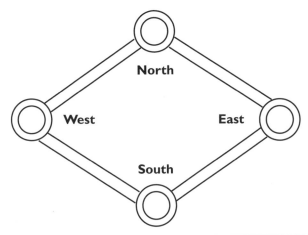

Position	Tower	Year	Original use
North			
East			
South			
West			

Starting tip:

CULTURED CANINES

A TV show devoted to clever pets presented one programme featuring dogs who could perform unusual feats. At the end of the show the four dogs and their owners lined up to take a bow in the positions lettered A to D in the diagram. Can you name the owner and breed of dog depicted in each of positions A to D and say what each dog did? NB Left and right are used throughout from the point of view of the TV audience.

Clues

1 As you look at the picture below, the dancing poodle is somewhere to the left of Katie's pet in the line-up.

2 The dog which walked across the studio floor on its hind legs is further right (as you look at the picture) than the labrador.

3 The dog that sang isn't the one lettered C and isn't owned by Bella.

4 Dog D is shown with his owner Pearl.

5 The samoyed, who appeared first in the show, was given position A in the line.

Owners:
Bella; Katie; Marina; Pearl

Breeds:
Collie; labrador; poodle; samoyed

Feats:
Counted; danced; sang; walked on hind legs

Dog	Owner	Breed	Feat
A			
B			
C			
D			

Starting tip:

Begin by placing the poodle.

GUEST BEERS

Each week our local pub features a guest beer, usually from a small local brewery. Can you discover the identity of last month's five beers - their names (all fictional), their strengths of each in terms of alcohol percentage by volume and the places in which they are brewed?

Clues

1 Black Cock is brewed in Bere Alston; it isn't 4.4% alcohol and it wasn't the guest beer in the week of the 17th.

2 Old Prior is the strongest of the five, but wasn't the first of last month's beers.

3 On the 24th the Malton beer arrived; it had a lower alcohol percentage than Ensign Ale, which we sampled on the 10th.

4 The beer from Ailsworth has 0.3% more alcohol than Castle Keep.

5 The ale from Brewham is lower in alcohol than Warlock.

6 The 4.2% pint was available from the 17th.

	Black Cock	Castle Keep	Ensign Ale	Old Prior	Warlock	4.2%	4.3%	4.4%	4.5%	4.6%	Ailsworth	Bere Alston	Brewham	Hopwood	Malton
3rd															
10th															
17th															
24th															
31st															
Ailsworth										
Bere Alston										
Brewham										
Hopwood										
Malton										
4.2%										
4.3%										
4.4%										
4.5%										
4.6%										

Wk beginning	Beer	% alcohol	Where brewed

POSH PROGENY

At the height of the Edwardian era, four nannies were pushing perambulators around Hyde Park, each pram containing the first-born son of a titled father. Can you name the nanny in charge of each of the prams numbered 1 to 4, name the infant each pram contained and work out his father's rank?

Clues

1 Pram 4 contained the progeny of a mere Baronet.

2 Thelma, whose charge wasn't Peter, wasn't pushing pram 1 and Jennifer's infant wasn't the Viscount's son.

3 Maureen was pushing a pram somewhere behind the one containing Gerald and somewhere ahead of the one transporting the Duke's heir.

4 Horatio's father was a belted Earl.

5 Simon wasn't the child in pram 3.

Nannies:
Clarice; Jennifer; Maureen; Thelma

Children:
Gerald; Horatio; Peter; Simon

Fathers:
Baronet, Duke, Earl; Viscount

Pram	Nanny	Child	Father
1			
2			
3			
4			

Starting tip:

First work out the number of the pram pushed by Maureen.

BATTLESHIPS

This puzzle is based on the old game of battleships. Your task is to find the vessels in the diagram. Some parts of boats or sea squares have already been filled in, and a number next to a row or column refers to the number of occupied squares in that row or column. The boats may be positioned horizontally or vertically, but no two boats or parts of boats are in adjacent squares – horizontally, vertically or diagonally.

Aircraft Carrier:

Battleships:

Cruisers:

Destroyers:

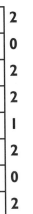

										2
										0
									◖	2
										2
										1
				≈						2
										0
					≈					2
										7
										2
3	1	3	1	0	6	0	2	0	4	

IN BLACK AND WHITE

Laurel and Hardy, Morecambe and Wise, Abbott and Costello, Flanagan and Allen, are names which go together like, say, fish and chips. But, at the height of the Hollywood era in the 1930s, there were other comedy pairings, less well remembered, who adorned the silver screen. Five such couples are featured here. Can you work out the full names of both halves of each pair?

Clues

1 None of the surnames involved form a natural pair, such as fish and chips.

2 Freddie Fortnum was a bright star of the black and white cinema.

3 Dick and Poney were a pair on the screen, though off it they detested each other.

4 Hal Hedges is one of the now forgotten Hollywood stars.

5 Benson wasn't Charlie, whose other half was called Motion, leading to corny posters advertising 'another Motion picture'.

6 Tom and Algy were together throughout the thirties. Algy's surname is listed two places before Sidney's in the alphabetical list.

7 The pairing of Chalk and Trapp didn't include Leslie or Wilbur, nor was Wilbur Leslie's partner on screen.

		1st surname					2nd forename					2nd surname				
		Benson	Chalk	Fortnum	Poney	Time	Algy	Dick	Hal	Sidney	Wilbur	Cheese	Hedges	Mason	Motion	Trapp
1st	Charlie															
	Eddie															
	Freddie															
	Leslie															
	Tom															
2nd	Cheese															
	Hedges															
	Mason															
	Motion															
	Trapp															
2nd	Algy															
	Dick															
	Hal															
	Sidney															
	Wilbur															

First forename	First surname	Second forename	Second surname

PILE UP

These piles of bricks aren't the random results of a child's play but clues to a final, at present blank, pile on the right. Like the rest, that one has six bricks each with a different one of the six letters.

The numbers below the piles tell you two things:

(a) The number of adjacent pairs of bricks in that column which also appear adjacent in the final pile.

(b) The number of adjacent pairs of bricks that make a correct pair but the wrong way up.

So:

would score one in the 'Correct' row if the final pile had an A directly above a C and a one in the 'Reversed' row if the final pile had a C on top of an A. From all this, can you create the final pile before it topples?

Correct	1	1	0	2	5
Reversed	0	1	0	0	0

IN THE YARDS

In the 25th century, the Luna Yards are one of the galaxy's leading starship repairers, able to handle anything from a simple air-leak to a complete rebuild on almost any known type of vessel. The clues below relate to a single day in the year 2467, when there were just five starships in the yards. Can you work out each one's name, type and planet of origin and say for what repair it was in?

Clues

1 The Terran vessel called the Berlin, which had no problem with its engines, wasn't the economy-class spaceliner.

2 Vantikar was a trading ship looking for new markets in the Sol Quadrant.

3 Qazzigo (not from G'Kall) was being decontaminated after encountering a corrosive gas cloud out beyond Centauri.

4 The name of the Styrian freighter has an even number of letters. It wasn't the vessel undergoing repairs after its hull had been breached by a collision.

5 The trampship had been towed in by a starforce cruiser after being discovered drifting in the Asteroid Belt and was having a long-overdue new engine fitted.

6 The starship from Cha-Vis, which wasn't called the Jentiro, was having its forcefield generator replaced.

Starship	Ship type	Planet of origin	Work

EURO SQUARE

Each of the sixteen small squares in the diagram contains one of the numbers 1 to 4 in words, in either English, French, German or Italian, as listed below. Can you write the correct word in each square?

Clues

1 Each of columns A, B, C and D contains a number in each of the four different languages.

2 Quatre is the number in square B2.

3 The number in B1 is double that in D2, both being in the same language.

4 Two is in the horizontal row next to and above that containing both zwei and due.

5 The even number in D3 isn't in French.

6 Tre is next to and right of four and next to and above vier.

7 Quattro is somewhere in column D.

8 The German number in column C is drei; but its right-hand neighbour isn't in German. D1 doesn't contain eins.

9 The number in A4 is one higher than that in A1, though, of course, the language is different.

10 The numbers in D1 and C3 are of the same language, the former being the higher of the two.

English:
One; two;
three; four

French:
Un; deux;
trois; quatre

German:
Eins; zwei;
drei; vier

Italian:
Uno; due;
tre; quattro

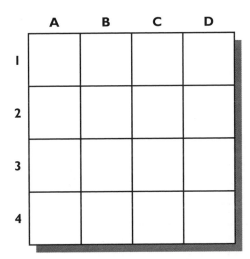

Starting tip:

First identify the number in B1.

BY THE WAY

Will Fixett, an AA patrolman, was called to five different minor breakdowns the other day. Can you name the member whose call he logged at each of the listed times, identify his or her vehicle and say where each breakdown occurred?

Clues

1 The 4.25 breakdown occurred on a major trunk road.

2 The vehicle which broke down on the motorway was the Peugeot; Will's next call after this one wasn't to the Hyundai.

3 Kirsten's call was received some time later than the one from the owner of the Saab, but some time earlier than the one from the member stranded in the drive at home.

4 Ida, whose car isn't the Lada, didn't break down in a city street and Mary didn't make the 3 o'clock call.

5 Philip was in a country lane when his car ground to a halt, but fortunately he had his mobile phone with him; his call wasn't logged at 12.15.

6 The Ford owner was the first member whose breakdown Will attended that day.

	Ida	Kirsten	Mary	Maurice	Philip	Ford	Hyundai	Lada	Peugeot	Saab	City street	Country lane	Home drive	Motorway	Trunk road
10.30															
12.15															
2.10															
3.00															
4.25															
City street											
Country lane											
Home drive											
Motorway											
Trunk road											
Ford						
Hyundai						
Lada						
Peugeot						
Saab						

Call time	Member	Car	Location

DUMPED BY DEBBIE

Debbie went through five boyfriends last year, each one being 'dumped' after approximately two months for various reasons. Can you name the youth whose company was dispensed with in each of the listed months, say what each did for a living and work out why he was given the elbow?

Clues

1 The pig farmer with acute halitosis isn't Alan, who was given his marching orders in the first half of the year.

2 Pete, who was always telling lies, was Debbie's next boyfriend after the teacher.

3 Jonathan wasn't dumped by Debbie in August.

4 Rex, the market trader, was the immediate predecessor of the butcher in Debbie's affections.

5 It was in April that her current boyfriend's irritating tuneless whistle finally became too much for Debbie.

6 The sloppy dresser was Debbie's next boyfriend after getting rid of the youth who was excessively clumsy, though he himself was soon traded in for the salesman.

	Alan	Jonathan	Pete	Rex	Steve	Butcher	Market trader	Pig farmer	Salesman	Teacher	Clumsy	Halitosis	Irritating whistle	Sloppy dresser	Told lies
February															
April															
June															
August															
October															
Clumsy															
Halitosis															
Irritating whistle															
Sloppy dresser															
Told lies															
Butcher															
Market trader															
Pig farmer															
Salesman															
Teacher															

Month	Name	Occupation	Reason

SIGN OF THE TIMES

The diagram shows a page in Samantha's autograph book, which contains the (sadly unrecognisable) signatures of the four members of her favourite pop group, The Skylarks. Can you work out the full name and group rôle of the men whose signatures appear in the positions marked?

Clues

1 Glen's autograph is towards the right-hand side of the page, as you look at it.

2 The signature of Lee, the vocalist, appears directly below Mickey's.

3 The guitarist signed Samantha's book in the position numbered 2.

4 Clyde Knowlson's autograph is diagonally across the page from that of the synthesiser player.

5 Padley's autograph is numbered one lower than that of Darren, who isn't the drummer.

Forenames:
Clyde; Darren; Glen; Mickey

Surnames:
Burrows; Knowlson; Lee; Padley

Rôles:
Drums; guitar; synthesiser; vocals

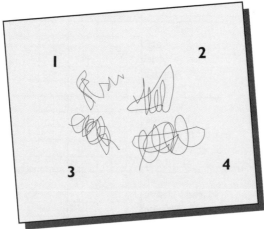

Signature	Forename	Surname	Rôle
1			
2			
3			
4			

Starting tip:

First work out the forename in position 3.

FOUR SEEN

A popular roadside advertising technique for local events is the positioning of a series of small signs each containing a single piece of information, making them easier to read from a moving car. Below are details of five groups of four notices I spotted locally last week – from the information given, can you discover the nature, day, venue and start time of each event?

Clues

1 'Table-top sale', 'Friday', began one sequence, with a start time half an hour after the event at the Crown Inn; 'Monday', 'Manor House', was part of another, starting half an hour before the car boot sale.

2 'Playing field' and '2.00pm', were together on one set of signs but didn't refer to the Sunday event.

3 'Craft fair' wasn't followed by 'Saturday'; the advertised time was before 2.30.

4 The event in the school was advertised as starting after 2 o'clock.

5 The Thursday event started at 2.30.

6 The last sign of the 'Flower festival' sequence advertised the earliest of the five start times.

	Monday	Thursday	Friday	Saturday	Sunday	Crown Inn	Manor House	Playing field	School	Village hall	1.00	1.30	2.00	2.30	3.00
Car boot sale															
Charity auction															
Craft fair															
Flower festival															
Table-top sale															
1.00															
1.30															
2.00															
2.30															
3.00															
Crown Inn															
Manor House															
Playing field															
School															
Village hall															

Event	Day	Venue	Start time

DELIVERY BOY

Ted, a recently retired senior citizen, supplements his income by delivering a free-sheet newspaper around the area where he lives. Can you work out the number of houses in each of the five streets he visits, say in which order he delivers there and work out which of his relatives coincidentally lives in which street?

Clues

1 Browning Street is the second of the five streets on Ted's itinerary.

2 The fourth street to which Ted delivers, which is where his brother lives, has fewer than 100 houses.

3 There are 85 papers to be delivered in Byron Street (not where Ted's cousin lives) which is earlier than Masefield Street on his round.

4 Ted's son lives on the street with the fewest houses, which comes somewhere before Tennyson Street on Ted's round.

5 The street with 107 houses is neither the third nor the fifth on Ted's delivery route.

6 Ted's married daughter lives in Kipling Street, where he delivers immediately after leaving the street with 71 houses.

	46	71	85	107	163	First	Second	Third	Fourth	Fifth	Brother	Cousin	Daughter	Sister	Son
Browning Street															
Byron Street															
Kipling Street															
Masefield Street															
Tennyson Street															
Brother															
Cousin															
Daughter															
Sister															
Son															
First															
Second															
Third															
Fourth															
Fifth															

Street	No of houses	Order	Relative

QUINTUPLE WEDDING

There was an unusual quintuple wedding at the church of St Heloise, Bellingdon, last week, when five friends each married their sisters – no, not their own sisters (that wouldn't be allowed!) but each others' sisters – I'm sure you understand. Can you work out the first name and surname of each groom and the first name and maiden name of his bride?

Clues

1 Mr Vance married the former Miss Dale, daughter of a local doctor.

2 The forename of Mark's bride appears two places after that of the newly married Mrs Addison in the alphabetical list.

3 Angela, née Vance, didn't marry Robin.

4 Ursula, now Mrs Onslow, is the sister of John, whose surname begins with a consonant.

5 Dennis is married to Fiona; the former Miss Addison now married to Bruce isn't Kate.

	Addison	Caxton	Dale	Onslow	Vance	Angela	Fiona	Kate	Paula	Ursula	Addison	Caxton	Dale	Onslow	Vance
Bruce															
Dennis															
John															
Mark															
Robin															
Addison															
Caxton															
Dale															
Onslow															
Vance															
Angela															
Fiona															
Kate															
Paula															
Ursula															

His forename	His surname	Her forename	Her surname

RED, WHITE AND BLUE

Each cell of the square below is coloured either red, white or blue.
Every row, column and each of the two long diagonals of six cells contains
exactly two cells of each colour. The information in each clue refers only
to the cells in that row or column. From the clues below, can you tell the
colour of every cell?

Clues

1 The reds are somewhere between the blues.
2 The whites are adjacent to one another.
3 The whites are somewhere between the reds.
4 The blues are further right than the reds.
5 No two squares of the same colour are adjacent to one another.
6 The blues are somewhere between the whites.

A The blues are adjacent to one another.
B Each white is next to and above a blue.
C No two squares of the same colour are adjacent to one another.
D The whites are somewhere above the reds.
E The whites are somewhere above the blues.
F The reds are somewhere above the whites.

	A	B	C	D	E	F
1						
2						
3						
4						
5						
6						

ON THE DOUBLE

The darts championship at our village pub, the Ring O'Bells, has been won by a different player in each of the last five years. Can you identify each year's champion and work out his occupation?

Clues

1 Matthew Tipp, who wasn't succeeded as champion by Leonard, won the title some time after the village postman.

2 The blacksmith was the Ring O'Bells darts champion the year before Wilfred.

3 The 1998 championship wasn't won by Flyte.

4 Ockey, who farms locally, was champion the year before Arrow.

5 Feather's win came in 1994; his first name isn't Leonard.

6 The doctor was the surprise winner in 1996.

7 Daniel operates a village taxi service.

	Daniel	Jeremy	Leonard	Matthew	Wilfred	Arrow	Feather	Flyte	Ockey	Tipp	Blacksmith	Doctor	Farmer	Postman	Taxi-driver
1994															
1995															
1996															
1997															
1998															
Blacksmith															
Doctor															
Farmer															
Postman															
Taxi-driver															
Arrow															
Feather															
Flyte															
Ockey															
Tipp															

Year	Forename	Surname	Occupation

MEN OF LETTERS

Below are details of five personalised car number plates. From the verse can you discover the registration letter, numbers and personalised letters on each plate and the make of car in each case?

Clues

The Volvo is the property of Philip Arthur Hobbs,
The number on the plate is the next lowest under Bob's.
Bob's car is an E-reg, but the number isn't 6 –
The E car's not a Rover and the Rover isn't Mick's:
Also Michael Johnson isn't in the Audi seen,
Whose reg isn't a vowel but whose number is 16.
The plate that starts R20 isn't fastened to a Merc;
The P-reg car doesn't belong to Derek Ronald Burke.
If 27 TOM begins with A or E
The Ford's reg is a consonant, a J or R or P;
If 27 TOM starts P or R or J
The Ford's reg is a vowel, that's to say an E or A.
Can you now sort out the letters and the numbers too,
To find out what is on each plate and which belongs to who?

NB – To make things crystal clear, the following is a list of people named in the verse and the car registration part to which they refer: Philip Arthur Hobbs, PAH; Bob, BOB; Michael 'Mick' Johnson, MPJ; Derek Ronald Burke, DRB.

	6	10	16	20	27	BOB	DRB	MPJ	PAH	TOM	Audi	Ford	Mercedes	Rover	Volvo
A															
E															
J															
P															
R															

Reg letter	Number	Letters	Make of car

HOME IMPROVEMENTS

A family consisting of a father, mother and teenage son and daughter were all agreed that there were six obvious ways in which their home could be improved. At a family conference each was asked to list these six improvements in order of priority and your task, from the clues given below, is to place the six in their correct positions on each of the four lists.

Clues

1 No item appeared in the same position on more than one list.

2 Father's top priority was a patio, though this was rated number 6 by another member of the family, whose third choice was the stereo system.

3 The son placed decorating the lounge higher than did his sister, but it wasn't the top item on his list, which was rated number 6 by his mother.

4 The son also rated the dining table as a higher priority than the stereo system, while his mother placed it in an even higher position.

5 Mother placed the stereo system fourth; she considered decorating the lounge as a more pressing improvement.

6 One male member of the family placed the new stair-carpet second, while the other rated it fourth.

7 The daughter only placed the stair-carpet third.

8 Mother's third choice was her daughter's fifth.

9 Father deemed the stereo system more urgent than the dining table, but he thought the kitchen bar less important than decorating the lounge.

Improvements: Decorating the lounge, dining table, kitchen bar, patio, stair-carpet, stereo system

	Father	Mother	Son	Daughter
First				
Second				
Third				
Fourth				
Fifth				
Sixth				

LADDIES FROM LANCASHIRE

Five brothers brought up in a Lancashire village in the 1930s each had a particular food preference and each grew up to follow a different local football team. Can you place them in their correct order in the family and work out each lad's culinary and sporting preference?

Clues

1 The youngest lad caused some concern in the family when he developed an unnatural taste for the pudding named after the rival county of Yorkshire; he didn't support Oldham Athletic.

2 Stanley, who by rights should have supported Accrington, chose Blackburn Rovers as his favourite team.

3 Frank, the black pudding addict, was immediately senior in the family to the Manchester City fan.

4 The Burnley supporter rated hotpot his top culinary item, while tripe wasn't the favourite dish of the second brother.

5 Henry was the fourth of the five brothers.

6 James didn't support either of the Manchester teams, though both his immediate senior and his immediate junior in the family did.

	Albert	Frank	Henry	James	Stanley	Black pudding	Fish and chips	Hotpot	Tripe	Yorkshire pudding	Blackburn Rovers	Burnley	Manchester City	Manchester United	Oldham Athletic
Eldest															
Second															
Third															
Fourth															
Youngest															
B'burn Rovers															
Burnley															
Man City															
Man United															
Oldham Ath															
Black pudding															
Fish and chips															
Hotpot															
Tripe															
Yorks pudding															

Family order	Name	Food	Team

THE LULU WARS

The Southshire Fusiliers spent five years fighting the Lulu tribe in Lululand and during that time five members of the regiment were decorated for valour. Can you work out the name and rank of each fearless Fusilier and where and when he won his medal?

Clues

1 The Battle of Beacon Hill wasn't in 1879, nor was it the year after Edgar Fidler earned his award.

2 The man decorated at the Battle of Quirk's Drift in 1882 wasn't Albert Buggins.

3 It was in 1881 that the Corporal won his decoration.

4 The battle for which Joseph Kneebone got his medal was earlier than the one at Blackoak Swamp.

5 The Lieutenant was decorated later than the Sergeant who won his medal at the battle of Swan's Creek.

6 Edgar Fidler's rank was Fusilier, equivalent to Private in a normal infantry regiment; he was decorated in an odd-numbered year.

7 The Lance-Corporal, who won his medal in the Eighties, wasn't Oscar Portwine, known as 'the hero of Kingstown'.

	Corporal	Fusilier	Lance-Corporal	Lieutenant	Sergeant	Beacon Hill	Blackoak Swamp	Kingstown	Quirk's Drift	Swan's Creek	1878	1879	1880	1881	1882
Albert Buggins															
Edgar Fidler															
Joseph Kneebone															
Oscar Portwine															
Sidney Tonkin															
1878															
1879															
1880															
1881															
1882															
Beacon Hill															
Blackoak Swamp															
Kingstown															
Quirk's Drift															
Swan's Creek															

Name	Rank	Battle	Year

WHOSE COUP?

In the middle years of the century the South American republic of Eldorado was ruled by a succession of military dictators. Can you work out the rank and full identity of the man who seized power in each of the listed years?

Clues

1 General Pasodoble led a successful coup to unseat the President named Pablo.

2 President Flamenco's term of office immediately preceded that of the Admiral.

3 The Field-Marshal seized power in the Revolution of 1961.

4 Ricardo Maracas wasn't an Admiral of any kind.

5 The leader of the 1952 coup was Ronaldo.

6 The Air-Marshal's first name was Enrico; he didn't declare himself President and Father of the Nation in 1954.

7 President Bossanova's rank wasn't Vice-Admiral.

	Admiral	Air-Marshal	Field-Marshal	General	Vice-Admiral	Arturo	Enrico	Pablo	Ricardo	Ronaldo	Bolero	Bossanova	Flamenco	Maracas	Pasodoble
1940															
1947															
1952															
1954															
1961															
Bolero															
Bossanova															
Flamenco															
Maracas															
Pasodoble															
Arturo															
Enrico															
Pablo															
Ricardo															
Ronaldo															

Year	Rank	Forename	Surname

ROLLIN', ROLLIN', ROLLIN'

If you should visit the leisure park at Little Trembling, Herts and you are tempted to go on the Monster Roller-Coaster, you will be hurtled over four tracks, each with different maximum heights and lengths. Can you enter in the table below the statistics of each track and the time it takes to complete each one?

Clues

1 The track with the lowest maximum height is neither the shortest in length nor the one which takes the least time.

2 The track which riders face second is higher than the third but not as long; neither of them takes exactly 55 seconds.

3 The fourth track takes less time than the first and isn't as long; the track which takes 60 seconds is both lower in height and shorter than the one which takes 55 seconds.

4 The 1500-yard track takes five seconds less than the 1600 and has a lower maximum height; the one with a maximum height of 190 feet is shorter than the 200-feet one but takes longer to complete.

5 The track which takes least time is a later one and shorter in length than that with the greatest maximum height.

Maximum heights:
170 feet; 190 feet; 200 feet; 220 feet

Lengths:
1400 yards; 1500 yards; 1600 yards; 1800 yards

Times:
50 seconds; 55 seconds; 60 seconds; 65 seconds

	Max height	Length	Time
First			
Second			
Third			
Fourth			

Starting tip:
Work out which maximum height corresponds to the time of 50 seconds.

HAPPY LANDING?

Five soldiers recently had their initiation into parachuting. Can you work out the order in which they jumped, the colour of each one's canopy and the place where each landed?

Clues

1 Lynagh jumped immediately after the man who landed in the silage pit and immediately before the one who had the green canopy.

2 The man who dropped on to the church roof had a single-coloured canopy, like Roope (who jumped later than him) but unlike Cordleigh, who jumped two places earlier than the man who fell on the church roof.

3 Neither Fell, the first man to jump (who is Fell's brother-in-law) nor the one who jumped immediately after Fell (and got himself impaled in the hedge) was the one with the blue and white canopy (who jumped next after the chap who finished up in the village pond).

4 There was the same number of jumpers (at least one) between Packer and the man with the orange canopy (who jumped in that order) as there was between the man who landed on the glasshouse and the one who had the white canopy (who also jumped in that order).

	Cordleigh	Fell	Lynagh	Packer	Roope	Blue and white	Green	Orange	Red and white	White	Church roof	Glasshouse	Hawthorn hedge	Silage pit	Village pond
First															
Second															
Third															
Fourth															
Fifth															
Church roof															
Glasshouse															
Hawthorn															
Silage pit															
Village pond															
Blue and white															
Green															
Orange															
Red and white															
White															

Order	Name	Canopy colour	Landing place

SUMMIT'S UP

The Apresh Climbing Club recently spent a week in the Fort William area, attempting six different peaks. Can you work out which peak was attempted on each of the days and how many climbers dropped out from each attempt?

Clues

1 Two more dropped out of the climb of Stob Coire Eassain than on Thursday. Two fewer dropped out on Saturday than on the climb up Stob Choire Claurigh. Neither Stob Coire Eassain nor Stob Choire Claurigh had a drop-out of 20.

2 The Tuesday drop-out number was next above that from the ascent of Aonach Moir. Neither the Tuesday ascent, nor the climb of Ben Nevis had the largest drop-out.

3 Friday's drop-out was two more than on the climb of Aonach Beag, but two fewer than on the climb of Binnein Moir.

4 The combined drop-out from the Wednesday climb and that of Aonach Beag was the same as the combined drop-out from the Tuesday climb and that of Stob Choire Claurigh; these are four different climbs.

Peaks:
Aonach Beag; Aonach Moir;
Ben Nevis; Binnein Moir;
Stob Choire Claurigh;
Stob Coire Eassain

Numbers of drop-outs:
8; 10; 12; 16; 18; 20

Day	Peak	Drop-outs

Starting tip:
Work out which climb had the highest number of drop-outs.

BATTLESHIPS

This puzzle is based on the old game of battleships. Your task is to find the vessels in the diagram. Some parts of boats or sea squares have already been filled in, and a number next to a row or column refers to the number of occupied squares in that row or column. The boats may be positioned horizontally or vertically, but no two boats or parts of boats are in adjacent squares – horizontally, vertically or diagonally.

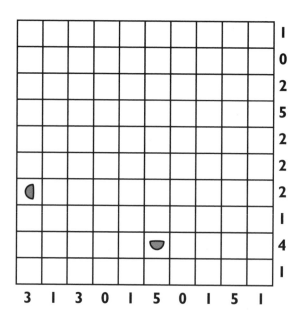

Aircraft Carrier:

Battleships:

Cruisers:

Destroyers:

STAND AND DELIVER

In the summer of 1938 a newspaper advertised by sending a chap under the name of Luddy Lobb round various seaside resorts where the first person to identify and challenge him correctly while producing a copy of the paper would win a crisp white £5 note. One week he was correctly challenged on six consecutive days at the resorts shown in the diagram. For each resort, can you state the day and time of the challenge there?

Clues

1 The place where he was spotted on Thursday is further east than the one where someone won £5 on Saturday.

2 The challenge at Eastbourne was more than a day later in the week but more than an hour earlier in the day than the one at Worthing.

3 The Monday challenge was at the resort next east to the one where he was challenged at 12.50 and next west to the one where he was confronted at 10.45.

4 The Wednesday sighting was neither at Folkestone nor at 4.40.

5 A holidaymaker at Hastings identified Luddy Lobb two days earlier in the week and more than one hour earlier in the day than another one did at Bognor.

6 The Tuesday challenge was at a time next but one after that at Bognor.

7 The resort where he was challenged at 4.00 is next west to the one where he was spotted at 12.50 one day later; neither of these incidents was at Worthing.

Days:
Monday; Tuesday; Wednesday; Thursday; Friday; Saturday

Times:
10.45; 11.15; 12.50; 3.05; 4.00; 4.40

Resort	Day	Time

Starting tip:

First work out in which resort the 4.00 challenge took place.

CONCERTED EFFORT

Three Italian composers whose works are rarely heard these days each wrote a different number of symphonies and a different number of concertos. Can you identify them and say how many of each type of work each man produced?

Clues

1 Benedetto wrote more symphonies, but fewer concertos, than Evilorri.

2 Domenico was the composer of nine concertos.

3 The man who wrote four symphonies composed ten concertos.

4 Verrisorri wrote more concertos than the man who wrote only three symphonies.

	Evilorri	Merziferri	Verrisorri	3 symphonies	4 symphonies	5 symphonies	8 concertos	9 concertos	10 concertos
Benedetto									
Domenico									
Pietro									
8 concertos									
9 concertos									
10 concertos									
3 symphonies									
4 symphonies									
5 symphonies									

Forename	Surname	Symphonies	Concertos

HAND OVER

Three young people have been knocking on the doors of residents of Lower Mandible this week seeking sponsorship for activities they are pursuing for various causes. Can you work out the full names of the young people, the activity each is undertaking and the cause for which they are raising money?

Clues

1 Mark, whose surname isn't Smith, is hoping to record a decent time in the Netherlipp marathon.

2 Dan Parker's good cause isn't the heart scanner.

3 Melanie (who doesn't play the guitar) hopes to collect money for sports equipment for her school.

	Jameson	Parker	Smith	Marathon run	Playing guitar	Swimming	Heart scanner	Sports equipment	Village hall
Dan									
Mark									
Melanie									
Heart scanner									
Sports equipment									
Village hall									
Marathon run									
Playing guitar									
Swimming									

Forename	Surname	Activity	Cause

BROADLY DISASTROUS

Puddock's Boats, who hire out motor cruisers on the Norfolk Broads, are used to receiving phone calls from boaters in trouble, but four problems reported the other day were a little – well, unusual. Can you work out the name of each boat, the name of the family that had hired it, where they had their problem and what – allegedly – occurred?

Clues

1 The cruiser which was apparently struck by lightning – out of a clear blue sky – while crossing Holton Broad was neither the Sardine (one of Puddock's smaller craft) nor the vessel which is two years older than the Sardine and which was hired by the Hawkins family.

2 The Prawn, hired by the Grenvilles, was neither the cruiser which got into trouble on the River Dure nor the one allegedly attacked by a submarine in less than five feet of water (which wasn't on the River Dure).

3 The Raleighs' boat, which they claimed had struck an iceberg, was neither the Haddock nor the cruiser which had a problem on Salthouse Broad; and neither of these latter two vessels was reported to have been boarded by pirates.

	Drake	Grenville	Hawkins	Raleigh	Holton Broad	River Dure	River Ent	Salthouse Broad	Attacked by submarine	Boarded by pirates	Hit iceberg	Struck by lightning
Dugong												
Haddock												
Prawn												
Sardine												
Attacked by sub												
Boarded/pirates												
Hit iceberg												
Struck/lightning												
Holton Broad												
River Dure												
River Ent												
Salthouse Broad												

Boat	Family	Location	Problem

SOCCER IT TO HER

Nancy Nette, regular goalie for the Queen's Head women's football team in Northchester, is on maternity leave and various other team members are having to fill in for her. Last month, there was a different woman keeping goal every week. From the clues below, can you work out who played in goal each week, what rôle she normally fills in the team and why she refused to play in goal ever again?

Clues

1 Midfielder Peggy Pools and the woman who usually plays as a striker took on the goalkeeper's rôle more than eight days apart.

2 The player who was used to defending the goal as a back took on the between-the-posts position two weeks before the woman who refused to be keeper a second time because she got a mouthful of mud while making a spectacular dive on a very wet day.

3 Beryl Boote got a black eye when she played as keeper – somebody's elbow caught her during a goalmouth scrimmage – and graciously declined the opportunity to sustain further damage.

4 The goalie on the 10th was neither the team's physiotherapist nor the woman who sprained her ankle, who wasn't Mitzi Match.

5 The woman who was in goal on the 24th broke a finger saving a shot and understandably, was reluctant to play there again.

	Beryl Boote	Gerty Ground	Mitzi Match	Peggy Pools	Back	Midfielder	Physiotherapist	Striker	Black eye	Broken finger	Mouthful of mud	Sprained ankle
3rd												
10th												
17th												
24th												
Black eye												
Broken finger												
Mouthful of mud												
Sprained ankle												
Back												
Midfielder												
Physiotherapist												
Striker												

Date	Player	Usual rôle	Problem

FINAL STAGES

At the close of this year's season, four stalwart members of Brightbourne's Pier Theatre Players will be retiring from the stage. From the clues below, can you work out each man's full name, what kind of performer he is and for how many summers he's been appearing at the Pier Theatre?

Clues

1 Mr Friday has been performing at the Pier Theatre for more than 24 years.

2 Clive is a magician, performing under the name of The Amazing Marvo.

3 The first name of the comedian surnamed Raye appears in the alphabetical list immediately after that of the man who's spent the last 28 summers at the Pier Theatre.

4 The pianist hasn't been a Pier Theatre Player as long as Andy Murphy.

5 Mr Joplin has been a regular at the Pier Theatre for the last 30 years.

	Friday	Joplin	Murphy	Raye	Comedian	Impressionist	Magician	Pianist	24 years	26 years	28 years	30 years
Andy												
Bill												
Clive												
Dick												
24 years												
26 years												
28 years												
30 years												
Comedian												
Impressionist												
Magician												
Pianist												

Forename	Surname	Act	Years

ROUND TABLE

The drawing below shows the round table at which representatives of four South American republics are discussing which of them should be given the disputed Campo du Patates region. Can you work out the title and name of each man at the table and say which country he represents?

Clues

1 The representative of the Republic of San Guinari, who isn't the General, is seated immediately clockwise from the man surnamed Gomez.

2 The man from Cafeteria – guess their main export! – is occupying seat D.

3 The Doctor representing Los Perros, who is acting as host for the talks, isn't in seat B.

4 Admiral Ruiz is seated directly opposite the delegate from the Democratic Republic of Bananaria.

5 The man called Torres occupies the seat marked A.

Titles:
Admiral; Doctor; General; Vice-President

Surnames:
Gomez; Mendoza; Ruiz; Torres

Republics:
Bananaria; Cafeteria; Los Perros; San Guinari

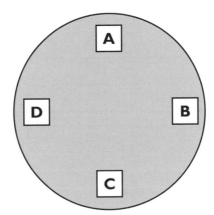

Seat	Title	Surname	Republic
A			
B			
C			
D			

Starting tip:

Work out from which Republic the man in seat B comes.

LOGI-PATH

Use your deductive reasoning to form a pathway from the box marked 'START' to the box marked 'FINISH', moving either horizontally or vertically (but not diagonally) from square to adjacent square. The number at the beginning of every row or column indicates exactly how many boxes in that row or column your pathway must pass through. The small diagram at the bottom of the page is given as an example of how it works.

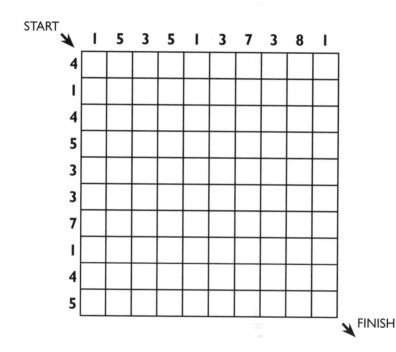

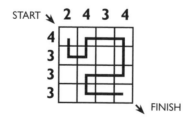

PILE UP

These piles of bricks aren't the random results of a child's play but clues to a final, at present blank, pile on the right. Like the rest, that one has six bricks each with a different one of the six letters.

The numbers below the piles tell you two things:

(a) The number of adjacent pairs of bricks in that column which also appear adjacent in the final pile.

(b) The number of adjacent pairs of bricks that make a correct pair but the wrong way up.

So:

would score one in the 'Correct' row if the final pile had an A directly above a C and a one in the 'Reversed' row if the final pile had a C on top of an A. From all this, can you create the final pile before it topples?

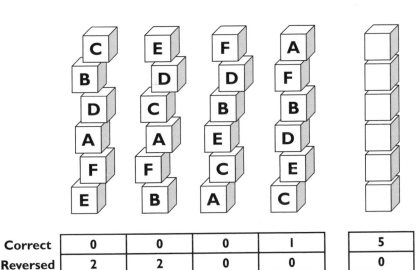

Correct	0	0	0	I		5
Reversed	2	2	0	0		0

GHOST STORIES

Five sports stars have recently published 'autobiographies' which were, in fact, entirely written by ghost writers. Can you match the stars with their sports and work out the full names of the authors who ghosted their life stories?

Clues

1 Olympic runner Gemma Crichton employed a male ghost writer, whose surname wasn't Scott.

2 Welsh took on the task of describing the soccer star's chequered career.

3 Graham wrote the rugby player's best-selling life story.

4 Christine Pearce didn't collaborate with the recently-retired snooker player.

5 Donald Fenton wasn't a boxer and his life story wasn't written by Laura.

6 Edwin wrote the autobiography of Carl Morrison.

7 Hardy was the surname of Fergus McKay's alter ego.

	Athletics	Boxing	Rugby	Snooker	Soccer	Christine	Edwin	Graham	Laura	Maurice	Green	Hardy	Pearce	Scott	Welsh
Carl Morrison															
Donald Fenton															
Fergus McKay															
Garry Rumbold															
Gemma Crichton															
Green															
Hardy															
Pearce															
Scott															
Welsh															
Christine															
Edwin															
Graham															
Laura															
Maurice															

Star	Sport	Forename	Surname

DRUNK AND DISORDERLY

One day in 1889 five cowboys found themselves in court in the Wild West town of Painted Rock, charged with being drunk and disorderly after a fight at the Silver Dollar Saloon the night before. Can you work out the full name of each man, the ranch for which he worked and to how many days in jail he was sentenced when it turned out he'd no money to pay a fine?

Clues

1 Barney Cooper was the first of the five rather battered and woebegone men to be sentenced.

2 Wayne was a tophand rider for the Rocking Chair ranch.

3 The Sabre ranch cowhand had been Christened Randolph, but was always known in Painted Rock as Randy.

4 The man from the Bar 7 ranch was sentenced to 7 days in jail; the Pitchfork cowboy was given a sentence two days shorter than Wolfie's.

5 The man known as Preacher got the longest sentence; he didn't work for the Lazy K.

6 Eastwood went to jail for 5 days; Gus had to serve one day less than Stewart.

	Cooper	Eastwood	McCrea	Stewart	Wayne	Bar 7	Lazy K	Pitchfork	Rocking Chair	Sabre	3 days	4 days	5 days	7 days	8 days
Barney															
Gus															
Preacher															
Randy															
Wolfie															
3 days															
4 days															
5 days															
7 days															
8 days															
Bar 7															
Lazy K															
Pitchfork															
Rocking Chair															
Sabre															

Forename	Surname	Ranch	Sentence

MISTRESSES IN RETIREMENT

A recent issue of a magazine for the more mature person carried an article about five retired schoolmistresses, all spinsters and the hobbies they have taken up since finishing work. Can you work out each woman's full name, where she lives and what she does as a hobby?

Clues

1 Cynthia lives in a cottage in Suffolk, while Miss Dyer has a house on the edge of the Yorkshire moors.

2 Miss Leach's forename isn't Violet and the retired teacher who writes historical novels doesn't live in West London.

3 Agatha has a six-letter surname, unlike the mistress who has become an enthusiastic gardener since retirement.

4 Miss Polton, who has built up quite a reputation as an amateur detective, doesn't live in London.

5 Judith has become a keen and expert angler since giving up teaching.

6 Phyllis Hickes isn't the mistress from Cheshire who has taken up water-colour painting.

	Dyer	Hickes	Leach	Polton	Sealey	Cheshire	South London	Suffolk	West London	Yorkshire	Amateur detective	Angler	Gardener	Novelist	Painter
Agatha															
Cynthia															
Judith															
Phyllis															
Violet															
Amateur det															
Angler															
Gardener															
Novelist															
Painter															
Cheshire															
South London															
Suffolk															
West London															
Yorkshire															

Forename	Surname	Location	Hobby

ALL OF A TWIST

When a new TV production of *Oliver Twist* was announced, five of the actors chosen for various adult parts were already familiar to viewers as regular characters in different television soaps. Can you work out the full name of the thespian chosen for each of the five featured rôles and say in which soap he or she normally appears?

Clues

1 Jemima, who, of course, is to play Nancy, isn't Richie, the Thameside regular.

2 Fraser Hewson, whose rôle will not be Fagin, has never appeared in Denverdale.

3 Parker was delighted when he received his invitation to appear in the new version of Oliver Twist.

4 Brian has a large following among fans of the 60s police soap Pulse.

5 Nelson's character in the new serial will be Mr Brownlow.

6 Fagin will be played by the star on temporary loan from Northenders, whose first name isn't James.

7 The star from Jubilee Terrace has not been booked to play Bill Sikes.

	Brian	Fraser	James	Jemima	Leslie	Drake	Hewson	Nelson	Parker	Richie	Denverdale	Jubilee Terrace	Northenders	Pulse	Thameside
Bill Sikes															
Bumble															
Fagin															
Mr Brownlow															
Nancy															
Denverdale															
Jubilee Terrace															
Northenders															
Pulse															
Thameside															
Drake															
Hewson															
Nelson															
Parker															
Richie															

Character	Forename	Surname	Soap

NAMES ON THE STREET

The town centre has been enhanced by commercial sponsorship of various amenities in the pedestrianised High Street. From the following details, can you work out how many of which item each company has sponsored and each company's sphere of activity?

Clues

1 Goldway has sponsored the hanging baskets; there are two fewer of these than the item that carries Premier's name.

2 The Midland and Northern Bank hasn't sponsored the trees; there are fewer flower-beds, sponsored by the garden centre, than there are trees.

3 Horton's has sponsored eight items.

4 The 15 benches don't carry the supermarket's name.

5 The chemist has sponsored 13 items.

6 There are not nine litter bins in the scheme.

	Benches	Flower-beds	Hanging baskets	Litter bins	Trees	Goldway	Horton's	Midland & Northern	Premier	Williams'	Bank	Chemist	Estate agents	Garden centre	Supermarket
6															
8															
9															
13															
15															
Bank															
Chemist															
Estate agents															
Garden centre															
Supermarket															
Goldway															
Horton's															
Midland/Northern															
Premier															
Williams'															

Quantity	Item	Company	Activity

GETTING TO GRIPS

There were five wrestling bouts at the Drill Hall last weekend. From the following information, can you discover the order of the bouts, the two wrestlers taking part and the number of rounds each bout lasted?

Clues

1 The first bout lasted four rounds.

2 The second bout lasted longer than the third one.

3 John Bull participated in the fourth bout, but not against King Kong, who took part in either the longest or shortest bout.

4 Mountain Rhodes was in the fifth bout.

5 Sid Samson's fight went to three rounds.

6 The fight between Iron Bloch and Mighty Mammoth lasted only half as many rounds as Mick Magog and his opponent, who wasn't Rocky Cliffe.

	Iron Bloch	King Kong	Mick Magog	Mountain Rhodes	The Bruiser	Hercules Hammond	John Bull	Mighty Mammoth	Rocky Cliffe	Sid Samson	Two rounds	Three rounds	Four rounds	Six rounds	Seven rounds
1															
2															
3															
4															
5															
Two rounds															
Three rounds															
Four rounds															
Six rounds															
Seven rounds															
Hercules Hammond															
John Bull															
Mighty Mammoth															
Rocky Cliffe															
Sid Samson															

Bout No	First	Second	No of rounds

DOMINO SEARCH

A standard set of dominoes has been laid out, using numbers instead of dots for clarity. With the aid of a sharp pencil and a keen brain, can you draw in the lines to show where each domino has been placed? You may find the check grid useful – crossing off each domino as you find it.

1	5	2	4	1	4	3	3
4	6	5	5	4	0	1	3
0	0	0	6	6	5	1	1
3	4	3	6	6	2	2	2
4	5	2	1	1	3	0	0
0	5	3	2	2	4	4	6
3	6	5	2	1	0	6	5

0							
1							
2							
3							
4							
5							
6							
	0	1	2	3	4	5	6

THE WORKS TEAM

The picture shows the two cars entered for this year's Melans 24-hour Motor Race by Cheetah Cars Ltd, each with the three drivers who will be taking turns at its wheel. Can you work out the full name of each driver and the colour or colours of his crash-helmet?

Clues

1 Figure 4 is wearing a gold and white helmet.

2 Marco Donesi, the Italian driver, is indicated by a number two higher than that marking the man in the black helmet; they will not be driving the same Cheetah Supersports in the race.

3 Gill, whose helmet is green, isn't figure 3. Hammett is indicated by an odd number which is higher than the number of Brewer.

4 Owen and the man in the blue and red helmet are members of the same car's crew.

5 The silver-helmeted driver, who is indicated by an even number, isn't Scott, who isn't figure 2, whose surname is Rowles.

6 Barry is figure 5 in the picture.

7 Geoff, whose helmet is fluorescent orange, will be sharing a drive with Tom.

Forenames:
Barry; Geoff; Jack; Marco; Tom; Scott

Surnames:
Brewer; Donesi; Gill; Hammett; Owen; Rowles

Helmet colours:
Black; blue/red; gold/white; green; orange; silver

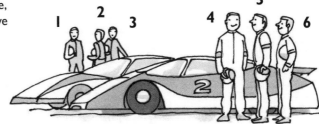

Number	Forename	Surname	Helmet
1			
2			
3			
4			
5			
6			

Starting tip:

BRONZED FIGURES

In the early years of this century five statues of local worthies were erected in the city centre. Can you discover who is commemorated by the statues erected in each year, his or her field of distinction and the location of his or her statue?

Clues

1 The statue to the distinguished local actor was erected outside the Royal Theatre; the figure isn't Sir George Turner and the year wasn't 1920.

2 The first of the five statues was set up on Market Hill; neither it nor the 1910 statue commemorates the author.

3 The statue to the MP is of more recent date than that to Lady Parry in Castle Square.

4 The effigy of Sir Henry Hunt was erected ten years after the statue in the churchyard.

5 The statue of the social reformer dates from 1907.

6 Major Ingleman found fame as a soldier.

	Edward Sherman	Lady Parry	Major Ingleman	Sir George Turner	Sir Henry Hunt	Actor	Author	MP	Social reformer	Soldier	Castle Square	Churchyard	Elmwood Park	Market Hill	Royal Theatre
1905															
1907															
1910															
1915															
1920															
Castle Square															
Churchyard															
Elmwood Park															
Market Hill															
Royal Theatre															
Actor															
Author															
MP															
Social reformer															
Soldier															

Date	Subject	Field	Location

A DATE WITH DESTINY

The diagram shows four fighting ships sailing off to fight the Spanish Armada. Can you name each of the vessels lettered A to D and fully identify her captain?

Clues

1 Collingham is master of the Corsair, which doesn't occupy position B in the flotilla.

2 Denzil's ship is next in line astern of Trueman's and immediately ahead of the Medusa.

3 Amethyst isn't leading the flotilla and she isn't captained by Rackham.

4 Francis is the captain of ship C, but Luke isn't in command of the Flamingo.

Ships:
Amethyst; Corsair; Flamingo; Medusa

Captains:
Denzil; Francis; Luke; Walter

Surnames:
Collingham; Rackham; Trueman; Wakefield

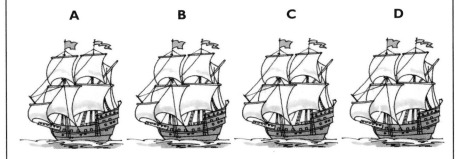

A   B   C   D

Ship	Ship's name	Captain	Surname

Starting tip:

Begin by working out which ship is Denzil's.

BROLLY BRIGADE

Five Allied airmen were shot down at various stages of the Second World War, but fortunately all were able to survive by using their parachutes. Can you match each flyer with the month and year of his unlucky flight and the location where he was shot down?

Clues

1 The pilot shot down in 1944 was flying over Holland at the time.

2 There was a three-year gap between the May incident and the one which took place over the English Channel.

3 Colin, who baled out over Vichy France, did so in a later month of a later year than the man who was shot down in 1941.

4 Desmond's war ended the year after another flyer was forced to eject over Northern France, which wasn't in 1940.

5 Sandy's plane came to grief in 1943, but not in February.

6 It was on a dark November night that Edwin's plane was hit.

7 June was the month when one man had to take to his parachute over Germany.

	February	May	June	October	November	1940	1941	1942	1943	1944	English Channel	Germany	Holland	Northern France	Vichy France
Colin															
Desmond															
Edwin															
Robert															
Sandy															
English Channel															
Germany															
Holland															
N France															
Vichy France															
1940															
1941															
1942															
1943															
1944															

Name	Month	Year	Location

TIMECHECK

Five women who each had an appointment to keep at 10.30 all used a different method of checking the time as the deadline approached. Can you match each woman with her appointment, work out the exact time when each carried out her check and say which method she used?

Clues

1 The teletext was used by the woman expecting a visitor at 10.30 prompt.

2 Janice checked the time at 10.29.

3 Delphine had the 10.30 appointment at the dentist's. She checked the time nearer to 10.30 than did Morag.

4 The grandfather clock showed exactly 10.25 when it was consulted.

5 The woman who checked the time on her wrist-watch did so two minutes before the one (not Janice) with the business appointment.

6 Penelope used her mobile phone to consult the speaking clock.

7 The woman hoping to catch the 10.30 train, who wasn't Eunice, carried out her time check at 10.26.

	Business appt	Bus to catch	Dental appointment	Expecting visitor	Train to catch	10.25	10.26	10.27	10.28	10.29	Grandfather clock	Mobile phone	Teletext	Town Hall clock	Wrist-watch
Delphine															
Eunice															
Janice															
Morag															
Penelope															
G'father clock															
Mobile phone															
Teletext															
Town Hall clock															
Wrist-watch															
10.25															
10.26															
10.27															
10.28															
10.29															

Name	Appointment	Time	Consulted

SOLUTIONS

Hair Line (No 1)

Frances works at The Hairport (clue 2). Joy Bunn, who isn't employed at Marcel's (clue 1), is the assistant at Making Waves, aged 19 (clue 3). Thus Bianca works at Marcel's and (clue 1) is 18, so Frances is 20. Her surname isn't Fringe (clue 2), so Curleigh. Bianca's is Fringe.

In summary:

Bianca Fringe, Marcel's, 18.
Frances Curleigh, The Hairport, 20.
Joy Bunn, Making Waves, 19.

The Gentle Sex (No 2)

Lila Kreiks works in Chicago (clue 4). Dilly Frith's city isn't Sheffield (clue 2), so Dublin and Karel Blayne's is Sheffield. Since Dilly Frith operates in Dublin, she isn't in the novel by Jane Shorrocks (clue 1) and as she's also not Melanie Pierce's investigator (clue 2), she appears in Penelope Gunn's book, Nowhere To Hide (clue 3). She Had To Pay doesn't feature Lila Kreiks (clue 4), so Karel Blayne and Lila Kreiks investigates the crime in Deadly Desire. The author of this book isn't Melanie Pierce (clue 2), so Jane Shorrocks. Melanie Pierce wrote She Had To Pay.

In summary:

Jane Shorrocks, Deadly Desire, Lila Kreiks, Chicago.
Melanie Pierce, She Had To Pay, Karel Blayne, Sheffield.
Penelope Gunn, Nowhere To Hide, Dilly Frith, Dublin.

A Hair of Difference (No 3)

The witness who said the thief's hair was shoulder-length didn't say he'd a goatee beard or a heavy moustache (clue 2), nor that he was clean shaven (clue 1), so said he'd a full beard. The painter didn't say he had a goatee beard or heavy moustache (clue 2), so described him as clean shaven and bald on top (clue 1). The passer-by, who said the thief's hair was greying, didn't say he had a full beard (clue 3) and the witness who said he had a goatee beard thought his hair was dark brown (clue 2), so the passer-by thought the thief had a heavy moustache; but not short hair (clue 3), so receding. The one who said the thief's hair was fair isn't the painter or shopkeeper (clue 1), so the customer. Thus the shopkeeper said he had dark brown hair and the painter said it was red brown. By elimination, the customer said he had a full beard and the shopkeeper said he had short hair.

In summary:

Customer, fair, shoulder-length, full beard.
Painter, red brown, bald on top, clean shaven.
Passer-by, greying, receding, heavy moustache.
Shopkeeper, dark brown, cut short, goatee beard.

Poppins-pourri (No 4)

George and Phoebe are brother and sister (clue 7). Oliver Carson (clue 5) is the brother of Alicia (clue 1). The Bagstock girl isn't Sarah (clue 3) or Phoebe (clue 7), so Ethel. Maud Potiphar looked after Ralph (clue 4) and Mavis Pomfret worked for the Dugdales (clue 6). The Carsons' nanny wasn't Martha Poggins (clue 2), so Mabel Ponsonby. George and Phoebe were the Alwyns' children (clue 7). By elimination, the Dugdales' daughter was Sarah and (clue 1) Ralph was Ethel's brother. Thus Sarah's brother was Henry and the Alwyns' nanny was Martha Poggins.

In summary:

Alwyns, George, Phoebe, Martha Poggins.
Bagstocks, Ralph, Ethel, Maud Potiphar.
Carsons, Oliver, Alicia, Mabel Ponsonby.
Dugdales, Henry, Sarah, Mavis Pomfret.

Gone Fishin' (No 5)

The man who caught one fish had his car stolen (clue 2). Three fish were caught at Bull's Bridge (clue 5), so (clue 1) Sam, who was bitten by a dog, caught no fish and the man who went to Mill Reach caught one fish. Chick fished at Jack's Island (clue 3), so Sam at The Pits. By elimination, Chick caught two fish. The man who caught three wasn't Keith (clue 5), so Percy and Keith caught one. Chick lost his rod (clue 4), so Percy fell in the river.

In summary:

Chick, Jack's Island, two, lost rod.
Keith, Mill Reach, one, car stolen.
Percy, Bull's Bridge, three, fell in river.
Sam, The Pits, none, bitten by dog.

Record Holders (No 6)

Bridge Over The Mersey came out in 1965 (clue 1). Far Side Of The Planet by Peter's Pilgrims wasn't released in 1966 (clue 4). The 1966 release wasn't Hearsay (clue 2), so was Born In The UK, which is record B (clue 3). The Faunas' record is A (clue 3), so Born In The UK is by the Rolling Bones. Thus Far Side Of The Planet is C (clue 4). Hearsay isn't by the Scarabs (clue 2), so the Faunas and (by elimination) the Scarabs recorded Bridge Over The Mersey, which is D. Hearsay was recorded in 1964 (clue 2), so Far Side Of The Planet in 1963.

In summary:

A, Hearsay, Faunas, 1964.
B, Born In The UK, Rolling Bones, 1966.
C, Far Side Of The Planet, Peter's Pilgrims, 1963.
D, Bridge Over The Mersey, Scarabs, 1965.

SOLUTIONS

Just Phenomenal (No 7)

Tristan is the singer (clue 2) and the keyboard player was writing to Bethany (clue 5), so Martin, who was writing to Sarah and who doesn't play a guitar (clue 1), is the drummer. The girl from Liverpool is Jenny (clue 2). Peter was writing to Glasgow (clue 3) and the lead guitarist was writing to Manchester (clue 6). Martin wasn't writing to Birmingham (clue 4), so London. Jenny hadn't written to Tristan (clue 2), so to the bass guitarist. Thus Peter is the keyboard player and Tristan's correspondent was the girl from Birmingham. She isn't Tina (clue 4), so Naomi and Tina is from Manchester. The lead guitarist isn't Jamie (clue 6), so Richard. Jamie is the bass guitarist.

In summary:
Jamie, bass guitarist, Jenny, Liverpool.
Martin, drummer, Sarah, London.
Peter, keyboard player, Bethany, Glasgow.
Richard, lead guitarist, Tina, Manchester.
Tristan, singer, Naomi, Birmingham.

In Divers Places (No 8)

Captain Jervis of the Wyvern is the only man with a name the same length as his ship's (clue 1) and Captain Popham's ship is in the Arctic Ocean (clue 6), so Gipsy in the North Sea (clue 3), is Captain Fisher's. Hunter isn't Captain Popham's (clue 1) or Captain Stark's (clue 4), so Captain Blake's and is raising the submarine (clue 5). Captain Stark's ship is the Diadem (clue 1) and Captain Popham's is the Orion, working on the airliner (clue 2). The vessel in the Tasman Sea working on the schooner (clue 1) is the Diadem and Wyvern is in the Indian Ocean. Wyvern is working on the freighter (clue 3) and the Gipsy is working on a galleon.

In summary:
Diadem, Captain Stark, Tasman Sea, schooner.
Gipsy, Captain Fisher, North Sea, galleon.
Hunter, Captain Blake, Aegean Sea, submarine.
Orion, Captain Popham, Arctic Ocean, airliner.
Wyvern, Captain Jervis, Indian Ocean, freighter.

It's a Dog's Life (No 9)

K9-5's dog is Columbo (clue 1), Dobermann drives for K9-4 (clue 2) and Schnauzer is handler in team K9-1 (clue 7). The team with Cairn as driver and Marlowe as dog isn't K9-1 or K9-2 (clue 5), so K9-3 and Basset is the handler In K9-2. The team with Husky as handler and Archer as dog (clue 6) is thus K9-4. K9-3's handler isn't Russell (clue 4), so Griffon and Russell's team is K9-5. The dog in K9-1 isn't Kojak (clue 7), so Starsky and Kojak is in K9-2. The K9-5 driver isn't Airedale (clue 1) or Pointer (clue 3), so Vizsla, since Pointer drives for K9-2 (clue 3) and Airedale for K9-1.

In summary:
K9-1, Airedale, Schnauzer, Starsky.
K9-2, Pointer, Basset, Kojak.
K9-3, Cairn, Griffon, Marlowe.
K9-4, Dobermann, Husky, Archer.
K9-5, Vizsla, Russell, Columbo.

Foreign Exchange (No 10)

Eva is staying with Sarah (clue 6), so (clue 2) Elsa is with Kathy. Elsa isn't from Dortmund (clue 1), Frankfurt (clue 2) or Hamburg (clue 3). She isn't going to the British Museum (clue 2), thus isn't from Stuttgart (clue 3), so Hannover and Heidi is from Hamburg. The girl from Stuttgart isn't Eva (clue 6) and isn't with Louise (clue 1) or Liz (clue 4), so she's Natalie. By elimination, Eva is from Frankfurt and Heidi is with Liz. The girl from Dortmund isn't Maria (clue 1), so Hannah. Maria is with Natalie. Louise and Hannah are going to the National Gallery (clue 1). The girl going to Stratford-upon-Avon isn't Elsa or Heidi (clue 5), so Eva. Elsa will visit Warwick Castle (clue 2) and Heidi is going to Windsor Castle.

In summary:
Kathy, Elsa, Hannover, Warwick Castle.
Liz, Heidi, Hamburg, Windsor Castle.
Louise, Hannah, Dortmund, National Gallery.
Natalie, Maria, Stuttgart, British Museum.
Sarah, Eva, Frankfurt, Stratford-upon-Avon.

Get Your Bearings (No 11)

The box containing 64 isn't 2 or 7 (clue 1) or 6 (clue 6). There are 8 ball-bearings in box 3 (clue 4), so that with 64 isn't 1 or 4 (clue 3), so box 5. Box 4 is blue (clue 2) and has one ball-bearing. The green box has 2 and isn't box 2 (clue 2), so it's box 1 and 3 is white. There are 4 in box 6 (clue 4), thus (clue 1) 16 in box 7 and 32 in box 2, which is thus pink (clue 4). Box 5 is red (clue 1). Box 6 is yellow (clue 5) and box 7 is brown.

In summary:
Box 1, green, 2.   Box 2, pink, 32.
Box 3, white, 8.   Box 4, blue, 1.
Box 5, red, 64.   Box 6, yellow, 4.
Box 7, brown, 16.

Their Number's Up (No 12)

No-one won on Friday. Thursday's prize was the microwave (clue 5) and Tuesday's lucky ticket was 83 (clue 6), so the whisky won with ticket 5 (clue 2), was Monday's prize and Neil won on Wednesday. Rose won the television (clue 4) and Cissie had ticket 24 (clue 1). The whisky wasn't won by Spencer (clue 3), so Bunny. Tuesday's prize wasn't Spencer's (clue 3), so Rose's. The tin of biscuits was won with ticket 66 by Neil (clue 3) and Spencer's number was 30. By elimination, Saturday's prize was the umbrella. Cissie won the umbrella (clue 6), so Spencer got the microwave.

SOLUTIONS

In summary:
Bunny, whisky, 5, Monday.
Cissie, umbrella, 24, Saturday.
Neil, tin of biscuits, 66, Wednesday.
Rose, portable television, 83, Tuesday.
Spencer, microwave, 30, Thursday.

Mack and Ms Knyfe (No 13)

The book about blackmail was written in June (clue 5) and the one set in Seattle was written in April (clue 6). The Denver-set book about the forgery wasn't written in August or November (clue 1), so January. Burning Heat was written in November (clue 2). Temptress which is set in Cleveland wasn't written in June (clue 5), so August. Femme Fatale was the murder case (clue 1), so was written in April. Siren Song wasn't written in January (clue 3), so the Denver-set book is Forbidden Fruit and Siren Song is about blackmail. It wasn't set in Pittsburgh (clue 3), so Miami and Pittsburgh is the setting for Burning Heat. The latter isn't about burglary (clue 4), so kidnapping and the burglary is in Temptress.

In summary:
Burning Heat, November, Pittsburgh, kidnapping.
Femme Fatale, April, Seattle, murder.
Forbidden Fruit, January, Denver, forgery.
Siren Song, June, Miami, blackmail.
Temptress, August, Cleveland, burglary.

Irrational Explanations (No 14)

The doctor's claim was made in 1981 (clue 3) and Mr Sayne is a teacher (clue 6). Mr Featon-Ground who made his claim in 1997 isn't the estate agent (clue 2) or librarian (clue 3), so the bus driver who claimed his children are aliens (clue 1). The claim of having been abducted by aliens was made eight years before Miss Clerehead's (clue 3), so not in 1989, nor were alien spacecraft seen in 1989 (clue 4). Someone claimed to have come from another planet in 1993 (clue 5), so 1989's claim was the body taken over by aliens by Mrs Sobers (clue 1). The 1981 claim wasn't made by Miss Clerehead (clue 3), so Mr Normhall. Miss Clerehead thus made her claim in 1993 (clue 3) and the 1985 story was Mr Sayne's. Mrs Sobers is the librarian (clue 3) and Mr Sayne claimed that he had been abducted by aliens. By elimination, Mr Normhall claimed that he'd seen alien spacecraft and Miss Clerehead is the estate agent.

In summary:
1981, Mr Normhall, doctor, saw alien spacecraft.
1985, Mr Sayne, teacher, abducted by aliens.
1989, Mrs Sobers, librarian, body taken over.
1993, Miss Clerehead, estate agent, another planet.
1997, Mr Featon-Ground, bus driver, children are aliens.

Hanging Matters (No 15)

The flower-pattern wallpaper was hung on Tuesday (clue 1) and Roland decorated the hall and stairs on Thursday (clue 2). The woodchip paper for the dining room wasn't put up on Monday or Friday (clue 5), so Wednesday. Roland used more than four rolls of flowered paper (clue 1). Five rolls were used on either Monday or Friday (clue 3) and six rolls were an embossed paper (clue 6), so seven rolls were used on Tuesday. Three were used in the kitchen (clue 4), so (clue 3) four were used on Wednesday and six on Thursday. Thus he used five rolls of the abstract paper on Monday or Friday (clue 2). By elimination, the kitchen wallpaper had a striped design and (clue 1) wasn't hung on Friday, so Monday. Five rolls were hung on Friday, but not in the sitting room (clue 1), so bedroom. The sitting room paper was hung on Tuesday.

In summary:
Monday, kitchen, three, stripes.
Tuesday, sitting room, seven, flowers.
Wednesday, dining room, four, woodchip.
Thursday, hall and stairs, six, embossed.
Friday, bedroom, five, abstract.

The Grimbold Story (No 16)

The economist is male (clue 3) and the occultist accused Grimbold of black magic (clue 6). The banker is George Hall (clue 4). Ann Bull put Grimbold's success down to luck and used his name in her book's title (clue 5), so she's not ex-partner (clue 5), so she's the journalist who wrote Grimbold's Millions (clue 7). Profit Without Honour alleges dishonesty (clue 4). The occultist's book isn't Grimbold or Money Machine (clue 6), so it's Gold Bug, written by Mark Lamb (clue 2). Rita Sharp isn't the male economist (clue 3), so she's the ex-partner and David Cory is the economist. The book which calls him a genius but isn't Grimbold (clue 1), is Money Machine, so Grimbold states that he did it all by hard work. Rita Sharp didn't write Money Machine (clue 1) or Grimbold (clue 5), so Profit Without Honour. David Cory didn't write Money Machine (clue 2), so Grimbold. George Hall wrote Money Machine.

In summary:
Ann Bull, journalist, Grimbold's Millions, luck.
David Cory, economist, Grimbold, hard work.
George Hall, banker, Money Machine, genius.
Mark Lamb, occultist, Gold Bug, black magic.
Rita Sharp, ex-partner, Profit Without Honour, dishonesty.

SOLUTIONS

Parbridge Parishes (No 17)

Parish B is St Anselm's (clue 2) and the Revd O Matthews is the minister of St Ebba's (clue 3). The Revd A Johnson's parish E isn't St Monica's (clue 1) or St Jude's (clue 6), so St Hubert's. Parish D's church is in West Square (clue 4), the Revd U Paul's is in Church Street (clue 5) and St Jude's is in Barr Hill (clue 6). St Hubert's isn't in Guild Lane (clue 1), so Market Street. St Jude's is thus in Barr Hill, which isn't the Revd I Marks' parish (clue 6), so the Revd E Lucas'. St Jude's isn't C (clue 2), so A. The Guild Lane church isn't in C (clue 1), so B and the Church Street church is in C. The church in parish C is thus St Monica's, the Revd I Marks's church is St Anselm's and St Ebba's is in West Square.

In summary:
A, St Jude's, Barr Hill, Revd E Lucas.
B, St Anselm's, Guild Lane, Revd I Marks.
C, St Monica's, Church Street, Revd U Paul.
D, St Ebba's, West Square, Revd O Matthews.
E, St Hubert's, Market Street, Revd A Johnson.

Rogues' Gallery (No 18)

The $3,000 reward was offered for the sheep stealer (clue 3) and $5,000 was featured on poster C (clue 7). The price put on the bank robber on F wasn't $1,000 or $2,000 (clue 1). Since $4,000 was offered for the capture of Artie Fishell (clue 6), $6,000 wasn't the reward for the bank robber (clue 1), who was thus Artie Fishell. Poster E featured the kidnapper (clue 6) and (clue 1) the reward for Rusty Nayle was $2,000. Brad Hall was wanted for murder (clue 2), so (by elimination) the reward for his capture was $5,000 and his portrait was thus on C. Billy Cann was on E (clue 2) with a reward of $6,000. The $5,000 wasn't for the stagecoach robber (clue 5), so Rusty Nayle robbed the stagecoach and the $1,000 reward was for the rustler's capture. The latter wasn't Hank Artz (clue 4), so Dan Druff. Thus $3,000 was offered for Hank Artz. Neither Rusty Nayle nor Dan Druff was on poster D (clue 5), so Hank Artz was on D, Dan Druff on A and Rusty Nayle on B.

In summary:
A, Dan Druff, rustling, $1,000.
B, Rusty Nayle, stagecoach robbery, $2,000.
C, Brad Hall, murder, $5,000.
D, Hank Artz, sheep stealing, $3,000.
E, Billy Cann, kidnap, $6,000.
F, Artie Fishell, bank robbery, $4,000.

In the Soap (No 19)

James Tyler has been in the series for 4 years (clue 1), so Adam Quinn has been in the show for 6 years (clue 4) and the person playing the market stallholder for 7 years. Adam's character is Clark Foster (clue 5). Jean Neville has played

Eileen Pascoe for 7 years (clue 3) and the publican has been in the soap for 4 years and is played by James Tyler (clue 1). Jack Stretton is the shopkeeper (clue 2) and the lorry driver is Fred Pascoe (clue 6), so Clark is the café owner and Alan Poole is Fred Pascoe. Jack Stretton has been in the cast for 10 years (clue 2), so Alan Poole for 5. Len Hooton is played by James Tyler (clue 1) and Mr Holland is played by Jack Stretton.

In summary:
Adam Quinn, Clark Foster, café owner, six years.
Alan Poole, Fred Pascoe, lorry driver, five years.
Jack Stretton, Mr Holland, shopkeeper, ten years.
James Tyler, Len Hooton, publican, four years.
Jean Neville, Eileen Pascoe, market stallholder, seven years.

Branches Everywhere (No 20)

Clive lives at number 1 (clue 5) and the Holts at number 5 (clue 4). Bradley Woods doesn't live at number 7, where the tree house is in the sycamore (clue 2), so at number 3. Darren's den in the beech tree (clue 1) is thus at number 5. Andrew lives at number 7. Bradley's tree house isn't in the horse chestnut (clue 3), so the walnut tree. Clive's is in the horse chestnut. His surname isn't Forrest (clue 3), so Spinney. Andrew's surname is Forrest.

In summary:
1, Clive Spinney, horse chestnut.
3, Bradley Woods, walnut.
5, Darren Holt, beech.
7, Andrew Forrest, sycamore.

Not Too Close (No 21)

The resident of number 1 isn't Nutbrown (clue 1), Ashburton, the former banker (clue 2) or Birchfield (clue 3), so Firman and the ex-solicitor lives at number 3, which is The Laurels (clue 4). Ashburton's house is thus number 2 (clue 2) and The Oaks is number 1. The Larches, owned by the retired publisher (clue 1) is number 4. By elimination, Firman is the retired judge and number 2 is The Elms. Nutbrown is the ex-solicitor (clue 1), so Birchfield owns The Larches.

In summary:
1, Mr Firman, judge, The Oaks.
2, Mr Ashburton, banker, The Elms.
3, Mr Nutbrown, solicitor, The Laurels.
4, Mr Birchfield, publisher, The Larches.

Memory Lane (No 22)

Bernard liked Tom And Jerry (clue 5). Roy is 36 (clue 2). The boy whose favourite was Bugs Bunny (clue 1) was thus Philip. The Flintstones was favoured by the 34-year-old (clue 3), who isn't Petula (clue 2), so Annie Mason (clue 1) and Philip is 33. Yogi Bear wasn't preferred by Petula

SOLUTIONS

(clue 2), so Roy. Petula preferred Huckleberry Hound. Bernard isn't 32 (clue 5), so 35 and Petula is 32. Mr/Ms Ryan isn't Bernard (clue 5), so Petula. Philip's surname isn't Short or Allen (clue 4), so Philip is Burton, Bernard is Short and Roy is Allen.

In summary:
Annie Mason, 34, The Flintstones.
Bernard Short, 35, Tom And Jerry.
Petula Ryan, 32, Huckleberry Hound.
Philip Burton, 33, Bugs Bunny.
Roy Allen, 36, Yogi Bear.

Looking Ahead (No 23)

The temperature on the unsettled day will be 20C (clue 4) and 21C when the wind is in the east (clue 5). The sunshine and showers day will have a temperature of at least 19C (clue 1), so the sunny day with the winds in the north east which will be warmer still (clue 2), is forecast for 22C. The 19C day doesn't have cloud mentioned in its forecast (clue 5), so sunshine and showers. Tuesday will be 18C (clue 1) and Thursday will see cloud and rain (clue 6). No rain has been mentioned for Friday (clue 4) and no sun for Wednesday (clue 3), so the 19C sunshine and showers is on Monday. Wednesday is thus the unsettled day and the sunny day is Friday. Wednesday's wind won't be in the west (clue 3) or south east (clue 4), so the south. The westerly wind won't blow when there's any rain (clue 4), thus is forecast for Tuesday and the south easterly wind will be on Monday. By elimination, Tuesday will be cloudy and Thursday's wind is in the east.

In summary:
Monday, sunshine and showers, SE, 19C.
Tuesday, cloudy, W, 18C.
Wednesday, unsettled, S, 20C.
Thursday, cloud and rain, E, 21C.
Friday, sunny, NE, 22C.

Neighbours (No 24)

Toby's wife is Janet (clue 1). Nick's wife isn't Shirley who lives at No 1 (clue 2) or Norma (clue 3), so Stella. They aren't at No 3 (clue 3), nor are they the Toyota owners at No 5 (clue 4), so they live at No 7. Toby and Janet live at No 3 (clue 1) and Shirley and her husband own the Volvo. The Fiat is at No 3 and Norma lives at No 5. Laurie isn't at No 5 (clue 4), so No 1. Patrick lives at No 5.

In summary:
Number 1, Laurie and Shirley, Volvo.
Number 3, Toby and Janet, Fiat.
Number 5, Patrick and Norma, Toyota.
Number 7, Nick and Stella, Peugeot.

Whoops! (No 25)

Gillian left on Thursday (clue 3) and Olive Tree was Wednesday's victim (clue 5), so (clue 1) Donna left on Friday after spilling something on Carol Singer. The gravy was spilled on Tuesday (clue 6) so (clue 4) Samantha dropped the trifle on Wednesday and red wine was spilled on Matt Finnish on Thursday. Rebecca's victim wasn't Dawn Brakes (clue 2), so Lord Sandladies. By elimination, Louise dropped something on Dawn Brakes on Monday. This wasn't chocolate sauce (clue 7), so tomato soup. Thus chocolate sauce was spilled on Friday and Rebecca spilled gravy.

In summary:
Monday, Louise, tomato soup, Dawn Brakes.
Tuesday, Rebecca, gravy, Lord Sandladies.
Wednesday, Samantha, trifle, Olive Tree.
Thursday, Gillian, red wine, Matt Finnish.
Friday, Donna, chocolate sauce, Carol Singer.

Valerie's Valentines (No 26)

The office boy signed 'John Doe' (clue 1) and 'mystery man' sent the card with a four-line verse (clue 4). The sales manager's card with the two-line verse wasn't signed 'secret admirer' or 'you-know-who' (clue 3), so 'Mr X' whose card had a heart (clue 5). The lovebirds card contained a limerick (clue 2). The picture on the card with the four lines of prose wasn't a teddy bear or a cupid (clue 6), so roses. It wasn't from the office boy (clue 1), the postman or Valerie's boss (clue 6), so her husband. The boss's card didn't show a cupid (clue 6), so lovebirds. By elimination, 'mystery man' was the postman whose card had a teddy bear and the office boy sent the cupid card, which thus contained only a greeting. The boss didn't sign his card 'you-know-who' (clue 2), so 'secret admirer'. Her husband signed himself 'you-know-who'.

In summary:
Cupid, greeting only, 'John Doe', office boy.
Heart, two lines verse, 'Mr X', sales manager.
Lovebirds, limerick, 'secret admirer', boss.
Roses, four lines prose, 'you-know-who', husband.
Teddy bear, four lines verse, 'mystery man', postman.

Doggy Decisions (No 27)

Remember throughout that each judge placed the dogs in a different position, nor was 1st place given by Ann to dog A, Barry to B, Chloë to C or David to D (intro and clue 1). Chloë placed dog B 3rd (clue 3). The judge who placed D 1st and B 4th (clue 7) wasn't David (clue 1), Chloë (clue 3) or Ann (clue 5), so Barry. D is the Labrador (clue 2). Ann placed Crusty 1st (clue 2), so Trusty the Samoyed (clue 4) who wasn't placed 1st by David, was chosen 1st by Chloë. He isn't

SOLUTIONS

dog C (clue 1), so A. David placed B 1st (clue 4), so Ann placed C 1st. By elimination, dog B was placed 2nd by Ann, so Dusty is dog D (clue 5), thus Rusty is B, placed 3rd by Chloë. Chloë didn't place C 4th (clue 3), so D 4th and C 2nd. By elimination, Ann placed A 4th and D 3rd and Barry placed A 2nd and C 3rd, thus David placed D 2nd, A 3rd and C 4th. Dog C isn't the Alsatian (clue 6), so the Dalmatian. The Alsatian is dog B.

In summary:
A, Trusty, Samoyed.
B, Rusty, Alsatian.
C, Crusty, Dalmatian.
D, Dusty, Labrador.
Ann, C, B, D, A.
Barry, D, A, C, B.
Chloë, A, C, B, D.
David, B, D, A, C.

Gasworks Cottage (No 28)
The £6.00 purchase was from the auction (clue 1) and the £27.00 buy was from the antique shop. Thus the china shop charged £3.00 (clue 5) and the auction was in Birmingham. The man who paid £6.00 (clue 5) wasn't Mr Grayson (clue 3), so Mr Jesmond. The £30.00 and £54.00 cottages weren't bought in Norwich (clue 2) or Hastings (clue 3), so St Alban's and/or Swindon. The £3.00 cottage wasn't bought in Hastings (clue 3), so Norwich and £27.00 was paid in Hastings. Mrs Welburn paid £30.00 (clue 3) and Mr Grayson £54.00. The junk shop wasn't in Swindon (clue 4), so St Alban's and the street market was in Swindon. The woman who shopped in St Alban's (clue 4) was Mrs Welburn and Mr Grayson went to Swindon. Miss Peabody spent £3.00 (clue 1) and Mrs Browning £27.00.

In summary:
Mrs Browning, £27.00, antique shop, Hastings.
Mr Grayson, £54.00, street market, Swindon.
Mr Jesmond, £6.00, auction, Birmingham.
Miss Peabody, £3.00, china shop, Norwich.
Mrs Welburn, £30.00, junk shop, St Alban's.

Class Distinction (No 29)
The year 7 pupils who are the youngest (intro) aren't taking maths (clue 1), German (clue 2), or English with Mrs Fiddle (clue 4), so history and (clue 2) year 8 are taking German. Mr Liddell isn't teaching maths or history (clue 1), so German. The history teacher isn't Miss Biddle (clue 2), so Mr Diddle. He's in room 3 (clue 4). By elimination, Miss Biddle is the maths teacher. She isn't in rooms 1 or 4 (clue 1), so room 2. Mr Liddell is in room 1 (clue 1), so Mrs Fiddle is in room 4. The year 10 class isn't in room 4 (clue 3), so room 2. The year 9 class is in room 4.

In summary:
Room 1, Mr Liddell, year 8, German.
Room 2, Miss Biddle, year 10, Maths.
Room 3, Mr Diddle, year 7, History.
Room 4, Mrs Fiddle, year 9, English.

Jubilee Terrace (No 30)
Denise is Mrs Fenner (clue 4). Mrs Lister whose husband is violent isn't Shirley (clue 2), so her name contains five letters. Thus her husband is Shane (clue 2). Mrs Lister isn't Penny (clue 5), nor is she Mandy, who is having an affair (clue 7), so she's Diane. Mrs Markham isn't Shirley (clue 3) or Penny (clue 5), so Mandy. Gordon who gambles isn't surnamed Markham or Renshaw (clue 1), so Mr Fenner. Shirley's surname isn't Gibson (clue 3), so Renshaw and Penny is Mrs Gibson. Darren's surname is Markham (clue 3) and Pete is Mr Renshaw. The woman who discovered a past secret isn't Shirley (clue 3), so Penny. Shirley and Pete have arguments.

In summary:
Arnold and Penny Gibson, past secret.
Darren and Mandy Markham, affair.
Gordon and Denise Fenner, gambling.
Pete and Shirley Renshaw, arguments.
Shane and Diane Lister, violence.

A Rewarding Time (No 31)
The apothecary turned in Hank Artz (clue 2) and Jack Knife was the bounty hunter (clue 4). Lou Tennant claimed the reward of $2,000 for Rusty Nayle (clue 1) and wasn't the mortician; nor (clue 6) was he the oil prospector, so he was the farmhand. Jim Crack made the third claim (clue 5), so Lou Tennant didn't make the second (clue 3). Nor was he the second claimant Jack Knife (clue 4). The second claimant captured Artie Fishell (clue 4), thus (reward of $4,000) wasn't the oil prospector (clue 6), so he was the mortician. Lou Tennant made the first claim (clue 1) and (clue 3) Bob Binns made the second. Chad Valley didn't make the fourth claim (clue 7), so the fifth and Jack Knife made the fourth. Jim Crack didn't turn in Hank Artz (clue 5), so he was the oil prospector and Chad Valley was the apothecary. Jack Knife's claim didn't relate to Dan Druff (clue 7), so Brad Hall. Jim Crack turned in Dan Druff.

In summary:
Artie Fishell, Bob Binns, mortician, second.
Brad Hall, Jack Knife, bounty hunter, fourth.
Dan Druff, Jim Crack, oil prospector, third.
Hank Artz, Chad Valley, apothecary, fifth.
Rusty Nayle, Lou Tennant, farmhand, first.

SOLUTIONS

Just Fêted (No 32)

The vicarage hosted the church fête (clue 1), the village green fête was in August (clue 3) and the marquee wasn't delivered to the June fête (clue 5). The Junior Soccer League's July fête wasn't at the football stadium (clue 1) or Town Hall (clue 2), so the Junior Soccer League's fête was at Valley Farm, where the speakers failed (clue 6) and the scouts' fête was in June. August's fête wasn't organised by the tennis club (clue 3), so the Women's Institute. September's was at the Town Hall (clue 2), so the church fête was in May, the scouts' was at the football stadium and the tennis club ran the September event. It rained in May (clue 4) and the power cut was in September.

In summary:

May, vicarage, church, rain.

June, football stadium, scouts, no marquee.

July, Valley Farm, Junior Soccer League, speakers failed.

August, village green, Women's Institute, no guest.

September, Town Hall, tennis club, power cut.

Taking Stock (No 33)

Since the time between the purchase of the shares in Albion Group and BBF was 10 minutes (clue 4), the first wasn't made at 9.00 and since the Euro-Amalgamated shares were acquired at 9.30 (clue 1), it wasn't 9.20. Thus the Albion shares were bought at 9.50 for 110p each (clue 5) and the BBF ones at 10.00. Gordon bought 600 BBF shares (clue 3). AD&G shares weren't purchased at 9.00 (clue 2), so 9.20 and cost 126p. By elimination, Imperial Holdings shares were thus bought at 9.00. The 400 shares cost 73p (clue 6), so the even number of hundreds of AD&G shares bought at 126p (clue 2) was the 200 block. The 600 weren't at 40p (clue 3), so 142p. Imperial Holdings shares were 73p (clue 1) and those in Euro-Amalgamated were 40p and amounted to 500. Thus 300 Albion shares were purchased.

In summary:

9.00, Imperial Holdings, 73p, 400.

9.20, AD&G, 126p, 200.

9.30, Euro-Amalgamated, 40p, 500.

9.50, Albion Group, 110p, 300.

10.00, BBF, 142p, 600.

Battleships (No 34)

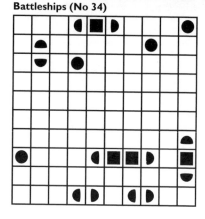

Logi-5 (No 35a)

D	A	C	E	B
E	C	B	D	A
A	B	D	C	E
C	E	A	B	D
B	D	E	A	C

ABC (No 35b)

B	C	A		
		B	A	C
	A	C		B
C			B	A
A	B		C	

Not-so-Grand Prix (No 36)

Croft had even numbers throughout (clue 2), so didn't finish first and start sixth (clue 7). He didn't start second (clue 2), so started fourth and finished second, thus his pit number was six. The drivers who finished sixth and/or seventh weren't Armendez (clue 4), Ortiz or Girling (clue 5) or Downes (clue 6), so Fetterman and/or Stottski. The person who started fifth finished third (clue 1) and the one who finished first started sixth (clue 7). Girling finished two places ahead of his starting position (clue 5), so started in seventh position and finished fifth. Thus Fetterman finished seventh (clue 3) and Stottski, sixth. Armendez finished fourth (clue 4). Thus Ortiz finished third and started fifth (clue 5) and Downes finished first and started sixth.

SOLUTIONS

Fetterman started first (clue 3) and the second and third starting places were those of Armendez and Stottski respectively (clue 4). Fetterman's pit number was five (clue 3), Downes' was four (clue 6), so Girling's was three (clue 1) and Ortiz's was two. Stottski wasn't in pit seven (clue 4), so in pit one. Armendez was in pit seven.

In summary (pit number - starting position - finishing position):

Armendez, seven, two, four.
Croft, six, four, two.
Downes, four, six, one.
Fetterman, five, one, seven.
Girling, three, seven, five.
Ortiz, two, five, three.
Stottski, one, three, six.

Cursing the Curse (No 37)

The visitor who saw the tomb on Monday wasn't Peter (clue 2), Rowena (clue 3), Barry or Marjorie (clue 5), so Julia. Rowena's visit was on Tuesday (clue 3). Julia's mishap wasn't losing the wallet, which happened to a man, or having an upset stomach (clue 1). Nor, since she visited the day before Rowena, could it have been losing spectacles, which happened to the person who visited the day before Peter (clue 2), or falling in the river (clue 3), so was breaking her ankle. Rowena didn't have the stomach upset (clue 1) or the fall into the river (clue 3), so lost her spectacles. Peter's visit was thus on Wednesday (clue 2). He didn't have the stomach upset (clue 1) or fall in the river (clue 3), so lost his wallet. The stomach upset was thus after Thursday's visit (clue 1) and Friday's visitor fell in the river. Julia's surname isn't King (clue 1), Holliday (clue 2), Sands (clue 4) or Cave (clue 5), so Palmer. Peter's is Sands (clue 4). Rowena's isn't Holliday (clue 2) or Cave (clue 5), so King. Barry's is Holliday (clue 5) and Marjorie's is Cave. Marjorie's visit was on Thursday (clue 5) and Barry's on Friday.

In summary:

Barry Holliday, Friday, fell in river.
Julia Palmer, Monday, broke ankle.
Marjorie Cave, Thursday, had stomach upset.
Peter Sands, Wednesday, lost wallet.
Rowena King, Tuesday, lost spectacles.

The Icing On The Cake (No 38)

The blue lettering on the horseshoe cake didn't celebrate a birthday (clue 2). The engagement cake was heart-shaped (clue 1) and the retirement cake bore the green inscription (clue 6). The blue lettering on the horseshoe cake wasn't for a birthday (clue 2), so it was made in November (clue 3) and (clue 2) the rectangular cake was made in December. The August cake wasn't heart-shaped (clue 1) or

round (clue 5), so square. The pink inscription was on the September cake (clue 4). The yellow inscription was written before October (clue 1), so in August. The retirement cake wasn't made in December (clue 6), so it was round and September's was heart-shaped. Thus the retirement cake was made in October and the inscription on December's cake was orange. The 18th birthday cake wasn't made in August (clue 5), so December. August's was for the 40th birthday.

In summary:

August, 40th birthday, square, yellow.
September, engagement, heart-shaped, pink.
October, retirement, round, green.
November, wedding, horse-shoe, blue.
December, 18th birthday, rectangular, orange.

Just the Ticket (No 39)

The winning ticket from the batch of two was 40 (clue 3), so that from the batch of five was 50 and the vase was won with ticket 30. The numbers on the winning tickets from the batches of twelve and six were both higher than 25 (clues 1 and 2), so ticket number 25 was from the batch of ten. The number from the batch of twelve wasn't 30 (clue 1), so 35. By elimination, the number 30 was from the batch of six. The winning ticket from the Drama Group was 30 (clue 1) and number 25 won the table mats. The lemonade was won with ticket 35 (clue 2). The wine was won with ticket 50 (clue 6) and the tin of beans with ticket 40. Ticket 35 wasn't bought from the church hall or church restoration stalls (clue 1), or from the Scouts stall (clue 5), so from the School Association stall. Ticket 25 came from the Scouts (clue 4). Ticket 50 wasn't bought in aid of the church restoration (clue 6), so was from the Church Hall stall. Ticket 40 came from the church restoration tombola.

In summary:

Church Hall, five, 50, bottle of wine.
Church restoration, two, 40, tin of beans.
Drama Group, six, 30, vase.
School Association, 12, 35, bottle of lemonade.
Scouts, ten, 25, table mats.

On Manoeuvres (No 40)

Dave was 25 minutes late (clue 4), so the driver of the Land-Rover wasn't late by 20 or 25 minutes (clue 1). The vehicle which was 15 minutes late was made in 1945 (clue 6). The Land-Rover was made in 1951 (clue 1), thus wasn't 5 minutes late (clue 2), so 10 minutes late. Geoff's lorry wasn't made in 1945 and he wasn't 5 minutes late (clue 2), so 20 minutes late. Barry was 15 minutes late (clue 1). Stephen wasn't 5 minutes late (clue 5), so 10 minutes late and Mike was 5 minutes late and drove the Jeep. It doesn't date from 1942 (clue 2) or 1943 (clue 3), so 1944. The lorry dates from 1943 (clue 3), so Dave's vehicle was made in 1942. This isn't the motor-cycle (clue 7), so the staff car and the motor-cycle is Barry's.

In summary:
Barry, motor-cycle, 1945, 15 minutes.
Dave, staff car, 1942, 25 minutes.
Geoff, lorry, 1943, 20 minutes.
Mike, Jeep, 1944, 5 minutes.
Stephen, Land-Rover, 1951, 10 minutes.

Lonely Vigils (No 41)

The man who served for 12 years wasn't Blunderbuss or Rictus (clue 1) or Hiatus (clue 4), so Voluminus. The man from Africa served for 11 years. Voluminus wasn't from Syria (clue 2) or Germania (clue 4), so Gallia and (clue 3) was on the west wall. Blunderbuss was on the east wall (clue 1). The man on the north wall had served for 9 years (clue 3) and wasn't Hiatus (clue 4), so Rictus. By elimination, Hiatus was on the south wall and (clue 4) Blunderbuss was on the east wall and served for 10 years. Rictus wasn't from Africa (clue 3), so Syria and Hiatus was from Africa.

In summary:
North, Rictus, Syria, nine years.
East, Blunderbuss, Germania, ten years.
South, Hiatus, Africa, eleven years.
West, Voluminus, Gallia, twelve years.

Second Thoughts (No 42)

The race in which Desmond's original choice was the winner was next before that in which it was second (clue 2); thus neither of his first choices in these two races ran in the 3.30 (clue 1). So his winning first choice didn't run in the 3.00, nor his second-place one in the 4.00 (clue 2). He didn't reject the first in the 2.00 (clue 1), so originally selected the first in the 2.30 and second in the 3.00. So Rallentando was backed in the 2.30 and Claredown in the 3.00 (clue 2). His first choice for the 4.00 was Cynosure (clue 7), so he didn't back Dinkum Lad in the 3.30 or 4.00 (clue 3), thus in the 2.00, missing a third place (clue 3). His original choice for the 2.30 was thus Trottophan (clue 3). The horse rejected in the 3.30 was fourth (clue 1), so he rejected the fifth-placed horse in the 4.00. The one he backed in the 2.30 was seventh (clue 1) and (clue 4) Great Scott was rejected in the 3.00. Thus Brunski wasn't his final choice for the 3.30 (clue 6), so in the 4.00 and he discarded Arivale in the 3.30 (clue 6). By elimination, he discarded Grey Mist in the 2.00 and backed Big Cheese in the 3.30. Big Cheese was eighth (clue 5). Claredown was ninth (clue 7) and Brunski tenth. Dinkum Lad was sixth.

In summary:
2.00, Grey Mist, third, Dinkum Lad, sixth.
2.30, Trottophan, first, Rallentando, seventh.
3.00, Great Scott, second, Claredown, ninth.
3.30, Arivale, fourth, Big Cheese, eighth.
4.00, Cynosure, fifth, Brunski, tenth.

Sporting Scholars (No 43)

Jones plays football (clue 6) and Nicholas plays baseball (clue 4), so Boyd Greaves, whose sport isn't athletics or ice hockey (clue 1), is studying tennis. Lincoln is at Parkleigh (clue 2) and O'Driscoll is at Gayle (clue 5). Boyd isn't at Harwell (clue 1) or Cornford (clue 3), so Stanburg. Jones isn't at Harwell (clue 6), thus (clue 1) the Harwell man plays baseball. O'Driscoll isn't Franklin (clue 5), so Warren and Franklin is at Cornford. Warren isn't the athlete (clue 5), so the ice hockey player. Lincoln isn't Lambert (clue 2) or Howard (clue 6), so Jones. By elimination, Franklin is studying athletics and (clue 6) he's Howard, so Nicholas is Lambert.

In summary:
Boyd Greaves, Stanburg, tennis.
Franklin Howard, Cornford, athletics.
Lincoln Jones, Parkleigh, football.
Nicholas Lambert, Harwell, baseball.
Warren O'Driscoll, Gayle, ice hockey.

Rapid Repertory (No 44)

The theatre where the company first performed wasn't the Alhambra (clue 2), Coliseum (clue 3), Forum (clue 4) or Royal (clue 6), so the Playhouse. The comedy's week wasn't the first (clue 1), fourth, fifth or second (clue 3), so third. The Coliseum thus staged the fifth play (clue 3). The farce wasn't the first, second or fourth in the repertoire (clue 2), so fifth, Flatt's comedy was third and the play at the Alhambra fourth (clue 2). The Forum didn't stage the second play (clue 4), so the third and Penman wrote the first. By elimination, the second play was at the Royal, so the first was the costume drama (clue 6). Archer didn't write the farce (clue 1) or whodunnit (clue 4), so the kitchen-sink play. Lines' play wasn't the second (clue 5), so the fifth. Boarder's wasn't second (clue 6), so fourth and Archer's was second. Boarder wrote the whodunnit.

In summary:
Comedy, Flatt, Forum, third.
Costume drama, Penman, Playhouse, first.
Farce, Lines, Coliseum, fifth.
Kitchen-sink play, Archer, Royal, second.
Whodunnit, Boarder, Alhambra, fourth.

SOLUTIONS

Lots and Lots (No 45)

The commodity with 294 lots isn't books and folios or jewellery (clue 1), furniture (clue 2), stamps or pictures (clue 3) so china and glass. The one with 271 lots isn't jewellery (clue 1), furniture (clue 2), pictures (clue 3) or stamps (clue 4), so books and folios. Thus Tuesday's auction is for china and glass (clue 1) and furniture will be sold on Wednesday (clue 2). The only numbers all of whose digits are present in the other numbers are 132 and 271 and since there are not 271 items of furniture (clue 2), there are 132 items in Wednesday's sale (clue 6). There aren't 185 or 223 pictures (clue 3), so 167 pictures and 185 stamps. By elimination, there are 223 items of jewellery, thus (clue 4) for Saturday's auction. Monday's items amount to either 167 or 185 (clue 5), so Friday's number isn't 271 (clue 6), thus Friday's has 185 items and Monday's has 167 (clue 5). Thursday's thus has 271.

In summary:
Monday, pictures, 167.
Tuesday, china and glass, 294.
Wednesday, furniture, 132.
Thursday, books and folios, 271.
Friday, stamps, 185.
Saturday, jewellery, 223.

Logi-Path (No 46)

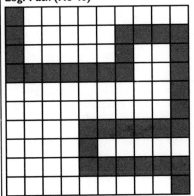

On the Ball (No 47)

Harold supports Brentford (clue 1) and Stanley supports Wolves (clue 5), so Mr Carter aged 83 who supports Preston (clue 3) is Ted. Edith's surname is Swift (clue 5). Alice is in seat E (clue 2), so she isn't Mrs Finney (clue 1), so Mrs Finney is Mavis. She isn't in seats E or F (clue 1) and isn't the resident aged 80 in seat C (clue 4). Nor is Mavis in seat D (clue 1), thus she's in B. Harold is in C (clue 1) and the resident in D is 91. Stanley is 86 and isn't in seat A (clue 5), so he's in F and

Edith is in D. Mavis isn't 95 (clue 6), so 78 and Alice is 95. By elimination, Ted is in seat A. Since the residents in both seats B and D are female, Harold in seat C isn't Matthews (clue 7), nor is he Franklin (clue 4), so he's Wright. Alice is Matthews (clue 7), so Stanley is Franklin.

In summary:
A, Ted Carter, 83.
B, Mavis Finney, 78.
C, Harold Wright, 80.
D, Edith Swift, 91.
E, Alice Matthews, 95.
F, Stanley Franklin, 86.

Domino Search (No 48)

6	6	4	4	4	3	6	6
5	0	1	2	5	4	0	2
0	0	3	4	5	2	5	0
1	5	1	1	1	2	5	2
1	4	3	0	6	1	4	3
2	5	5	2	2	3	3	1
6	6	0	3	4	0	6	3

Scotch Mist (No 49)

Paul and Joyce are one couple (clue 4), so Jenny who suffered a heat wave and who isn't married to Peter (clue 3) is the wife of Patrick and Peter's wife is Joan. Patrick and Jenny didn't go to Scotland where the mist descended (clue 1), and didn't visit Spain (clue 2), so went to Italy. Peter and Joan didn't encounter floods (clue 5), so Scotch mist. Thus Paul and Joyce went to Spain and encountered the floods.

In summary:
Patrick, Jenny, Italy, heat wave.
Paul, Joyce, Spain, floods.
Peter, Joan, Scotland, mist.

Say it with Flowers (No 50)

One card showed four roses (clue 3). Janet's didn't have three freesias (clue 2), so five freesias. By elimination, one card had three sunflowers. Daphne didn't send the one with roses (clue 3), so sunflowers and Karen's had the roses. Janet doesn't live in Preston (clue 1) or Lincoln (clue 2), so Bristol. Karen is from Lincoln (clue 1) and Daphne from Preston.

In summary:
Daphne, Preston, sunflowers, three.
Janet, Bristol, freesias, five.
Karen, Lincoln, roses, four.

A Walk in the Sun (No 51)

Adam's third stop was at Cragfoot (clue 3). Beckford, where he ate the pork pie, can't have been his first or second stop (clue 2), so was the fourth, and (clue 2) Moortop was the second stop, where he had a cheese roll (clue 4). By elimination, the first stop was Tarnside. The King's Head where he ate the sausage roll (clue 1), isn't in Cragfoot (clue 3), so Tarnside and his Cragfoot snack was a ham sandwich. The Fox and Pheasant isn't in Moortop (clue 2) or Cragfoot (clue 3), so Beckford. The Moortop pub isn't the Red Cow (clue 4), so the Black Bear. The Red Cow is in Cragfoot.

In summary:
First, Tarnside, King's Head, sausage roll.
Second, Moortop, Black Bear, cheese roll.
Third, Cragfoot, Red Cow, ham sandwich.
Fourth, Beckford, Fox and Pheasant, pork pie.

Sunken Subs (No 52)

UXS-3 sank in Cuxhaven (clue 1) and UXS-4 sank in a storm (clue 2). The U-boat which sank in the Irish Sea after being attacked by a whale, which wasn't UXS-2 (clue 3), was UXS-1. Von Kee's boat wasn't UXS-1 or UXS-4 and didn't spring a leak (clue 4), so it was in a collision. Von Derful's U-boat sank in the Skagerrak (clue 5). Von Kee's didn't sink in the Wash (clue 4), so Cuxhaven. By elimination, UXS-2 sprung a leak. UXS-4 sank in the Wash (clue 4). By elimination, Von Derful's U-boat was the UXS-2. The UXS-4's captain wasn't Von Nadose (clue 2), so Von Atatime. Von Nadose's was the UXS-1.

In summary:
UXS-1, Von Nadose, Irish Sea, attacked by whale.
UXS-2, Von Derful, Skagerrak, sprang leak.
UXS-3, Von Kee, Cuxhaven, collision.
UXS-4, Von Atatime, Wash, sank in storm.

Transports of Delight (No 53)

The model for the Jan–March issue isn't Roberta, who's pictured with the sports car (clue 2), Michelle (clue 3) or Denise (clue 5), so Jackie. The background of her picture isn't the barn (clue 1), pub or windmill (clue 6), so the railway station. The gypsy caravan's background is the windmill (clue 3), so Jackie (not with the pony and trap, clue 4) is pictured at the wheel of the jeep. Denise thus appears on the April-June cover (clue 5). This is the second quarter, so (clue 2) Roberta is on the cover of the fourth quarter's (Oct–Dec) issue. By elimination, the July–Sept model is Michelle, and (clue 3) Denise is with the gypsy caravan; thus Michelle is with the pony and trap. The pub is on the Oct–Dec cover (clue 1) and the July–Sept issue shows the barn.

In summary:
Jan–March, Jackie, jeep, railway station.
April–June, Denise, gypsy caravan, windmill.
July–Sept, Michelle, pony and trap, barn.
Oct–Dec, Roberta, sports car, pub.

Four Men in a Boat (No 54)

Since Harding is two positions in front of Jakeman in boat B (clue 5), Lewis and Carroll aren't in that boat (clue 1). Nor, since Baker is number 1 in boat C and number 3 in that boat has a six-letter name (clue 7), are Lewis and Carroll in boat C; thus they're in A. Davies is number 2 in A (clue 3), so, (clue 1) Lewis is number 4 and Carroll number 3. Edwards' position in C isn't 4 (clue 2), 1 or 3 (clue 7), so 2 and Anson is number 3 in B (clue 2). Harding is number 2 (clue 5) and Jakeman number 4 in B. Kelly and Farrow (clue 4) are thus in C. Kelly isn't number 3 (clue 7), so 4 and Farrow is number 3. Giles is number 1 in A (clue 6) and Morgan is number 1 in B.

In summary:
A, 1 Giles, 2 Davies, 3 Carroll, 4 Lewis.
B, 1 Morgan, 2 Harding, 3 Anson, 4 Jakeman.
C, 1 Baker, 2 Edwards, 3 Farrow, 4 Kelly.

Criminal Masterminds (No 55)

Ted Wallace's detective is Insp Gower (clue 3) and Damon Gardner's script is set in Liverpool (clue 6), so the script featuring Sgt Tyrrel and set in Newcastle, which is also by a man (clue 2), is the work of Paul Sayers. Chief Insp Denny features in Sons Of Eve (clue 4). Anna Creasey who wrote Out of Sight didn't create Dr Evans (clue 5), so Supt Verges. Walk in Fear is set in Brighton (clue 3). Out of Sight isn't set in rural Norfolk (clue 1), so rural Devon. Ted Wallace's isn't set in Brighton (clue 3), so rural Norfolk. By elimination, Walk in Fear was written by Kate Marsh and features Dr Evans; and Sons of Eve was written by Damon Gardner. Paul Sayers didn't write Born To Die (clue 6), so Life For Life. Ted Wallace wrote Born To Die.

In summary:
Anna Creasey, Out Of Sight, Supt Verges, rural Devon.
Damon Gardner, Sons Of Eve, Chief Insp Denny, Liverpool.
Kate Marsh, Walk In Fear, Dr Evans, Brighton.
Paul Sayers, Life For Life, Sgt Tyrrel, Newcastle.
Ted Wallace, Born To Die, Insp Gower, rural Norfolk.

Pub Entertainment (No 56)

The pub in Oslo Square is presenting performing fish (clue 4), Mildmay Place is in EC4 (clue 3) and the Duke of Dorset is in Bute Terrace (clue 6). Boomerang throwers can be seen at the Hansom Cab, which isn't in Paxton Court nor in a district numbered higher than 3 (clue 2), so is in Knight Street. Knight Street isn't in W1 (clue 1) and the flea circus is performing in NW3 (clue 3), so the Hansom Cab is in WC2. Since both the pubs with one-word names have higher postal district numbers than this, the Wellington is in SW5 (clue 5) and the Antelope is in NW3 and is presenting the flea circus (clue 3). The Antelope is (by elimination) in Paxton Court, so the Old Hat is in EC4, the Wellington is in Oslo Square and the Duke of Dorset is in W1. The Duke of Dorset isn't presenting the fruit-juggling (clue 1), so Albanian folk music. The Old Hat is presenting fruit-juggling.

In summary:
Antelope, Paxton Court, NW3, flea circus.
Duke of Dorset, Bute Terrace, W1, Albanian folk music.
Hansom Cab, Knight Street, WC2, indoor boomerangs.
Old Hat, Mildmay Place, EC4, fruit-juggling.
Wellington, Oslo Square, SW5, performing fish.

Banns Substance (No 57)
Paul's surname is Wright (clue 1) and Mr McLaren is marrying Miss Tucker (clue 3). Mark is marrying Miss Piper and his surname is neither Walton nor Hobbs (clue 5), so Searle. Miss Piper is Laura (clue 3). Philip is marrying Tara (clue 4) and Jonathan's fiancée's name begins with C (clue 2), so Rachel, who isn't marrying Paul (clue 1), is marrying Michael. Miss Ramsey's future husband isn't Paul or Michael (clue 1), Jonathan (clue 2) or Mark (clue 5), so Philip. Mr McLaren isn't Jonathan (clue 3), so Michael. Mr Hobbs isn't Philip (clue 4), so Jonathan. Philip is Mr Walton. Jonathan isn't marrying Miss Newman (clue 4), so Miss Brennan, whose name is Catherine (clue 6). Paul is marrying Charlotte Newman.

In summary:
Jonathan Hobbs, Catherine Brennan.
Mark Searle, Laura Piper.
Michael McLaren, Rachel Tucker.
Paul Wright, Charlotte Newman.
Philip Walton, Tara Ramsey.

Jump-off (No 58)
Miss Maggie got round in 2 minutes 14 seconds (clue 5) and the horse whose time was 2 minutes 20 seconds had 8 faults (clue 4), so Anne Melton, who collected 3 faults and whose time was four seconds slower than Silver King, went round in 2 minutes 22 seconds and thus Silver King's time was 2 minutes 18 seconds (clue 2). Shadow Lad was ridden by Malcolm Quinn (clue 6). Anne Melton wasn't on Coral River who had 12 faults (clue 3), so she rode Diamante. By elimination, Coral River collected 12 faults in 2 minutes 16 seconds; and Shadow Lad managed 8 faults in 2

minutes 20 seconds. Miss Maggie didn't manage a clear round (clue 5), so got 4 faults and Silver King went clear. George Farrow didn't ride Miss Maggie (clue 5), but his round was faster than Jane Warwick's (clue 1), so he rode Coral River and Jane Warwick rode Silver King. Miss Maggie was ridden by Graham Stewart.

In summary:
Anne Melton, Diamante, 3 faults, 2 min 22 sec.
George Farrow, Coral River, 12 faults, 2 min 16 sec.
Graham Stewart, Miss Maggie, 4 faults, 2 min 14 sec.
Jane Warwick, Silver King, clear, 2 min 18 sec.
Malcolm Quinn, Shadow Lad, 8 faults, 2 min 20 sec.

Domino Theory (No 59)
The spots on domino A total four (clue 2). This isn't a double 2 (clue 6), nor, since one 4 is on the upper half of domino E and the other accompanies a 1 (clue 3), has domino A a 4 and a blank, so it shows a 3 and a 1. Since the only 2 is on the lower half of C (clue 1), the number of spots on the upper half of domino C (clue 5) is 6 and the 3 is on the upper half of A, with the 1 on the lower half. There is another 6 accompanying the 4 on domino E (clue 5), thus it's on the lower half. The only blank, which is to the left of the double (clue 6) is on either B or D, so (clue 3) it's the 4/1 and the double is on F. It isn't a double 5 (clue 8), nor a double 2 or blank, both of which occur only once. There are two 1s and two 4s somewhere to the left of domino F and since no number of spots occurs more than three times in all (clue 4), the double is thus double 3. There is a 1 on the upper half of B (clues 2 and 4). There is a 5 somewhere (clue 7). Since one of the two combinations left is 4/1, the 5 is with the blank. Thus the lower half of B has 4 spots (clue 3). By elimination, D is 5/blank, with (clue 8) the 5 on the lower half and the blank on the top half.

In summary (upper half/lower half):
3/1, 1/4, 6/2, 0/5, 4/6, 3/3.

Le Autres Mousquetaires (No 60)
The overweight Musketeer's vice was eating (clue 2) and that of the man from Provence was duelling (clue 5). The bow-legged Burgundian didn't drink or gamble (clue 6), so his vice was women and he was thus Silvis (clue 3). Maximos was very large (clue 5), so the man with big ears whose name began with a consonant (clue 1) was Damos. The man with red hair wasn't the drinker (clue 4), so wasn't Archamos from Normandy. Thus Archamos was the overweight eater and Uramis had red hair and was from Provence. Damos wasn't the gambler (clue 3), so he was

the drinker and Maximos was the gambler. Damos wasn't from Picardy (clue 2), so Touraine. Maximos was from Picardy.

In summary:
Archamos, Normandy, overweight, eating.
Damos, Touraine, big ears, drinking.
Maximos, Picardy, very large, gambling.
Silvis, Burgundy, bow-legged, women.
Uramis, Provence, red hair, duelling.

Battleships (No 61)

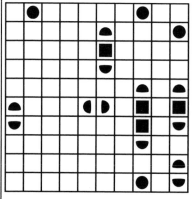

Pile Up (No 62)
From the top:
C, E, D, B, A, F.

Doggy Do (No 63)
The Irish setter came first (clue 2) and the springer spaniel belongs to Ann Darling (clue 4). Liz Pope's second-placed dog (clue 5) wasn't the Dalmatian called Spots (clue 1) or the poodle (clue 3), so the boxer. Mickey belongs to Robin Scott (clue 2), Liz's dog isn't Bosun (clue 3) or Topsy (clue 5), so Fitz. Bosun wasn't first or second (clue 3), so third, Frank Grey's dog was fourth and the poodle was fifth. So Spots was fourth and Ann Darling's dog is Bosun. Mickey wasn't first (clue 2), so fifth and first prize went to Topsy, owned by John Lamb.

In summary:
First, Topsy, Irish setter, John Lamb.
Second, Fitz, boxer, Liz Pope.
Third, Bosun, springer spaniel, Ann Darling.
Fourth, Spots, Dalmatian, Frank Grey.
Fifth, Mickey, poodle, Robin Scott.

A Question of Quizzes (No 64)
The TV presenter isn't Alan Ashley, Tony Turpin or Roy Rumford (clue 1) or Don Darrell (clue 3), so Martin Moor. Tony Turpin, who will be asking questions about famous people (clue 4) is on Comeback (clue 1). The Quizzicle quizmaster

isn't Don Darrell or Roy Rumford (clue 2) or Martin Moor (clue 6), so Alan Ashley. Double, Double's questions are on showbiz (clue 6) and (clue 2) the show's quizmaster is either Don Darrell or Roy Rumford. Martin Moor, the TV presenter, isn't asking questions on recent history (clue 4), or general knowledge (clue 6), so sport. Alan Ashley's won't be on general knowledge (clue 6), so recent history. He isn't the film actor or the TV actor (clue 2) or the radio presenter (clue 4), so the newsreader. Don Darrell's not the TV actor (clue 3) or radio presenter (clue 3), so the film actor. Roy Rumford's not the radio presenter (clue 3), so the TV actor and the radio presenter is Tony Turpin. Don Darrell's questions aren't on general knowledge (clue 5), so showbiz and Roy Rumford is asking general knowledge questions, not on Third Degree (clue 5), so Under Pressure. Martin Moor's is Third Degree.

In summary:
Alan Ashley, newsreader, Quizzicle, recent history.
Don Darrell, film actor, Double, Double, showbiz.
Martin Moor, TV presenter, Third Degree, sport.
Roy Rumford, TV actor, Under Pressure, general knowledge.
Tony Turpin, radio presenter, Comeback, famous people.

Signs of the Times (No 65)
Hilda's husband is an Aries (clue 6), so Hazel the Libra subject (clue 1) is married to the Capricorn. Hetty and Alfred aren't the Sagittarius/Cancer pairing (clue 4) and Alan is a Pisces (clue 2), so Alfred's sign is Scorpio. Hazel's husband isn't Arthur (clue 2). Albert's wife is a Gemini (clue 5), so Hazel's husband is Anthony. By elimination, Albert is the Aries subject and Arthur is the Cancerian. Holly isn't Alan's wife (clue 2), so she's married to Arthur and Alan's wife is Helen. Hetty's sign isn't Taurus (clue 3), so Leo and Helen's is Taurus.

In summary:
Hazel, Libra, Anthony, Capricorn.
Helen, Taurus, Alan, Pisces.
Hetty, Leo, Alfred, Scorpio.
Hilda, Gemini, Albert, Aries.
Holly, Sagittarius, Arthur, Cancer.

Census Sensibility (No 66)
Tom Wheeler has seat 4 (clue 3) and seat 5 is a man's (clue 5), so (clue 10) Lucy Graham has seat 1 and Esther Lyon is in seat 3. Harriet Smith isn't in 2 (clue 1), so 6 and the person looking at the Newcastle records has seat 5 (clue 7). William Dane isn't in 2 (clue 2), so 5 and John Alden is in 2. Thus (clue 8) Lucy Graham is checking the

SOLUTIONS

Leeds records. The man examining the Bristol records is immediately right of someone checking North London or West London records (clue 9), so he's thus in seat 4. John Alden isn't checking the North London or West London records (clue 4), so those from Salisbury. Harriet Smith isn't looking at the North London records (clue 6), so West London records and Esther Lyon is checking the North London ones.

In summary:
1, Lucy Graham, Leeds.
2, John Alden, Salisbury.
3, Esther Lyon, North London.
4, Tom Wheeler, Bristol.
5, William Dane, Newcastle.
6, Harriet Smith, West London.

Suffering Cats (No 67)

Hannah went in third (clue 4) and David owns Tiny Tim (clue 5). Catullus, seen first, isn't Sarah's (clue 2) or Michael's (clue 1), so Katy's and (clue 7) had a cut paw and Oedipus was seen second and thus had cat flu (clue 6). He isn't Michael's (clue 1), so Sarah's. Mitzi had the broken tooth (clue 3). The cat which had the injections wasn't Sam (clue 1), so Tiny Tim. Tiny Tim wasn't seen fifth (clue 1), so fourth. Michael's cat was seen fifth and isn't Sam (clue 1), so Mitzi. Hannah's pet is Sam and suffers an abscess.

In summary:
David, Tiny Tim, injections, fourth.
Hannah, Sam, abscess, third.
Katy, Catullus, cut paw, first.
Michael, Mitzi, broken tooth, fifth.
Sarah, Oedipus, cat flu, second.

In the Frame (No 68)

Nigel is in stall C (clue 3), so (clue 1) Jackie is in B. Derek Raynes isn't in D (clue 2), so A and the jockey in D is Paddy, riding Saturday Night (clue 4). Silk is Nigel (clue 1) and Mr Jingle is the mount of Derek Raynes. Nigel's horse isn't Sea Fret (clue 3), so Placebo. Jackie's is Sea Fret. Paddy isn't Mount (clue 4), so Ryder. Jackie is Mount.

In summary:
A, Mr Jingle, Derek Raynes.
B, Sea Fret, Jackie Mount.
C, Placebo, Nigel Silk.
D, Saturday Night, Paddy Ryder.

In Business (No 69)

Mr Bailey is the decorator (clue 1) and Mr Andrews paid for box C (clue 4). The plumber whose advert is in box D isn't Mr Rogers (clue 5), so Mr Kilroy who trades in South Lane (clue 2). Bailey didn't place the box A advertisement for the Station Road business (clue 3), so placed B. The address in box C is Main Street (clue 1), so Mr Bailey's is the business in Church Street. By elimination, Mr Rogers' is in Station Road. Mr Andrews isn't the florist (clue 4), so the landscape gardener. Mr Rogers is the florist.

In summary:
Box A, Rogers, florist, Station Road.
Box B, Bailey, decorator, Church Street.
Box C, Andrews, landscape gardener, Main Street.
Box D, Kilroy, plumber, South Lane.

I Do... Again (No 70)

Oscar Lavisch was the financier (clue 5) and Dean Richland was husband number three (clue 2), so Ga-Ga's fifth husband who was in oil but who wasn't Buck Pyle (clue 3) and who wasn't Barney Silverspoon (clue 4), was Harvey Cashmore, with his personal wealth of $20 million (clue 6). The property magnate was worth more than Buck Pyle (clue 4), so wasn't the second husband, worth $14 million (clue 1), or the first (clue 4). He immediately followed Barney Silverspoon as Ga-Ga's husband (clue 4), so wasn't her fourth. Thus the third was the property magnate and the second was Barney Silverspoon. The husband who made his money in computers was worth $18 million (clue 1), so Barney was in shipping. By elimination, the $18 million man was Buck Pyle. Oscar Lavisch was worth less than $20 million (clue 5), so $16 million and the husband worth $22 million was property-owner Dean Richland. Buck Pyle wasn't Ga-Ga's first husband (clue 1), so her fourth. Her first was Oscar Lavisch.

In summary:
First, Oscar Lavisch, financier, $16 million.
Second, Barney Silverspoon, shipping, $14 million.
Third, Dean Richland, property, $22 million.
Fourth, Buck Pyle, computers, $18 million.
Fifth, Harvey Cashmore, oil, $20 million.

They Also Serve (No 71)

Paul reached the semi-final (clue 5), so the man who served at 131 mph, who was the next to be eliminated after Mark Svensson (clue 2), isn't Martin, the defeated finalist (clue 1). The man serving at 130 mph went out in the third round (clue 4), so (clue 1) Martin served at 132 mph. The player beaten in the first round didn't serve at 131 mph (clue 2), or 129 mph (clue 6), so 128 mph. The second-round loser wasn't Mark (clue 2), Charles (clue 3) or Simon (clue 6), so Harry. Martin isn't Simon (clue 6), so Charles. Harry is Willis (clue 3) who served at 131 mph; so Paul served at 129 mph. Simon was eliminated in the third round (clue 6) and thus served at 130 mph. Mark Svensson thus served at 128 mph. Simon isn't Jourdain (clue 6), so Bradley and Paul is Jourdain.

SOLUTIONS

In summary:
Charles Martin, 132 mph, final.
Harry Willis, 131 mph, second round.
Mark Svensson, 128 mph, first round.
Paul Jourdain, 129 mph, semi-final.
Simon Bradley, 130 mph, third round.

Over the Garden Wall (No 72)

Since Mrs Gabbey lives at number 10 (clue 2), the woman at number 12 isn't Madge, who is talking to Mrs Gossip about her sister (clue 1), or the woman talking about her son (clue 5). The resident of number 6 is speaking about her husband (clue 4), so the one at number 12 is talking about her daughter. She isn't Mrs Gossip (clue 1), thus Madge doesn't live at number 10, so at number 8. Mrs Gossip is at number 6 (clue 1), so Mrs Gabbey is talking about her son. Pat Chatham (clue 3) lives at number 12. Annie isn't at number 10 (clue 3), so she's Mrs Gossip and Zoë is Mrs Gabbey. Madge's surname is Tattle.

In summary:
Number 6, Annie Gossip, husband.
Number 8, Madge Tattle, sister.
Number 10, Zoë Gabbey, son.
Number 12, Pat Chatham, daughter.

Strangers in Town (No 73)

Cal Coulan was the bronco buster (clue 6), so Frank Forman from Comanche Butte wasn't the rancher (clue 5). Nor was he the buffalo hunter or gambler (clue 1), so he was the Texas Ranger going to Spanish Springs (clue 2). By elimination, Joe Jarvis was the rancher. 'Alabama' Abney, was going to Comanche Butte (clue 4), thus wasn't the buffalo hunter (clue 1), so the gambler. 'Grizzly' Gates was the buffalo hunter from Eagle Ridge (clue 1). The man travelling from Fort Hood to Eagle Ridge wasn't Joe Jarvis (clue 3), so Cal Coulan. Joe Jarvis wasn't coming from or going to Mustang City (clue 5), so was travelling from Spanish Springs to Fort Hood. By elimination, 'Alabama' Abney came from Mustang City and 'Grizzly' Gates was going there.

In summary:
'Alabama' Abney, gambler, Mustang City, Comanche Butte.
Cal Coulan, bronco buster, Fort Hood, Eagle Ridge.
Frank Forman, Texas Ranger, Comanche Butte, Spanish Springs.
'Grizzly' Gates, buffalo hunter, Eagle Ridge, Mustang City.
Joe Jarvis, rancher, Spanish Springs, Fort Hood.

Educational Excursion (No 74)

The $15 was lost at the Treasure Island (clue 5). The loss at the Golden Nugget on Tuesday (clue 2) wasn't $22 (clue 3), so $12. The $35 was won on the Wheel of Fortune (clue 1). The game of roulette at the Sahara (clue 3) didn't involve a loss of $22 (clue 2), so a win of $25. Baccarat was played on Wednesday (clue 6). Roulette wasn't played on Thursday or Friday (clue 3), so Monday and $22 was lost on Wednesday. This wasn't at the Circus (clue 6), so the Mirage and the Wheel of Fortune was at the Circus. This was on Thursday (clue 4) and $15 was lost on Friday at black jack. Video poker was played on Tuesday.

In summary:
Monday, Sahara, roulette, won $25.
Tuesday, Golden Nugget, video poker, lost $12.
Wednesday, Mirage, baccarat, lost $22.
Thursday, Circus, Wheel of Fortune, won $35.
Friday, Treasure Island, black jack, lost $15.

Domino Search (No 75)

1	0	3	4	5	1	2	4
6	5	0	0	0	2	3	4
3	1	6	1	2	4	4	6
6	1	5	5	0	3	3	2
6	4	0	4	5	6	3	5
5	3	2	1	3	1	0	5
6	0	1	6	2	2	2	4

Retiring Types (No 76)

Derek Gordon got the CD player (clue 1). The man retiring after 18 years was presented with a camera and isn't Len Rogers (clue 3), so was George Doughty of Sales (clue 4). Beryl Peacock retired after 24 years (clue 4) and Derek Gordon had been with the firm for more than 30 years (clue 1). The employee with 16 years' service wasn't Jean Kelly (clue 2), so Len Rogers. The person from Accounts had worked for the company for 33 years (clue 5). The Export employee hadn't been there for 16 years (clue 2), so neither was Len Rogers. Nor was Len retiring from Personnel (clue 3), so from Purchasing and was presented with the clock (clue 6). Beryl Peacock wasn't given the video player (clue 4), so garden furniture. Jean Kelly got the video player. The person from Export wasn't Derek Gordon (clue 1) or Jean Kelly (clue 2), so Beryl Peacock. Jean Kelly didn't work in Personnel (clue 2), so Accounts. Derek Gordon was in Personnel.

In summary:
Beryl Peacock, Export, 24 years, garden furniture.
Derek Gordon, Personnel, 31 years, CD player.
George Doughty, Sales, 18 years, camera.
Jean Kelly, Accounts, 33 years, video player.
Len Rogers, Purchasing, 16 years, clock.

Punnet of Strawberries (No 77)

The phone number 100775 is for Rose Cottage, where either Bernard or Felicity lives (clue 4), so Vernon's house in Mill Lane has 100670 (clue 6) and the number for Badger's Holt in The Street is 100635 (clue 6). The number for Snow Hill ends in a zero (clue 3), so it's 100740. Rose Cottage isn't in Church Green (clue 4), so London Road and the number for the Church Green house is 100845. Prudence's house isn't Valley View and her number isn't 100845 (clue 2), so it's 100740 and Valley View is in Snow Hill. Vernon's house isn't Oakhurst (clue 1), so Moonrakers and Oakhurst is in Church Green. It isn't Julian's (clue 1) or (lower phone number than Bernard's, clue 5) Felicity's, so Bernard's is Oakhurst. Rose Cottage belongs to Felicity (clue 4), so Badger's Holt to Julian.

In summary:
Bernard, Oakhurst, Church Green, 100845.
Felicity, Rose Cottage, London Road, 100775.
Julian, Badger's Holt, The Street, 100635.
Prudence, Valley View, Snow Hill, 100740.
Vernon, Moonrakers, Mill Lane, 100670.

Square Dances (No 78)

Thirty are watching the act in the centre of the Square (clue 2) and 140 are watching Danny (clue 5). Carly is on the south side but hasn't an audience of 80 (clue 1) or 120 (clue 3), so 60. The north side audience isn't of 120 (clue 3) or 140 people (clue 5), so 80. The 120 people aren't watching Wizzo the magician (clue 3) or Lisa (clue 6), so Darren. Lisa isn't on the north side (clue 6), so she's in the centre and Wizzo is on the north side. The tumbler hasn't an audience of 120 or 140 (clue 6), so 60. The juggler is on the east side (clue 4). Lisa isn't the unicyclist (clue 2), so the mime artist. Darren isn't the unicyclist (clue 2), so the juggler. Danny is the unicyclist.

In summary:
Carly, south side, tumbler, 60.
Danny, west side, unicyclist, 140.
Darren, east side, juggler, 120.
Lisa, centre, mime artist, 30.
Wizzo, north side, magician, 80.

Hooke, Lyne, Sinker (and all) (No 79)

Tony is angler B (clue 3), thus (clue 1) Sinker, who caught no fish, isn't D. Paul caught 3 (clue 7). Angler E caught 2 (clue 6), so (clue 5) Grant Reel caught 5. Thus angler D caught 3 (clue 5). Hooke in position A (clue 2) thus caught 4. Angler E isn't Fergus (clue 1) or Dave (clue 6), so Andy. Grant Reel isn't C (fewer than Bates, clue 4), so F. Sinker isn't B (clue 1), so C and Fergus is Hooke. By elimination, Tony caught one fish and Sinker is Dave. Bates isn't B or D (clue 4), so E. Tony isn't Lyne (clue 3), so Rodd. Paul is Lyne.

In summary:
A, Fergus Hooke, 4.
B, Tony Rodd, 1.
C, Dave Sinker, 0.
D, Paul Lyne, 3.
E, Andy Bates, 2.
F, Grant Reel, 5.

By a Babbling Brook (No 80)

Jason is in tent 4 (clue 4) and Lesley in tent 2 (clue 2). Tent 1 is blue (clue 5), thus (clue 1) John and Sally are in tent 1 and tent 3 is green. Tent 4 is grey (clue 3) and Tara is in tent 3. Tent 2 is brown and Kelly is in tent 4. Patrick isn't in tent 3 (clue 3) so 2. Alan is in tent 3.

In summary:
Tent 1, John and Sally, blue.
Tent 2, Patrick and Lesley, brown.
Tent 3, Alan and Tara, green.
Tent 4, Jason and Kelly, grey.

First Impressions (No 81)

Each performer impersonated a star of his or her own sex (clue 1). The cook performed third (clue 6). Sally appeared second (clue 7) and isn't the woman who did the Madonna impression, who was on immediately before Rod, the mechanic (clue 2), so Sally impersonated Cilla Black and Lindsey impersonated Madonna. Rod didn't perform first (clue 2), so he was fourth or fifth and Lindsey third or fourth, ie the person who was fourth is either Rod or Lindsey. Thus (clue 3) Colin performed third. Lindsey was fourth (clue 2) and Rod fifth; so Geoff was first. The milk deliverer whose subject was Jon Bon Jovi (clue 5) is Geoff. Lindsey is the teacher (clue 4) and Sally the chiropodist. Colin impersonated Sting (clue 3), so Rod impersonated Stevie Wonder.

In summary:
Colin, third, Sting, cook.
Geoff, first, Jon Bon Jovi, milk deliverer.
Lindsey, fourth, Madonna, teacher.
Rod, fifth, Stevie Wonder, mechanic.
Sally, second, Cilla Black, chiropodist.

Mine's a Mini (No 82)

Jeremy's car is J registered (clue 4) and Pat's has the Union Jack roof (clue 5). The M registered Mini with chrome wheel-trims (clue 7) isn't Dave's (clue 1), or Anne's (clue 3), so Sally's and (clue 2) is silver. The red Mini has a K registration (clue 6), thus (clue 3) the yellow car is Jeremy's. The letter of the pink Mini with nudge bars isn't B (clue 1), so F and Dave owns the B registered car. Anne's car is pink (clue 3) and Dave's has extra lights. Jeremy's has the musical horn and Pat's is red, so Dave's is green.

In summary:
Anne, pink, F, nudge bars.
Dave, green, B, extra lights.
Jeremy, yellow, J, musical horn.
Pat, red, K, Union Jack roof.
Sally, silver, M, chrome wheel-trims.

Party Lines (No 83)

Jade's party made £165 (clue 1) and the hostess who chose the clock had sales of £140 (clue 5), so Ruby's total, which was less than £200 and was accompanied by the candelabra gift (clue 3), was £180. The Monday party at which the ring was chosen (clue 2), wasn't hosted by Jade (clue 1), Beryl (clue 2) or Pearl (clue 4), so by Gemma. The £260 party took place on Wednesday (clue 6), so Monday's total was £230. Jade didn't choose the wine glasses (clue 1), so the cuddly toy and the wine glasses were chosen on Wednesday. Jade's party was on Thursday (clue 1). Ruby's was on Friday (clue 4) and Pearl's on Wednesday. Beryl's was on Tuesday and had sales of £140.

In summary:
Monday, Gemma, £230, ring.
Tuesday, Beryl, £140, clock.
Wednesday, Pearl, £260, wine glasses.
Thursday, Jade, £165, cuddly toy.
Friday, Ruby, £180, candelabra.

Hitting the Headlines (No 84)

Holtby's story appeared on Friday (clue 2) and Ronald was featured in Thursday's paper (clue 6). Tuesday's reported the retirement (clue 7), so (clue 1) featured Daniel Perry and Monday's story was the paragliding accident. Edgar's tale wasn't told on Monday or Friday (clue 4), so Wednesday. Janice formed the action group (clue 3), so Emma had the paragliding accident and Janice's surname is Holtby. Emma's is Chambers (clue 4) and Ronald is the new bishop. Edgar stopped the runaway horse. His surname isn't Vernon (clue 5), so Leeson. Ronald's is Vernon.

In summary:
Daniel Perry, Tuesday, retirement.
Edgar Leeson, Wednesday, stopped runaway horse.
Emma Chambers, Monday, paragliding accident.
Janice Holtby, Friday, formed action group.
Ronald Vernon, Thursday, named bishop.

A-haunting We Will Go (No 85)

The apparition first seen in 1493 wasn't the mastiff (clue 1), the white boar (clue 2), the monk (clue 3) or the grey lady (clue 4), so the headless man and the monk was first seen in 1549 (clue 5). The abbey apparition is the headless man (clue 3). The monk doesn't haunt the manor (clue 2), monastery or rectory (clue 3), so the hall. The

grey lady is in Grimlyn (clue 4). The abbey isn't in Aarghyll (clue 1), Dredleigh (clue 2) or Fantoume (clue 3), so Raith. The 1670 apparition is an animal (clue 4), not the mastiff (clue 1), so the boar. Thus the Dredleigh apparition is the monk (clue 2). The Grimlyn grey lady was first seen in either 1721 or 1807, as was the Fantoume apparition (clue 3), so the Aarghyll sighting was in 1670. The mastiff was first seen in 1721 (clue 1). By elimination, the grey lady was first seen in 1807 and the mastiff is in Fantoume. The boar haunts the monastery (clue 3). The rectory apparition was first seen in 1721 (clue 4), so the grey lady haunts the manor.

In summary:
Grey lady, manor, Grimlyn, 1807.
Headless man, abbey, Raith, 1493.
Large mastiff, rectory, Fantoume, 1721.
Monk, hall, Dredleigh, 1549.
White boar, monastery, Aarghyll, 1670.

On the Beach (No 86)

Mr Kidd came by van (clue 2) and Mr Burr is with Dawn (clue 4), so Jane who came by car and isn't with Mr Ross (clue 6) is with Mr Watt. Kate's surname is Swan (clue 3) and she isn't with Mr Ross (clue 6), so Mr Kidd. Thus Mrs Ross who's with her husband (clue 6) is Zena. Tony who's with Ms Clay (clue 4) is Mr Watt, so Dawn's surname is Hunt. Jack is the man in couple A (clue 5). Tony and Jane aren't couple B (clue 4) or couple D (clue 6), so C and (clue 6) Zena and her husband are D. Thus Mr Ross isn't Alan (clue 1), so Gary. He didn't travel by train (clue 1), so coach. Mr Burr travelled by train. Alan is the man in couple B. Alan is thus Mr Kidd (clue 4) and Jack is Mr Burr.

In summary:
A, Jack Burr, Dawn Hunt, train.
B, Alan Kidd, Kate Swan, van.
C, Tony Watt, Jane Clay, car.
D, Gary Ross, Zena Ross, coach.

Give Me a Ring (No 87)

Adam made the third visit (clue 6). The fifth wasn't made by Graeme and Natalie (clue 1), Darren (clue 2) or Jonathan, who bought the opal ring (clue 5), so by Gareth. Since the second couple chose the sapphire (clue 4), the first male visitor, who accompanied Miranda (clue 3), wasn't Darren, whose visit immediately preceded that of Sharon, who chose a ruby ring (clue 2), thus Jonathan was first. Penny was one of the second couple (clue 5), so her fiancé is Darren. By elimination, Graeme and Natalie made the fourth visit, and (clue 1) the emerald ring was bought by Gareth. By elimination, Sharon was engaged to Adam, Natalie chose the diamond and Gareth's fiancée is Zoë.

In summary:
Adam, Sharon, ruby, third.
Darren, Penny, sapphire, second.
Gareth, Zoë, emerald, fifth.
Graeme, Natalie, diamond, fourth.
Jonathan, Miranda, opal, first.

Logi-5 (No 88a)

A	B	E	C	D
D	A	B	E	C
C	D	A	B	E
E	C	D	A	B
B	E	C	D	A

ABC (No 88b)

	B	C		A
		A	B	C
A	C			B
C		B	A	
B	A		C	

House Points (No 89)

Peacocks won the egg and spoon race (clue 2) and in the race that Herons won, Peacocks came third (clue 6), so the sprint, where Eagles came third (clue 3), wasn't won by either Peacocks or Herons. Nor was it won by Kingfishers (clue 3), so by Mallards and (clue 5) Kingfishers came second. Herons came second in the skipping race (clue 1). Third place in the skipping race didn't go to Kingfishers, so Mallards (clue 1) and Herons came second. Herons didn't win the relay race (clue 4), so third place didn't go to Peacocks, Kingfishers (clue 4), Eagles or Mallards, so to Herons. By elimination, Kingfishers came third in the egg and spoon race. Second place didn't go to Mallards (clue 2), so to Eagles. By elimination, Herons won/Peacocks came third in the sack race. Mallards thus came second in the sack race and Peacocks came second in the relay. The winner of the relay wasn't Kingfishers (clue 3), so Eagles. Kingfishers won the skipping race.

In summary:
Egg and spoon, Peacocks, Eagles, Kingfishers.
Relay, Eagles, Peacocks, Herons.
Sack, Herons, Mallards, Peacocks.
Skipping, Kingfishers, Herons, Mallards.
Sprint, Mallards, Kingfishers, Eagles.

International Calls (No 90)

Jim Hart phoned from Bombay (clue 5). Rick Plotkin rang from the USA but not from Chicago (clue 4), so either Los Angeles or New York. Neither of these calls was on Sunday (clues 2 and 5). Sunday's call wasn't from Chicago (clue 4), so either Bombay or Sydney. Kate Nilson called on Saturday (clue 2). Sunday's call wasn't from Cliff Brown (clue 2) or Sally Thynn (in the USA, clue 3), so was from Jim Hart in Bombay and the call from Los Angeles was on Tuesday (clue 5). The New York call wasn't on Saturday (clue 2), so Cliff Brown's wasn't on Thursday. The publisher didn't call on Saturday (clue 1), so Sally Thynn's call wasn't on Thursday (clue 3). Thus Rick Plotkin called on Thursday from New York. Cliff Brown called on Wednesday (clue 2) and Bob's stepchild called from Los Angeles. By elimination, the stepchild is Sally Thynn. Bob's old friend didn't call on Wednesday (clue 1) and Kate Nilson's and Rick Plotkin's were both business calls (clue 2 and 4), so the old friend is Jim Hart. The lawyer didn't call on Thursday or Saturday (clue 4), so Wednesday. The call from Chicago was Kate Nilson's (clue 4), so Cliff Brown's was from Sydney. The client's agent called after the publisher (clue 1), so Kate Nilson is the client's agent and Rick Plotkin is the publisher.

In summary:
Sunday, Jim Hart, Bombay, old friend.
Tuesday, Sally Thynn, Los Angeles, stepchild.
Wednesday, Cliff Brown, Sydney, lawyer.
Thursday, Rick Plotkin, New York, publisher.
Saturday, Kate Nilson, Chicago, client's agent.

Pandemonium Enterprises (No 91)

The owner of the firm with 24 workers wasn't Extranius (clue 1), Nonplus (clue 3) or Surplus (clue 4), so Uncius. The man with 28 wasn't Nonplus (clue 3) or Surplus (clue 4), so Extranius. The firm with 12 wasn't Fitted Furniture (clue 3), Venison Burgers (clue 4) or Mosaic Tiles (clue 5), so Herbal Remedies. Extranius's company wasn't Venison Burgers (clue 4) or Mosaic Tiles (clue 5), so Fitted Furniture. The firm in unit 4 wasn't Fitted Furniture (clue 1), Herbal Remedies (clue 2), or Mosaic Tiles (clue 5), so Venison Burgers. The firm in unit 3 wasn't Fitted Furniture (clue 3) or Herbal Remedies (clue 2), so Mosaic Tiles. The latter had 24 employees (clue 5) and Venison Burgers had 18. Fitted Furniture was in unit 2 (clue 1) and Herbal Remedies in unit 1. Surplus doesn't own Venison Burgers (clue 4), so Herbal Remedies. Nonplus owns Venison Burgers.

In summary:
Unit 1, Herbal Remedies, Surplus, 12.
Unit 2, Fitted Furniture, Extranius, 28.
Unit 3, Mosaic Tiles, Uncius, 24.
Unit 4, Venison Burgers, Nonplus, 18.

SOLUTIONS

Crafty Ladies (No 92)

Room C had 25 items (clue 6). Room D had either 20 or 23 (clue 2) and since neither A nor E had 30 (clue 1), the 30 were in B. Thus Gillian's room was A and the hand-knitting exhibition was in C (clue 1). Angela's room wasn't B (clue 4). Christine wasn't in B or C and Susan wasn't in B (clue 5), so Marie was the woman in B. The person in E wasn't Susan (clue 3) or Angela (clue 4), so Christine and (clue 5) there were 23 items in D. Christine's display hadn't 28 items (clue 5), so 20. By elimination, there were 28 items in A and (clue 2) these were of hand-weaving. The tapestry exhibition isn't in D or E (clue 4), so B. Angela didn't display oil paintings or knitting (clue 4), so quilting in (by elimination) room D. Susan hand-knitted the 25 items and Christine exhibited oil paintings.

In summary:

A, Gillian, hand-weaving, 28.
B, Marie, tapestry, 30.
C, Susan, hand-knitting, 25.
D, Angela, quilting, 23.
E, Christine, oil painting, 20.

Wheelie Difficult (No 93)

The mishap which befell the cyclist who wore No 6 wasn't the skid (clue 2), puncture (clue 3), collision with the hedge (clue 4) or the snapped chain (clue 5), so was falling in the ditch. The withdrawal at 31 miles wasn't due to the puncture (clue 3), collision, fall or skid (clue 7), so to the chain snapping. Peddler dropped out at 25 miles (clue 5). Spokesworth thus went 31 miles (clue 6). No 21's problem wasn't the skid (clue 2), collision (clue 4) or broken chain (clue 5), so the puncture. Chayne was No 6 (clue 3). The first man to withdraw wasn't Treddwell (clue 1) or Chayne (clue 3), so Saddler. Peddler's number wasn't 40 or 53 (clue 5), so 32. He didn't collide with the hedge (clue 4), so was the victim of the skid. Treddwell's departure was at 19 miles (clue 1), so Chayne fell in the ditch after 16 miles. Saddler had a puncture (clue 3). Spokesworth's number wasn't 40 (clue 5), so 53. Treddwell's was 40 and he collided with the hedge.

In summary:

Chayne, No 6, fell in ditch, 16 miles.
Peddler, No 32, skidded, 25 miles.
Saddler, No 21, puncture, 14 miles.
Spokesworth, No 53, chain snapped, 31 miles.
Treddwell, No 40, collided with hedge, 19 miles.

Home and Away (No 94)

Sandfield were the visitors in the game covered by Pass (clue 2) and the visiting team in Bill's match were Lingmoor (clue 7). Danny Ruck didn't report on the Winstone v Markwell match (clue 4), nor that involving Fenborough (clue 3), so he watched Dagford, who weren't at Boringham (clue 5). Gordon reported from Rawfleet (clue 1) and Tackle from Tibleigh (clue 6), so Dagford were at Thrumley. The visitors watched by Tackle weren't Fenborough (clue 3), so Lingmoor and Tackle is thus Bill. Boringham's home game wasn't reported by Chris (clue 5), so by Sandy and Chris covered the Winstone v Markwell game. Sandy is Pass (clue 5) and Chris is Boot. Gordon is Maul and saw Rawfleet v Fenborough.

In summary:

Bill Tackle, Tibleigh v Lingmoor.
Chris Boot, Winstone v Markwell.
Danny Ruck, Thrumley v Dagford.
Gordon Maul, Rawfleet v Fenborough.
Sandy Pass, Boringham v Sandfield.

An All-round Test (No 95)

No 1 had two even figures (clue 2). He wasn't Cloutov (clue 1), Pullov (two odd figures, clue 2), Nokov or Smitov (clue 4), or Swipov (clue 5), so Pinchitov. Pinchitov didn't concede 14 runs (clue 5), so (clues 2 and 4) 20. Smitov scored 18 runs (clue 4), so (clues 2 and 3) Pinchitov scored 12. His combined figure was thus 32, so (clue 6) Nokov's was 33 (17+16) and Pullov's 34 (21+13). Cloutov's figures were 15 and 14 (clue 1), so Pullov's were 21 and 13. Smitov scored 18 and conceded 19 (clue 4), so Swipov scored 10 and conceded 11. He was No 2 (clue 5) and No 4 was Smitov (clue 1). Nokov was No 6 (clue 4). Cloutov was No 3 (clue 5), so Pullov was No 5.

In summary:

No 1, Pinchitov, 12, 20.
No 2, Swipov, 10, 11.
No 3, Cloutov, 15, 14.
No 4, Smitov, 18, 19.
No 5, Pullov, 21, 13.
No 6, Nokov, 17, 16.

After Hours (No 96)

The surname of the speaker whose talk drew an audience of 36 wasn't Copeland (clue 1), Britton (clue 3), Granger (clue 4) or Richards (clue 5), so Wanstead. The surname of the one whose talk was attended by 46 wasn't Copeland (clue 1), Britton (clue 3) or Richards (clue 5), so Granger. Wanstead's first name isn't Kenneth (clue 1), Philip (clue 2), or John (clue 3). Since John's talk wasn't on Steam Railways, Wanstead isn't David (clues 2 and 3), so Bertrand and David gave the talk on Steam Railways. His audience wasn't 43 or 46 (clue 3). Nor was Philip's or Kenneth's audience 46 (clue 4). Thus John had the audience of 46 and David's was 41 (clue 4). Philip's wasn't

SOLUTIONS

43 (clue 4), so 38 and Kenneth's was 43. Philip is thus Copeland (clue 1). Local Castles was Britton's topic (clue 2) and since it attracted a bigger audience than Richards' talk (clue 5), it drew 43. By elimination, David's surname is Richards. Geology of Yorkshire was attended by 36 (clue 1). The talk on the River Tees wasn't by Philip (clue 4), so John. Philip's topic was Coastal Erosion.

In summary:
Bertrand Wanstead, Geology of Yorkshire, 36.
David Richards, Steam Railways, 41.
John Granger, River Tees, 46.
Kenneth Britton, Local Castles, 43.
Philip Copeland, Coastal Erosion, 38.

Fast Forward (No 97)

The stage one patient at bed 3 was a man and at bed 6 a woman (clue 5). Since it was only at stage two that there were women in opposite beds (clue 4), there was a man in bed 1 at stage one. Thus there was a woman in 2 at stage one (clue 2) and men in 2 at stages two and three. The two men opposite each other in stage one were in 3 and 4 (clue 4). Bed 4 thus had a woman at stage two (clue 5). With beds 1 and 6 having opposite sequences of bed occupancy (clue 5), bed 1 had a woman at stage three and bed 6, a man. The two stages where a man's bed was between two women's beds were two and three (clue 3). At stage three, this could only have happened with beds 1, 2 and 3, so bed 3 was occupied by a woman. This wasn't a stage where two women were opposite each other (clue 4), so there was a man in bed 4. Beds 1 and 6 were occupied by persons of the same sex at stage two (clue 5). If these had been men, there would have been two pairs of opposite men, which isn't possible (clue 4). So 1 and 6 were women's beds and (clue 4) there was a man in bed 3.

In summary:
Bed 1, man, woman, woman.
Bed 2, woman, man, man.
Bed 3, man, man, woman.
Bed 4, man, woman, man.
Bed 5, man, man, man.
Bed 6, woman, woman, man.

Figure It Out (No 98)

3	6	8	2	3	4
1	4	6	3	5	2
9	3	8	4	1	8
2	5	9	5	7	1
9	8	7	6	5	4
2	7	1	7	9	6

Logi-Path (No 99)

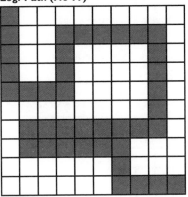

Drones at Ascot (No 100)

The Hon Sybilla is Miss Ponsonby (clue 1) and Edward accompanied Miss Wotherspoon (clue 6). Caroline, who went to Ascot with Montague (clue 5), isn't Miss Cullompton (clue 3), or Miss Rockingham (clue 4), so Miss Beauchamp and (clue 2) wore the blue hat. Miss Rockingham isn't Heather (clue 3) or Ariadne (clue 4), so Diana, who wore the primrose hat (clue 7). Ariadne wore the cream hat (clue 4). Sybilla's hat wasn't pink (clue 1), so beige hat and Heather's was pink. Heather's escort was Archie (clue 1), so she's Miss Cullompton and Ariadne is Miss Wotherspoon. The Hon Sybilla was escorted by Gerald (clue 5) and Rupert escorted Diana.

In summary:
Archie Fotheringhay, Heather Cullompton, pink.
Edward Tanqueray, Ariadne Wotherspoon, cream.
Gerald Huntington, Hon Sybilla Ponsonby, beige.
Montague Ffolliott, Caroline Beauchamp, blue.
Rupert de Grey, Diana Rockingham, primrose.

Floral Tributes (No 101)

Violet's husband Jeremy didn't give her roses (clue 3) or violets (clue 1), so lilies. Rose didn't get roses (clue 1), so violets and Lily got roses. John Flowers didn't buy the violets (clue 2), so his wife is Lily, thus Rose's husband is James. Mr Bloom isn't Jeremy (clue 4), so James. Jeremy is Mr Plant.

In summary:
Lily Flowers, John, roses.
Rose Bloom, James, violets.
Violet Plant, Jeremy, lilies.

Sackcloth and Ashes (No 102)

McNee's dismissal came after 40 minutes (clue 4), so Legge's, which wasn't after 25 minutes (clue 3), was after 65 and he's the striker (clue

1). Midfielder Foote (clue 2) thus went after 25 minutes and McNee is the defender. Legge didn't use his elbow as an offensive weapon (clue 1) or execute a damaging trip (clue 3), so was jostling the referee. Nor was the trip offence Foote's (clue 2), so it was McNee's and Foote jabbed an opponent with his elbow.

In summary:
Foote, 25 minutes, use of elbow, midfielder.
Legge, 65 minutes, jostling referee, striker.
McNee, 40 minutes, tripping, defender.

Logi-5 (No 103a)

C	D	A	E	B
B	E	D	A	C
A	C	E	B	D
E	B	C	D	A
D	A	B	C	E

ABC (No 103b)

	C	B		A
A			C	B
C		A	B	
	B	C	A	
B	A			C

Mayday! (No 104)

The Cygnet's propeller is fouled (clue 3) and the boat in a collision is at Wroxham (clue 1), so the Neptune which is moored at Ludham Bridge but hasn't a jammed rudder (clue 4) has water in the fuel. The Orchid isn't at Wroxham (clue 1), so has a jammed rudder and the Emerald is at Wroxham. The boat at Oulton Broad has 2 berths (clue 2). The Orchid has 5 (clue 1), so it's at Burgh Castle. The boat at Oulton Broad is Cygnet. The Neptune has 3 berths (clue 3), so the Emerald has 4.

In summary:
Cygnet, 2-berth, Oulton Broad, propeller fouled.
Emerald, 4-berth, Wroxham, collision.
Neptune, 3-berth, Ludham Bridge, water in fuel.
Orchid, 5-berth, Burgh Castle, rudder jammed.

Tung Street (No 105)

Mrs Jones lives at number 1 (clue 2) and Mrs Williams talked about Mrs Davies (clue 4) and Mrs Jones lives at number 1 (clue 2). Miss Taylor was gossiped about by a woman whose house number is two higher than that of Mrs Brown, who related that one resident was behind with the rent (clue 3), so Miss Taylor was gossiped about by Mrs Smith. Thus the allegation that Mrs Robinson was carrying on (clue 1) came from Mrs Jones and Mrs Brown talked about Mr Miller. Mrs Smith isn't at number 5 (clue 2), so number 7 and Mrs Brown is at number 5 (clue 3), thus Mrs Williams is at number 3. She didn't say Mrs Davies was in trouble with the law (clue 4), so drinking again and Miss Taylor was alleged to be in trouble with the law.

In summary:
Mrs Brown, No 5, Mr Miller, behind with rent.
Mrs Jones, No 1, Mrs Robinson, carrying on.
Mrs Smith, No 7, Miss Taylor, trouble with law.
Mrs Williams, No 3, Mrs Davies, drinking again.

Car-ry on Rallying (No 106)

The Alvis is Harry Innes's car (clue 2) and the Delahaye arrived on a van trailer (clue 4). The Connaught isn't Iris James's blue car (clue 1) nor does it belong to Ron Stirling (clue 3), so it's Frank Graham's. The yellow car which was driven to the event is the Alvis (clue 5). The vehicle which arrived on a car trailer isn't the Bristol (clue 3), so the Connaught and Ron Stirling's car is the Bristol. Iris James's is thus the Delahaye and the Bristol came on a lorry. It isn't white (clue 3), so green and the Connaught is white.

In summary:
Alvis, yellow, Harry Innes, driven.
Bristol, green, Ron Stirling, on lorry.
Connaught, white, Frank Graham, on car trailer.
Delahaye, blue, Iris James, on van trailer.

Indian File (No 107)

The translation of Gantuma includes Yellow (clue 3). The English equivalent of Kiawewe begins with Black but doesn't include Desert Flower (clue 1). The Black name also doesn't include Singing (clue 1) and another begins Long Mountain (clue 5), so the name is Black Running something. It isn't Feather (clue 1). One of the names is Happy something Wind (clue 4) and the third word of the translation of Haranto is Thunder (clue 6), so it's Black Running Elk. The second word of the name beginning Happy isn't Yellow (clue 3), so Singing. By elimination, Haranto means Long Mountain Thunder and Gantuma is something Yellow Feather. The translation of Tecume doesn't include Singing (clue 2), so it's something Desert Flower, leaving Happy Singing Wind as the meaning of Chalako. Tecume's translation doesn't begin with Big (clue 2), so it's Little Desert Flower and Yellow Feather follows the word Big in the translation of Gantuma.

SOLUTIONS

In summary:
Chalako, Happy Singing Wind.
Gantuma, Big Yellow Feather.
Haranto, Long Mountain Thunder.
Kiawewe, Black Running Elk.
Tecume, Little Desert Flower.

Pile Up (No 108)
From the top:
F, D, B, C, A, E

The Chips are Down (No 109)
Francesca is with Count Zaleski (clue 1) and
Lisette's companion has placed a £15,000 bet
(clue 4). Sir Brian Ranby has bet £25,000 (clue
2), thus he isn't with Isabella (clue 3) or Cecilia
(clue 6), so Sacha. The £5,000 bet is on number
12 (clue 5), so Isabella's companion has bet
£10,000 (clue 3). Thus Count Zaleski has a bet of
£20,000 on number 20 (clue 1). Prince Werther
placed £15,000 on number 32 (clue 2), so Sir
Brian Ranby has bet on number 16 and number
12 was chosen by Cecilia's companion. He isn't
Sir Vincent Tate (clue 6), so Lord Langridge. Sir
Vincent is accompanied by Isabella and has bet on
number 24.

In summary:
Count Zaleski, Francesca, 20, £20,000.
Lord Langridge, Cecilia, 12, £5,000.
Prince Werther, Lisette, 32, £15,000.
Sir Brian Ranby, Sacha, 16, £25,000.
Sir Vincent Tate, Isabella, 24, £10,000.

Miss Raffles at The Royal (No 110)
Kirk Mooney is in room 5 (clue 4) and Brian
Davis is in Z Files (clue 6). The star of The Law in
room 1 isn't Vince Young (clue 1) or Peter Stone
(clue 2), so Glenda James, who's playing Miss
Raffles (clue 3). The actor playing Tom Wright
is in room 2 (clue 5). The man playing Vorzinski
has a room numbered two higher than that of
the actor from Londoners (clue 2), so can't
be in room 3. Nor is room 3 that of the man
playing Inspector McKee (clue 5), so the man in
room 3 is the one who plays A J Raffles in Chaps
Misbehaving (clue 6). Kirk Mooney isn't the star
of Londoners (clue 2), so he's in Hammerdale
and the star of Londoners is in room 2. Peter
Stone is in room 3 (clue 2) and the man in room
4 plays Vorzinski. By elimination, he's Brian Davis,
the Londoners star is Vince Young and Kirk
Mooney plays Inspector McKee.

In summary:
Room 1, Glenda James, The Law, Miss Raffles.
Room 2, Vince Young, Londoners, Tom Wright.
Room 3, Peter Stone, Chaps Misbehaving, A J
Raffles.
Room 4, Brian Davis, Z Files, Vorzinski.
Room 5, Kirk Mooney, Hammerdale, Insp McKee.

Mission Accomplished (No 111)
The plane which ran out of fuel landed at 1340
(clue 3) and Rick, whose rudder was shot off,
also made an afternoon landing (clue 2). The
1030 landing wasn't made by the plane whose
undercarriage was shot off (clue 6) nor (clue 1)
by the pilot who blacked out after the balloon-
busting mission, so the plane whose engine had
seized made its landing at 1030. The man who
blacked out had been balloon busting (clue 1)
and the 1520 incident involved the pilot who
had been strafing enemy lines (clue 5). Billy's
emergency wasn't at 1115 or 1705 (clues 1 and
3) or 1520 (clue 5), so 1030. Thus (clue 1) the
blackout pilot made the 1115 landing. Dennis had
been artillery spotting (clue 4). Billy hadn't been
on escort patrol (clue 7), so a reconnaissance
flight. Dennis didn't land at 1705 (clue 4), so he
ran out of fuel. The 1705 landing didn't involve
the shot-away undercarriage (clue 6), so the
missing rudder. By elimination, the plane with
its undercarriage shot away landed at 1520 and
Rick's mission was as escort patrol. Jim didn't
land at 1520 (clue 5), so 1115 and Ben landed at
1520.

In summary:
Ben, strafing enemy lines, undercarriage shot off,
1520.
Billy, reconnaissance, engine seized, 1030.
Dennis, artillery spotting, ran out of fuel, 1340.
Jim, balloon busting, blacked out, 1115.
Rick, escort patrol, rudder shot off, 1705.

Inter Relations (No 112)
Constance's name is on headstone 2 (clue 4).
Ellen's isn't on stone 1 (clue 1), so 3 and Maud's
is on stone 1. James's isn't on stones 1 or 2 (clue
6), so 3. Samuel's wife died in 1894 (clue 2) and
Mrs Tombs died in 1899 (clue 5). Samuel wasn't
Stones (clue 2), so Graves. Thus (clue 4) he was
Maud's husband. Adam who died in 1891 (clue
3) was married to Constance. Ellen died in 1887
(clue 4), so Mrs Tombs was Constance. James
and Ellen were the Stones. James didn't die in
1896 (clue 3), so 1884 and Samuel died in 1896.

In summary:
Stone 1, Graves, Samuel, 1896, Maud, 1894.
Stone 2, Tombs, Adam, 1891, Constance, 1899.
Stone 3, Stones, James, 1884, Ellen, 1887.

Backing Out (No 113)
Robin hit the garage door (clue 3) and Mark's
father is Greg (clue 6), so Michael's son who hit
the dog (clue 1), is James. Diane had passed ten
days ago (clue 2) and Henry's offspring five days
ago (clue 5). Mark hadn't been driving for two
or twelve days (clue 6), so seven and James for
two. The lawn mower was hit by the driver with
twelve days' experience (clue 4). Mark didn't hit

his brother's bike (clue 6), so the gatepost. By elimination, Robin was driving for five days, Diane hit the bike and Emma the lawn mower. Emma's father isn't Roger (clue 4), so John. Diane's is Roger.

In summary:
Greg, Mark, gatepost, 7 days.
Henry, Robin, garage door, 5 days.
John, Emma, lawn mower, 12 days.
Michael, James, dog, 2 days.
Roger, Diane, brother's bike, 10 days.

The High Life (No 114)

The Belgian climber was homesick (clue 6) and Paul was defeated by gales (clue 7). Dieter the German didn't have the nose bleed (clue 1), nor is he the asthma sufferer who reached 4,600 metres (clues 1 and 4), so he was defeated by the severe cold. The Briton gave up at 4,200 metres (clue 8) and Peter at 4,400 (clue 5). Dieter didn't give up at 4,000 (clue 3), so 3,800 metres and (clue 1) the nose bleed occurred at 4,000 metres. Thus the Belgian gave up at 4,400 metres and he's Peter; and Paul gave up at 4,200 metres, so he's the British climber. The Frenchman reached 4,600 metres (clue 2) and the Dutch climber 4,000. Frank is Dutch (clue 2) and Richard is French.

In summary:
Dieter, German, 3,800 metres, cold.
Frank, Dutch, 4,000 metres, nose bleed.
Paul, British, 4,200 metres, gales.
Peter, Belgian, 4,400 metres, homesick.
Richard, French, 4,600 metres, asthma.

Logi-Path (No 115)

En Garde, Mousquetaire! (No 116)

Gorille was the 7.30 opponent (clue 5) and Archamos fought with Bourricot (clue 7), so Silvis who fought at 8.00 (clue 2) and who thus didn't fight Dingue (clue 4) or Laideron (clue 8),

fought Balourd who had kicked his horse (clue 6). The insult to the King led to the 6.30 duel (clue 4). The 6.00 duel wasn't caused by a personal insult (clue 1) nor was it Uramis' fight about the ugly beard (clue 8), so it was about the splashed tunic. The challenger wasn't Maximos (clue 3) or Damos (clue 4), so Archamos. The 6.30 challenger wasn't Damos (clue 4), so Maximos and Damos was personally insulted. Dingue didn't fight at 6.30 (clue 4), so 7.00 and Laideron at 6.30. Damos fought at 7.30 (clue 4) and Uramis at 7.00.

In summary:
6.00, Archamos, Bourricot, splashed tunic.
6.30, Maximos, Laideron, insulted King.
7.00, Uramis, Dingue, ugly beard.
7.30, Damos, Gorille, personal insult.
8.00, Silvis, Balourd, kicked horse.

Playing Away (No 117)

The score was 1-2 at St Johns (line 6) and Benfield play at Stamford Green (lines 13-14). The 3-0 game at Horton Road (lines 3-4) wasn't against Armley or Denton (lines 1-5), so Westhampton. I didn't attend the match with Paul (lines 9-10), Pete, with whom I travelled to Denton (line 1), Keith, who was with me for the 2-2 draw (line 7), or Don, who was with me at The Elms (line 8), so Steve. As Denton do not play at Old Mill (line 2), their ground is Craven Hall. The score there wasn't 3-0, 2-2 or 1-2. Nor was it 1-0 (lines 11-12), so Pete joined me to watch us beat Denton 2-0. Paul wasn't at the 1-0 game (line 11), so the 1-2 game. By elimination, the 1-0 match was at The Elms with Don, playing Armley. Thus I went to Benfield with Keith and with Paul to St Johns' ground at Old Mill.

In summary:
Don, Armley, The Elms, 1-0.
Keith, Benfield, Stamford Green, 2-2.
Paul, St Johns, Old Mill, 1-2.
Pete, Denton, Craven Hall, 0-2.
Steve, Westhampton, Horton Road, 3-0.

February Fun (No 118)

Since 26 is in C2 (clue 1), the horizontal sequence 5, 20, 14 (clue 2) isn't in A2, B2 or C2. F2 contains an odd number (clue 5), so the 5, 20, 14 sequence doesn't start in D2 or E2, so isn't in row 2. Nor is it in row 3 (clue 2). Since C4 also contains an odd number (clue 5), the 5, 20, 14 sequence isn't in A4 or B4. Nor can the 5 be in C4, since the 7 isn't in F2 (clues 5 and 7). The 3 is in F4 (clue 1), so the 5, 20, 14 sequence isn't in D4 or E4, thus it isn't in row 4, so in row 1. The 5 isn't in A1 (clue 4) and the 18 is in E1 (clue 1), so the sequence cannot start in C1, D1 or E1, which leaves its only possible starting square as B1. The 10 is thus in B4 and the 15 in B2 (clue 9), the 20 is in C1 and the 14 in D1. The 21 is in B3 (clue 10). We now know that C1, D1 and E1 all contain two-digit numbers, so the only other one in that row is the 13 (clue 8), which isn't in A1 or G1 (clue 4), so F1. The single-digit numbers in A1 and G1 (clues 4 and 8), are either 8 and 4, 4 and 2 or 2 and 1. The five numbers already placed in row 1 total 70, so 4 and 2 would make 76 and 2 and 1, 73, neither of which are possible (clue 8). So the 8 is in A1 and the 4 in G1. Since the 7 isn't in row 1, the 12 isn't in row 1 or row 2 (clue 7). Nor is it in row 4 (clue 3), so it's in row 3 and the 7 and 11 in row 2 (clue 7). Since the 26 is in C2, the 7 isn't in A2. Nor is it in E2 (clue 6), so (clue 7) it's in D2, the 11 is in F2 and the 12 in D3. The number in D4 is 23 (clue 6) and (clue 10) the 27 is in F3. The 17 isn't in column E (clue 6), or C (clues 6 and 7), so A and the 9 in column C (clue 7). The 1 is in C3 (clue 11) and the 9 in C4, so the 17 is in A4 and the 6 in A3 (clue 7). The 19 isn't in column E (clue 6) or G (clue 10), so A. The only odd number yet unplaced is 25, so this is in G4 (clue 4). The only single-digit number yet unplaced is 2, so it's in E2 (clue 5). The 24 isn't in E4 (clue 3), so (clue 12) it's in E3 and the 28 is in E4. The 22 is in G2 (clue 3) and the 16 in G3.

In summary:

8	5	20	14	18	13	4
19	15	26	7	2	11	22
6	21	1	12	24	27	16
17	10	9	23	28	3	25

Logi-5 (No 119a)

A	E	D	C	B
C	B	E	A	D
E	D	C	B	A
B	C	A	D	E
D	A	B	E	C

ABC (No 119b)

A			C	B
	B	A		C
C			B	A
B	A	C		
	C	B	A	

Detective Works (No 120)

Philippa Dean's books are set in London (clue 2) and Charlotte Neill's fictional detective is Rosie Rycroft (clue 1), so Scotland-based Sgt Currie, whose author is a woman (clue 4), is the creation of Susan Dewar. The eight books are the work of a man (clue 4) and the ten are set in Cornwall (clue 5), so Philippa Dean (clue 2) has written twelve. Four books feature Inspector Crisp (clue 6), so Susan Dewar has written six. By elimination, Charlotte Neill has written ten. The novels with the Norfolk setting are the eight written by a man (clue 1). By elimination, the Inspector Crisp novels are set in Manchester. They aren't the work of Ernest Bradley (clue 3), so Ian Lenton and Ernest Bradley wrote eight. His detective isn't Lady Lavinia Poole (clue 3), so Henry Madison. Philippa Dean created Lady Lavinia Poole.

In summary:

Charlotte Neill, Rosie Rycroft, ten books, Cornwall.

Ernest Bradley, Henry Madison, eight books, Norfolk.

Ian Lenton, Inspector Crisp, four books, Manchester.

Philippa Dean, Lady Lavinia Poole, twelve books, London.

Susan Dewar, Sgt Currie, six books, Scotland.

Domino Search (No 121)

1	3	6	2	4	0	5	6
5	2	0	2	1	1	0	2
4	4	0	2	4	6	0	3
5	0	6	5	6	3	5	5
2	3	0	4	1	4	5	0
1	6	6	6	2	1	3	1
1	2	3	4	4	5	3	3

Water Babies (No 122)

Samantha in lane 3 is third (clue 2), so Sonia Herring is either first in lane 2, or second in lane 1 (clue 1). Thus the swimmer for the greens isn't fourth in lane 4 or first in lane 2 (clue 1). The blues are in lane 1 (clue 4), so the green team is using lane 3 and are represented by Samantha. Sonia is second in lane 1 (clue 1) and is the blues' swimmer. Wendy isn't swimming for the yellows (clue 3), so the reds and Jenny represents the yellows. Jenny isn't in lane 4 (clue 3), so is first in lane 2 and Wendy is in lane 4. Samantha's surname is Codd (clue 5). Wendy's is Seal (clue 3), so Jenny's is Fish.

SOLUTIONS

In summary:
Lane 1, Sonia Herring, blue.
Lane 2, Jenny Fish, yellow.
Lane 3, Samantha Codd, green.
Lane 4, Wendy Seal, red.

Busking in the Sun (No 123)
Busker C plays the violin (clue 5). The Science student who plays the pan pipes hasn't pitch A or D (clue 1), so is Eleanor on pitch B (clue 3) and (clue 1) Rosalie is on pitch C. Jonathan the Classics student doesn't play the harmonica (clue 2), so the ukulele and Donald plays the harmonica. Jonathan hasn't pitch D (clue 4), so A and D is Donald's. Rosalie isn't reading Theology (clue 5), so Law. Theology is Donald's subject.
In summary:
A, Jonathan, Classics, ukulele.
B, Eleanor, Science, pan pipes.
C, Rosalie, Law, violin.
D, Donald, Theology, harmonica.

Lecture Tour (No 124)
Dr Searle's lecture begins at 10 o'clock (clue 4) and Dr Keenan's starts later than Dr Garvey's (clue 1). The 9 o'clock lecture isn't being given by Mr Blake or Mrs Newell (clue 5), so is Dr Garvey's on Medieval History (clue 1). Mrs Newell is in room 3 (clue 3). The 9.15 lecture in room 2 isn't being given by Mr Blake (clue 2), so Dr Keenan. The Romantic Poets lecture is in room 1 (clue 2), so Dr Garvey's is in room 4 (clue 1). Mr Blake's lecture isn't in room 1 (clue 2), so room 5, Dr Searle's is in room 1 and Mr Blake's starts at 10.45. The 10.45 subject is French Literature (clue 6). By elimination, Mrs Newell's lecture starts at 11 o'clock. Its subject isn't Calculus (clue 3), so Biophysics and the Calculus lecturer is Dr Keenan.
In summary:
9.00, room 4, Dr Garvey, Medieval History.
9.15, room 2, Dr Keenan, Calculus.
10.00, room 1, Dr Searle, Romantic Poets.
10.45, room 5, Mr Blake, French Literature.
11.00, room 3, Mrs Newell, Biophysics.

Just Managing (No 125)
Nesbitt is in charge of building 2 (clue 7) and Mervyn of building 3 (clue 3). Neither the jewellers nor Nathan Lucas' businesses are in 1 or 4 (clue 1), so they're in 5 and 6. Since 6 is the hotel (clue 5), the jewellers is in 5 (clue 1) and Nathan Lucas manages the hotel. Terry's computer store isn't on the same side of the street as the furniture store, so Terry's isn't in 2 (clue 2), so 4 and the furniture store is in 2. Building 3 houses the travel agency (clue 4), building 1 is the bank, managed by Brett and Mervyn's surname is Barrymore. Nesbitt isn't

Arnold (clue 7), so Robert and Arnold manages the jewellers. Brett is Walker (clue 6), Arnold is Coombes and Terry is Gilroy.
In summary:
1, bank, Brett Walker.
2, furniture store, Robert Nesbitt.
3, travel agents, Mervyn Barrymore.
4, computer store, Terry Gilroy.
5, jewellers, Arnold Coombes.
6, hotel, Nathan Lucas.

Logi-5 (No 126a)

E	B	A	D	C
D	C	E	A	B
C	E	D	B	A
B	A	C	E	D
A	D	B	C	E

ABC (No 126b)

B		C	A	
	A		B	C
A	C			B
		B	C	A
C	B	A		

Thrilling Words (No 127)
The vet chose book number 2 (clue 5) and Wendy is the optician (clue 1). Killer At Large, taken out by the nurse (clue 3), isn't book 3 selected by Olive, whose title has an even number of words (clue 4), so Olive is the barmaid. Thus book 2 is Death In The Rough (clue 2) and Joyce chose book 1, so Joyce is the nurse. By elimination, the vet is Mary and Wendy took out book 4. Olive's book wasn't Nemesis (clue 4), so Mayday Murder. Nemesis was chosen by Wendy.
In summary:
Book 1, Killer At Large, Joyce, nurse.
Book 2, Death In The Rough, Mary, vet.
Book 3, Mayday Murder, Olive, barmaid.
Book 4, Nemesis, Wendy, optician.

Buenos Dias (No 128)
Maria Benavento was the Thursday client (clue 1) and Felipe San Martin was the policeman (clue 5), so the Monday client, who was an engineer (clue 3) and who wasn't Rosita Jimenez (clue 2) or Pablo Machado from Mexico (clue 4), was Carlos Perez. The novelist was from Spain (clue 5). Pablo Machado wasn't the surgeon (clue 4), so banker. The Uruguayan was Wednesday's client

(clue 1). Carlos Perez wasn't from the Philippines (clue 2), so Costa Rica and Rosita Jimenez was Tuesday's client. Thus Wednesday's was Felipe San Martin, Pablo Machado was the Friday client and the surgeon was from the Philippines. The latter wasn't seen on Thursday (clue 4), so Tuesday. Maria Benavento was from Spain.

In summary:
Monday, Carlos Perez, Costa Rica, engineer.
Tuesday, Rosita Jimenez, Philippines, surgeon.
Wednesday, Felipe San Martin, Uruguay, policeman.
Thursday, Maria Benavento, Spain, novelist.
Friday, Pablo Machado, Mexico, banker.

Local Misgovernment (No 129)
George Flint was a company director (clue 1) and the estate agent ran a property racket (clue 5). The garage owner who was the 1998 Mayor (clue 4) wasn't the solicitor or Ann Chester who misused the car (clue 7), so Ann Chester was the publican. Susan Ryde, Mayor in 1994 (clue 2) wasn't the solicitor (clue 7), so the estate agent who ran the property racket. Ann Chester wasn't Mayor in 1995 (clue 3) or 1997 (clue 7), so 1996, the solicitor was Mayor in 1997 and George Flint in 1995. George Flint didn't have an affair with the Town Clerk (clue 1), nor was he involved in smuggling (clue 6), so he embezzled funds. The smuggler wasn't the solicitor (clue 6), so garage owner and the solicitor had the affair. Trevor Wells wasn't Mayor in 1998 (clue 4), so 1997 Mayor and John Lincoln was the 1998 Mayor.

In summary:
1994, Susan Ryde, estate agent, property racket.
1995, George Flint, company director, embezzlement.
1996, Ann Chester, publican, misused car.
1997, Trevor Wells, solicitor, affair with Town Clerk.
1998, John Lincoln, garage owner, smuggling ring.

Vee Short Interviews (No 130)
The balloonist born in the Eastland area was female (clue 3). She wasn't Alison Byrd, whose connection was her first job (clue 1) or Louise Mann, the novelist (clue 2), so was Jill Keevil. Vee's 12.30 interview was with Paul Quiller (clue 4), so her 9.30 appointment with the person whose mother is their connection (clue 6) wasn't with the inventor (clue 5). Nor was it with Louise Mann (clue 2), Jill Keevil (clue 5) or the pop singer (clue 6), so with the tennis player. Thus the 9.30 interviewee was Simon Tees. Louise Mann's connection wasn't her school (clue 2), so her grandfather and the school was

the connection for Paul Quiller. Vee saw Louise Mann at 2.00 (clue 2) and the inventor at 12.30 (clue 5), so Jill Keevil at 3.30. By elimination, Alison Byrd was interviewed at 11.00 and was the pop singer.

In summary:
9.30am, Simon Tees, tennis player, mother.
11.00am, Alison Byrd, pop singer, first job.
12.30pm, Paul Quiller, inventor, school.
2.00pm, Louise Mann, novelist, grandfather.
3.30pm, Jill Keevil, balloonist, birthplace.

Uncle Derek's Club (No 131)
Hannah is 11 (clue 1) and MacMahon is 12 (clue 6). The ninth birthday was on Thursday (clue 5), so (clue 3) Cheryl Vickers is the 9-year-old and the Monday birthday was an eighth. Adam's birthday was on Wednesday (clue 2). Hannah's wasn't on Friday (clue 7), so Tuesday. Waites is 8 (clue 1) and Hannah's surname is Temple (clue 4). By elimination, Fellowes is 10. Friday's birthday was MacMahon's (clue 7), so Adam's surname is Fellowes. MacMahon isn't Dean (clue 6), so Belinda and Dean is Waites.

In summary:
Monday, Dean Waites, 8.
Tuesday, Hannah Temple, 11.
Wednesday, Adam Fellowes, 10.
Thursday, Cheryl Vickers, 9.
Friday, Belinda MacMahon, 12.

Clubland (No 132)
Sir Peter Rowse has malt whisky (clue 1), so the banker with gin and tonic who is neither a peer nor Bernard Golding (clue 3), is Sir Anthony Grant who has The Times (clue 1). Lord Newbury has brandy and soda (clue 4), so Lord Redman has whisky and soda (clue 2) and Mr Golding has sherry. Lord Redman has the Daily Telegraph (clue 5). Mr Golding hasn't the Independent (clue 3) or Herald Tribune (clue 2), so the Guardian and he's the industrialist (clue 6). Sir Peter Rowse isn't reading the Herald Tribune (clue 4), so the Independent and Lord Newbury has the Herald Tribune. Sir Peter Rowse isn't in horse-racing (clue 4) and isn't the shipping magnate (clue 6), so he's the economist. The shipping magnate isn't Lord Newbury (clue 4), so Lord Redman. Lord Newbury is in horse-racing.

In summary:
Bernard Golding, Guardian, sherry, industrialist.
Lord Newbury, Herald Tribune, brandy and soda, horse-racing.
Lord Redman, Daily Telegraph, whisky and soda, shipping.
Sir Anthony Grant, The Times, gin and tonic, banker.
Sir Peter Rowse, Independent, malt whisky, economist.

SOLUTIONS

Battleships (No 133)

Domino Search (No 134)

1	5	0	5	6	5	6	2
3	2	4	3	0	5	3	0
1	5	1	3	2	3	1	6
4	6	0	0	0	4	1	4
4	2	2	2	5	3	4	5
1	6	4	6	6	1	2	0
5	2	3	1	4	3	6	0

Floor Show (No 135)

The girl in area C was given a 9.9 (clue 4), so the girl doing the floor exercises in area B (clue 1) was given a 9.8 and Gerda's top mark was 9.6. Natalie in area D (clue 2) was thus given a 9.7. Lara on the parallel bars (clue 3) was given the 9.9. By elimination, Gerda was in area A and the girl doing floor exercises is Barbara. Gerda wasn't on the beam (clue 5), so the vault and Natalie was on the beam.

In summary:
A, Gerda, vault, 9.6.
B, Barbara, floor, 9.8.
C, Lara, bars, 9.9.
D, Natalie, beam, 9.7.

Foreign Food (No 136)

Agich and Ruom's and the Green Fort are both in Domes (clue 4) and Proj-Ka's is totally dark (clue 5).The restaurant in Tunnel J3A which serves live food isn't the Violet Planet (clue 2), so the 19 Brothers. The Graypecian restaurant with a methane atmosphere isn't Agich and Ruom's (clue 6), or the Green Fort which serves Slanian food (clue 4), so the Violet Planet. Since only one of the restaurants with a non-oxygen

atmosphere is in a Dome (clue 1), the other is in Tunnel C7, thus it's the Violet Planet. Thus the eatery with a chlorine atmosphere is in a Dome – not the Port Dome (clue 1) or Old Dome (clue 3), so the Market Dome. Proj-Ka's isn't in the Port Dome (clue 5), so the Old Dome. Its cuisine isn't Adomphan (clue 3) or Purian (clue 5), so Karakatian. By elimination, the restaurant in the Port Dome serves poisonous food. This isn't Adomphan (clue 1) or Purian (clue 5), so Slanian. By elimination, the chlorine-atmosphered eatery in the Market Dome is Agich and Ruom's. Its cuisine isn't Adomphan (clue 3), so Purian and the Adomphan restaurant is the 19 Brothers.

In summary:
Agich and Ruom's, Market Dome, Purian, chlorine atmosphere.
Green Fort, Port Dome, Slanian, poisonous food.
19 Brothers, Tunnel J3A, Adomphan, live food.
Proj-Ka's, Old Dome, Karakatian, totally dark.
Violet Plant, Tunnel C7, Graypecian, methane atmosphere.

Over the Ditch (No 137)

Guy Fenton worked with Argent (clue 5) and Trudy Vane went to Dijon (clue 4). The agent who worked with Serin in Lille wasn't Dinah Ewart (clue 5) or Alec Cooper (clue 2), so Jack Moody. Serin was a mechanic (clue 4). The agent sent to Toulouse wasn't Alec Cooper or Guy Fenton (clue 3), so Dinah Ewart. Faucon was a dentist (clue 1). The police sergeant's codename wasn't Levrier (clue 3) or Argent (clue 5), so Pelerin. The police inspector wasn't Levrier (clue 3), so Argent and Levrier was the café owner. The agent who worked with Pelerin, wasn't Trudy Vane (clue 4) or Dinah Ewart (clue 5), so Alec Cooper, who wasn't sent to Rouen (clue 3), so Avignon. By elimination, Guy Fenton went to Rouen. Faucon didn't operate in Dijon (clue 1), so Toulouse and Levrier was in Dijon.

In summary:
Alec Cooper, Avignon, Pelerin, police sergeant.
Dinah Ewart, Toulouse, Faucon, dentist.
Guy Fenton, Rouen, Argent, police inspector.
Jack Moody, Lille, Serin, mechanic.
Trudy Vane, Dijon, Levrier, café owner.

On and Off (No 138)

Five passengers boarded at 10.05 (clue 6). The library was the 10.14 stop (clue 5). Thus 3 passengers got on at 10.08 (clue 2), the bus stopped at Odeon Corner at 10.11 and 9 alighted at the library at 10.14. Six left the bus at the shopping mall (clue 4), so (clue 7) 8 alighted at the post office and (clue 3) 2 boarded there. Seven got off at 10.11 (clue 7). By elimination, the bus stopped at the post office at 10.17. The number who got on at the library wasn't 4 (clue

SOLUTIONS

5), so 6 and 4 boarded at Odeon Corner. The number which got off at 10.05 is 6 (clue 1) and 5 got off at 10.08 at the station.

In summary:
Library, 10.14, 6 on, 9 off.
Odeon Corner, 10.11, 4 on, 7 off.
Post office, 10.17, 2 on, 8 off.
Shopping mall, 10.05, 5 on, 6 off.
Station, 10.08, 3 on, 5 off.

Gone Viking (No 139)

Snorri's wife was Gudrid (clue 2) and Thorwald had been missing for 3 years (clue 5). Thorhild's husband missing for a year wasn't Eyjolf (clue 2) or Eric (clue 7), so Bjarni, whose ship was the Ice Dragon (clue 1). Freydis' husband's ship, also named after a dragon (clue 6) was the Great Dragon. Vigdis' husband's was the Stormrider (clue 3). The wife of the Seasnake's captain wasn't Sigrid (clue 7), so Snorri. By elimination, Sigrid's husband was on the Black Shark which had been missing for 7 years (clue 4), so (clue 3) Vigdis' husband was gone for 5 years. By elimination, Snorri was missing for 6 years and Thorwald was Freydis' husband. Eyjolf wasn't 7 years (clue 2), so 5 and Sigrid's husband was Eric.

In summary:
Freydis, Thorwald, Great Dragon, 3 years.
Gudrid, Snorri, Seasnake, 6 years.
Sigrid, Eric, Black Shark, 7 years.
Thorhild, Bjarni, Ice Dragon, 1 year.
Vigdis, Eyjolf, Stormrider, 5 years.

Down Under (No 140)

The Antarctic expedition was in December (clue 1) and Victor went to the Indian Ocean (clue 6). Auguste's April expedition wasn't to the North or South Atlantic (clue 3), so the South Pacific. The July expedition was organised by Didier Pieuvre (clue 2). Requin explored the South Atlantic (clue 5), so Didier the North Atlantic. The October expedition was Hippocampe's (clue 4), so Requin set out in March. By elimination, Hippocampe's trip was to the Indian Ocean. Requin isn't Bruno (clue 5), so Emmanuel and Bruno explored the Antarctic. Calmar isn't Auguste (clue 5), so Bruno and Auguste is Soumarin.

In summary:
Auguste Soumarin, South Pacific, April.
Bruno Calmar, Antarctic, December.
Didier Pieuvre, North Atlantic, July.
Emmanuel Requin, South Atlantic, March.
Victor Hippocampe, Indian, October.

Bar of Judgment (No 141)

Matt's in seat 3 (clue 2). The drinker in seat 4 isn't Alison, who thinks the show 'excellent' (clue 4) or Tracey (clue 5), so Jack. He doesn't think the show's 'disappointing' (clue 1) or 'not bad' (clue 5), so 'rubbish'. The one who thinks the show's 'not bad' isn't Tracey (clue 5), so Matt and Tracey thinks it 'disappointing'. Tracey is in seat 2 (clue 5) drinking mineral water (clue 3) and Jack in seat 4 is drinking red wine. By elimination, Alison is in seat 1. She isn't drinking gin and tonic (clue 4), so white wine and Matt has gin and tonic.

In summary:
1, Alison, white wine, 'excellent'.
2, Tracey, mineral water, 'disappointing'.
3, Matt, gin and tonic, 'not bad'.
4, Jack, red wine, 'rubbish'.

Logi-Path (No 142)

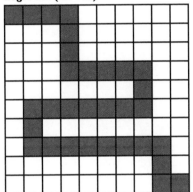

Because it was There (No 143)

Horatio's expedition was in 1861 (clue 3) and Rathbone's was in 1857 (clue 5). Solomon's wasn't in 1865 (clue 1), so 1857 and Wickstead's trip to the Amazonian forest was in 1853. Handyside's first name was Leopold (clue 2). Gideon explored Western Australia (clue 6), so Wickstead was Marmaduke. Gideon's surname wasn't Boswell (clue 6), so Prothero and Boswell was Horatio. Leopold's expedition wasn't in 1849 (clue 2), so 1865 and Gideon's was in 1849. Horatio went to the Canadian north (clue 2) and Solomon to Darkest Africa (clue 4), thus Leopold went to Tibet.

In summary:
Gideon Prothero, Western Australia, 1849.
Horatio Boswell, Canadian north, 1861.
Leopold Handyside, Tibet, 1865.
Marmaduke Wickstead, Amazon forest, 1853.
Solomon Rathbone, Darkest Africa, 1857.

Tea Time (No 144)

Monday's trip was to Ashdene (clue 6). Fruit cake was eaten on Sunday (clue 3), so Wednesday's visit was to Millwood and jam was sampled on Monday (clue 2). Thus the Inglenook is in Ashdene. Meringues were eaten in Oakmeadow but not on Saturday (clue 3), so Tuesday. Saturday's trip wasn't to Stoneybrook (clue 1), so Sunday's was to Stoneybrook and clotted cream from the Wishing Well was enjoyed on Saturday. By elimination, Saturday's trip was to Thatchleigh and chocolate cake was the speciality of the Millwood tea-room. The Copper Kettle wasn't visited on Wednesday or Tuesday (clue 4), so Sunday. Wednesday's tea wasn't at the Tudor Cottage (clue 5), so the Mulberry Tree. The Oakmeadow tea-rooms were visited on Tuesday.

In summary:
Saturday, Wishing Well, Thatchleigh, clotted cream.
Sunday, Copper Kettle, Stoneybrook, home-made fruit cake.
Monday, Inglenook, Ashdene, home-made jam.
Tuesday, Tudor Cottage, Oakmeadow, meringues.
Wednesday, Mulberry Tree, Millwood, chocolate cake.

Puzzle it Out (No 145)

A woman does the Bugle crossword (clue 1), Emma buys the Globe (clue 7) and the giant crossword appears in the Planet (clue 5). Rodney's cryptic crossword isn't in the Watchman (clue 3), so the Clarion, on Wednesday (clue 6). The paper whose general knowledge puzzle is published on Thursday isn't the Bugle (clue 1) or the Watchman (clue 3), so the Globe. Kevin's paper isn't the Bugle (clue 1) or the Planet (clue 5), so the Watchman. Caroline does the Sunday crossword (clue 2), so (clue 3) Kevin's is on Monday. The Planet isn't the Sunday paper (clue 5), so Saturday's and Sunday's is the Bugle. By elimination, Janice does the Saturday crossword. The skeleton crossword isn't in the Watchman (clue 4), so the Bugle and the thematic crossword is in the Watchman.

In summary:
Caroline, skeleton, Sunday, Bugle.
Emma, general knowledge, Thursday, Globe.
Janice, giant, Saturday, Planet.
Kevin, thematic, Monday, Watchman.
Rodney, cryptic, Wednesday, Clarion.

Aiming High (No 146)

The rocket launched on September 21st wasn't Hybus (clue 2), Rekniz (clue 3), Superlox V (clue 5) or Lopez II (clue 6), so DZQ. It didn't reach 10 miles (clue 1), but went further than 5.5 miles, since at least two rockets were less successful. Ruritania's rocket went further (clue 1), so wasn't sent up on January 7th (clue 4). Nor was January 7th the date of the launch by Banania (clue 3), Balonia (clue 5) or Columnia (clue 6),

so was Gondwanaland's and Hybus went up on March 29th. The 3-mile failure, which preceded the 8.5-mile one (clue 4) wasn't on July 10th (clue 2), so DZQ returned to earth from 6 miles. These first two rockets were both less successful than DZQ. The January 7th one didn't reach 3 miles (clue 4), so 5.5 miles. Thus Hybus failed at 3 miles, the rocket launched on May 16th reached 8.5 and the one launched on July 10th, 10 miles. Balonia sent up its rocket before July but not on May 16th (clue 5), so March 29th. Superlox V was launched on January 7th (clue 5). Columnia's didn't reach 8.5 miles (clue 6), so 6 miles. Rekniz was launched on May 16th (clue 3) and Banania's rocket on July 10th. By elimination, Banania's was Lopez II and Rekniz was Ruritania's.

In summary:
January 7th, Gondwanaland, Superlox V, 5.5 miles.
March 29th, Balonia, Hybus, 3 miles.
May 16th, Ruritania, Rekniz, 8.5 miles.
July 10th, Banania, Lopez II, 10 miles.
September 21st, Columnia, DZQ, 6 miles.

Prodigy Close (No 147)

Bright plays chess (clue 1), Linda is the runner (clue 2) and the pianist at number 2 is a girl (clue 5). Matthew Best is neither the violinist nor the swimmer (clue 4), so the tennis player. The Marvells live at number 3 (clue 3) and Kieron at number 5 (clue 6). The violinist doesn't live at number 6 (clue 5). Matthew doesn't live at number 6 (clue 7), so the violinist lives at number 3 (clue 4) and Matthew at number 1. Kieron isn't the swimmer (clue 4), so plays chess and (clue 1) Jamie lives at number 6. Thus Jamie is the swimmer and Linda lives at number 4. The Dazzlers' house is number 4 (clue 7), Linda is Dazzler and Mary is at number 2. Naomi is thus the violinist. Mary's surname isn't Tallant (clue 5), so Nonesuch and Jamie's is Tallant.

In summary:
1, Best, Matthew, tennis.
2, Nonesuch, Mary, piano.
3, Marvell, Naomi, violin.
4, Dazzler, Linda, running.
5, Bright, Kieron, chess.
6, Tallant, Jamie, swimming.

Who Goes There? (No 148)

The driver of car 4 wasn't John (clue 1), Betty (clue 3) or Maggie (clue 4), so Dick and is a Vauxhall (clue 2) and car 3 was heading for village D, which is Dimbourne (intro and clue 2). Neither of the first two cars was making for village B (clue 1), so Dick was going there and (clue 3) Betty was going to C, Kidwell. Betty and/ or John drove either cars 1 and/or 2 (clue 1), so car 3 is Maggie's and Betty's car is the Fiat. Village B is Walbury (clue 4) so A is Brigthorpe and was

John's destination. The Citroën isn't car 1 (clue 5), so either 2 or 3. If John's is car 1, then car 2 is Betty's Fiat (clue 1), which (clue 5) isn't possible. So John's is car 2 and (above) Betty's is car 1. Car 3 is the Citroën (clue 5), so John has a Rover.

In summary:
Car 1, Betty, Fiat, village C, Kidwell.
Car 2, John, Rover, village A, Brigthorpe.
Car 3, Maggie, Citroën, village D, Dimbourne.
Car 4, Dick, Vauxhall, village B, Walbury.

The Empire Looks Back (No 149)

Picture A is of Kevin Kaye (clue 5) and picture E is from The Bird From Gozo (clue 4). The picture of Tom Briscoe in Whitehouse has a shot of Sandra Singer one place clockwise from it (clue 6), so isn't F. Nor is it B or C (clue 1), so it's D and thus shows him as Dr Boswell (clue 2). E is of Sandra Singer (clue 6) and C shows the star playing Kit Shannon and is from Comrade Abel. Michelle Hammond's clockwise neighbour is playing Xantipon (clue 3) and C is of a woman (clue 1), so C shows Emma Eastley and B shows Charlie Cotman as Jean Gaudier (clue 7). F is of Michelle Hammond (clue 7) in The Third Woman. Charlie Cotman isn't in Henry VI (clue 1), so The 40th Step and Kevin Kaye is the star of Henry VI. Sandra Singer didn't play Sergeant Fox (clue 4), so Ginger and Michelle Hammond played Sergeant Fox.

In summary:
A, Kevin Kaye, Xantipon, Henry VI.
B, Charlie Cotman, Jean Gaudier, The 40th Step.
C, Emma Eastley, Kit Shannon, Comrade Abel.
D, Tom Briscoe, Dr Boswell, Whitehouse.
E, Sandra Singer, Ginger, The Bird From Gozo.
F, Michelle Hammond, Sergeant Fox, The Third Woman.

Battleships (No 150)

Logi-5 (No 151a)

C	E	B	D	A
E	B	D	A	C
B	D	A	C	E
D	A	C	E	B
A	C	E	B	D

ABC (No 151b)

C		A	B	
B		C		A
A	B			C
	C	B	A	
	A		C	B

Cutting Remarks (No 152)

The first customer wasn't Ginger (clue 3), Curly (clue 4), Shorty or Baldie (clue 5), so Blondie. He isn't Harry (clue 1), Jack (clue 3), Fred or Roy (clue 5), so Peter. Pybus was the 9.50 customer (clue 2) who (clue 5) is Fred and the 10.30 customer was Baldie. Pybus isn't Curly or Shorty (clue 2), so Ginger. Baldie is Jack (clue 3). Harry's turn wasn't at 11.40 (clue 3), so 11.00 and Farmer's was at 11.40. By elimination, Farmer's first name is Roy. He isn't Shorty (clue 1), so Curly and Harry is Shorty. Harry isn't Dowson or Walker (clue 5), so Spoors. Walker isn't Jack (clue 5), so Peter and Jack is Dowson.

In summary:
Fred, Pybus, Ginger, 9.50.
Harry, Spoors, Shorty, 11.00.
Jack, Dowson, Baldie, 10.30.
Peter, Walker, Blondie, 9.20.
Roy, Farmer, Curly, 11.40.

Photo Development (No 153)

The location of the photograph at A isn't Salcombe (clue 1), Little Haven (clue 3), Milford-on-Sea or Swanage (clue 4), so Tenby. She wasn't 1 or 3 (clue 2) or 5 or 6 on that holiday (clue 4), so 4. Thus she was 5 at Milford (clue 4) and 6 at Swanage. She wasn't 3 at Little Haven (clue 3), so 3 at Salcombe and 1 at Little Haven. The Salcombe photograph is D (clue 2) and the Little Haven E (clue 3). The one taken at Swanage is C (clue 1) and the Milford photograph is B.

In summary:
A, Tenby, 4.
B, Milford-on-Sea, 5.
C, Swanage, 6.
D, Salcombe, 3.
E, Little Haven, 1

SOLUTIONS

The Engine Room (No 154)

The country where the man of 38 is working isn't France (clue 1), Sweden (clue 2), Scotland (clue 3) or England (clue 4), so Germany. The 50-year-old isn't Kurt or Mark (clue 2), Adolph (clue 3) or Kon (clue 4), so Fitz. The 38-year-old isn't Kurt or Mark (clue 2), or Adolph (clue 3), so Kon Fetti. The 41-year-old isn't Kurt (older than Mark, clue 2) or Adolph (clue 3), so Mark. Thus the road construction engineer is 38 (clue 2). The 41-year-old isn't in France (clue 1), Sweden (2) or Scotland (clue 3), so England. Fitz isn't in France (clue 1) or Sweden (clue 5), so Scotland. Thus Kurt isn't 47 (clue 2), so 44 and Adolph is 47. Kurt isn't in Sweden (clue 2), so France and Adolph is in Sweden. The marine engineer is Mark (clue 1) and (clue 5) the railway engineer is Fitz. The concrete expert isn't Kurt (clue 1), so Adolph. Kurt is in aircraft design.

In summary:
Adolph Finn, 47, reinforced concrete, Sweden.
Fitz Anstarts, 50, railway engines, Scotland.
Kon Fetti, 38, road construction, Germany.
Kurt Manners, 44, aircraft design, France.
Mark Thyme, 41, marine salvage, England.

Farmers' Arms (No 155)

The name of the man in seat 3 is alphabetically next after that of the man in seat 1 and next before that of the man in seat 4 (clue 5), so neither Stockman nor Syloh was in seat 1, neither Barlie nor Syloh was in 3 and neither Barlie nor Chook was in 4. Barlie wasn't in 1, Giles wasn't in 3 and Grayne wasn't in 4 (clue 1), so (clue 5) Chook wasn't in 1 or 3, thus Giles wasn't in 4. Oates ('same side of the table as', clue 4) wasn't in 1 or 5, so Stockman wasn't in 3 and Syloh wasn't in 4 (clue 5). Since Barlie wasn't in 1 (clue 1), the potato-grower wasn't in 5 and Stockman wasn't in 4 (clue 2). Oates wasn't in 3 (clue 5) and Haynes wasn't in 1. Thus the man in 1 was either Giles or Grayne, the man in 3 was Grayne or Haynes and the man in 4 was Haynes or Oates. If Grayne was in 1, then the fruit grower opposite him was in 5 (clue 4) and Syloh was in 3. But the man in 3 was Grayne or Haynes (above). Thus Grayne was in 3, Giles in 1 and Haynes in 4. The fruit grower was in 7 (clue 4), the corn grower in 6, Syloh in 5, the wheat grower in 2 and Oates in 8. The pig farmer was in 1 (clue 2), the cattle farmer in 8 and Barlie in 7 (clue 3). Chook was in 6 (clue 2), the poultry farmer in 4, the potato-grower in 3 and Stockman in 2. By elimination, Syloh grows rapeseed.

In summary:

1, Giles, pigs.	2, Stockman, wheat.
3, Grayne, potatoes.	4, Haynes, poultry.
5, Syloh, rapeseed.	6, Chook, corn.
7, Barlie, fruit.	8, Oates, cattle.

Domino Search (No 156)

1	6	3	6	0	6	0	2
6	2	2	6	6	5	3	1
2	4	1	2	4	4	0	0
0	5	5	3	0	4	5	3
4	1	3	1	4	5	3	3
1	5	0	0	1	6	4	2
6	2	3	2	1	4	5	5

Logi-5 (No 157a)

C	D	E	B	A
B	A	D	C	E
A	E	B	D	C
D	C	A	E	B
E	B	C	A	D

ABC (No 157b)

A	B		C	
C	A	B		
B		C		A
		A	B	C
	C		A	B

Down on the Farm (No 158)

Plowman works for Wiles (clue 4). Eddie Drill isn't employed by Giles (clue 3), so Stiles at Toft Farm (clue 1). Harrow works for Giles. Giles isn't at Nutwood Farm (clue 2), so Hilltop Farm and Wiles is at Nutwood Farm. Ben doesn't work at Hilltop Farm (clue 5), so he's Plowman and Jack is Harrow.

In summary:
Ben Plowman, Wiles, Nutwood Farm.
Eddie Drill, Stiles, Toft Farm.
Jack Harrow, Giles, Hilltop Farm.

Annual Event (No 159)

The nemesia plants were bought by the occupant of No 17 (clue 1). The person who bought both begonias and lobelias doesn't live at No 15 (clue 4), so No 21. The pansies were bought by the occupant of No 15 and (clue 2) Mr Green lives at No 17. Mr Raikes doesn't live at No 21 (clue 3), so No 15 and Mr Dibber at No 21. Mr Raikes didn't buy geraniums (clue 3), so impatiens. Mr Green chose geraniums.

SOLUTIONS

In summary:
Raikes, 15, impatiens, pansies.
Green, 17, geraniums, nemesia.
Dibber, 21, begonias, lobelia.

Pile Up (No 160)
From the top:
B, C, D, A, E, F

Tame Shrink (No 161)
Dr Twist was on Albion TV at 12 noon (clue 3), so (clue 5) the talk with Alison Reid about UFOs wasn't at 10.00am. Triskaidekaphobia was the topic of the 4.00pm talk (clue 2). The 10.00am talk wasn't about chocolate (clue 4), so stress. Thus the 12 noon talk was about chocolate and the 2.00pm talk was on UFOs. The talk on Radio 29 was at 4.00pm (clue 5). The chat with Clair Payne of City Radio (clue 1) was at 10.00am, so the 2.00pm piece was on Welkin-TV. Kay Sampson's wasn't on chocolate (clue 4), so triskaidekaphobia. Liz Twyford's was on chocolate.

In summary:
10.00am, Clair Payne, City Radio, stress.
12 noon, Liz Twyford, Albion TV, chocolate.
2.00pm, Alison Reid, Welkin-TV, UFOs.
4.00pm, Kay Sampson, Radio 29, triskaidekaphobia.

Misses Grundy (No 162)
The sister having an affair with a pop star was meant to be an accountant (clue 4) and the photographer was meant to be a banker (clue 2). Angela wasn't intended to be a banker or lawyer and is embarking on her fourth marriage (clue 3), so was expected to go into medicine. The sister who went into the theatre posed for a nude portrait (clue 1) and Daphne went into journalism (clue 2), so Angela is in advertising. The sister who posed nude isn't Cherry (clue 1), so Brenda and Cherry is the sister intended for banking who went into photography (clue 2). Brenda posed for the nude portrait, she wasn't intended for accountancy, so for the law and the sister meant for accountancy was Daphne. Thus Cherry wrote her kiss and tell memoirs.

In summary:
Angela, medicine, advertising, fourth marriage.
Brenda, law, theatre, nude portrait.
Cherry, banking, photography, kiss and tell memoirs.
Daphne, accountancy, journalism, affair with pop star.

If Music be the Food... (No 163)
Jack spent £44 at the Magnolia (clue 4). The £50 bill wasn't from the Old Bull (clue 1) or Trivett's (clue 5), so the Blue Moon. Jack spent £48 on

Sunday (clue 2), but not at the Old Bull (clue 1), so Trivett's. Thursday dinner during which the gipsy violinist played cost £50 (clue 5) and was thus at the Blue Moon. Saturday's was at the Old Bull (clue 1) and Tuesday's at the Magnolia. Saturday's bill was £46. Tuesday's music wasn't from the pianist (clue 3) or folk trio (clue 4), so the string quartet. The folk trio didn't play on Sunday (clue 2), so Saturday. The pianist played on Sunday.

In summary:
Sunday, Trivett's, £48, pianist.
Tuesday, Magnolia, £44, string quartet.
Thursday, Blue Moon, £50, gipsy violinist.
Saturday, Old Bull, £46, folk trio.

XX MD (No 164)
The 11.30am patient had a knife wound (clue 3), the agent from Hong Kong who saw Dr XX at 10.00am was male (clue 5) and Julian Bond had the 9.30am appointment (clue 7), so (clue 1) Sally Leamas saw Dr XX at 9.00am, Julian Bond was in Tangiers and the man from Hong Kong had a bullet wound. Basil Oakes was in Rio de Janeiro (clue 2) and Walter Ashenden had a broken arm (clue 6), so Rex Hannay saw Dr XX at 10.00am (clue 5). The agent from Moscow with the cracked rib (clue 4) saw him at 10.30am and (by elimination) is Helen Palmer. Walter Ashenden's appointment wasn't at 11.30am (clue 3), so 11.00am and Basil Oakes's was at 11.30am. Julian Bond didn't have a broken leg (clue 7), so a common cold and Sally Leamas had the broken leg. Walter Ashenden wasn't from Budapest (clue 6), so East Berlin. Sally Leamas was from Budapest.

In summary:
9.00am, Sally Leamas, broken leg, Budapest.
9.30am, Julian Bond, common cold, Tangiers.
10.00am, Rex Hannay, bullet wound, Hong Kong.
10.30am, Helen Palmer, cracked rib, Moscow.
11.00am, Walter Ashenden, broken arm, East Berlin.
11.30am, Basil Oakes, knife wound, Rio de Janeiro.

Nursery Rhyme (No 165)
Mrs McKay purchased the weedkiller (line 1). The rose bush and packet of seeds were bought together (line 2) and a woman bough the peat (line 11), so Mr Munroe who bought ivy (line 7) but not terracotta pots (lines 9-10) also bought the watering-can. Mr Moore didn't buy the rose bush and seeds (line 3), so terracotta pots as part of his £8.84 purchase (line 4). The person who spent £6.00 bought peat (line 11). The one buying mint spent £3.10 (line 5) and (by elimination) weedkiller. Mr Munroe didn't spend £4.50 (line 8), so £5.20 and £4.50 was for the rose bush and

SOLUTIONS

seeds. The purchase that included the poppies didn't total £6.00 (lines 11-12), so they were bought by Mr Moore and the bulbs were bought with the peat, not by Mrs Benn (line 6), so Mrs Watts. Mrs Benn bought the rose bush and seeds.

In summary:

Mr Moore, poppies and terracotta pots, £8.84.
Mr Munroe, ivy and watering-can, £5.20.
Mrs Benn, rose bush and packet of seeds, £4.50.
Mrs McKay, mint and weedkiller, £3.10.
Mrs Watts, bulbs and peat, £6.00.

It's True... (No 166)

The air hostess was the second mistress (clue 1). The first wasn't Marilyn the dancer (clue 2), Ms Sefton the researcher (clue 3) or the businesswoman (clue 4), so was the secretary. Helen was the fifth and wasn't the businesswoman (clue 4), so the researcher and (clue 3) Ann was the third mistress and was the businesswoman. By elimination, Marilyn was the fourth mistress. Ann is Mrs Oliver (clue 2). Marilyn is Miss Philpott (clue 6). Beatrice Macfarlane is the secretary (clue 5) and Carol is the air hostess and her surname is Large.

In summary:

Ann Oliver, businesswoman, third.
Beatrice Macfarlane, secretary, first.
Carol Large, air hostess, second.
Helen Sefton, researcher, fifth.
Marilyn Philpott, dancer, fourth.

Petts' Teachers (No 167)

Miss Cudlipp was supposed to be an ex-spy (clue 4) and Mr Acroyd's nickname was Curly (clue 6). Ginger, believed to be a bigamist, wasn't Mr Ennion (clue 1) or Mrs Dancey (clue 5), so Mrs Bowsher, who ran the Camera Club (clue 5). Since the poet was also a woman (clue 6), she was Mrs Dancey. A man ran the football team (clue 2) and whoever ran the school orchestra was thought to be an ex-convict (clue 3). Mrs Dancey didn't run the Drama Club (clue 5), so the Cycling Club and was thus Freckles (clue 2). Miss Cudlipp thus ran the Drama Club. Her nickname wasn't The Yank (clue 3), so Dasher and Mr Ennion was The Yank. He wasn't the alleged circus performer (clue 3), so ex-convict and Mr Acroyd was thought to have been a circus performer and ran the football team.

In summary:

Mr Acroyd, Curly, football team, circus performer.
Mrs Bowsher, Ginger, Camera Club, bigamist.
Miss Cudlipp, Dasher, Drama Club, spy.
Mrs Dancey, Freckles, Cycling Club, poet.
Mr Ennion, The Yank, school orchestra, convict.

Visitors (No 168)

Peace's visitor is his sister (clue 6). Dick Crippen's isn't the mother named Gloria (clue 1), nor the daughter in cubicle D (clues 1 and 3), so his girlfriend and (clue 6) he's the burglar. Sandra isn't the sister or girlfriend (clue 6), so the daughter and Peace is in cubicle C. Dick Crippen's cubicle isn't A or D (clue 1), so B. Gloria is in A (clue 1) and the fraudster is in C. The car thief isn't in D (clue 4), so A and the man in D was convicted of assault. Sean is in C (clue 4). Cyril is in A (clue 2) and Bobby in D. Bobby isn't Adams (clue 5), so Christie. Cyril is Adams. Dick's visitor isn't Debbie (clue 7), so Amy and Sean's is Debbie.

In summary:

A, Cyril Adams, car theft, Gloria, mother.
B, Dick Crippen, burglary, Amy, girlfriend.
C, Sean Peace, fraud, Debbie, sister.
D, Bobby Christie, assault, Sandra, daughter.

Battleships (No 169)

Logi-5 (No 170a)

B	C	D	A	E
A	D	E	C	B
C	E	B	D	A
E	A	C	B	D
D	B	A	E	C

ABC (No 170b)

	A	B		C
B			C	A
A	C		B	
	B	C	A	
C		A		B

SOLUTIONS

Come Rain, Come Shine (No 171)

Harry ran to Woodtoft on Tuesday (clue 2). It was fine all day Wednesday (clue 5), so (clue 1) he didn't run the 17 miles to Springwell on Monday or Thursday. Nor did he do so on Wednesday (clue 5), so on Friday. It rained steadily on Thursday (clue 1) when he ran 19 miles (clue 6), but not to Broadleigh (clues 1 and 2) or Thorpe Green (clue 6), so Jerningham and he ran 20 miles to Thorpe Green. He ran 16 miles to Woodtoft (clue 2) and 18 to Broadleigh. It was overcast on the day he ran to Broadleigh (clue 4), so this was on Monday and he ran 20 miles on Wednesday. Tuesday wasn't frosty (clue 3), so showery and Friday was frosty.

In summary:
Monday, Broadleigh, 18 miles, overcast.
Tuesday, Woodtoft, 16 miles, showery.
Wednesday, Thorpe Green, 20 miles, fine.
Thursday, Jerningham, 19 miles, steady rain.
Friday, Springwell, 17 miles, frosty.

Have I Shown You These? (No 172)

Mrs Gushing's grandchild is Rebecca (clue 1) and Nellie's is Esther (clue 6). Betty Proudley's isn't Elizabeth (clue 3) or Jack, aged 3 months (clues 3 and 7), so Thomas. Laura's grandchild aged 11 months (clue 5) isn't Elizabeth (clue 3), so Rebecca. Mrs Boast's grandchild is 7 months old (clue 2). Thomas isn't 5 months old (clue 3), so 9 months and Elizabeth is thus 7 months old. Esther is 5 months old, thus her grandmother isn't Mrs Bragg (clue 4), so Mrs Strutt and Jack's is Mrs Bragg. She isn't Amy (clue 7), so Stella and Amy is Mrs Boast.

In summary:
Amy Boast, Elizabeth, 7 months.
Betty Proudley, Thomas, 9 months.
Laura Gushing, Rebecca, 11 months.
Nellie Strutt, Esther, 5 months.
Stella Bragg, Jack, 3 months.

Taken for a Ride (No 173)

Sam paid on the Dodgems (clue 3) and Debbie was paid for on the Waltzer (clue 4). Cathy didn't treat Sam on the Chairplanes (clue 1) or the Ghost Train (clue 6), so the Big Wheel. She wasn't paid for on the Ghost Train which was the fifth ride (clue 6) and Liz was paid for on the fourth (clue 2), so Laura was paid for on the Ghost Train. The girl who treated her wasn't Liz (clue 5), so Debbie. Liz paid for the third ride (clue 5) and wasn't treated by Laura (clue 2), so Sam. By elimination, Cathy was paid for on the Chairplanes. Cathy's/Sam's ride on the Big Wheel wasn't the second (clue 1), so first. The second ride wasn't on the Chairplanes (clue 1), so the Waltzer. The third ride was thus on the Chairplanes and Laura paid for Debbie.

In summary:
Big Wheel, Cathy and Sam, first.
Chairplanes, Liz and Cathy, third.
Dodgems, Sam and Liz, fourth.
Ghost Train, Debbie and Laura, fifth.
Waltzer, Laura and Debbie, second.

Avant les Mousquetaires (No 174)

Nicolas wanted to be a poet (clue 2) and Gaston was Maximos (clue 4). Uramis who wanted to be a priest wasn't Pierre (clue 6) or Augustin (clue 1), so Fernand whose surname was Rollin (clue 1). The man who wanted to be a physician wasn't Augustin (clue 1) or Gaston (clue 4), so Pierre. Silvis' surname was Saint-Simon (clue 5). Augustin's didn't contain 'Saint' (clue 1) and he wasn't Archamos (clue 5), so he was Damos. He didn't want to be an architect (clue 3), so a courtier and Maximos wanted to be an architect. Archamos didn't want to be a physician (clue 4), so a poet and Pierre wanted to be a physician. Saint-Denis wasn't Damos or Maximos (clue 3), so Archamos. Maximos' wasn't De La Fresnay (clue 4), so Du Bartas and Damos was De La Fresnay. Silvis was Pierre.

In summary:
Archamos, Nicolas, Saint-Denis, poet.
Damos, Augustin, De La Fresnay, courtier.
Maximos, Gaston, Du Bartas, architect.
Silvis, Pierre, Saint-Simon, physician.
Uramis, Fernand, Rollin, priest.

Carved in Stone (No 175)

Lord Sanglier and his wife Lady Elfreda are in tomb 2 (clue 6). The man in tomb 4 isn't Sir Guy Gargrave (clue 1), Lord Dealtry (clue 2), Lord Bovill or Sir Rhys Redlaw (clue 5), so Sir Bruce Baynard and (clue 1) the man in tomb 6 is Sir Guy Gargrave. The man in tomb 1 isn't Lord Dealtry (clue 2) or Lord Bovill (clue 4), so Sir Rhys Redlaw. Lord Bovill is in tomb 5 (clue 5) and Lady Anthea in tomb 6 (clue 4). By elimination, tomb 3 is Lord Dealtry's so (clue 2) Lady Helen's is tomb 1. Lady Margaret was the wife of Sir Bruce Baynard (clue 3) and Lord Dealtry was married to Lady Muriel, so Lord Bovill was married to Lady Vanessa.

In summary:
1, Sir Rhys Redlaw, Lady Helen.
2, Lord Sanglier, Lady Elfreda.
3, Lord Dealtry, Lady Muriel.
4, Sir Bruce Baynard, Lady Margaret.
5, Lord Bovill, Lady Vanessa.
6, Sir Guy Gargrave, Lady Anthea.

Web Sites (No 176)

Sixteen flies were caught in the web attached to the shed (clue 5) and Webfield caught 20 (clue 6), so the web stretching from the conifer to the rose bush caught 8 (clue 2) and Webster caught 16. The web attached to the fence caught 24 (clue 4), so Webbington's which was attached to the trellis (clue 1) caught 12. Webley's started from the apple tree (clue 1), so the one from the conifer was Webber's and Webley's caught 24 and stretched to the fence. Webfield's was attached to the bicycle and Webster's to the wall (clue 3). Webbington's was attached to the wheelbarrow.

In summary:
Webber, conifer to rose bush, 8 flies.
Webbington, wheelbarrow to trellis, 12 flies.
Webfield, bicycle to garage, 20 flies.
Webley, apple tree to fence, 24 flies.
Webster, shed to wall, 16 flies.

Hello, Campers (No 177)
The family of four was in chalet 2 (clue 2) and the Plaistow family had chalet 3 (clue 3), so Mrs Castle and her two children, forming the family of three didn't have chalet 4 (clue 1). There weren't two in chalet 4 (clue 3) so five. The Islingtons were in chalet 4 (clue 4) and the Beach family in chalet 2. The family of two weren't in chalet 1 (clue 5), so chalet 3 and the Castles were in chalet 1. The Beaches were from Ealing (clue 1), so the Castles were from Dulwich. The family from Plaistow wasn't the Buckets (clue 3), so the Spades and the Buckets were from Islington.

In summary:
Chalet 1, Castle, Dulwich, three.
Chalet 2, Beach, Ealing, four.
Chalet 3, Spade, Plaistow, two.
Chalet 4, Bucket, Islington, five.

It's Quicker by Tube (No 178)
Kirk is number 3 (clue 4) and passenger 4 is going to South Ealing (clue 3). Norbert going to Acton Town is number 2 (clue 1) and Crisp is number 1. Crisp isn't going to Earl's Court (clue 2), so Hammersmith and Kirk is going to Earl's Court. Crisp is Edmund (clue 2), so number 4 is Denzil. Kirk isn't Easton (clue 2) or Roberts (clue 4), so Mills. Passenger 2 isn't Roberts (clue 4), so Easton and Roberts is number 4.

In summary:
1, Edmund Crisp, Hammersmith.
2, Norbert Easton, Acton Town.
3, Kirk Mills, Earl's Court.
4, Denzil Roberts, South Ealing.

Follow the Signs (No 179)
The Sagittarian was told to follow her instincts (clue 4) and Mrs Fish's sign is Taurus (clue 7). Mrs Crabbe was told it would be a good day for her finances and isn't Sybil, the Pisces subject (clue 6), nor is her sign Cancer (clue 1), so it's Libra. The sign of Rosemary Archer (clue

3) isn't Sagittarius (clue 1), so Cancer. Glenda was advised to make no commitments (clue 2). Rosemary wasn't warned of domestic squalls (clue 3), so to expect a phone call. Mrs Crabbe isn't Patricia (clue 5), so Marjorie. Glenda's sign is thus Taurus. By elimination, Patricia's is Sagittarius and Sybil was warned of domestic squalls. Patricia isn't Mrs Scales (clue 5), so Mrs Bull and Sybil is Mrs Scales.

In summary:
Glenda Fish, Taurus, make no commitments.
Marjorie Crabbe, Libra, good day for finances.
Patricia Bull, Sagittarius, follow instincts.
Rosemary Archer, Cancer, expect phone call.
Sybil Scales, Pisces, domestic squalls.

Domino Search (No 180)

1	3	0	3	3	5	4	6
2	0	0	1	1	4	4	2
5	2	2	4	3	6	5	5
2	0	6	6	4	0	5	2
4	0	6	3	1	0	1	4
5	3	6	3	5	6	1	4
1	2	1	5	2	3	6	0

Logi-Path (No 181)

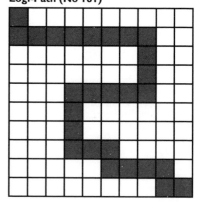

Spaced Out (No 182)
The Csertik is Mostian (clue 4). The Quaroquep isn't Rigarthic and since its engines are less powerful than those of the Novilmu (clue 5), it isn't the Jarromian vessel whose name means Not Scared By Anything (clue 3). The Quaroquep isn't Vortican (clue 6), so Bodian. Hosadifi means Gigantic (clue 4). Quaroquep doesn't mean Conquest (clue 1) or Evening Star (clue 5), so

SOLUTIONS

Short Shift and it's the freighter (clue 2). The mining ship is the Zapikniar (clue 2). The Novilmu isn't the survey ship (clues 1 and 5). The Novilmu is the Vortican spaceliner and the Hosadifi is the battlecruiser (clue 6). By elimination, the Hosadifi is Rigarthic and the mining ship is Jarromian, so the Csertik is the survey ship. Csertik doesn't mean Evening Star (clue 5), so Conquest and Novilmu means Evening Star.

In summary:
Csertik, Conquest, survey ship, Mostian.
Hosadifi, Gigantic, battlecruiser, Rigarthic.
Novilmu, Evening Star, spaceliner, Vortican.
Quaroquep, Short Shift, freighter, Bodian.
Zapikniar, Not Scared By Anything, mining ship, Jarromian.

On the Mat (No 183)

Mat A was red (clue 5) and B was Carl's (clue 4). Cliff's was orange (clue 6), so his mat and the one with the horseshoe design were either D or E. Mat C depicted the car (clue 7). The green mat with the bottle design isn't F (clue 2), so B and Rhys's was D. Thus Cliff's was E and the horseshoe design is on mat D. Bryn's teddy bear mat wasn't F (clue 1), so A. The girl design was on E (clue 3) and F was brown, thus featured a cat. Gareth's wasn't C (clue 7), so F and Owen's was C. C was pink (clue 7), so D was blue.

In summary:
A, Bryn, red, teddy bear.
B, Carl, green, bottle.
C, Owen, pink, car.
D, Rhys, blue, horseshoe.
E, Cliff, orange, girl.
F, Gareth, brown, cat.

Wallingfen Busts (No 184)

The 3rd Duke's bust came from France (clue 2). The 6th Duke's bust of Aristotle (clue 3) wasn't from Greece (clue 1) or Italy (clue 4), so Germany. The 5th Duke didn't acquire D (clue 5), so the Duke who acquired a bust in Italy was the 5th and D was acquired by the 6th Duke (clue 4). By elimination, the 4th bought his bust in Greece. The 5th Duke bought either B or C (clue 5). Bust A wasn't bought by the 4th Duke (clue 3), so by the 3rd. The bust of Napoleon isn't C (clue 6) or A (clue 1), so B. Bust A isn't of Galileo (clue 3), so Beethoven and C is of Galileo. C wasn't bought by the 5th Duke (clue 1), so the 4th and the 5th Duke bought B.

In summary:
A, Beethoven, 3rd Duke, France.
B, Napoleon, 5th Duke, Italy.
C, Galileo, 4th Duke, Greece.
D, Aristotle, 6th Duke, Germany.

Silly Season (No 185)

The Times reporter is on the pterodactyl story (clue 3) and the Gazette reporter is in Barstead (clue 6). The reporter covering the Downbury tiger story isn't from the Free Press nor is the Free Press reporter covering the ghost story (clue 4), so the reporter in Downbury isn't from the Inquirer. Thus he/she is from the Herald and (clue 5) is Ian Jones. The reporter on the ghost story is from the Gazette (clue 4) and Annie Brown is in Jugford (clue 6). Edna Finch isn't in Fenfield (clue 1) or Barstead (clue 6), so Hillwood. Geoff Hall is covering the monster story (clue 5), so he's in Fenfield and the Gazette reporter is Colin Dawes. Geoff Hall isn't from the Inquirer (clue 2), so the Free Press and the Inquirer reporter is covering the UFOs. The Times reporter isn't Edna Finch (clue 3), so Annie Brown and Edna Finch is the Inquirer reporter.

In summary:
Annie Brown, Times, Jugford, pterodactyl.
Colin Dawes, Gazette, Barstead, ghost.
Edna Finch, Inquirer, Hillwood, UFOs.
Geoff Hall, Free Press, Fenfield, monster.
Ian Jones, Herald, Downbury, tiger.

Wanted No More (No 186)

The arrest for passing a forged dollar was in a Fairview (clue 3) and that in New Hope was for littering (clue 6). Gorilla Gieriger was arrested for illegal parking (clue 2). Scarface Sporco was arrested in Oak Grove but not for swearing (clue 5), so speeding. Tuesday's arrest was for passing a forged dollar (clue 3), so Lucky Le Base wasn't arrested on Monday (clue 4). Big Al Baddman was arrested on Thursday (clue 1). The arrest in New Hope was the day after Machinegun McSwine's (clue 6), so Machinegun wasn't arrested on Monday. The man arrested on Monday wasn't Gorilla (clue 2), so Scarface. The Midway arrest was on either Wednesday or Thursday (clue 4) and Lucky's was on Tuesday or Wednesday. Friday's wasn't of Machinegun (clue 6), so Gorilla. It wasn't in Fairview, Massachusetts (clue 2), so Fairview, New York. Thus the arrest in Fairview, Massachusetts was on Tuesday (clue 3) and the Midway arrest was for swearing. The latter was on Thursday (clue 5) and (clue 4) Lucky was arrested on Wednesday, thus in New Hope. Machinegun was arrested on Tuesday.

In summary:
Monday, Scarface Sporco, Oak Grove, speeding.
Tuesday, Machinegun McSwine, Fairview (Mass), passing forged dollar.
Wednesday, Lucky LeBase, New Hope, littering.
Thursday, Big Al Baddman, Midway, swearing.
Friday, Gorilla Gieriger, Fairview (NY), illegal parking.

Pop Shots (No 187)

Rachel has 54 photos of a male star (clue 6) and someone owns 65 photos of Rackstraw (clue 4), so (clue 1) the girl whose favourite is Alma Lincoln has 58 photos of her. Kerry's favourite is Hawkes and she hasn't 47 photos (clue 7), so 42. Rachel's male star isn't Malone (clue 6), so his surname is Hyssop and Malone's fan has 47 photos (clue 1). Julia's favourite is Garry (clue 2). Rachel's isn't Rick (clue 3), so Calvin. Rackstraw isn't Rick (clue 3) or Melanie (clue 4), so Garry. Hannah has 58 photos (clue 5), so Angie has 47 of Malone. Malone isn't Melanie (clue 5), so Rick and Melanie is Hawkes.

In summary:
Alma Lincoln, Hannah, 58.
Calvin Hyssop, Rachel, 54.
Garry Rackstraw, Julia, 65.
Melanie Hawkes, Kerry, 42.
Rick Malone, Angie, 47.

On the March (No 188)

The only letters which occur three times are A and S. A5 doesn't contain an A (clue 1), so, (clue 3) S is in A5, B2 and D3 and (clue 8) Q is in D5. Thus the odd-numbered column with the downward sequence A, U, F (clue 6) isn't column 5. Since D3 contains an S and A3 cannot contain an A (clue 1) the A, U, F sequence isn't in column 3, so column 1. The A isn't in A1 (clue 1), so B1, the U is in C1 and the F in D1. A6 contains E (clue 2) and C3 contains D. Also in row D is an R and an O (clue 7), thus they're in D2 and/or D4. There are three As (clue 1), so one is in row D, thus in D6. Since B3 contains a vowel (clue 9), the A two places to the left of the K (clue 4) isn't the one in B1. The third A is in row C (clue 1). Since C4 contains a vowel (clue 9), the A isn't in C2, so (clue 4) it's in C4 and the K is in C6. The R in row D (clue 10) isn't in D4, so, (clue 7) it's in D2 and the O is in D4. The sequence C, O, H doesn't start in A1 or B4 (clue 11), nor in B3 (clue 9), so A2 contains the C, A3 the O and A4 the H. The I is in C2 (clue 12), the T in C5 and the P in A1. The only spaces remaining are in row B and the unused letters are C, E, R and U. The R isn't in B3 (clue 9), B4 or B5 (clue 10), so B6. B4 contains the U (clue 5), so B3 has the E and B5 has the C.

In summary:

P	C	O	H	S	E
A	S	E	U	C	R
U	I	D	A	T	K
F	R	S	O	Q	A

The five words are: FORCED, HARE, PAST, QUICK and SOUSA.

Blitz (No 189)

The Browns house was damaged on the 9th (clue 3) and a house was damaged by an incendiary bomb on the 14th (clue 5). Thus the Smiths' house was wrecked by blast on the 20th (clue 4). Number 10 was hit by shrapnel (clue 6). The Lees were at number 6 (clue 2), so number 4 wasn't hit by a 50-kg bomb (clue 2). Number 4 was damaged on the 17th (clue 3), so by a 250-kg bomb and (clue 1) the Wilsons lived at number 2. The Smiths lived at number 8. The Hills weren't at number 10 (clue 2), so number 4 and number 2 was hit by a 50-kg bomb on the 11th. By elimination, the Lees' home was damaged on the 14th, the 50-kg bomb hit the Wilsons' home and the Browns were at number 10.

In summary:
Browns, No 10, 9th, shrapnel.
Hills, No 4, 17th, 250-kg bomb.
Lees, No 6, 14th, incendiary bomb.
Smiths, No 8, 20th, blast.
Wilsons, No 2, 11th, 50-kg bomb.

Going for a Song (No 190)

Lot 56 was the tea-set (line 11) and the bookcase cost £60 (line 9). Lot 77 wasn't £60 (line 4) and wasn't the golf-clubs (line 5) or table and chairs (line 6), so the clock. Miss Langham bought the table and chairs (lines 6 and 7) and Mr Ayres lot 10 (line 8). The clock wasn't sold to Mrs Bryce (lines 1 and 2) or Mr Dawson (line 13), so Miss Newton. Mr Dawson paid £200 (line 14). Miss Newton didn't pay £100 (line 3) or £150 (line 16), so £180. The bookcase wasn't bought by Mrs Bryce or Mr Ayres. Mrs Bryce didn't pay £100 (lines 2 and 3), so £150 and Miss Langham paid £100. She didn't buy lot 30 (line 10), so the table and chairs were lot 47 and lot 30 was the golf-clubs. Lot 30 didn't fetch £150 (line 15), so £200 and the tea-set was £150.

In summary:
Lot 10, bookcase, Mr Ayres, £60.
Lot 30, golf-clubs, Mr Dawson, £200.
Lot 47, table and chairs, Miss Langham, £100.
Lot 56, tea-set, Mrs Bryce, £150.
Lot 77, clock, Miss Newton, £180.

Pile Up (No 191)
From the top:
B, D, A, F, E, C

Out of Court (No 192)

Player 6 isn't the barrister (clue 1), the court usher or Philip the solicitor (clue 2), Wilmott the judge (clue 4) or the judge's clerk (clue 5), so he's the QC. His opponent on court 3 isn't the barrister (clue 1), usher or solicitor (clue 2) and player 5 isn't the judge's clerk (clue 5), so the QC's opponent is Wilmott. Marcus is player 3 (clue 3) and Henry is Barlow (clue 1). Mr Wilmott isn't Bryan (clue 4) or Wilfred (clue 5), so Christopher. Henry is the barrister's opponent (clue 1). The QC isn't Wilfred (clue 5), so Bryan. Player 1 is Douglas (clue 3) and Horne's opponent isn't Christopher (clue 5). The QC isn't Rushby (clue 1), so Price. Wilfred isn't Horne or Rushby (clue 5), so Douglas, thus Horne is player 3 (clue 5) and Philip's surname is Rushby. Player 4 isn't the barrister (clue 1), court usher (clue 2) or judge's clerk (clue 5), so he's the solicitor and (clue 2) the court usher is Horne. Henry is player 2. Wilfred is the barrister (clue 1), so Henry is the judge's clerk.

In summary:
1, Wilfred Douglas, barrister.
2, Henry Barlow, judge's clerk.
3, Marcus Horne, court usher.
4, Philip Rushby, solicitor.
5, Christopher Wilmott, judge.
6, Bryan Price, QC.

Logi-5 (No 193a)

C	A	B	D	E
D	B	E	C	A
E	C	D	A	B
A	E	C	B	D
B	D	A	E	C

ABC (No 193b)

C		B	A	
A			C	B
	C	A	B	
B	A			C
	B	C		A

Multiple Choice (No 194)

The gardening programme didn't first figure in his choices until more than a day after consumer advice (clue 5) and wasn't decided upon on consecutive days (clue 1), so his decisions to tape or watch the gardening programme came on Friday and Sunday. The decision about consumer advice on Wednesday (clue 5) wasn't to tape it (clue 2), so watch it. He didn't tape it on Thursday (clue 1), Friday or Sunday (clue 5), so Saturday and (clue 2) watched the archaeology programme on Friday. Thus on Friday he decided to tape the gardening programme and on Sunday to watch it. He didn't watch the holiday programme on Thursday (clue 6), so Saturday and taped it on Thursday. By elimination, he saw the film on Thursday. He didn't tape it on

Wednesday (clue 3), so Sunday, thus taped the archaeology programme on Wednesday.

In summary:
Wednesday, watch consumer advice, tape archaeology.
Thursday, watch film, tape holiday.
Friday, watch archaeology, tape gardening.
Saturday, watch holiday, tape consumer advice.
Sunday, watch gardening, tape film.

On the Road (No 195)

Mike Stand will be presenting on Wednesday (clue 2). Friday's show won't be presented by Fay D'Oute (clue 1), Vee Aitcheff (clue 2) or Lynne Cupp (clue 5), so it's Ann Ouncer's Great Aymouth show (clue 6). Luckstowe will be visited on Tuesday (clue 4). Monday's venue isn't Tickton Pier (clue 3) or Baddon (clue 5), so Deepstoft. Fay D'Oute isn't presenting on Tuesday (clue 4) or Monday (clue 5), so Thursday and (clue 1) Friday's show is from North Quay. Fay's isn't from Baddon (clue 5), so Tickton and Baddon is Wednesday's venue. Lynne Cupp will be at Marine Parade (clue 5). The King's Park show won't be hosted by Vee Aitcheff (clue 2), so Mike Stand and Vee's is on Tuesday at The Croft. The Marine Parade show is thus from Deepstoft.

In summary:
Monday, Deepstoft, Lynne Cupp, Marine Parade.
Tuesday, Luckstowe, Vee Aitcheff, The Croft.
Wednesday, Baddon, Mike Stand, King's Park.
Thursday, Tickton, Fay D'Oute, Pier.
Friday, Great Aymouth, Ann Ouncer, North Quay.

In Theory (No 196)

Malachi produced the Theory of Inactivity (clue 3) and Rubinstein's was produced in 1933 (clue 5). Harry's work appeared three years after Bierstein's Theory of Proclivity (clue 1) and Isaac's was published three years after Goldstein's (clue 6). The 1936 Theory of Sensitivity wasn't the work of Theodore Rothstein (clue 2), so Rudolf. Bierstein isn't Harry (clue 1), so Isaac. His theory wasn't published in 1942 (clue 1) or 1930 (clue 6), so 1939. Harry's was produced in 1942 (clue 1). Goldstein is thus Rudolf (clue 6). By elimination, Harry is Epstein, Malachi is Rubinstein and Rothstein's work was published in 1930. Harry's wasn't the Theory of Passivity (clue 4), so the Theory of Productivity. Theodore's was the Theory of Passivity.

In summary:
Harry Epstein, Theory of Productivity, 1942.
Isaac Bierstein, Theory of Proclivity, 1939.
Malachi Rubinstein, Theory of Inactivity, 1933.
Rudolf Goldstein, Theory of Sensitivity, 1936.
Theodore Rothstein, Theory of Passivity, 1930.

That's my Line (No 197)

Rachel's item was the nightie (clue 4), the shorts were either in 16th or 18th place (clue 5) and the white shirt was further down the line than 7th (clue 1). Mum's item was 7th and wasn't a T-shirt (clue 2), so trousers. Terry's red item was more than seven places nearer the top of the line than the white shirt (clue 1), so it was the T-shirt. It wasn't 1st on the line (clue 2), so 9th. The white shirt was 18th (clue 1) and the shorts 16th, so the nightie was 1st. The pink item was nearer the top of the line than 9th (clue 2) and wasn't the trousers (clue 6), so it was the nightie. The shorts weren't blue (clue 5), so green and the trousers were blue. The shorts didn't belong to Adam (clue 3), so Caroline and the white shirt was Adam's.

In summary:

1st, nightie, pink, Rachel.
7th, trousers, blue, mum.
9th, T-shirt, red, Terry.
16th, shorts, green, Caroline.
18th, shirt, white, Adam.

Into Battle (No 198)

Phalanx sold 5 papers (clue 4) and Lucy sold 10 (clue 6), so (clue 1) Ruth sold 12 copies in the Coronet and Paperweight and Rank is Lucy. Major Van Guard sold 8 papers in the Toad and Harrow (clue 2). Ruth isn't Fyle (clue 3), so Cannon, thus Fyle sold 7 copies. Patsy sold 8 (clue 3). Naomi isn't Phalanx (clue 5), so Fyle and Rose is Phalanx who sold her papers in the Lady of Shallott. Lucy's weren't sold in the Ironmonger's Arms (clue 6), so the Grey Donkey and Naomi went to the Ironmonger's Arms.

In summary:

Lucy Rank, Grey Donkey, 10 copies.
Naomi Fyle, Ironmonger's Arms, 7 copies.
Patsy Van Guard, Toad and Harrow, 8 copies.
Rose Phalanx, Lady of Shallott, 5 copies.
Ruth Cannon, Coronet and Paperweight, 12 copies.

Book Trade (No 199)

Phil's 9.30 appointment was in Reading (clue 1), he took an order for £100 at Booker (clue 2) and the appointment in Pagie Hill was in the afternoon (clue 3). The 11.30 appointment where he took an order worth over £200 wasn't in Leafield (clue 2), so Wordsley. That order wasn't worth £300 (clue 5), so £500, thus was at Brought to Book (clue 6). The Chapterhouse bookshop is in Pagie Hill (clue 3) and his 3.00 appointment was at The Bookshelf (clue 4). His 9.30 call wasn't at Speak Volumes (clue 1), so New Leaf. It wasn't worth £25 (clue 1) or £300

(clue 5), so £175. The remaining orders are £25, £100 and £300. The 3.00 order was thus £300 (clue 4) and the 4.30 order was £100, thus the £25 order was at 1.30; not at Speak Volumes (clue 1), so Chapterhouse. Thus he went to Speak Volumes at 4.30 and Leafield at 3.00.

In summary:

9.30, New Leaf, Reading, £175.
11.30, Brought to Book, Wordsley, £500.
1.30, Chapterhouse, Pagie Hill, £25.
3.00, The Bookshelf, Leafield, £300.
4.30, Speak Volumes, Booker, £100.

Pisa the Action (No 200)

The artist in 3B produces ceramics (clue 3). The artist in B who produces textiles (clue 2) isn't Patrick in 2B (clue 4), so is in 1B and is thus Millais (clue 5). Dorothy's surname is Landseer (clue 6) and Ellen produces sculptures. Millais isn't Joan (clue 1) or Martin (clue 2), so Winnie. Ellen's studio is on the left of the building, thus the artist in 3B is Dorothy (clue 6) and (clue 8) Sickert and the etcher are in 2A and/or 2B. Ellen isn't in 2A (clue 6), so she isn't Sickert. Browne produces action paintings (clue 7), so Sickert creates collages. Browne isn't in 1A (clue 7), so 3A. Thus Browne isn't Joan (clue 1), so Martin. Ellen's surname isn't Beardsley (clue 6), so Turner. Thus Beardsley produces etchings and (clue 4) is Patrick, so Joan is Sickert and is in 2A.

In summary:

1A, Ellen Turner, sculptures.
1B, Winnie Millais, textiles.
2A, Joan Sickert, collages.
2B, Patrick Beardsley, etchings.
3A, Martin Browne, action paintings.
3B, Dorothy Landseer, ceramics.

Just Fine (No 201)

The fifth man wasn't fined £70 or £75 (clue 1), nor can he be Pratt, fined £60 (clue 3). Hogg who ignored the stop sign wasn't fined £60 so the fifth offender wasn't fined £50 (clue 1), thus he had to pay £40 and Hogg was fined £50. Riskett was the fourth to appear and wasn't fined £75 (clue 4), so £70 and the second defendant £75. The second wasn't Knott-Fussey (clue 2), so Blythe and Knott-Fussey was the fifth. Thus the first defendant who was charged with having defective tyres (clue 2) was Pratt and Hogg was the third. Blythe was accused of careless driving (clue 3). Knott-Fussey had defective lights (clue 5), so Riskett was convicted of speeding.

In summary:

First, Pratt, defective tyres, £60.
Second, Blythe, careless driving, £75.
Third, Hogg, ignoring stop sign, £50.
Fourth, Riskett, speeding, £70.
Fifth, Knott-Fussey, defective lights, £40.

SOLUTIONS

Battleships (No 202)

Logi-5 (No 203a)

D	A	C	E	B
A	B	E	D	C
B	E	D	C	A
C	D	A	B	E
E	C	B	A	D

ABC (No 203b)

C		B	A	
A			C	B
	B	A		C
	C		B	A
B	A	C		

Gig Guide (No 204)

The Stag's Head is in Wharf Lane (clue 1). Stir's Newland Square venue isn't the Leather Bottle and they aren't the first or last band to perform (clue 2), so aren't appearing at the Britannia (clue 6), nor is their venue the Five Bells (clue 4), so it's McGinty's. Stir's gig doesn't start at 9.00 (clue 2), so 9.30 (clue 1), the gig at the Leather Bottle starts at 9.00 and the one at the Cambridge Street venue at 10.30 (clue 2). The Rosettes are on at 9.00 (clue 1) and the Stag's Head gig starts at 8.30. The Wood Street gig starts at 9.00 (clue 6). The 10.30 band isn't Cobra (clue 3) or Relish (clue 5), so Shock Troupe. The 8.00 band isn't Relish (clue 5), so Cobra. By elimination, Cobra are playing in Market Street and Relish is performing at 8.30. Cobra's venue isn't the Five Bells (clue 4), so the Britannia and Shock Troupe are at the Five Bells.

In summary:
Cobra, Britannia, Market Street, 8.00.
Relish, Stags Head, Wharf Lane, 8.30.
Shock Troupe, Five Bells, Cambridge St, 10.30.
Stir, McGinty's, Newland Square, 9.30.
The Rosettes, Leather Bottle, Wood St, 9.00.

Parish Pumps (No 205)

The Courier isn't edited by Sarah (clue 5) or Alan (clue 6). The magazine edited by Sarah isn't the Bugle, Clarion or Grapevine (clue 6), so it's Contact, Alan's is the Clarion and the Newthorpe journal is the Bugle. The editor is female (clue 3), so she's Dorothy Johnson. Mrs Young is Sarah (clue 2). Alan lives in Kelwick (clue 6) and the Courier is based in Dunsford. The Crayston magazine isn't Contact (clue 1), so Grapevine and Contact is based in Barnby. Kitson's village isn't Kelwick (clue 1) or Crayston (clue 2), so Dunsford. Attwater doesn't edit the Clarion (clue 4), so Grapevine. By elimination Alan is Pybus, who lives in Kelwick. Thomas' village isn't Dunsford (clue 7), so Crayston and Keith lives in Dunsford.

In summary:
Barnby, Sarah Young, Contact.
Crayston, Thomas Attwater, Grapevine.
Dunsford, Keith Kitson, Courier.
Kelwick, Alan Pybus, Clarion.
Newthorpe, Dorothy Johnson, Bugle.

Ruling Classes (No 206)

The ruler who belonged to the XVIIth dynasty wasn't the one who didn't marry (clue 1). He hadn't 3 wives (clue 1), 4 wives (clue 3) or one (clue 5), so had 2. Snafu-Pet's dynasty was the XIVth (clue 5) and the ruler from the XIIIth dynasty reigned for 14 years. He wasn't Tip-Re-Bel (clue 1), Rum-Chef (clue 3) or Hot-Instep (clue 4), so Pelmel-Motif. Snafu-Pet ruled for 16 years (clue 2). The reign of the king from the XVth didn't last 8 or 10 years (clue 4), so 12. He wasn't thus Tip-Re-Bel (clue 1) or Hot-Instep (clue 4), so Rum-Chef. Hot-Instep reigned for 8 years (clue 4) and Tip-Re-Bel for 10. The king from the XVIth dynasty hadn't 3 wives (clue 6), so Tip-Re-Bel wasn't from the XVIIth dynasty (clue 1), thus the king from that dynasty was Hot-Instep. Rum-Chef had 3 wives (clue 4) and Snafu-Pet had 4 (clue 5). Tip-Re-Bel was the XVIth dynasty king who thus had one wife (clue 1) and Pelmel-Motif didn't marry.

In summary:
Hot-Instep, XVIIth, 8 years, two wives.
Pelmel-Motif, XIIIth, 14 years, no wives.
Rum-Chef, XVth, 12 years, three wives.
Snafu-Pet, XIVth, 16 years, four wives.
Tip-Re-Bel, XVIth, 10 years, one wife.

SOLUTIONS

Logi-Path (No 207)

Domino Search (No 208)

6	6	1	2	1	3	6	5
3	2	0	1	2	2	3	6
6	0	0	0	5	4	2	6
6	4	0	0	3	1	5	6
2	2	4	4	3	5	1	4
5	5	5	3	3	2	5	4
3	4	4	1	1	1	0	0

Chain of Command (No 209)

Town 5 is Maywell (clue 5) and the store in town 3 is in the High Street (clue 7), so Stackley where the store is in King's Parade and which is indicated by an odd number (clue 2) is town 1. Middleton is the manager in town 2 (clue 3). Stokes in Market Square is in town 5 (clue 6) and Dilby is town 6. Thus town 3 is Newfield, where the manager is Landers (clue 1) and Scott Street is in town 4. Nelson Avenue isn't in town 6 (clue 4), so town 2 and the store in town 6 is in Lincoln Lane. Town 2 isn't Rockbury (clue 4), so Warnford and town 4 is Rockbury, where the manager is Riches (clue 4). Fowler is in Dilby (clue 8) and Fulton is in Stackley.

In summary:
1, Stackley, King's Parade, Fulton.
2, Warnford, Nelson Avenue, Middleton.
3, Newfield, High Street, Landers.
4, Rockbury, Scott Street, Riches.
5, Maywell, Market Square, Stokes.
6, Dilby, Lincoln Lane, Fowler.

Going Up (No 210)

Roberta's room is 69 (clue 3). The occupant of room 61 isn't Alice Sibley (clue 1) or Monica whose position in the lift is 4 (clues 1 and 4),

so Genevieve. Dixon is passenger 3 (clue 2), so Alice is passenger 2 (clue 1) and Genevieve is passenger 1. By elimination, Roberta is Dixon and Monica's room is on the fifth floor, so (clue 4) Genevieve is Collins and Monica is Rowland. Monica has room 51 (clue 2) and room 59 is Alice's.

In summary:
1, Genevieve, Collins, Room 61.
2, Alice, Sibley, Room 59.
3, Roberta, Dixon, Room 69.
4, Monica, Rowland, Room 51.

Unmatched Pairs (No 211)

Julia Cameron's partner dressed as Tarzan (clue 4). Joanne Brock dressed as Hannah Snell (clue 3). Her partner didn't dress as Robin Hood (clue 2), Superman or Sir Lancelot (clue 3), so Romeo. Adrian Towers' partner was Rosemary Weston who didn't dress as Julia Cameron (clue 1), Aphra Behn (clue 5) or Queen Maria (clue 6), so Queen Edith. The man dressed as Sir Lancelot wasn't Adrian Towers nor did he partner Denise Moody or Pauline Wolfe (clue 3), so Sir Lancelot was Virginia Sampson's partner. Since Virginia and Rosemary have the same number of letters, Rosemary's partner didn't dress as Superman (clue 3), so Robin Hood. Denise Moody's dressed as Superman (clue 4). Denise Moody didn't dress as Queen Maria (clue 6), so Aphra Behn. By elimination, Julia Cameron was Pauline Wolfe and Queen Maria was Virginia Sampson, whose partner was thus Christian Spicer (clue 6). Pauline Wolfe's partner wasn't Nigel Ward or Sebastian White (clue 6), so Jason Carey. Sebastian White didn't partner Denise Moody (clue 5), so Joanne Brock and Nigel Ward partnered Denise Moody.

In summary:
Adrian Towers, Robin Hood, Rosemary Weston, Queen Edith.
Christian Spicer, Sir Lancelot, Virginia Sampson, Queen Maria.
Jason Carey, Tarzan, Pauline Wolfe, Julia Cameron.
Nigel Ward, Superman, Denise Moody, Aphra Behn.
Sebastian White, Romeo, Joanne Brock, Hannah Snell.

Rough Rounds (No 212)

George's Monday total wasn't 109 (clue 2), 114 or 121 (clue 3) or 127 (clue 4), so 116. On Tuesday his worst hole was either the third or fifteenth (clue 5), thus his Tuesday total wasn't 127 (clue 2), so 121 (clue 4) was the third (clue 3). Thus Monday's score at his worst hole was 9 (clue 3) and Tuesday's was 11 (clue 4). Wednesday's total was 114 (clue 3).

His worst hole score wasn't 7 on Friday (clue 1) or Wednesday (clue 4), so Thursday. His round of 127 wasn't on Friday (clue 1), so Thursday and Friday's total was 109. Wednesday's worst hole was the fifteenth (clue 3), so Friday's was the twelfth when he scored 10 (clue 6) and Thursday's was the sixth. Thus Monday's worst was the tenth and he scored 8 on Wednesday.

In summary:
Monday, 116, tenth, 9.
Tuesday, 121, third, 11.
Wednesday, 114, fifteenth, 8.
Thursday, 127, sixth, 7.
Friday, 109, twelfth, 10.

On Show (No 213)

A man bought car E (clue 6). Mrs Austin's red car isn't A or F (clue 1), C or D which cost £3,500 (clue 5), so B. The buyer of car E wasn't Mr Bentley (clue 4). The grey car cost £4,250 (clue 3), so (clue 2) Mr Ford who paid £3,750 isn't the man who bought E, who paid £500 less than the price of the green car (clue 6). So car E was bought by Mr Rolls. He didn't spend £4,000 (clue 2), £4,500 or £4,750 (clue 6), so £4,250 and the green car was £4,750. Car A wasn't £4,500 or £4,750 (clue 1) or £4,000 (clue 2), so £3,750. Car C wasn't bought by Mr Bentley (clue 4) or Mrs Morris (clue 7), so Mrs Jowett. Mr Bentley didn't buy F (clue 4), so D and Mrs Morris bought F which is green. Mrs Austin paid £4,000 (clue 1) and Mrs Jowett £4,500. D wasn't light blue or dark blue (clue 5), so white. Car A was dark blue (clue 2) and C was light blue.

In summary:
A, Mr Ford, £3,750, dark blue.
B, Mrs Austin, £4,000, red.
C, Mrs Jowett, £4,500, light blue.
D, Mr Bentley, £3,500, white.
E, Mr Rolls, £4,250, grey.
F, Mrs Morris, £4,750, green.

Numbers Up (No 214)

Eric didn't choose 7 or 19 (clue 4) and his three numbers weren't 31, 38 and 47 (clue 1), so his lowest was 23. Thomas didn't choose 19 (clue 4), so his lowest was 7. Since neither Arthur nor Philip had 23 (clue 4), the other two with that number (clue 1) were Charles and Thomas. The 7 was chosen three times (clue 1), not by Charles (clue 3), so Arthur and Philip chose 7. Eric didn't have both 31 and 38 (clue 1), so had one of these together with 47. The two with 19 (clues 1, 2 and 4) were Charles and Philip. Arthur and Charles had no number in common (clue 2), so weren't the consecutive two with 38 (clue 5) and since there weren't three alphabetically consecutive 38's, Charles, Eric and Thomas had 38. Thus

Arthur and Philip had 31 Arthur had 47.
In summary:
Arthur, 7, 31, 47.
Charles, 19, 23, 38.
Eric, 23, 38, 47.
Philip, 7, 19, 31.
Thomas, 7, 23, 38.

Guided Tour (No 215)

The party had lunch at the King's Head on Wednesday (clue 5). The day for lunching at the Pheasant Inn wasn't Monday, Thursday or Friday (clue 3), so Tuesday and on Monday they went round the castle. The lunch at the Travellers' Rest was on Monday (clue 4). By elimination, the lunches at the Black Lion and the Wheatsheaf were on either Thursday and/or Friday, so the building they looked at on Tuesday wasn't the church (clue 1) or the priory (clue 2). Nor was it the abbey (clue 4), so it was the hall. They were in Newholm on Monday (clue 5). Wadby wasn't the site of the church, abbey or priory (clue 2), so the hall. Friday's visit wasn't to Belham (clue 1) or Egton (clue 4), so Storton. The church was visited on Thursday (clue 1), they went to Belham on Wednesday and lunched at the Black Lion on Friday. By elimination, they lunched at the Wheatsheaf on Thursday and saw the priory on Wednesday (clue 2), so went to the abbey on Friday and to Egton on Thursday.

In summary:
Monday, Newholm, castle, Travellers' Rest.
Tuesday, Wadby, hall, Pheasant Inn.
Wednesday, Belham, priory, King's Head.
Thursday, Egton, church, Wheatsheaf.
Friday, Storton, abbey, Black Lion.

Pile Up (No 216)
From the top:
B, C, F, D, E, A

Penny Whistle (No 217)

Encastle is Wednesday morning's location (clue 4). Branbury isn't visited on Wednesdays (clue 6), so (clue 2) the afternoon session in Dunford is on Wednesday, Tuesday morning's is in Cragleigh and Thursday evening's in Branbury. The Branbury morning session isn't on Thursday (clue 1) or Monday (clue 9), so Friday. The Angleton morning class isn't on Thursday (clue 9), so Monday and (by elimination) Thursday morning's session is in Dunford. The day when the Cragleigh evening class follows the afternoon session in Branbury (clue 8) isn't Tuesday or Friday (clue 1), so Monday and Wednesday evening's class is in Angleton. The evening class in Encastle isn't on Tuesday (clue 7), so Friday and Tuesday evening's is in Dunford. Tuesday afternoon's isn't in Angleton (clue 5), so Encastle (clue 1). Friday afternoon's isn't in Angleton (clue 3), so Cragleigh and Thursday afternoon's is in Angleton.

In summary:
Monday, Angleton, Branbury, Cragleigh.
Tuesday, Cragleigh, Encastle, Dunford.
Wednesday, Encastle, Dunford, Angleton.
Thursday, Dunford, Angleton, Branbury.
Friday, Branbury, Cragleigh, Encastle.

Generation Game (No 218)

Alan's wife is the youngest daughter (clue 3), so David's wife, who is younger than William's mother (clue 1), is the middle daughter and William is the child of the eldest daughter, who (by elimination) is married to Peter. Emma is the middle daughter (clue 4). Since Bridget is Janet's child (clue 2), her father is neither Peter nor David, so Alan and Janet is thus the youngest daughter. Thus Eleanor is Emma's daughter and William's mother is Rachel.

In summary:
Emma, middle, David, Eleanor.
Janet, youngest, Alan, Bridget.
Rachel, eldest, Peter, William.

Clinical Commitments (No 219)

The September appointment isn't with Patel (clue 1) or Ryder (clue 2), so Philips. The July appointment isn't with the cardiologist (clue 1) or orthopaedic consultant (clue 2), so is with the general medical doctor who (clue 3) has been seen four times previously. He isn't Dr Ryder (clue 2), so Dr Patel and the appointment with Dr Ryder is in August. Ryder isn't the orthopaedic consultant (clue 2), so cardiologist and Mr Philips is the orthopaedic consultant. Dr Ryder was seen twice before (clue 2) and Mr Philips, three times.

In summary:
July, Dr Patel, general medical, four.
August, Dr Ryder, cardiologist, two.
September, Mr Philips, orthopaedic, three.

Messing About in Boats (No 220)

Graham went out with Rachel (clue 1), Carol was in the sailing dinghy (clue 2) and Helen was in the boat that caught fire (clue 3). John wasn't in the sailing dinghy but was in the boat which ran aground (clue 4), so was with Amanda. David's vessel was the canoe (clue 5) and John's wasn't the rowing boat, so motor boat. The sailing dinghy didn't overturn (clue 2), so sank. The girl who went out with David was thus Helen and the canoe caught fire. By elimination, Carol went with Alan and Graham's boat overturned.

In summary:
Alan, Carol, sailing dinghy, sank.
David, Helen, canoe, caught fire.
Graham, Rachel, rowing boat, overturned.
John, Amanda, motor boat, ran aground.

Logi-Path (No 221)

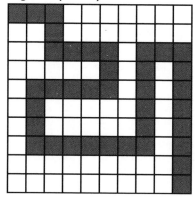

Winners (No 222)

Ivor's win on Autumn Venture owned by Mrs Steed wasn't in the 3.30 race (clue 1), in which he wore mauve and white (clue 3) or the 3.00 race (clue 2). Nor was the 3.30 winner Mr Dobbin's (clue 1) or Lord Palfrey's (clue 4), so it was Miss Colt's. The 2.00 winner wasn't Mr Dobbin's (clue 1) or Lord Palfrey's (clue 4), so Mrs Steed's. Mr Dobbin's won the 2.30 (clue 1) and Lord Palfrey owns the 3.00 winner, Coral Dancer (clue 2). The 3.30 winner was Marshal Hart (clue 4) and Mr Dobbin's colours were blue and orange. By elimination, the 2.30 winner was Golden Gain. Ivor's colours in the 3.00 weren't purple and pink (clue 2), so red and gold. Purple and pink were worn in the 2.00.

In summary:
2.00, Autumn Venture, Mrs Steed, purple and pink.
2.30, Golden Gain, Mr Dobbin, blue and orange.
3.00, Coral Dancer, Lord Palfrey, red and gold.
3.30, Marshal Hart, Miss Colt, mauve and white.

On Assignment (No 223)

Mick Nash has been sent to North London (clue 2). The film premiere is in West London (clue 4). The boxing match Hannah Jay will photograph isn't in South London (clue 5), so East London. The person going to West London isn't Don Ellis (clue 4), so Wally Young and Don Ellis is going to South London with Rob Shelley (clue 5). Amy Burton is covering the railway accident (clue 1). The reporter going to West London isn't Gordon Hope (clue 3), so Kate Lister. By elimination, Hannah Jay is accompanying Gordon Hope, Amy Burton is going with Mick Nash, the railway accident is in North London and the political speech in South London.

In summary:

Amy Burton, Mick Nash, North London, railway accident.

Gordon Hope, Hannah Jay, East London, boxing match.

Kate Lister, Wally Young, West London, film premiere.

Rob Shelley, Don Ellis, South London, political speech.

Bushrangers (No 224)

Picture 3 shows Edward (clue 1) and picture 1 is Tiger (clue 2). Picture 4 doesn't show Sailor Hobart (clue 4) or Bluey (clue 5), so Jock, thus Edward in picture 3 is Bluey (clue 5) and (by elimination) Sailor Hobart is in picture 2. Nicholas is in picture 1 (clue 4). Alfred Darwin (clue 3) is Jock, so William is Sailor Hobart. Edward isn't Cairns (clue 5), so Bendigo and Nicholas is Cairns.

In summary:

Picture 1, Nicholas Tiger Cairns.

Picture 2, William Sailor Hobart.

Picture 3, Edward Bluey Bendigo.

Picture 4, Alfred Jock Darwin.

Flavour of the Lunch (No 225)

Claire has cheese and onion crisps (clue 3). Anne doesn't have the curried chicken sandwich and smoky bacon crisps, the roast chicken crisps (clue 1) or the prawn cocktail crisps, as the name of their owner is alphabetically later than that of the child with the smoked ham spread sandwich (clue 2), so Anne's are salt and vinegar flavour and her yoghurt strawberry (clue 5). Jessica has prawn spread sandwich (clue 2). The girl with the chicken sandwich and raspberry yoghurt (clue 3) is thus Claire. Jessica's crisps aren't prawn cocktail (clue 2), so roast chicken. The child with prawn cocktail crisps hasn't smoked ham spread sandwich (clue 2), so tuna spread, and Anne has smoked ham sandwich. The tuna sandwich isn't David's (clue 4), so belongs to Ben who has black cherry yoghurt (clue 6) and the curried chicken sandwich is David's. His yoghurt isn't mango (clue 1), so banana and Jessica's is mango.

In summary:

Anne, smoked ham, salt and vinegar, strawberry.

Ben, tuna, prawn cocktail, black cherry.

Claire, chicken, cheese and onion, raspberry.

David, curried chicken, smoky bacon, banana.

Jessica, prawn, roast chicken, mango.

First Scenes (No 226)

Cedric Doone was the dustman (clue 1) and the bank clerk's screen name is Nick Maxim (clue 2). Muriel Nutter alias Cleo Blaize wasn't the shop assistant (clue 3) or the cleaner (clue 5), so the traffic warden. Liz Monroe is Alice Bowells (clue 1). Nick Maxim's real name isn't Victor Wallop (clue 2), so Joseph Kettle. The pub customer is Sean Turpin (clue 3), the second soldier is Victor Wallop (clue 4) and the third gipsy will be played by the ex-cleaner (clue 5). Joseph Kettle isn't playing a cyclist (clue 2), so first zombie. Victor Wallop wasn't a cleaner (clues 4 and 5), so a shop assistant and the cleaner was Alice Bowells. By elimination, Cedric Doone is Sean Turpin, Muriel Nutter is playing a cyclist and Victor Wallop's screen name is Carl Dumain.

In summary:

Alice Bowells, cleaner, Liz Monroe, third gipsy.

Cedric Doone, dustman, Sean Turpin, pub customer.

Joseph Kettle, bank clerk, Nick Maxim, first zombie.

Muriel Nutter, traffic warden, Cleo Blaize, cyclist.

Victor Wallop, shop assistant, Carl Dumain, second soldier.

Paradrops (No 227)

The third agent carried money (clue 2), Perroquet dropped fourth (clue 3) and the second agent was dropped at Honbert (clue 4). Vaurien who jumped immediately before the agent who parachuted into Doubourg with a radio (clue 6) thus dropped third and the agent who jumped into Doubourg was fourth. Loir who dropped into Lancy wasn't fifth (clue 5), so first and the second agent carried explosives. Javelot had medicines (clue 1), so was Choriste was second and Javelot fifth. By elimination, Loir carried guns. Javelot didn't jump over St Andre (clue 1), so Touriers and Vaurien jumped over St Andre.

In summary:

First, Loir, Lancy, guns.

Second, Choriste, Honbert, explosives.

Third, Vaurien, St Andre, money.

Fourth, Perroquet, Doubourg, radio.

Fifth, Javelot, Touriers, medicines.

Trail Drive (No 228)

Dusty provided 93 cows (clue 3) and Young provided 145 (clue 4), so (clue 1) Paddy O'Reilly provided 187. Hickory from the Diamond Star (clue 7) provided fewer than Fraser (clue 5), so wasn't Young. Young's nickname wasn't Lobo (clue 4), so Buffalo. Fraser's ranch was the Rocking B (clue 5). Buffalo's wasn't the Lazy K (clue 4) or the Sabre (clue 6), so the Cactus and (clue 2) Morgan's was the Sabre. Paddy's was the

Lazy K and Hickory was Smith. The man who provided 68 cows wasn't Morgan (clue 2) or Fraser (clue 5), so Smith and Fraser provided 84, so Fraser was Lobo and Dusty was Morgan.

In summary:
Buffalo Young, Cactus, 145.
Dusty Morgan, Sabre, 93.
Hickory Smith, Diamond Star, 68.
Lobo Fraser, Rocking B, 84.
Paddy O'Reilly, Lazy K, 187.

Battleships (No 229)

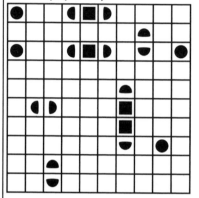

To be a Pilgrim (No 230)

Geoffrey is a soldier (clue 2), so the potter is Gilbert (clue 4) and Geoffrey is pilgrim 2. Hugh is pilgrim 4 (clue 5) and pilgrim 6 is the woodcutter (clue 7). The shepherd's number isn't 1 or 7 (clue 1), 3 or 5 (clue 5), so 4. Lionel is pilgrim 3 (clue 1) and Robin pilgrim 5. Simon who is two positions behind the baker (clue 3) isn't pilgrim 1 or pilgrim 6, so 7 and the baker is Robin. Gilbert is thus pilgrim 1 and pilgrim 6 is Jacob. Lionel isn't the farmer (clue 6), so farrier and Simon is the farmer.

In summary:
1, Gilbert, potter.
2, Geoffrey, soldier.
3, Lionel, farrier.
4, Hugh, shepherd.
5, Robin, baker.
6, Jacob, woodcutter.
7, Simon, farmer.

The Prodigies (No 231)

Antonio Bambino was 6 when he wrote his first piece (clue 3) and the tone poem was written by a 9-year-old (clue 6). The composer of the symphony who was two years younger than virtuoso clarinetist Joachim Kiddi (clue 1) wasn't 4, 6 or 11, so 7 and Joachim was 9. Josef Neubörn who wrote the overture wasn't 11 (clue 4), so 4. The opera composer was two

years older than the virtuoso oboist (clue 5), so 6 and Josef was the oboist. By elimination, the 11-year-old wrote the piano concerto and thus was the virtuoso pianist (clue 2). He isn't Wolfgang Todlür (clue 2), so Otto von Tott and Wolfgang was 7. Bambino was the flautist (clue 3), so Wolfgang was the violin virtuoso.

In summary:
Antonio Bambino, 6, opera, flute.
Joachim Kiddi, 9, tone poem, clarinet.
Josef Neubörn, 4, overture, oboe.
Otto von Tott, 11, piano concerto, piano.
Wolfgang Todlür, 7, symphony, violin.

Firm Foundations (No 232)

The college founded in 1385 is noted for its chapel (clue 6). Lionel Don's college was founded in 1440 (clue 5) and St Peter's in 1426 (clue 3), so (clue 1) the college with the tower, which was founded next before Plantagenet whose Master is Alfred Chaplain, doesn't date from 1401, 1426 or 1463 and is thus the 1440 foundation. Plantagenet was founded in 1463 (clue 1). Lazarus College noted for its library (clue 2) was founded in 1401 and Colin Fellows is the Master of the college with the chapel. This isn't Cordwainers (clue 4), so Princes and Cordwainers is Lionel Don's college. The gardens are at St Peter's (clue 4) and the fountain is at Plantagenet. Robert Proctor is Master of Lazarus (clue 4), so Angus Dean is Master of St Peter's.

In summary:
Cordwainers, Lionel Don, 1440, tower.
Lazarus, Robert Proctor, 1401, library.
Plantagenet, Alfred Chaplain, 1463, fountain.
Princes, Colin Fellows, 1385, chapel.
St Peter's, Angus Dean, 1426, gardens.

Steeped in History (No 233)

Theodore lectures at Cordwainers (clue 2) and Dry at Lazarus (clue 3). The man at St Peter's is Fogey or Fossil (clue 7). Arthur Old isn't the Civil War specialist at Princes (clue 1), so Arthur is Plantagenet. Cedric's topic is 19th-century Europe (clue 4) and Fogey's specialist area is Roman Britain (clue 6). The man at Princes isn't Sebastian (clue 5), so Basil. His surname isn't Fossil (clue 5), so Yore. Arthur Old's subject isn't Social History (clue 8), so the Reformation. Fossil isn't Theodore (clue 5), so Theodore is Fogey and Fossil is at St Peter's. He isn't Sebastian (clue 5), so Cedric and Sebastian is Dry whose subject is Social History.

In summary:
Cordwainers, Theodore Fogey, Roman Britain.
Lazarus, Sebastian Dry, Social History.
Plantagenet, Arthur Old, The Reformation.
Princes, Basil Yore, Civil War.
St Peter's, Cedric Fossil, Europe in 19th century.

SOLUTIONS

The Regulars (No 234)

Alpha 2's passenger will be going to Bridge House (clue 3), Col O'Dowd will be going to Stag Lodge (clue 5). The person going from Saxby House to East Street won't be in Bravo 1 or Bravo 2 (clue 2). Mr Todd will be picked up by Bravo 2 and won't be going to York Road (clue 4), so Chaucer Road. Cllr Clark will be picked up at the Town Hall (clue 6). Mr Todd won't be picked up from the Mill Hotel (clue 1) or the Post Office (clue 4), so the railway station. Cllr Clark won't be going to Bridge House (clue 6), so York Road. Alpha 2's passenger won't be Mr Lang (clue 3), so Mrs Usher and Mr Lang is going to East Street. Mrs Usher isn't being picked up from the Mill Hotel (clue 1), so the Post Office and Col O'Dowd from the Mill Hotel. Mr Lang isn't being picked up by Bravo 1 (clue 2) or Alpha 1 (clue 3), so Charlie 1. The cab that picks up Cllr Clark won't be Alpha 1 (clue 6), so Bravo 1 and Alpha 1 will pick up Col O'Dowd.

In summary:
Alpha 1, Colonel O'Dowd, Mill Hotel, Stag Lodge.
Alpha 2, Mrs Usher, Post Office, Bridge House.
Bravo 1, Councillor Clark, Town Hall, York Road.
Bravo 2, Mr Todd, railway station, Chaucer Road.
Charlie 1, Mr Lang, Saxby House, East Street.

Car Boot Tale (No 235)

The owner of car E bought the ladder (clue 3) and Car D is Rob's (clue 6). Tim's car isn't B (clue 7), so F (clue 1) and the owner of H bought the doors. The owner of car A hasn't a five-letter name (clue 8) and Henry bought wallpaper (clue 2), so Henry's car is C and B is Vince's. Neil's is H (clue 4) and Owen's G. Alec's isn't A (clue 5), so E, A is Mac's, Rob bought the cupboard and Tim the tiles. The man who bought the electric drill isn't Mac or Vince (clue 7), so Owen. The paint wasn't bought by Vince (clue 2), so Mac and Vince bought the shelves.

In summary:
A, Mac, paint.
B, Vince, shelves.
C, Henry, wallpaper.
D, Rob, cupboard.
E, Alec, ladder.
F, Tim, tiles.
G, Owen, electric drill.
H, Neil, doors.

Not from Dock Green (No 236)

The officer with 16 years' service wasn't the Detective Sergeant (clue 2), the Police Constable (clue 3), the Sergeant (clue 4) or the Detective Inspector (clue 5), so the Inspector. The officer with 10 years' service wasn't Gordon or Geoffrey (clue 1), Georgina (clue 2) or Grace (clue 4), so Graham. His rank wasn't Detective Sergeant (clue 2), Police Constable (clue 3) or Detective Inspector (clue 5), so Sergeant and (clue 4) Grace served for 11 years. Geoffrey didn't serve for 13 or 14 years (clue 1), so 16 and Gordon for 14. By elimination, Georgina served for 13 years. The Detective Sergeant served for 11 years (clue 2) and the South Yorkshire officer for 10. Thus the Devon and Cornwall officer served for 13 years (clue 1) and wasn't the Detective Inspector (clue 5), so the Police Constable, thus the Detective Inspector was Gordon. Grace didn't belong to the West Midlands force (clue 4) and wasn't from Norfolk (clue 5), so belonged to the Thames Valley force. The Norfolk officer was Geoffrey (clue 5) and the West Midlands officer was Gordon.

In summary:
Geoffrey Dixon, Inspector, Norfolk, 16 years.
Georgina Dixon, Police Constable, Devon/C'wall, 13 years.
Gordon Dixon, Detective Inspector, W Midlands, 14 years.
Grace Dixon, Detective Sergeant, Thames Valley, 11 years.
Graham Dixon, Sergeant, S Yorkshire, 10 years.

On Your Bike (No 237)

The Mountie is bike 4 (clue 3) and bike 1 is red (clue 4), so (clue 1) Colin's blue bike is 2 and the Rambler is 3. The Mudlark ridden by Craig (clue 5) is bike 1, so bike 2 is the Comet. The Mountie isn't Clyde's (clue 3), so Clint's. It isn't yellow (clue 2), so green and Clyde has the yellow Rambler.

In summary:
Bike 1, Craig, Mudlark, red.
Bike 2, Colin, Comet, blue.
Bike 3, Clyde, Rambler, yellow.
Bike 4, Clint, Mountie, green.

Vintage Stuff (No 238)

The Stackard was built in 1903 (clue 5). The 1908 model was neither the yellow Deauville nor the Mascara (clue 4), so the Gentley. Card 18 featured the 1905 car (clue 3), so the Gentley is on card 17 (clue 1) and the red car on card 19. The Deauville is on card 18 (clue 4). The green car is on card 20 (clue 2) and the red one was built in 1912 and (by elimination) is the Mascara, so the Stackard is green and the Gentley is black.

In summary:
Card 17, Gentley, black, 1908.
Card 18, Deauville, yellow, 1905.
Card 19, Mascara, red, 1912.
Card 20, Stackard, green, 1903.

Another Door Opens (No 239)

Walter's seat was Onyerbyke (clue 4). The loser at Gowing West whose first name has six letters and who is now a bank chairman (clue 1), isn't Morgan (clue 3), so Lester Burns (clue 6). Terence is the publisher (clue 5). O'Leary, former MP for Upson Downs isn't Morgan (clue 3), so Noel. He isn't the barrister (clue 7) and the company director's surname is Carroll (clue 2), so Noel is the TV pundit. Reeves isn't the barrister (clue 7), so the publisher and the barrister's surname is Pearce. He isn't Morgan (clue 3), so Walter and Morgan is Carroll. Terence didn't represent Cutloose (clue 7), so Casterside and Morgan represented Cutloose.

In summary:
Lester Burns, Gowing West, bank chairman.
Morgan Carroll, Cutloose, company director.
Noel O'Leary, Upson Downs, TV pundit.
Terence Reeves, Casterside, publisher.
Walter Pearce, Onyerbyke, barrister.

Cut for Deal (No 240)

The fourth card wasn't cut by Clara (clue 1), Betty (clue 3) or Adam (clue 4), so Dave. So the man referred to in clue 2 is Adam, whose card was a heart (clue 4). The second cut was of a black card (clue 5), so Adam's was third (clue 2) and Dave's was a diamond, so (clue 4) was the 10. Card 2 was the 3 (clue 2). Clara didn't draw card 1 and cut card 2 (clue 1) and Adam's was the king, so card 1 was the 7, which (by elimination) was cut by Betty. It wasn't a club (clue 3), so a spade and Clara's was a club.

In summary:
Card 1, 7 of spades, Betty.
Card 2, 3 of clubs, Clara.
Card 3, king of hearts, Adam.
Card 4, 10 of diamonds, Dave.

Windows of Opportunity (No 241)

Mrs O'Brien is paying her phone bill (clue 1) and the person at window 3 is buying stamps (clue 3). Mr Shelton at window 1 isn't collecting his pension (clue 5) or sending a parcel (clue 2), so paying his car tax. Mr Malone heads the line of 5 people (clue 2), so (clue 4) Mr Shelton's queue has 3 people and there are 6 at window 5. Mrs O'Brien's queue has 4 people (clue 1). The customer at window 5 isn't Miss Evans (clue 3), so Mrs Greenwood and there are 10 people in Miss Evans' queue. The person at window 3 isn't Miss Evans (clue 3), so Mr Malone. The parcel isn't being sent by Mrs Greenwood (clue 2), so Miss Evans and Mrs Greenwood is collecting her pension. Mrs O'Brien isn't at window 4 (clue 1), so window 2 and Miss Evans is at window 4.

In summary:
Window 1, three people, Mr Shelton, car tax.
Window 2, four people, Mrs O'Brien, phone bill.
Window 3, five people, Mr Malone, stamps.
Window 4, ten people, Miss Evans, parcel.
Window 5, six people, Mrs Greenwood, pension.

Holy Rota (No 242)

Mr S Robertson will be sidesman on the 30th (clue 6). Mrs Newton is doing the flowers on the 2nd (clue 1). The flowers on the 30th won't be done by Mrs Leonard (clue 1), Mrs Talbot (clue 4) or Miss Stark (clue 5), so Miss Woodcock. Mrs Fox is reading on the 9th (clue 2). The reader on the 2nd won't be Miss Woodcock (clue 3), Mr Howe (clue 4) or Mrs Gray (clue 5), so Mr R Robertson, who is also the sidesman on the 2nd (also clue 2). Miss Stark and Mr Webb are on flower and sidesman duty on the same Sunday (clue 5). Mr Talbot won't be the sidesman when Mrs Talbot is doing flowers (clue 3), so Mrs Leonard is on flower duty that Sunday and Mr Swain is sidesman when Mrs Talbot is on the flower rota. The flowers on the 16th won't be done by Mrs Leonard or Mrs Talbot (clue 3), so Miss Stark. Mrs Gray will read on the 23rd (clue 5). Miss Woodcock will do the flowers on the 30th and (clue 3) Mr Howe will read on the 30th, thus Miss Woodcock will read on the 16th. Mr Swain is sidesman on the 23rd (clue 4), so Mr Talbot is sidesman on the 9th.

In summary:
2nd, Mrs Newton, Mr R. Robertson, Mr R. Robertson.
9th, Mrs Leonard, Mr Talbot, Mrs Fox.
16th, Miss Stark, Mr Webb, Miss Woodcock.
23rd, Mrs Talbot, Mr Swain, Mrs Gray.
30th, Miss Woodcock, Mr S. Robertson, Mr Howe.

Domino Search (No 243)

3	2	3	3	5	3	2	3
6	4	2	1	1	0	1	2
2	2	6	6	6	3	2	5
2	3	0	4	1	1	0	0
1	5	5	0	5	4	0	0
6	1	4	5	5	1	4	4
3	4	6	0	6	6	5	4

Willing Workhorse (No 244)

Aristide was in Marseille in July (clue 6) and was involved in the fraud case in August (clue 4). June and September have 30 days, so the robbery in Bordeaux was in May (clue 3). The Gauloise butt was found during the kidnap inquiry (clue 1) and the smell of perfume helped him in Clermont-Ferrand (clue 2). His vital clue in May wasn't the broken wine glass (clue 5) or Champagne cork (clue 7), so the orange peel and (clue 8) the murder case was in June. September's case wasn't blackmail (clue 5), so kidnap, July's involved blackmail and August's clue was the broken wine glass. By elimination, perfume was June's clue and the Champagne cork was July's. The kidnapping wasn't in Orleans (clue 1), so Nantes and August's case was in Orleans.

In summary:
May, Bordeaux, robbery, orange peel.
June, Clermont-Ferrand, murder, perfume.
July, Marseille, blackmail, champagne cork.
August, Orleans, fraud, broken wine glass.
September, Nantes, kidnap, Gauloise butt.

Great Expectations (No 245)
Michelle is the social worker (clue 4). Suki isn't the saleswoman (clue 3) or the teacher in seat A (clues 1 and 3), so Suki is the nursery nurse. She isn't in seat B (clue 5), so C (clue 3) and is expecting her fourth child (clue 2). The teacher isn't Penny (clue 1), so Eleanor and Penny is the saleswoman. Michelle isn't in seat D (clue 4), so B and Penny is in D. Michelle is expecting her first child (clue 3). The woman expecting her second isn't in seat A (clue 1), so D and Eleanor is expecting her third child.

In summary:
A, Eleanor, teacher, third.
B, Michelle, social worker, first.
C, Suki, nursery nurse, fourth.
D, Penny, saleswoman, second.

Please Repeat (No 246)
Norma prefers South Pacific (clue 1), the 52-year-old The Sound Of Music (clue 3) and Mrs Lerner's My Fair Lady (clue 5), so (clue 1) Mrs Stein prefers Oklahoma. She isn't Sally who is 54 (clues 1, 2 and 3) and Mrs Lowe is 56 (clue 2). Mrs Stein isn't 58 (clue 7), so 60 and (clue 1) Norma is 58. Rhoda is Mrs Hammer (clue 4), so Norma is Mrs Rogers. Mrs Stein isn't Jill (clue 6), so Greta. By elimination, Sally is Mrs Lerner, Rhoda is 52 and Jill is Mrs Lowe, whose favourite is The King And I.

In summary:
Greta Stein, 60, Oklahoma.
Jill Lowe, 56, The King And I.
Norma Rogers, 58, South Pacific.
Rhoda Hammer, 52, The Sound Of Music.
Sally Lerner, 54, My Fair Lady.

Pile Up (No 247)
From the top:
A, B, D, C, F, E

Puppy Love? (No 248)
The day Buddy weed in the washing-basket was either Thursday or Saturday (clue 1) and the day he chewed the TV remote control and left a puddle in the kitchen wasn't Monday (clue 5). On Monday, he didn't disgrace himself under the dining-table (clue 4) or have the chocolate biscuit and wee on the armchair (clue 2), so on Monday he had an accident on the hearth-rug. By elimination, on the slipper-chewing day he stole some bacon, but didn't disgrace himself in the washing-basket (clue 1) or wet the hearth-rug (clue 3), so left a puddle under the dining-table. This wasn't on Thursday (clue 3), so was Sunday and he chewed the newspaper on Saturday (clue 4). The day he chewed the welly wasn't the day he weed in the washing-basket (clue 1) or wet the armchair (clue 2), so he left a puddle on the hearth-rug and (clue 2) he wet the armchair on Wednesday which (by elimination) was the day he chewed the chair leg. By elimination, he chewed the TV remote and weed in the kitchen on Thursday, so (clue 1) the puddle in the washing-basket was on Saturday. On Saturday, he didn't steal the sausage (clue 1) or cake (clue 6), so the cheese sandwich. On Thursday, he didn't take the sausage (clue 5), so the cake and he took the sausage on Monday.

In summary:
Monday, welly, sausage, hearth-rug.
Wednesday, chair leg, chocolate biscuit, armchair.
Thursday, TV remote control, cherry cake, kitchen.
Saturday, newspaper, cheese sandwich, washing-basket.
Sunday, slipper, bacon, under dining-table.

Bouncing About (No 249)
The garden party started at 2.00 (clue 5), so (clue 7) the village carnival at 11.00 and the Glebeton event at 10.30. The wedding party was at Bloomwell (clue 2). The birthday party didn't start at 10.30 (clue 3), so August's holiday gala (clue 1) was in Glebeton. The July event in Oakdown wasn't the birthday party (clue 3) or carnival (clue 7), so the garden party. The birthday party started at 4.00 (clue 3) and the wedding party at 1.30. The birthday party was in April (clue 4), the wedding party in June and the carnival in May. The birthday party was in Fernleigh (clue 6) and the village carnival in Brookfield.

In summary:
April, birthday party, Fernleigh, 4.00pm.
May, village carnival, Brookfield, 11.00am.
June, wedding party, Bloomwell, 1.30pm.
July, garden party, Oakdown, 2.00pm.
August, holiday gala, Glebeton, 10.30am.

SOLUTIONS

On the Trail (No 250)

Jack had a cheese roll at 3.00 (clue 4) and Mick had a doughnut at 9.00 (clue 5). Gilly had a sausage roll at midday (clues 1 and 6). The hiker who had a sausage roll at 9.00 and a doughnut at 3.00 wasn't Patsy (clues 2 and 7), so Dave. The hiker who had a ham roll at 3.00 wasn't Patsy (clues 7 and 4) or Gilly (clue 6), so Mick. By elimination, Patsy had the 3.00 sausage roll and Gilly's 3.00 snack was a chocolate bar. Mick's midday snack wasn't a chocolate bar (clues 3 and 5), so cheese roll. Whoever had a ham roll at midday had a chocolate bar at 9.00 (clue 3), so Dave had a chocolate bar at midday. The person who had a ham roll at 9.00 didn't have a doughnut at midday (clue 2), so a sausage roll at noon. Jack's 9.00 snack was (by elimination) a chocolate bar and Patsy had a doughnut at midday and a cheese roll at 9.00am.

In summary:
Dave, sausage roll, chocolate bar, doughnut.
Gilly, ham roll, sausage roll, chocolate bar.
Jack, chocolate bar, ham roll, cheese roll.
Mick, doughnut, cheese roll, ham roll.
Patsy, cheese roll, doughnut, sausage roll.

The Rhyme's the Thing (No 251)

Bruce died in 1944 (clue 2) and Arthur in Madagascar (clue 3), thus the man killed in Hong Kong in 1938 (clue 5) wasn't Dennis (clue 3). Nor was he Charles, agent 028 (clue 1), so Edgar. Agent 042 who died in 1961 (clue 4) wasn't Dennis (clue 3), so Arthur and Dennis died in 1955, so Charles in 1949. Bruce was killed in the Bahamas. Dennis didn't die in Greece (clue 6), so Algeria and Charles in Greece. Bruce was agent 21 (clue 2) and Dennis was agent 014, so Edgar was agent 035.

In summary:
Arthur, 042, 1961, Madagascar.
Bruce, 021, 1944, Bahamas.
Charles, 028, 1949, Greece.
Dennis, 014, 1955, Algeria.
Edgar, 035, 1938, Hong Kong.

Screened Off (No 252)

The cinema opened in 1933 closed in 1974 (clue 4) and the Empire opened in 1936 (clue 6), thus (clue 3) the cinema closed in 1984 was built in 1934 and the Astoria in 1935. The cinema closed in 1992 is now a community church (clue 4). The one opened in 1931 didn't close in 1979 or 1992 (clue 1), so 1967. It wasn't the Palace (clue 1) or Rivoli (clue 5), so the Essoldo, which (clue 2) is now a furniture store. The Astoria didn't close in 1979 (clue 3), so 1992. The Salvation Army citadel isn't in the cinema closed in 1979 or 1984 (clue 3), so 1974 and wasn't the Palace (clue 1), so the Rivoli. The Palace thus closed in 1984. It

isn't used for light engineering (clue 2), so as a car showroom and the Empire is now used for light engineering.

In summary:
Astoria, 1935, 1992, community church.
Empire, 1936, 1979, light engineering.
Essoldo, 1931, 1967, furniture store.
Palace, 1934, 1984, car showroom.
Rivoli, 1933, 1974, Salvation Army citadel.

A Taste for Literature (No 253)

The boy who liked Treasure Island was born in 1913 (clue 2) and the lad born in 1915 grew up to admire Ellery Queen (clue 5), so the one who liked both Robin Hood and Dr Thorndyke, not the oldest or the youngest (clue 1), was born in 1917. Clarence's adult hero was Hercule Poirot (clue 4). The boy born in 1915 wasn't Benjamin (clue 4), Percival (clue 5) or Charles, who was the immediate senior of the lad who read Swiss Family Robinson (clue 6), so he was Adrian, whose favourite wasn't Tarzan (clue 3). Benjamin's favourite was Robinson Crusoe (clue 4), so Adrian's was Swiss Family Robinson. Charles was born in 1913 and his adult preference wasn't for Father Brown (clue 6), so Lord Peter Wimsey. By elimination, Percival was born in 1917 and Benjamin's favourite detective was Father Brown. Thus Clarence preferred Tarzan, so (clue 3) he was born in 1920 and Benjamin in 1910.

In summary:
Adrian, 1915, Swiss Family Robinson, Ellery Queen.
Benjamin, 1910, Robinson Crusoe, Father Brown.
Charles, 1913, Treasure Island, Lord Peter Wimsey.
Clarence, 1920, Tarzan, Hercule Poirot.
Percival, 1917, Robin Hood, Dr Thorndyke.

Fire! (No 254)

Jim drove to location 1 (clue 2) and the chimney fire was at location 3 (clue 4). Gordon and his crew rescued the cat but not at location 4 (clue 3), so location 2. This wasn't at Scorchford (clue 3), or Sparkton (clue 5). The incident at Blazeborough was the factory fire (clue 1), so the cat was in Flamewell. Reg didn't go to location 3 (clue 4), so 4 and Frank went to location 3. Thus (clue 1) the incident at location 1 was the chip pan fire. Scorchford wasn't location 1 (clue 3), so location 3. Sparkton was location 1.

In summary:
1, Sparkton, Jim, chip pan fire.
2, Flamewell, Gordon, cat up tree.
3, Scorchford, Frank, chimney fire.
4, Blazeborough, Reg, factory fire.

SOLUTIONS

Triangulation (No 255)

The letter in triangle 1 appears in triangle 12 (clue 1), so it isn't G, L, O, R or U. Nor is it T, since those two letters occur in triangles numbered eight apart (clue 9). The two Is both appear in inverted triangles (clue 5) and one of the two Ns is in triangle 8 (clue 7), so triangles 1 and 12 both contain an A. The G is in triangle 13 (clue 2). There isn't an I in triangle 6 (clue 6) or 15 (clue 8), so the Is are in 3 and 11 (clue 5). The two Ts aren't in triangles 2 and 10 (clue 4), so either 6 and 14 or 7 and 15. There is a 60° somewhere in the bottom row (clue 3), so it's in triangle 14 (clues 4 and 8) and (above) the two Ts are in 7 and 15. Triangle 6 doesn't contain a vowel (clue 6), so the O is in triangle 5 (clue 10) and the U in triangle 9. There is a 60° in that row (clue 3), so it's in triangle 6. The 60° in the row above isn't in triangle 2 (clue 3), so triangle 4. Since there are two Ns, the second one is in 2 (clue 4), the L is in 16 and the R in 10.

In summary:
1 A; 2 N; 3 I; 4 60°; 5 O; 6 60°; 7 T; 8 N; 9 U; 10 R; 11 I; 12 A; 13 G; 14 60°; 15 T; 16 L.

Criminal Pursuit (No 256)

The author of book 4 isn't Jane D'Eath (clue 1), Dulcie Coughen (clue 3) or Simon Gore (clue 5), so Al Leith. It isn't Love Lies Bleeding (clue 1), or Murder At Twilight (clue 5). The detective in book 3 isn't Sergeant Spotforth (clue 4), so book 4 isn't The Melon Seller (clue 2), thus it's The Aspidistra Deaths. Its detective isn't Blair (clue 4), so D'Eath's book isn't 1 or 3 (clue 1), thus D'Eath's is 2 and Blair is in book 3. Book 1 is thus Love Lies Bleeding (clue 1). Inspector Sharp isn't in 1 or 2 (clue 5), so 4. Gore didn't write book 3 (clue 5), so book 1 and Coughen wrote book 3. Murder At Twilight is book 2 (clue 5) and The Melon Seller is 3. Spotforth is in Murder At Twilight (clue 2) and Clewes in Love Lies Bleeding.

In summary:
1, Love Lies Bleeding, Simon Gore, Chief Inspector Clewes.
2, Murder at Twilight, Jayne D'Eath, Sergeant Spotforth.
3, The Melon Seller, Dulcie Coughen, Superintendent Blair.
4, The Aspidistra Deaths, Al Leith, Inspector Sharp.

Raising Canes (No 257)

Mr Delving grows blackcurrants (clue 2), so Michael Trench grows raspberries (clue 3) and Mr Mulch strawberries. Michael grows parsnips (clue 4). Mr Delving thus grows artichokes (clue 2), and Mr Mulch marrows. Derek is Mr Delving (clue 1) and Robin is Mr Mulch.

In summary:
Derek Delving, artichokes, blackcurrants.
Michael Trench, parsnips, raspberries.
Robin Mulch, marrows, strawberries.

Pile Up (No 258)
From the top:
A, E, B, C, F, D

Steady Does It (No 259)

The starting price of the winner wasn't 3-1 (clue 1) or 6-4 (clue 2), so 7-2 and was Franchard (clue 3). Franchard wasn't in the 2.30 (clue 1) or 3.30 races (clue 3), so the 3.00. Mr Gilly wasn't third (clue 2), so second and Klondyke was third. Mr Gilly's starting price was 3-1 and ran in the 3.30 (clue 2), so Klondyke's was 6-4 in the 3.30.

In summary:
2.30, Klondyke, third, 6-4.
3.00, Franchard, first, 7-2.
3.30, Mr Gilly, second, 3-1.

Course You Can! (No 260)

Donna Lyons got tangled in the net (clue 2) and Eddie March was helped by Sgt Grant (clue 3). Sgt Hart's celebrity who refused to climb the wall wasn't Carl Kirkby (clue 4), so Fiona Niven. Eddie March wasn't the council chairperson who got jammed in the tunnel (clue 3), so he fell into a pond. By elimination, Carl Kirkby was the council chairperson. The swimmer was helped by Sgt Wood (clue 1) and Fiona Niven the radio reporter. Thus Eddie March is the novelist, the swimmer is Donna Lyons and Carl Kirkby was helped by Sgt Moore.

In summary:
Carl Kirkby, council chairperson, Sgt Moore, jammed in tunnel.
Donna Lyons, swimmer, Sgt Wood, tangled in net.
Eddie March, novelist, Sgt Grant, fell into pond.
Fiona Niven, radio reporter, Sgt Hart, refused to climb wall.

Seeing the Sights (No 261)

Pete Van Hool's coach went to Windsor (clue 2). Mick Leyland's coach, which carried 51 passengers, didn't tour Historic London (clue 3) or Oxford (clue 4), so Brighton and was thus the X1 (clue 1). The X3 had 48 passengers (clue 4) and the Oxford coach 45. Pete Van Hool's had 48 (clue 2) and Billy Dennis' had 54. Thus the coach to Oxford was driven by Jim Guy and Billy Dennis took the Historic London tour. Jim Guy's coach wasn't the X4 (clue 1), so the X2 and the X4 was Billy Dennis'.

SOLUTIONS

In summary:

X1, Mick Leyland Brighton, 51.

X2, Jim Guy, Oxford, 45.

X3, Pete Van Hool, Windsor, 48.

X4, Billy Dennis, Historic London, 54.

Too Many Chiefs (No 262)

The Chief with 18 officers wasn't Chief Gore (clue 3), Chief Panzer (clue 4) or Chief Keems (clue 5), so Chief Durkin and (clue 2) the Arkansas force had 12 officers. The Minnesota force didn't have 8 or 14 (clue 5), so 18 and Chief Keem's force had 14. The Kentucky force had 8 officers, so Chief Keems' force were from Riverside in Texas (clue 1). The force of 8 wasn't from Pleasant Hill (clue 3) or Georgetown (clue 4), so Five Points. They were headed by Chief Gore (clue 3) and there were 12 officers at Pleasant Hill. Chief Panzer wasn't from Georgetown (clue 4), so Pleasant Hill and Chief Durkin was from Georgetown.

In summary:

Chief Durkin, Georgetown, Minnesota, 18 officers.

Chief Gore, Five Points, Kentucky, 8 officers.

Chief Keems, Riverside, Texas, 14 officers.

Chief Panzer, Pleasant Hill, Arkansas, 12 officers.

The Fortune Wheel (No 263)

The tan segment is lettered F (clue 5) and the 800 points are on segment D (clue 3). Both B (clue 6) and E (clue 4) also bear numerals, so the legend BANKRUPT, on a black background which isn't on segment A (clue 1), is on C. The 500 isn't on F (clue 2), E (clue 4) or B (clue 6), so A and (clue 2) B is yellow. The 300 isn't on E (clue 4) or B (clue 6), so F. The orange segment is D (clue 7) and E is pink, so A is green. B shows 250 (clue 8) and the 450 is on E.

In summary:

Segment A, 500, green.

Segment B, 250, yellow.

Segment C, BANKRUPT, black.

Segment D, 800, orange.

Segment E, 450, pink.

Segment F, 300, tan.

Hot Shots (No 264)

F Stopp owns a Nippon (clue 6) and Otto Folkus' work was Commended (clue 1). The 1st prize photograph taken with a Gunn (clue 4) wasn't Poynton Shute's (clue 4) or Ivor Leitmeter's (clue 5), so Len Scapp's. Bleak Mid-winter won 2nd prize (clue 3), Golden Harvest was submitted by Poynton Shute (clue 4) and White Water was taken with a Sushi (clue 6). Len's picture wasn't Sandy Shore (clue 2), so Morning Mist. Second prize wasn't given to Ivor Leitmeter (clue 5), so F Stopp. Ivor Leitmeter was 4th (clue 5) and the

Zeus-user 3rd. By elimination, the latter was Poynton Shute. Ivor's picture wasn't Sandy Shore (clue 2), so White Water and Sandy Shore was by Otto Folkus and taken with a Hitax.

In summary:

F Stopp, Bleak Mid-winter, 2nd, Nippon.

Ivor Leitmeter, White Water, 4th, Sushi.

Len Scapp, Morning Mist, 1st, Gunn.

Otto Folkus, Sandy Shore, Commended, Hitax.

Poynton Shute, Golden Harvest, 3rd, Zeus.

Public Demonstrations (No 265)

The audience of 6 people watched the demonstration on the ground floor (clue 1) and 12 marvelled at Markaway easy-clean carpets (clue 6), so Clout power tools being demonstrated on the 3rd floor but not to an audience of 15 or 18 (clue 4), attracted 9 and Suzanne spoke to 15. Derek's 2nd floor demonstration wasn't to 18 (clue 3), so 12. Sandra demonstrated Emotions perfumery (clue 2). Paul didn't have an audience of 9 and wasn't demonstrating Shimmer window-cleaner (clue 5), so demonstrated Pinnacle cookware. Sandra wasn't on the ground or first floor (clue 2), so the basement and Suzanne was on the first floor. By elimination, Sandra's audience numbered 18. Paul demonstrated cookware, so Suzanne was Shimmer's demonstrator and Clive demonstrated Clout power tools.

In summary:

Basement, Emotions perfumery, Sandra, 18.

Ground floor, Pinnacle cookware, Paul, 6.

1st floor, Shimmer window-cleaner, Suzanne, 15.

2nd floor, Markaway easy-clean carpets, Derek, 12.

3rd floor, Clout power tools, Clive, 9.

Logi-5 (No 266a)

B	C	E	D	A
E	B	C	A	D
A	D	B	E	C
C	A	D	B	E
D	E	A	C	B

ABC (No 266b)

B			C	A
C			A	B
	A	C	B	
	B	A		C
A	C	B		

Extra Time (No 267)

The two days' work was as a restaurant patron (clue 5), so the soldier job occupied four days (clue 2) and the August job two days. The April thriller took one day (clue 4). The job of footballer was in May (clue 6). April's wasn't playing a pub customer (clue 3), so a market trader. Shooting in the pub took five days and his rôle as a footballer three days (clue 3). The historical epic in which he played a soldier wasn't filmed in June (clue 6), so July and the five-day stint was in June. In the comedy he was neither a restaurant patron nor a pub customer (clue 5), so a footballer. His part in the filming of the classic novel took five days (clue 1), so he played a pub customer for five days and a restaurant patron in the romance.

In summary:

April, thriller, market trader, one day.
May, comedy, footballer, three days.
June, classic novel, pub customer, five days.
July, historical epic, soldier, four days.
August, romance, restaurant patron, two days.

Snowsauruses (No 268)

The 5-year-old's father made the snow pterodactyl (clue 3) and Igg's son is 7 (clue 6). Agg made the snow mammoth and his son isn't 3 or 4 (clue 2), so 6 and Pigg is 4. Legg whose father built the snow sabre-toothed tiger (clue 5) is thus 7. Agg's son isn't Wagg (clue 1) or Cogg (clue 4), so Dugg. Cogg's father isn't Ogg (clue 1) or Egg (clue 4), so Ugg. Ugg didn't build the snow brontosaurus (clue 4), or the snow stegosaurus (clue 7), so the snow pterodactyl. By elimination, Wagg is 3. His father didn't make the snow stegosaurus (clue 7), so the snow brontosaurus and the stegosaurus was made for Pigg. Wagg's father isn't Ogg (clue 5), so Egg and Pigg's is Ogg.

In summary:

Agg, mammoth, Dugg, 6.
Egg, brontosaurus, Wagg, 3.
Igg, sabre-toothed tiger, Legg, 7.
Ogg, stegosaurus, Pigg, 4.
Ugg, pterodactyl, Cogg, 5.

Say Cheese (No 269)

Tybalt is played by the medical student (clue 5). Tim whose subject is Geology isn't Tooley, who plays Mercutio (clue 1), so Tim's is the remaining male rôle, that of Romeo. Adam's surname is Benfield (clue 3) and the English student is playing the Nurse. This female rôle isn't played by Jenny, whose University subject is Spanish (clue 6), so Rosamund and Jenny is Juliet. By elimination, Mercutio is Simon, whose subject is Classics. Rosamund isn't Ostler (clue 2) or Hemmings (clue 4), so Cooke. Jenny is Ostler (clue 6) and Tim is Hemmings.

In summary:

Juliet, Jenny Ostler, Spanish.
Mercutio, Simon Tooley, Classics.
Nurse, Rosamund Cooke, English.
Romeo, Tim Hemmings, Geology.
Tybalt, Adam Benfield, Medicine.

You're Nicknamed! (No 270)

'Dalek' taught on Wednesday (clue 2). The Monday lesson wasn't with 'Gromit' (clue 3) or 'Bunny' (clue 4), nor was it French with 'Froggy' (clue 1) , so it was with 'Delia' Smith (clue 4) and with 'Bunny' on Tuesday. English was on Thursday (clue 5), so French was on Friday. By elimination, 'Gromit' taught on Thursday. Mr Benton's PE lesson was on Wednesday (clue 3). Mr Thorn's lesson wasn't on Thursday (clue 5) or Tuesday (clue 6), so Friday. The maths teacher's name is shorter than that of the English teacher (clue 5), so Mrs Johnson taught English. Thus Mrs Waren was 'Bunny'. She didn't teach history (clue 6), so maths and 'Delia' taught history.

In summary:

Monday, 'Delia' Smith, History.
Tuesday, 'Bunny' Waren, Maths.
Wednesday, 'Dalek' Benton, PE.
Thursday, 'Gromit' Johnson, English.
Friday, 'Froggy' Thorn, French.

Grandsons' Treat (No 271)

The Fardels went to Broadwell on Friday (clue 1) and at Widebridge they spent the morning at the motor museum (clue 5). Tuesday morning's boat trip wasn't at Deepford or Highstone (clue 6), so Longsands, where they spent the afternoon on the beach (clue 3). Monday afternoon was spent at the aircraft museum (clue 6), so the cinema trip was on Wednesday afternoon (clue 4), the castle trip was on Friday morning and Friday afternoon's was to the country park. The safari park wasn't visited on Thursday (clue 2) or Wednesday morning (clue 5), so Monday morning. They didn't go to Highstone on Monday (clue 2), so the safari park and aircraft museum are in Deepford. The motor museum wasn't visited on Thursday morning (clue 5), so Wednesday morning. Thus Thursday's destination was Highstone, to the windmill in the morning and the funfair in the afternoon.

In summary:

Monday, Deepford, safari park, aircraft museum.
Tuesday, Longsands, boat trip, beach.
Wednesday, Widebridge, motor museum, cinema.
Thursday, Highstone, windmill, funfair.
Friday, Broadwell, castle, country park.

SOLUTIONS

Miss Raffles' Secret (No 272)

Miss Raffles lived as Mrs Morris in Liverpool (clue 2) and in a semi-detached house in York (clue 3). In Oxford she also lived in a house (clue 4). The flat where she lived as Miss Porter wasn't in Bristol (clue 5), so Birmingham and Miss Porter was thus the 'actress' (clue 1). The house in Oxford was either detached or terraced (clue 4) and the name she used there was either Mrs Atkins or Mrs Wilson. Mrs Wilson was the 'Colonel's widow' (clue 7), so she didn't live in the terraced house occupied by the 'Bishop's sister' (clue 6), nor was Mrs Wilson's home a detached house (clue 7), so Mrs Atkins lived in Oxford, but not in a terraced house (clue 6), so a detached house. Mrs Morris' home wasn't the cottage (clue 2), so a terraced house and the cottage was in Bristol. The house in York wasn't home to Miss Forbes' (clue 3), so Mrs Wilson and Miss Forbes lived in Bristol. Miss Raffles didn't pose as a novelist in Oxford (clue 4), so a 'peer's mistress' and was a 'novelist' in Bristol.

In summary:
Mrs Atkins, detached house, Oxford, peer's mistress.
Miss Forbes, cottage, Bristol, novelist.
Mrs Morris, terraced house, Liverpool, Bishop's sister.
Miss Porter, flat, Birmingham, actress.
Mrs Wilson, semi-detached house, York, Colonel's widow.

To the Ouache Basin (No 273)

The explorer is in charge of navigation (clue 2) and Raoul St Simon is in charge of communications (clue 5). Biologist Heinrich Von Haller isn't the Parisian language specialist (clue 7) or the cook (clue 1), so is in charge of first aid. Jacques Laplace comes from Brussels (clue 3) and the geologist is from Cape Town (clue 6). Heinrich Von Haller isn't from Montreal (clue 4) so New York. The geologist isn't in charge of cooking (clue 1), so communications. The man acting as cook isn't the reporter (clue 1), so photographer. He isn't Mikhail Novikov (clue 1) or Jacques Laplace (clue 3), so Andre Benoit. By elimination, Jacques Laplace is the explorer, Andre Benoit is from Montreal and the linguist is Mikhail Novikov and he's a reporter.

In summary:
Andre Benoit, Montreal, photographer, cooking.
Heinrich Von Haller, New York, biologist, first aid.
Jacques Laplace, Brussels, explorer, navigation.
Mikhail Novikov, Paris, reporter, languages.
Raoul St. Simon, Cape Town, geologist, communications.

Towers of Strength (No 274)

Rollo's Tower is to the north (clue 3) and the eastern tower was completed in 1100 (clue 4). The one built in 1080 isn't to the south (clue 1) or west (clue 2), so north and the Jerusalem Tower, containing the servants' quarters, is to the east. The Lion Tower isn't to the south (clue 1), so west and the Prince's Tower is to the south. It didn't house the armoury (clue 1) or food store (clue 5), so the guardhouse. The armoury was in Rollo's Tower (clue 1) and the food store in the Lion Tower. The Lion Tower was built in 1120 (clue 1) and the Prince's Tower in 1140.

In summary:
North, Rollo's Tower, 1080, armoury.
East, Jerusalem Tower, 1100, servants' quarters.
South, Prince's Tower, 1140, guardhouse.
West, Lion Tower, 1120, food store.

Cultured Canines (No 275)

Pearl owns dog D (clue 4) and A is the samoyed (clue 5), so (clue 1) the poodle which danced is B and Katie owns C. The labrador isn't D (clue 2), so C; thus D walked on its hind legs and is the collie. C didn't sing (clue 3), so the samoyed sang. Its owner wasn't Bella (clue 3), so Marina and Bella owns the poodle.

In summary:
A, Marina, samoyed, sang.
B, Bella, poodle, danced.
C, Katie, labrador, counted.
D, Pearl, collie, walked on hind legs.

Guest Beers (No 276)

Old Prior is 4.6% in strength (clue 2) and Ensign Ale was guest beer on the 10th (clue 3). The 4.2% beer featured on the 17th (clue 6) wasn't Black Cock (clue 1) or Warlock (clue 5), so Castle Keep. The beer from Ailsworth is 4.5% (clue 4). Black Cock which is brewed in Bere Alston isn't 4.4% (clue 1) so 4.3%. The Malton beer which arrived on the 24th wasn't 4.6% (clue 3) or 4.2% (clue 6), so 4.4%. Ensign Ale is thus 4.5% (clue 3) and Warlock is from Malton. The beer from Brewham isn't Old Prior (clues 2 and 5), so Castle Keep and Old Prior is from Hopwood. Old Prior was the choice for the 31st (clue 2), so Black Cock for the 3rd.

In summary:
3rd, Black Cock, 4.3%, Bere Alston.
10th, Ensign Ale, 4.5%, Ailsworth.
17th, Castle Keep, 4.2%, Brewham.
24th, Warlock, 4.4%, Malton.
31st, Old Prior, 4.6%, Hopwood.

SOLUTIONS

Posh Progeny (No 277)

The baronet's son was in pram 4 (clue 1), so Maureen was pushing pram 2 (clue 3), Gerald was in pram 1 and the Duke's son in pram 3. The Earl's son was Horatio (clue 4), so Gerald was the Viscount's son and pram 2 contained Horatio. Simon wasn't in pram 3 (clue 5), so 4 and Peter was in 3. Thelma thus pushed pram 4 (clue 2) and Jennifer pram 3. Thus Clarice pushed pram 1.

In summary:

1, Clarice, Gerald, Viscount.
2, Maureen, Horatio, Earl.
3, Jennifer, Peter, Duke.
4, Thelma, Simon, baronet.

Battleships (No 278)

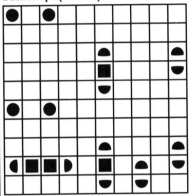

In Black and White (No 279)

Freddie was Fortnum (clue 2) and Chalk and Trapp were a pair (clue 7). Charlie whose partner was Motion (clue 5), wasn't Time (clue 1) or Benson (clue 5), so Poney and (clue 3) Dick was Motion. Hal was Hedges (clue 4). Trapp wasn't Algy (clue 6) or Wilbur (clue 7), so Sidney. Tom's partner Algy was Mason (clue 6) and Wilbur's surname was Cheese. Chalk wasn't Leslie (clue 7), so Eddie. Leslie's partner wasn't Wilbur (clue 7), so Hal Hedges and Freddie's was Wilbur. Leslie wasn't Benson (clue 1), so Time and Tom was Benson.

In summary:

Charlie Poney and Dick Motion.
Eddie Chalk and Sidney Trapp.
Freddie Fortnum and Wilbur Cheese.
Leslie Time and Hal Hedges.
Tom Benson and Algy Mason.

Pile Up (No 280)
From the top:
B, A, C, D, F, E

In the Yards (No 281)

Vantikar was a trader (clue 2) and Berlin was from Terra (clue 1), so (clue 4) the freighter from Styrios was Mharba. The starship from Cha-Vis was getting a new generator (clue 6). Qazzigo which was being decontaminated wasn't from G'Kall (clue 3), so Najrun. The ship from Cha-Vis wasn't Jentiro (clue 6), so Vantikar and Jentiro was from G'Kall. The tramp was getting a new engine and wasn't Mharba (clue 5). Mharba wasn't having hull repairs (clue 4), so having a routine service. The Berlin wasn't the liner or the tramp (clues 1 and 5), so the ore-carrier. By elimination, the vessel from G'Kall was the tramp ship, Qazzigo was the liner and Berlin was having a hull repair.

In summary:

Berlin, ore-carrier, Terra, hull repair.
Jentiro, tramp, G'Kall, new engine.
Mharba, freighter, Styrios, routine service.
Qazzigo, liner, Najrun, decontamination.
Vantikar, trader, Cha-Vis, new generator.

Euro Square (No 282)

The number in B1 is 2 or 4 in one of the four languages (clue 3), but not French, since quatre is in B2 (clues 1 and 2), vier (clue 6) or quattro (clue 7). The German drei is in column C (clue 8), so vier isn't in C (clue 1) and (clue 6) four isn't in B1. So B1 contains a 2, not zwei or due (clue 4), so two is in B1 and (clue 3) one in D2. Zwei and due are both in row 2 (clue 4). Zwei isn't C2 (clues 1 and 8), so in A2 and due is in C2. Tre is in row 3 (clue 6) but not in column A (clue 6) or C (clue 1). D3 contains an even number (clue 5), so tre is in B3. Four is in A3 (clue 6) and vier in B4. The even number in D3 isn't French (clue 5), so it's quattro. Uno is in column A (clue 1), but isn't in A4 (clue 9), so A1. The remaining 2 is deux in (clue 9) A4. Eins is in D4 (clues 1 and 8). The number in D1 is French (clue 1), so (clue 10) trois is in D1 and un in C3. Drei isn't in C4 (clue 8), so C1 and three is in C4.

In summary:

uno	two	drei	trois
zwei	quatre	due	one
four	tre	un	quattro
deux	vier	three	eins

By the Way (No 283)

The 4.25 breakdown was on the trunk road (clue 1) and the Ford broke down at 10.30 (clue 6), so (clue 3) Kirsten called at 2.10, the Saab broke down at 12.15 and the member stranded in the drive called at 3.00. Thus the Peugeot which broke down on the motorway (clue 2) is

Kirsten's car, the Hyundai was the subject of the 4.25 call and the Lada was the car in the drive which refused to start. Philip broke down in a country lane (clue 5). His call wasn't at 12.15 (clue 5), so 10.30. By elimination, the Saab broke down on a city street. Ida's car is the Hyundai (clue 4) and Mary's is the Saab, so the Lada is Maurice's.

In summary:
10.30, Philip, Ford, country lane.
12.15, Mary, Saab, city street.
2.10, Kirsten, Peugeot, motorway.
3.00, Maurice, Lada, home drive.
4.25, Ida, Hyundai, trunk road.

Dumped by Debbie (No 284)

The youth with the irritating whistle was dispensed with in April (clue 5), so (clue 6) Debbie dropped the sloppy dresser in August. The clumsy youth was got rid of in June (clue 6) and the salesman in October. The pig farmer had halitosis (clue 1), so was dumped in February and the salesman was Pete who told lies (clue 2). The teacher dressed sloppily (clue 2). Rex the market trader was dropped in April (clue 4) and the butcher in June. Alan wasn't the pig farmer nor was he dumped in August (clue 1), so he was the butcher. Jonathan wasn't the teacher (clue 3), so the pig farmer and Steve was the teacher.

In summary:
February, Jonathan, pig farmer, halitosis.
April, Rex, market trader, irritating whistle.
June, Alan, butcher, clumsy.
August, Steve, teacher, sloppy dresser.
October, Pete, salesman, told lies.

Sign of the Times (No 285)

The guitarist's autograph is No 2 (clue 3). No 3's signature isn't Glen's (clue 1), Mickey's (clue 2) or Clyde Knowlson's (clue 4), so Darren's. No 2 is Padley's (clue 5) and Padley plays the guitar. Darren doesn't play the synthesiser (clue 4) or drums (clue 5), so he's the vocalist. Thus his surname is Lee and signature No 1 is Mickey's (clue 2). By elimination, Clyde's is No 4. Mickey plays the synthesiser (clue 4), so Clyde plays the drums. By elimination, Glen's forename is Padley and Mickey's surname is Burrows.

In summary:
1, Mickey Burrows, synthesiser.
2, Glen Padley, guitar.
3, Darren Lee, vocalist.
4, Clyde Knowlson, drums.

Four Seen (No 286)

The table-top sale was advertised for Friday (clue 1), the playing field event began at 2.00 (clue 2) and the craft fair started before 2.30 (clue 3). The flower festival started at 1.00 (clue 6). The

car boot sale began half an hour later than the Monday event in the Manor House (clue 1), so Thursday's 2.30 event (clue 5) was the charity auction. The 3.00 event was thus for the table-top sale and the event at the Crown Inn was at 2.30 (clue 1). The 2.00 event wasn't on Sunday (clue 2), so Saturday and (clue 3) wasn't the craft fair, so the car boot sale. Thus Monday's event started at 1.30 (clue 1) and was the craft fair. The event in the school began at 3.00 (clue 4), so the 1.00 event was on Sunday in the village hall.

In summary:
Car boot sale, Saturday, playing field, 2.00.
Charity auction, Thursday, Crown Inn, 2.30.
Craft fair, Monday, Manor House, 1.30.
Flower festival, Sunday, village hall, 1.00.
Table-top sale, Friday, school, 3.00.

Delivery Boy (No 287)

Browning Street is the second to be visited (clue 1). Ted's brother lives at the fourth to be visited (clue 2). Ted's daughter lives in Kipling Street which isn't the first (clue 6), so either the third or fifth. Thus it hasn't 107 houses (clue 5) or 71 (clue 6). Byron Street has 85 (clue 3) and Ted's son lives in the street with 46 houses (clue 4), so there are 163 in Kipling Street. The first isn't Masefield Street (clue 3) or Tennyson Street (clue 4), so Byron Street. The street with 107 houses isn't the fourth (clue 2), third or fifth (clue 5), so second. Kipling Street isn't the third (clue 6), so fifth and the fourth has 71 houses. By elimination, Ted's son lives in the third street, so (clue 4) Tennyson Street is the fourth and Masefield Street the third. Ted's cousin lives in Browning Street (clue 3) and Ted's sister in Byron Street.

In summary:
Browning Street, 107, second, cousin.
Byron Street, 85, first, sister.
Kipling Street, 163, fifth, daughter.
Masefield Street, 46, third, son.
Tennyson Street, 71, fourth, brother.

Quintuple Wedding (No 288)

Dennis married Fiona and Bruce married Miss Addison (clue 5). Angela Vance didn't marry Robin (clue 3) or Mark (clue 2), so John. His sister Ursula is Mrs Onslow and John's surname begins with a consonant (clue 4), so isn't Addison. Since John married Angela Vance, Ursula wasn't the Miss Dale who married Mr Vance (clue 1), so John's surname is Caxton. Miss Addison wasn't Kate (clue 5), so Paula. Mark didn't marry Kate (clue 2), so Ursula and Kate married Robin who is Addison. Miss Dale is thus Fiona and Mr Vance is Dennis. By elimination, Bruce's surname is Dale and Kate is the former Miss Onslow.

SOLUTIONS

In summary:
Bruce Dale, Paula Addison.
Dennis Vance, Fiona Dale.
John Caxton, Angela Vance.
Mark Onslow, Ursula Caxton.
Robin Addison, Kate Onslow.

Red, White and Blue (No 289)

B	R	R	W	W	B
B	W	W	B	R	R
R	B	B	W	W	R
W	W	R	R	B	B
R	B	W	B	R	W
W	R	B	R	B	W

On the Double (No 290)

The doctor won in 1996 (clue 6). The 1998
winner wasn't the postman (clue 1), the
blacksmith (clue 2) or Ockey the farmer (clue
4), so Daniel, the taxi-driver (clue 7). Matthew
is Tipp (clue 1). Feather who won in 1994 isn't
Leonard (clue 5) or Wilfred (clue 2), so Jeremy.
Daniel's surname isn't Flyte (clue 3), so Arrow.
Ockey won in 1997 (clue 4). He isn't Wilfred
(clue 2), so Leonard. Matthew didn't win in 1996
(clue 1), so 1995. By elimination, the doctor's full
name is Wilfred Flyte. Matthew is the blacksmith
(clue 2), so Jeremy is the postman.

In summary:
1994, Jeremy Feather, postman.
1995, Matthew Tipp, blacksmith.
1996, Wilfred Flyte, doctor.
1997, Leonard Ockey, farmer.
1998, Daniel Arrow, taxi-driver.

Men of Letters (No 291)

The plate with the number 16 has a consonant
registration letter (line 6), so the personalised
letters aren't BOB which is on the E-reg car (line
3), or MPJ (lines 5 and 6). As the car is an Audi
(lines 5 and 6), the letters aren't PAH (which are
on a Volvo, line 1) or TOM (which accompany
the number 27, lines 9–12), so DRB. Thus the
registration letter is neither P (line 8) nor R,
which precedes the number 20 (line 7), so Mr
Burke's plate is J16 DRB. Bob's E-reg BOB plate
hasn't the number 6 (line 3), so it's E10 BOB.
Thus the PAH plate has the number 6 (lines
1–2). By elimination, the number 20 precedes
Mick Johnson's personalised MPJ and the plate
is thus R20 MPJ. Mick's car isn't a Rover (line 4)
or Mercedes (line 7), so a Ford. The A-reg car
is A27 TOM (lines 9–12) and the P-reg car is Mr
Hobbs's P6 PAH Volvo. E10 BOB isn't a Rover
(line 4), so a Mercedes and the A-reg car is the
Rover.

In summary:
A27 TOM, Rover.   E10 BOB, Mercedes.
J16 DRB, Audi.   P6 PAH, Volvo.
R20 MPJ, Ford.

Home Improvements (No 292)

The father placed the patio first (clue 2), the
mother placed the stereo system fourth (clue
5) and the daughter rated the stair-carpet third
(clue 7). The person who placed the patio
sixth and stereo system third (clue 2) is thus
the son who (clue 4) placed the dining table
second and his mother placed the dining table
first. The father placed the stair-carpet second
(clue 6) and the son placed it fourth. The son
placed decorating the lounge fifth (clue 3) and
the daughter placed it sixth. By elimination, the
son placed the kitchen bar first, so (clue 3) his
mother placed this sixth. The mother's third
choice wasn't the stair-carpet or decorating the
lounge (clue 8), so the patio, which her daughter
placed fifth. The mother's second choice was
decorating the lounge (clue 5), so her fifth was
the stair-carpet. The daughter's first choice
wasn't the dining table or kitchen bar (clue 1),
so the stereo system. Her second wasn't the
dining table (clue 1), so kitchen bar and the dining
table was her fourth. The father didn't place the
stereo system third or fourth (clue 1), so (clue
9) fifth and the dining table sixth. By elimination,
he placed decorating the lounge third and the
kitchen bar fourth.

In summary (in order first to sixth):
Father: patio, stair-carpet, decorating lounge,
kitchen bar, stereo system, dining table.
Mother: dining table, decorating lounge, patio,
stereo system, stair-carpet, kitchen bar.
Son: kitchen bar, dining table, stereo system,
stair-carpet, decorating lounge, patio.
Daughter: stereo system, kitchen bar, stair-
carpet, dining table, patio, decorating lounge.

Laddies from Lancashire (No 293)

Henry was the fourth brother (clue 5), so
(clue 6) the youngest brother didn't support
Manchester City or Manchester United. Nor
was he the Oldham fan (clue 1). His food
preference was Yorkshire pudding (clue 1) and
the Burnley supporter favoured hotpot (clue 4),
so the youngest supported Blackburn Rovers
and he's thus Stanley (clue 2). Frank the black
pudding lover was the immediate senior of the
Manchester City fan (clue 3), so (clue 6) James
is the third brother and (clues 3 and 6) the
Manchester United fan is Henry, the Manchester
City fan is the second brother and Frank is the
eldest. Thus Albert is the second brother, James

prefers hotpot and Frank's team is Oldham Athletic. The tripe lover isn't Albert (clue 4), so Henry and Albert's dish is fish and chips.

In summary:
Eldest, Frank, black pudding, Oldham Athletic.
Second, Albert, fish and chips, Manchester City.
Third, James, hotpot, Burnley.
Fourth, Henry, tripe, Manchester United.
Youngest, Stanley, Yorkshire pudding, Blackburn Rovers.

The Lulu Wars (No 294)

The Corporal got his medal in 1881 (clue 3), so Fusilier Edgar Fidler was decorated in 1879 (clue 6). The man decorated in 1878 wasn't the Lieutenant (clue 5) or Lance-Corporal (clue 7), so the Sergeant who (clue 5) won at Swan's Creek. Oscar Portwine won his medal at Kingstown (clue 7). The man who won a medal at Quirk's Drift in 1882 wasn't Albert Buggins (clue 2) or Joseph Kneebone (clue 4), so Sidney Tonkin. Edgar's medal wasn't earned at Beacon Hill (clue 1), so Blackoak Swamp and (clue 4) Joseph was the Sergeant. Thus Albert won his medal at Beacon Hill, but not in 1880 (clue 1), so 1881 and Oscar's was in 1880. The Lance-Corporal wasn't Oscar (clue 7), so Sidney and Oscar was the Lieutenant.

In summary:
Albert Buggins, Corporal, Beacon Hill, 1881.
Edgar Fidler, Fusilier, Blackoak Swamp, 1879.
Joseph Kneebone, Sergeant, Swan's Creek, 1878.
Oscar Portwine, Lieutenant, Kingstown, 1880.
Sidney Tonkin, Lance-Corp, Quirk's Drift, 1882.

Whose Coup? (No 295)

The General's surname was Pasodoble (clue 1) and the Air-Marshal was Enrico (clue 6). Ricardo Maracas wasn't the Admiral or Vice-Admiral (clue 4), so the Field-Marshal who led the 1961 coup (clue 3). Ronaldo led the 1952 coup (clue 5). The 1954 coup wasn't Pablo's (clue 1) or Enrico's (clue 6), so Arturo's. General Pasodoble isn't Arturo or Pablo (clue 1), so Ronaldo. Pablo's coup was in 1947 (clue 1) and Enrico's in 1940. He's Flamenco (clue 2) and Pablo is the Admiral. By elimination, Arturo's rank is Vice-Admiral, so (clue 7) he isn't Bossanova. Thus Pablo is Bossanova and Arturo is Bolero.

In summary:
1940, Air-Marshal Enrico Flamenco.
1947, Admiral Pablo Bossanova.
1952, General Ronaldo Pasodoble.
1954, Vice-Admiral Arturo Bolero.
1961, Field-Marshal Ricardo Maracas.

Rollin', Rollin', Rollin' (No 296)

The track which accounts for 50 seconds hasn't a maximum height of 170 feet (clue 1), 190 (clue 4) or 220 (clue 5), so 200 feet. Its length isn't 1400 yards (clue 1), 1600 (clue 4) or 1800 (clue 5), so 1500. The track of 1600 yards takes 55 seconds (clue 4), so the 1400-yard track takes 60 seconds (clue 3) and the 1800-yard track takes 65. The 1400-yard track hasn't a maximum height of 170 feet (clue 1) or 220 feet (clue 5), so 190 feet and the 1600-yard track has a maximum height of 220 feet (clue 3). By elimination, the track with the height of 170 feet is 1800 yards long. The 1600-yard track isn't second or third (clue 2) or fourth (clue 5), so first. The fourth track thus takes 50 seconds (clue 3). The track with the 170-feet maximum height isn't second (clue 2), so third and the 190-feet one is second.

In summary:
First, 220 feet, 1600 yards, 55 seconds.
Second, 190 feet, 1400 yards, 60 seconds.
Third, 170 feet, 1800 yards, 65 seconds.
Fourth, 200 feet, 1500 yards, 50 seconds.

Happy Landing? (No 297)

The first jumper's parachute wasn't green (clue 1), blue and white (clue 3) or orange or white (clue 4), so red and white. The second jumper's wasn't green (clue 1), orange or white (clue 4), so blue and white. The first jumper landed in the village pond (clue 3). The fifth wasn't Lynagh (clue 1), Cordleigh (clue 2), Fell (clue 3) or Packer (clue 4), so Roope. His landing place wasn't the silage pit (clue 1), church roof (clue 2) or glasshouse (clue 4), so the hawthorn hedge. The fourth jumper didn't land in the silage pit (clue 1) or on the glasshouse (clue 4), so on the church roof. Cordleigh jumped second (clue 2) and (clue 3) Fell jumped fourth. The first jumper wasn't Lynagh (clue 1), so Packer and Lynagh jumped third. Cordleigh thus landed in the silage pit and Fell had the green canopy (clue 1). Roope's canopy was white (clue 4), so Lynagh landed on the glasshouse and his canopy was orange.

In summary:
First, Packer, red and white, village pond.
Second, Cordleigh, blue and white, silage pit.
Third, Lynagh, orange, glasshouse.
Fourth, Fell, green, church roof.
Fifth, Roope, white, hawthorn hedge.

Summit's Up (No 298)

The climb from which there was a drop-out of 20 wasn't of Stob Coire Eassain or Stob Choire Claurigh (clue 1), Aonach Moir or Ben Nevis (clue 2) or Aonach Beag (clue 3), so Binnein Moir. Thus 18 dropped out of the Friday climb and 16 out of the ascent of Aonach Beag (clue 3), which wasn't on Tuesday or Wednesday (clue 4). The possible combined numbers of combined

SOLUTIONS

drop-outs as mentioned in clue 4 are 26 (10+16 and 8+18) and 28 (8+20, 10+18 and 12+16). Stob Choire Claurigh hadn't a drop-out of 8 (clue 1), so the combined number was 28 and 12 dropped out on Wednesday (clue 4). Tuesday's drop-out total wasn't 20 (clue 2), so the combination is 10+18, with Tuesday's figure being 10 and the drop-out on Stob Choire Claurigh 18. Thus 8 dropped out from Aonach Moir (clue 2) and 16 from the Saturday climb (clue 1). The 20 drop-out wasn't on Thursday (clue 1), so Monday and 8 dropped out on Thursday. There was a 10-climber drop-out from Stob Coire Eassain (clue 1), so Wednesday's climb was Ben Nevis.

In summary:
Monday, Binnein Moir, 20.
Tuesday, Stab Coire Eassain, 10.
Wednesday, Ben Nevis, 12.
Thursday, Aonach Moir, 8.
Friday, Stob Choire Claurigh, 18.
Saturday, Aonach Beag, 16

Battleships (No 299)

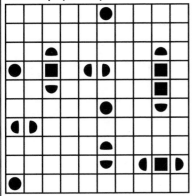

Stand and Deliver (No 300)

The place where Luddy Lobb was challenged at 4.00 wasn't Worthing (clue 7) and wasn't Eastbourne (clue 2), Hastings (clue 5) or Folkestone (clue 7). The 4.00 encounter was next west to the 12.50 one which wasn't at Worthing (clue 7), so the 4.00 one was at Brighton and he was challenged at 12.50 at Eastbourne. Monday's sighting was at Hastings (clue 3) and the 10.45 one at Folkestone, so Wednesday's was at Bognor (clue 5). This wasn't at 11.15 (clue 5) or 4.40 (clue 4), so 3.05. The time of the Hastings challenge was at 11.15 (clue 5) and the Worthing one at 4.40 on Tuesday (clue 6). On Saturday he wasn't identified at Folkestone (clue 1), so Eastbourne (clue 7) and Friday's challenge was in Brighton. Thursday's was thus in Folkestone.

In summary:
Bognor, Wednesday, 3.05
Worthing, Tuesday, 4.40.
Brighton, Friday, 4.00.
Eastbourne, Saturday, 12.50.
Hastings, Monday, 11.15.
Folkestone, Thursday, 10.45.

Concerted Effort (No 301)

Domenico wrote 9 concertos (clue 2), so (clue 1) Benedetto wrote 8 and Pietro 10. Pietro wrote 4 symphonies (clue 3). Benedetto wrote 5 symphonies (clue 1), so Domenico wrote 3. Verrisorri isn't Benedetto or Domenico (clue 4), so Pietro. Benedetto isn't Evilorri (clue 1), so he's Merziferri and Domenico is Evilorri.

In summary:
Benedetto Merziferri, 5 symphonies, 8 concertos.
Domenico Evilorri, 3 symphonies, 9 concertos.
Pietro Verrisorri, 4 symphonies, 10 concertos.

Hand Over (No 302)

Dan's surname is Parker (clue 2). Mark's isn't Smith (clue 1), so Jameson and Melanie is Smith. Mark will run in the marathon (clue 1). Melanie doesn't play the guitar (clue 3), so she's undertaking a sponsored swim and Dan will play the guitar. Melanie's cause is the purchase of sports equipment for her school (clue 3). Dan is collecting for the village hall (clue 2) and Mark for the heart scanner.

In summary:
Dan Parker, playing guitar, village hall.
Mark Jameson, marathon run, heart scanner.
Melanie Smith, swimming, sports equipment.

Broadly Disastrous (No 303)

The cruiser which got into trouble on Salthouse Broad didn't hit an iceberg and wasn't boarded by pirates (clue 3), nor was it struck by lightning (clue 1), so it was attacked by a submarine. The Haddock wasn't attacked by a submarine, nor did it have a problem with an iceberg or pirates (clue 3), so it was struck by lightning on Holton Broad (clue 1). The Raleighs' boat hit an iceberg (clue 3). The Prawn which had been hired by the Grenvilles wasn't attacked by a submarine (clue 2), so boarded by pirates. This didn't occur on Salthouse Broad or the River Dure (clue 2), so the River Ent. The boat hired by the Hawkins wasn't the Haddock or the Sardine (clue 1), so the Dugong. Thus the Sardine was hired by the Raleighs and the Haddock by the Drakes. By elimination, the Dugong was attacked by a submarine and the iceberg was on the River Dure.

SOLUTIONS

In summary:
Dugong, Hawkins, Salthouse Broad, attacked by submarine.
Haddock, Drake, Holton Broad, struck by lightning.
Prawn, Grenville, River Ent, boarded by pirates.
Sardine, Raleigh, River Dure, hit iceberg.

Soccer it to Her (No 304)

The goalie on the 24th broke a finger (clue 5), so (clue 2) the goalie on the 3rd normally played as a back and the one on the 17th got a mouthful of mud. Since the goalie on the 10th didn't sprain her ankle (clue 4), she got a black eye and was thus Beryl Boote (clue 3). By elimination, the woman who played in goal on the 3rd sprained her ankle. The midfielder was Peggy Pools (clue 1). Beryl Boote wasn't the physiotherapist (clue 4), so the striker. Peggy Pools was in goal on the 24th (clue 1). By elimination, the physio was in goal on the 17th. Mitzi Match got a mouthful of mud (clue 4), so Gerty Ground sprained her ankle.

In summary:
3rd, Gerty Ground, back, sprained ankle.
10th, Beryl Boote, striker, black eye.
17th, Mitzi Match, physiotherapist, mouthful of mud.
24th, Peggy Pools, midfielder, broken finger.

Final Stages (No 305)

Clive is the magician (clue 2) and the comedian's surname is Raye (clue 3). Andy Murphy isn't the pianist (clue 4), so he's the impressionist. Joplin who's been at the Pier for 30 years (clue 5), isn't the pianist (clue 4), so the magician. By elimination, the pianist's surname is Friday. He hasn't spent 24 seasons at the Pier (clue 1), or 28 (clue 4), so 26. Raye hasn't lasted for 28 years (clue 3), so 24 and Andy for 28. Bill's surname is Raye (clue 3), so Dick's is Friday.

In summary:
Andy Murphy, impressionist, 28 years.
Bill Raye, comedian, 24 years.
Clive Joplin, magician, 30 years.
Dick Friday, pianist, 26 years.

Round Table (No 306)

Torres is in seat A (clue 5) and the man from Cafeteria is in seat D (clue 2). The man in B isn't the Doctor from Los Perros (clue 3), nor is he from San Guinari (clue 1), thus he's from Bananaria and (clue 4) Admiral Ruiz is in D and represents Cafeteria. Gomez isn't in C (clue 1), so B and the man from San Guinari is in C. By elimination, the Doctor is Torres and the San Guinarian is Mendoza. He's not the General (clue 1), so the Vice-President and the General is Gomez.

In summary:
Seat A, Doctor Torres, Los Perros.
Seat B, General Gomez, Bananaria.
Seat C, Vice-President Mendoza, San Guinari.
Seat D, Admiral Ruiz, Cafeteria.

Logi-Path (No 307)

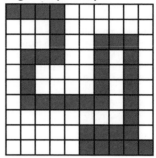

Pile Up (No 308)
From the top:
A, B, C, D, E, F

Ghost Stories (No 309)

Graham wrote for the rugby player (clue 3) and Edwin for Carl Morrison (clue 6), so the man who worked for athlete Gemma Crichton (clue 1) was Maurice. Welsh worked for the soccer star (clue 2), Pearce is Christine (clue 4) and Hardy wrote for Fergus McKay (clue 7). Maurice isn't Scott (clue 1), so Green. Christine didn't write about snooker (clue 4), so boxing. The boxer wasn't Donald Fenton (clue 5), so Garry Rumbold. Donald wasn't assisted by Laura (clue 5), so Graham and Laura's surname is Hardy. By elimination, Edwin's surname is Welsh, Fergus McKay plays snooker and Graham is Scott.

In summary:
Carl Morrison, soccer, Edwin Welsh.
Donald Fenton, rugby, Graham Scott.
Fergus McKay, snooker, Laura Hardy.
Garry Rumbold, boxing, Christine Pearce.
Gemma Crichton, athletics, Maurice Green.

Drunk and Disorderly (No 310)

Randy worked for the Sabre (clue 3). The man from the Bar 7 got 7 days and the one from the Pitchfork received a shorter sentence than Wolfie (also clue 4), so Preacher, who got 8 days and didn't work for the Lazy K (clue 5) was the Rocking Chair cowboy, whose surname was Wayne (clue 2). Eastwood got 5 days (clue 6), so Gus got 3 days and Stewart 4. Barney Cooper (clue 1) thus got 7 days. The Pitchfork cowboy wasn't Wolfie (clue 4), so Gus and Wolfie worked on the Lazy K. Wolfie was Eastwood (clue 6), so Randy was Stewart and Gus was McCrea.

SOLUTIONS

In summary:
Barney Cooper, Bar 7, 7 days.
Gus McCrea, Pitchfork, 3 days.
Preacher Wayne, Rocking Chair, 8 days.
Randy Stewart, Sabre, 4 days.
Wolfie Eastwood, Lazy K, 5 days.

Mistresses in Retirement (No 311)
Miss Dyer lives in Yorkshire (clue 1) and the painter in Cheshire (clue 6), so Miss Polton the amateur detective, who doesn't live in South London or West London (clue 4), lives in Suffolk and (clue 1) is Cynthia (clue 1). Miss Hickes is Phyllis (clue 6). Agatha isn't Dyer or Leach (clue 3), so Sealey. Miss Leach isn't Violet (clue 2), so she's Judith the angler (clue 5) and Violet is Miss Dyer who (clue 3) is the gardener. The painter from Cheshire isn't Phyllis (clue 6), so Agatha and Phyllis is the novelist. She doesn't live in West London (clue 2), so South London and Judith lives in West London.

In summary:
Agatha Sealey, Cheshire, painter.
Cynthia Polton, Suffolk, amateur detective.
Judith Leach, West London, angler.
Phyllis Hickes, South London, novelist.
Violet Dyer, Yorkshire, gardener.

All of a Twist (No 312)
Fraser is Hewson (clue 2) and Parker is also male (clue 3). Nelson will play Mr Brownlow (clue 5). Nancy's partner Jemima isn't Richie the Thameside star (clue 1), so Drake. The actor who will play Fagin isn't Fraser (clue 2) nor, since he's a Northenders star (clue 6) Richie, so Parker. Brian who appears in Pulse (clue 4) is Nelson. Fraser's soap isn't Denverdale (clue 2), so Jubilee Terrace. Thus his rôle will be Bumble (clue 7). By elimination, Jemima Drake is from Denverdale and Richie will play Bill Sikes. James isn't Parker (clue 6), so Richie and Leslie is Parker.

In summary:
Bill Sikes, James Richie, Thameside.
Bumble, Fraser Hewson, Jubilee Terrace.
Fagin, Leslie Parker, Northenders.
Mr Brownlow, Brian Nelson, Pulse.
Nancy, Jemima Drake, Denverdale.

Names on the Street (No 313)
Horton's have sponsored eight items (clue 3), so (clue 1) Goldway has sponsored 13 hanging baskets and Premier 15 items which (clue 4) are benches (clue 5) and Goldway is the chemist (clue 5). The flower beds are sponsored by the garden centre (clue 2), so the Northern Bank sponsor litter bins. Premier isn't the supermarket (clue 4), so the estate agency. There aren't nine litter bins (clue 6), so the bank sponsored six. By elimination, Williams' sponsored nine items and the supermarket sponsored the trees. There are eight flower beds (clue 2), so nine trees carrying Williams' logo.

In summary:
Six, litter bins, Northern, bank.
Eight, flower-beds, Horton's, garden centre.
Nine, trees, Williams', supermarket.
Thirteen, hanging baskets, Goldway, chemist.
Fifteen, benches, Premier, estate agency.

Getting to grips (No 314)
Sid Samson was in the three-round contest (clue 5), so the Iron Bloch/Mighty Mammoth bout lasted two rounds (clue 6) and Mick Magog was in the four-round fight, thus (clue 1) his was the first bout (clue 1). King Kong was in the seven-round contest (clue 3) and John Bull in the fourth. Mountain Rhodes was in the fifth bout (clue 4). John Bull's opponent wasn't King Kong (clue 3), so The Bruiser, for (by elimination) six rounds. By elimination, Sid Samson fought Mountain Rhodes. Mick Magog didn't fight Rocky Cliffe (clue 6), so Hercules Hammond and Rocky Cliffe fought King Kong. The second bout lasted for seven rounds (clue 2), so the third lasted two rounds.

In summary:
1, Mick Magog, Hercules Hammond, four rounds.
2, King Kong, Rocky Cliffe, seven rounds.
3, Iron Bloch, Mighty Mammoth, two rounds.
4, The Bruiser, John Bull, six rounds.
5, Mountain Rhodes, Sid Samson, three rounds.

Domino Search (No 315)

1	5	2	4	1	4	3	3
4	6	5	5	4	0	1	3
0	0	0	6	6	5	1	1
3	4	3	6	6	2	2	2
4	5	2	1	1	3	0	0
0	5	3	2	2	4	4	6
3	6	5	2	1	0	6	5

The Works Team (No 316)
Figure 5 is Barry (clue 6), so (clue 2) the man in the black helmet is figure 2 and Marco Donesi is 4 and has the gold and white helmet (clue 1). Figure 2 is Rowles (clue 5) and the silver helmet is worn by 6, who (clue 5) isn't Scott. Geoff and Tom are co-drivers (clue 7) in the other car, so figure 6 is Jack. Gill has a green helmet (clue

SOLUTIONS

3), Hammett's number is odd and Brewer's number is lower than Hammett's, so Jack is Owen and (clue 4) Barry's helmet is blue/red. Barry's surname isn't Gill or Brewer (clue 3), so Hammett. Figure 2 isn't Scott (clue 5) or Geoff whose helmet is orange (clue 7), so he's Tom. Gill isn't figure 3 (clue 3), so 1 and Geoff is 3. By elimination, Scott's surname is Gill and Geoff's is Brewer.

In summary:
1 Scott Gill, green.
2 Tom Rowles, black.
3 Geoff Brewer, orange.
4 Marco Donesi, gold/white.
5 Barry Hammett, blue/red.
6 Jack Owen, silver.

Bronzed Figures (No 317)

The 1905 statue was erected on Market Hill (clue 2), so Sir Henry Hunt's statue dates from 1920 (clue 4) and the 1910 statue is in the churchyard. Lady Parry's statue is in Castle Square (clue 3). Sir Henry Hunt's statue isn't the actor's outside the Royal Theatre (clue 1), so it's in Elmwood Park. By elimination, the 1907 statue to the social reformer (clue 5) is of Lady Parry and the statue to the actor dates from 1915. Major Ingleman was the soldier (clue 6). The actor wasn't Sir George Turner (clue 1), so Edward Sherman. The author's statue wasn't erected in either 1905 or 1910 (clue 2), so 1920. By elimination, Sir George Turner was an MP. His statue doesn't date from 1905 (clue 3), so 1910 and the 1905 statue is of Major Ingleman.

In summary:
1905, Major Ingleman, soldier, Market Hill.
1907, Lady Parry, social reformer, Castle Square.
1910, Sir George Turner, MP, churchyard.
1915, Edward Sherman, actor, Royal Theatre.
1920, Sir Henry Hunt, author, Elmwood Park.

A Date with Destiny (318)

Francis is captain of ship C (clue 4), so (clue 2) Denzil's vessel is ship B, Trueman's is A and C is the Medusa. The Corsair is captained by Collingham and isn't B (clue 1), so D. The Amethyst isn't A (clue 3), so B and A is the Flamingo. Trueman isn't Luke (clue 4), so Walter and Luke is Collingham. Denzil isn't Rackham (clue 3), so Wakefield and Francis is Rackham.

In summary:
A, Flamingo, Walter Trueman.
B, Amethyst, Denzil Wakefield.
C, Medusa, Francis Rackham.
D, Corsair, Luke Collingham.

Brolly brigade (319)

Sandy baled out in 1943 (clue 5) and the 1944 incident occurred over Holland (clue 1), so Colin who baled out over Vichy France (clue 3) did so in 1942. Edwin was shot down in November (clue 6) and the June incident was over Germany (clue 7). Colin didn't bale out in May (clue 2) or February (clue 3), so October. The incident over Northern France wasn't in 1940 or 1941 (clue 4), so 1943 and Desmond was shot down in 1944. By elimination, Edwin was shot down over the Channel and Robert baled out over Germany. Sandy's shooting down wasn't in February (clue 5), so May and Desmond was shot down in February. Edwin baled out in 1940 (clue 2), so Robert in 1941.

In summary:
Colin, October 1942, Vichy France.
Desmond, February 1944, Holland.
Edwin, November 1940, English Channel.
Robert, June 1941, Germany.
Sandy, May 1943, Northern France.

Timecheck (320)

The woman expecting a visitor used teletext (clue 1) and the one with a train to catch checked the time at 10.26 (clue 7). The grandfather clock was consulted at 10.25 (clue 4), not by Delphine who had the dental appointment (clue 3) or by the woman with the business appointment (clue 5), so by the woman with a bus to catch. Janice who checked the time at 10.29 (clue 2) didn't have the business appointment (clue 5), so was expecting a visitor. The woman who checked at 10.27 didn't have the business appointment (clue 5), so the dental appointment; thus the woman with the business appointment checked at 10.28 and the woman with the train to catch consulted her wrist-watch. Penelope used her mobile phone (clue 6), so had the business appointment. By elimination, Delphine looked at the Town Hall clock. The woman catching a train wasn't Eunice (clue 7), so Morag and Eunice was catching a bus.

In summary:
Delphine, dental appointment, 10.27, Town Hall clock.
Eunice, bus to catch, 10.25, grandfather clock.
Janice, expecting visitor, 10.29, teletext.
Morag, train to catch, 10.26, wrist-watch.
Penelope, business appointment, 10.28, mobile phone.